R. Gupta's®

Popular Master Guide

UNIVERSITY OF DELHI

B. Tech
Information Technology & Mathematical Innovations
(IT & M)

Entrance Exam

2019
EDITION

RAMESH PUBLISHING HOUSE, New Delhi

Published by
O.P. Gupta *for* Ramesh Publishing House

Admin. Office
12-H, New Daryaganj Road, Opp. Officers' Mess,
New Delhi-110002 ① 23261567, 23275224, 23275124

E-mail: info@rameshpublishinghouse.com
Website: www.rameshpublishinghouse.com

Showroom
● Balaji Market, Nai Sarak, Delhi-6 ① 23253720, 23282525
● 4457, Nai Sarak, Delhi-6, ① 23918938

Book Code: R-1830

ISBN: 978-93-5012-824-4

HSN Code: 49011010

Scheme of Examination

Course – **B.Tech. Information Technology and Mathematical Innovations (IT & M) at <u>Cluster Innovation Center</u> (CIC)**

- A **written MCQ based entrance test** will be conducted at centers identified by the university.

- The written entrance test of two hours duration will be based on **Mathematics, Reasoning and Analytical Abilities** at 10+2 levels.

- The marking pattern will be as specified by the university. In case, each course have to decide individually, there will be 100 questions and for each correct answer a student shall score +4 marks and for each negative response there will be −1 mark.

- Admission will be done according to the merit list prepared on the basis of the marks secured in the entrance test and Interview.

- The weightage for the written examination–75%

- The weightage for Interview–25%.

Contents

University of Delhi
B.TECH – Information Technology and Mathematical Innovations (IT & M)
Entrance Exam-2017

SECTION–A

1. If $f : X \to Y$, defined by $f(x) = \sqrt{3} \sin x + \cos x + 4$ is one-one and onto, then the interval of Y is:
   - A. $[1, 4]$
   - B. $[2, 5]$
   - C. $[1, 5]$
   - D. $[2, 6]$

2. Let $f : [-1, 2] \to [0, \infty)$ be a continuous function such that $f(x) = f(1 - x)$ for all $x \in [-1, 2]$. If $R_1 = \int_{-1}^{2} xf(x)dx$ and R_2 is the area of the region bounded by $y = f(x)$, $x = -1$, $x = 2$ and x-axis. Then,
   - A. $R_1 = 2R_2$
   - B. $R_1 = 3R_2$
   - C. $2R_1 = R_2$
   - D. $3R_1 = R_2$

3. If x is a real number in $[0, 1]$, then the values of $f(x) = \lim\limits_{m \to \infty} \lim\limits_{n \to \infty} \{1 + \cos^{2m}(n!\pi x)\}$ is given by
   - A. 2 or 1 according x is rational or irrational
   - B. 1 or 2 according as x is rational or irrational
   - C. 1 for all x
   - D. 2 or 1 for all x

4. If $f(x)$ is continuous for all real values of 'x' and satisfies $\int_{n}^{n+1} f(x)dx = \dfrac{n^2}{2}, \forall n \in I$, then $\int_{-3}^{5} f(|x|)dx$ is equal to:
   - A. $\dfrac{19}{2}$
   - B. $\dfrac{35}{2}$
   - C. $\dfrac{17}{2}$
   - D. $\dfrac{15}{2}$

5. See the picture below. Only one box contains a car and only one statement is true. Which box has the car?

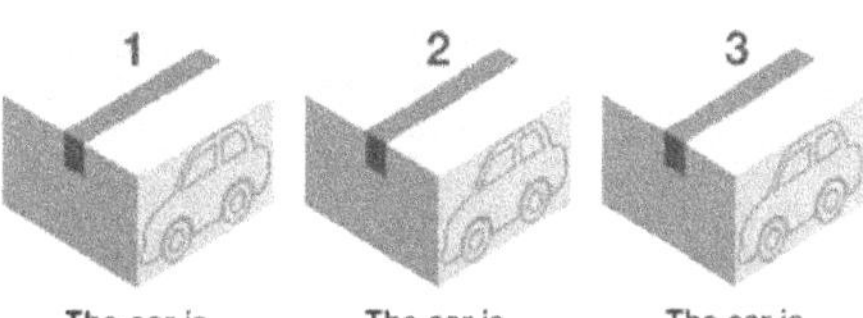

   - A. 1
   - B. 2
   - C. 3
   - D. Not enough information

6. $f(x)$ is a function defined on the interval $[-1, 1]$ such that $f(\sin 2x) = \sin x + \cos x$.

   Statement I :

   If $x \in \left[-\dfrac{\pi}{4}, \dfrac{\pi}{4}\right]$, then $f(\tan^2 x) = \sec x$

   Statement II :

   $f(x) = \sqrt{1 + x}, \forall x \in [-1, 1]$.
   - A. Statement I is true, Statement II is true.
   - B. Statement I is false, Statement II is false.
   - C. Statement I is true, Statement II is false.
   - D. Statement I is false, Statement II is true.

7. The vectors $\vec{a}$, $\vec{b}$ and $\vec{c}$ are equal in length and make equal angles when taken pairwise. If $\vec{a} = \hat{i} + \hat{j}$, $\vec{b} = \hat{j} + \hat{k}$ and $\vec{c}$ makes an obtuse angle with $\hat{i}$, then $\hat{c} =$

A. $\hat{i} + \hat{k}$

B. $-\hat{i} + 4\hat{j} - \hat{k}$

C. $-\dfrac{1}{3}\hat{i} + \dfrac{4}{3}\hat{j} - \dfrac{1}{3}\hat{k}$

D. $-\dfrac{1}{3}\hat{i} + \dfrac{4}{3}\hat{j} + \dfrac{1}{3}\hat{k}$

8. If $f(x)$ and $g(x)$ are periodic functions with period 7 and 11 respectively. Then the period of $F(x) = f(x)g\left(\dfrac{x}{5}\right) - g(x)f\left(\dfrac{x}{3}\right)$ is:

A. 177

B. 222

C. 433

D. 1155

9. There are 2 mothers, 2 daughters, 1 grandmother, 1 granddaughter. How many people are there?

A. 3

B. 4

C. 5

D. 6

10. If $A = \left\{ x : -\dfrac{2}{5} \le x \le \dfrac{\pi - 2}{5} \right\}$,

B = {y: − 1 ≤ y ≤ 1} and $f(x) = \cos(5x + 2)$, the mapping $f : A \to B$ is

A. one-one but not onto

B. onto but not one-one

C. both one-one and onto

D. neither one-one nor onto

11. Let $f(x)$ be a function defined by

$$f(x) = \int_1^x x(x^2 - 3x + 2)\,dx, \; 1 \le x \le 4.$$

Then,

A. Maximum value of $f(x)$ is $\dfrac{53}{4}$

B. Maximum value of $f(x)$ is $\dfrac{63}{4}$

C. Maximum value of $f(x)$ is $-\dfrac{1}{2}$

D. Maximum value of $f(x)$ is $-\dfrac{1}{3}$

12. If $f(x)$ be a continuous function defined for $1 \le x \le 3$ as $f(x) \in Q \; \forall \; x \in [1, 3], f(2) = 10$, (where Q is a set of all rational numbers) then $f(1.8)$ is:

A. 1

B. 5

C. 10

D. 20

13. An isosceles triangle ABC has the same perimeter as triangle ABP but twice the area of triangle ABP. The length of CP is

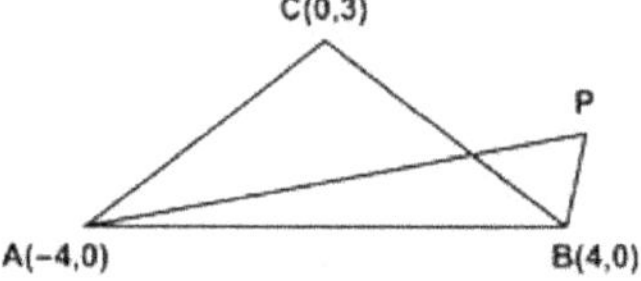

A. $\sqrt{21}$ units

B. $\sqrt{11}$ units

C. $\sqrt{5}$ units

D. $\sqrt{7}$ units

14. Let $S = \left\{ x \in (-\pi, \pi) : x \ne 0, \pm\dfrac{\pi}{2} \right\}$. The sum of all distinct solution of the equation $\sqrt{3}\sec x + \csc x + 2(\tan x - \cot x) = 0$ in the set S is equal to:

A. $-\dfrac{7\pi}{9}$

B. $-\dfrac{2\pi}{9}$

C. 0

D. $\dfrac{5\pi}{9}$

15. Statements : No women teacher can play.
Some women teachers are athletes.

Conclusions : I. Male athletes can play.
II. Some athletes can play.

A. Only conclusion I follows

B. Only conclusion II follows

C. Either I or II follows

D. Neither I nor II follows

16. A curve has a horizontal tangent at $x = 0$ and a tangent with slope 1 at $x = 1$. If the curve also satisfies the differential equation $y''' + 2x + 1$, then:

A. The curve has two points of local minima and one point of local maxima.

B. The curve has one point of local minima and two points of local maxima.

C. The curve has only one point of local minima and no point is a local maxima.

D. The curve has only one point of local maxima and no point is a local minima.

17. Let $S = \{1, 2, 3, ..., 20\}$. The probability of choosing a subset of three numbers from the set S so that no two consecutive numbers are in the set is:

A. 0.9

B. 0.1

C. $\dfrac{68}{95}$

D. $\dfrac{76}{95}$

18. Here are some words translated from an artificial language, godabim means kidney stones, romzbim means kidney beans, romzbako means wax beans. Which word could mean "wax statue"?

A. godaromz

B. lazbim

C. wasibako

D. romzpeo

19. Mrs. Susheela celebrated her wedding anniversary on Tuesday 30th September, 1997. When will she celebrate her next wedding anniversary on the same day (Tuesday)?

A. 30 September, 2002

B. 30 September, 2003

C. 30 September, 2004

D. 30 October, 2003

20. A function $y = f(x)$ is concave up if its derivative function $f'(x)$ is increasing and $y = f(x)$ is concave down if its derivative function $f'(x)$ is decreasing. Then:

Statement I : If $f(x)$ is increasing function with concavity upwards, then concavity of $f^{-1}(x)$ is also upwards.

Statement II : If $f(x)$ is decreasing function with concavity upwards then concavity of $f^{-1}(x)$ is also upwards.

A. Statement I is true, Statement II is true

B. Statement I is false, Statement II is false

C. Statement I is true, Statement II is false

D. Statement I is false, Statement II is true

21. The perimeter of a circle centered at the origin and inscribed in the parabola $y = x^2 - 3$ is:

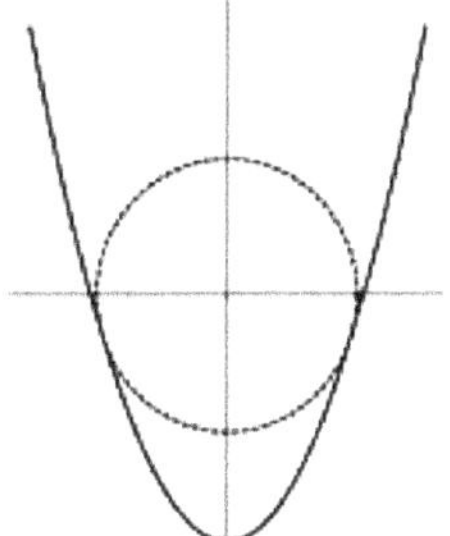

A. $\pi\sqrt{12}$ units

B. 2π units

C. $\pi\sqrt{3}$ units

D. $\pi\sqrt{11}$ units

22. There are three students X, Y and Z. One of them is Alpha who always tells truth. Beta always lies and Gamma can tell truth as well as lie. X declares that he is not Beta. Y says he is Beta. Z says he is not Beta. Who is Gamma?

A. X

B. Y

C. Z

D. Not enough information

23. Let $f(x) = \begin{cases} [x], & -2 \leq x \leq -\dfrac{1}{2} \\ 2x^2 - 1 & -\dfrac{1}{2} < x \leq 2 \end{cases}$

where [.] represents the greatest integer function.

The number of points where $f|x|$ is discontinuous is:

A. 4

B. 5

C. 2

D. 3

24. If the system of linear equations:

$x + 4ay + az = 0$

$x + 3by + bz = 0$

$x + 2cy + cz = 0$

have a non-trivial solution, then a, b, c

A. are in H.P.

B. are in G.P.

C. are in A.P.

D. satisfy $a + 2B + 3C = 0$

25. For all complex numbers z_1, z_2 satisfying $|z_1| = 12$ and $|z_2 - 3 - 4i| = 5$, the minimum value of $|z_1 - z_2|$ is:

A. 0   B. 2
C. 7   D. 17

26. The minimum value of the sum of real numbers a^{-5}, a^{-4}, a^{-3}, a^{-3}, a^{-3}, 1, a^8, a^{10} with $a > 0$ is:

A. 6   B. 7
C. 8   D. 9

27. By filling the black squares with either '+' or '−', in how many ways can you get the result?

$$1 \blacksquare 2 \blacksquare 3 \blacksquare 4 \blacksquare 5 \blacksquare 6 \blacksquare 7 \blacksquare 8 = 9$$

A. 0   B. 1
C. 2   D. 3

28. There are 10 halting stations on a circular road in a city. On the route, a bus will stop at any three stations so that no two stations are adjacent. The number of such possible bus routes are:

A. 50   B. 60
C. 70   D. 80

29. If $P_i(\alpha_i, \beta_i)$ are points on the circle $x^2 + y^2 = a^2$ such that the magnitude of the product $\alpha_i \beta_i$ is maximum, then:

A. P_i are points on a square inscribed in the circle $x^2 + y^2 = a^2$.
B. P_i are points on a rectangle inscribed in the circle $x^2 + y^2 = a^2$ whose length is twice the breadth.
C. P_i are points on an equilateral triangle inscribed in the circle $x^2 + y^2 = a^2$.
D. P_i are points on an isosceles triangle inscribed in the circle $x^2 + y^2 = a^2$ with equal sides twice the third side.

30. Eight students have to be split into two teams of four for a relay race. The number of ways this can be done is:

A. 70   B. 35
C. 140   D. 21

31. An efficient study of the morning shift at a factory indicates that the number of units produced by an average worker t hours after 8.00 A.M. may be modelled by the formula $Q(t) = -t^3 + 3t^2 + 9t$. At what time in the morning is the worker performing most efficiently?

A. 11 A.M.   B. 12 A.M.
C. 10 A.M.   D. 9 A.M.

32. If z is a complex number and $|z + 4| \leq 3$, then the maximum value of $|z + 1|$ is:

A. 6   B. 0
C. 4   D. 10

33. If $f(x) = \cos ax + \sin x$ is periodic, then a cannot be:

A. π B. 0.3
C. 0.5   D. 5

34. In a hexagon two diagonals are drawn at random. The probability that they intersect inside the hexagon (like the left hand side figure) and not on the hexagon (like the right hand side figure) is:

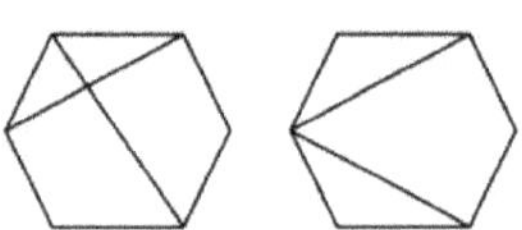

A. $\dfrac{5}{12}$ B. $\dfrac{1}{2}$

C. $\dfrac{5}{9}$ D. $\dfrac{2}{5}$

35. B_2CD, _?_, BCD_4, B_5CD, BC_6D

A. B_2C_2D B. BC_3D
C. B_2C_3D D. BCD_7

36. ABCD is a square of side length 1 cm. E, F, G and H are points on the side AB, BC, CD and DA respectively such that AE : EB = 1 : 1, BF : FC = 1 : 2, CG : GD = 1 : 3 and DH : HA = 1 : 4. The area of the quadrilateral EFGH is:

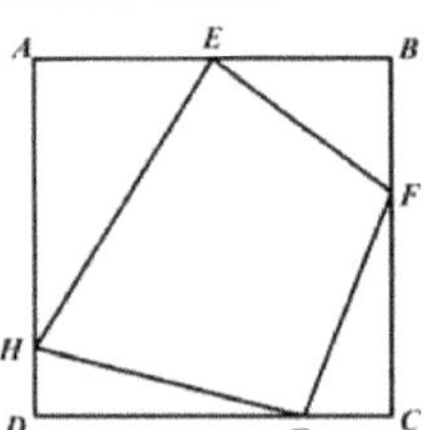

A. $\dfrac{19}{40}$ sq. cm.   B. $\dfrac{67}{120}$ sq. cm.

C. $\dfrac{1}{2}$ sq. cm.   D. $\dfrac{3}{5}$ sq. cm.

37. If $\sum_{r=1}^{k}\cos^{-1}\beta_r = \dfrac{k\pi}{2}$ for any $k \geq 1$ and

$A = \sum_{r=1}^{k}(\beta_r)^r$, then $\lim\limits_{x\to A}\dfrac{(1+x)^{\frac{1}{3}}-(1-2x)^{\frac{1}{4}}}{x+x^2}$

is equal to:

A. 0 B. $\dfrac{1}{2}$

C. $\dfrac{\pi}{2}$ D. $\dfrac{5}{2}$

38. In a survey for judging the popularity of three players X, Y and Z, 50% of the fans below the age 30 voted for X, 20% voted for Y and the rest voted for Z. 40% of the fans above the age 30 voted for X and the remaining voted equally for Y and Z. If the number of fans below the age of 30 is half of the number of fans above the age 30 who participated, which player is more popular?
A. Player X
B. Player Y
C. Player Z
D. Not enough information

39. The number of ways integers 1, 2, 3, 4, 5, 6 can be arranged so that 5 is neither adjacent to 4 nor to 6 is:
A. 240
B. 288
C. 430
D. 432

40. A packet containing 80 tennis balls has this declaration "all the balls have identical weight except one". If we have a weighing balance, minimum how many weighing we need to find the odd ball?
A. 4   B. 5
C. 6   D. 7

41. Which of the following figure has a point symmetry about the origin?

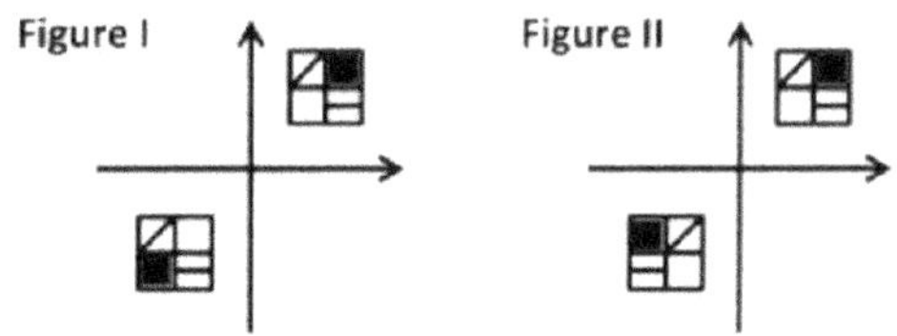

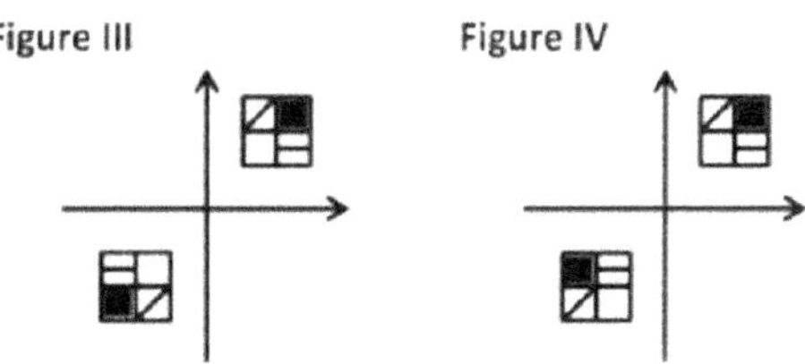

A. Figure I   B. Figure II
C. Figure III   D. Figure IV

42. If the adjoint of a 3×3 matrix P is $\begin{bmatrix} 1 & 4 & 4 \\ 2 & 1 & 7 \\ 1 & 1 & 3 \end{bmatrix}$, then the possible values of the determinant of P are:
A. ± 2 B. ± 1
C. ± 3 D. ± 4

43. A real number x is chosen randomly from the interval [1, 12]. If [.] denotes the greatest integer function, then the probability that $\left[\dfrac{x}{2}\right]$ is even is:

A. $\dfrac{1}{2}$ B. $\dfrac{1}{3}$

C. $\dfrac{4}{11}$ D. $\dfrac{1}{4}$

44. Two points are randomly selected on the circumference of a circle of radius 2 cms. The probability that the two points are more than 2 cms apart is:

A. $\dfrac{2}{3}$ B. 1

C. $\dfrac{5}{6}$ D. $\dfrac{1}{2}$

45. If the function $f: [1, \infty) \to [1, \infty)$ is defined by $f(x) = 2^{x(x-1)}$, then $f^{-1}(x)$ is:

A. $\left(\dfrac{1}{2}\right)^{x(x-1)}$

B. $\dfrac{1}{2}\left(1 + \sqrt{(1 + 4\log_2 x)}\right)$

C. $\dfrac{1}{2}\left(1 - \sqrt{(1 - 4\log_2 x)}\right)$

D. $\left(\dfrac{1}{2}\right)^{x(x+1)}$

46. The number of solutions of the equation $9x^2 - 18\,|x| + 5 = 0$ belonging to the domain of $\log_e [(x + 1)(x + 2)]$ is:

A. 1   B. 2

C. 3   D. 4

47. Let $f(x) = x \sin \pi x$, $x > 0$. Then for all natural numbers n, $f'(x)$ vanishes at:

A. A unique point in the interval $\left(n, n + \dfrac{1}{2}\right)$

B. A unique point in the interval $\left(n + \dfrac{1}{2}, n + 1\right)$

C. Two points in the interval $\left(n, n + \dfrac{1}{2}\right)$

D. Two points in the interval $(n, n + 1)$

48. 17 : 19 : : 47 : ?

A. 53   B. 59

C. 41   D. 34

49. What should be placed on the right side of the bottom scale in order to make it balance?

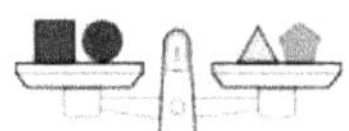

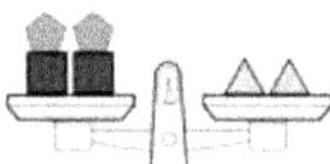

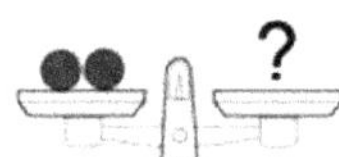

A. 3 pentagons B. 4 pentagons
C. 4 triangles   D. 5 triangles

50. The figure shows two ellipses whose major axis are perpendicular to each other. Each ellipse passes through the foci of the other ellipse that forms the vertices of a square. The shaded square encloses an area of 16 square units.

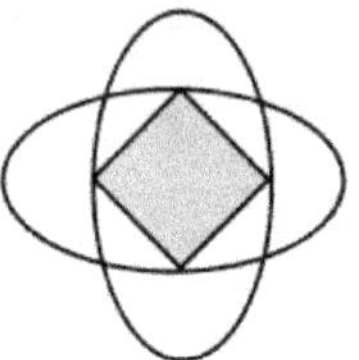

The area of one of the ellipse is:

A. $16\pi\sqrt{2}$ B. 16π

C. $8\pi\sqrt{2}$ D. 8π

51. The distinct linear function(s) which map(s) $[-1, 1]$ onto $[0, 2]$ is/are:

A. $X + 1, -X + 1$ B. $X - 1, X + 1$
C. $-X - 1$ D. None of these

52. Number of possible tangents to the curve $y = \cos(x + y)$, $-3\pi \le x \le 3\pi$, that are parallel to the line $x + 2y = 0$, is:

A. 1   B. 2

C. 3   D. 4

53. If $84 \times 13 = 8$, $37 \times 13 = 6$, $26 \times 11 = 6$, then $56 \times 22 = ?$

A. 36   B. 39

C. 7   D. 11

54. Given that I. The prices of petrol and diesel in the domestic market have remained unchanged for the past few months. II. The crude oil prices in the international market have gone up substantially in the last few months.

A. Statement I is the cause and statement II is its effect

B. Statement II is the cause and statement I is its effect

C. Both the statements I and II are independent causes

D. Both the statements I and II are effects of independent causes

55. Two persons lie on three days of the week and remain honest on other days. First person lies on Fridays, Saturdays and Sundays and the second person lies on Tuesdays, Wednesdays and Thursdays. On which day of the week can both of them say "I will lie tomorrow"?

A. Monday   B. Thursday
C. Friday   D. Sunday

56. DCXW, FEVU, HGTS, JIRQ, ?

A. LKPO   B. ABYZ
C. JLRQ   D. LMRS

57. A closed curve is defined parametrically as

$$x = \frac{1-t^2}{1+t^2} \text{ and } y = \frac{2t}{1+t^2}.$$ The area enclosed by the curve is equal to:

A. π sq. units   B. $\dfrac{\pi}{2}$ sq. units

C. $\dfrac{3\pi}{4}$ sq. units   D. $\dfrac{3\pi}{2}$ sq. units

58. The number of eight digit positive integers the sum of whose digits is 4 is:

A. 119   B. 120
C. 198   D. 105

59. Following information is given:

All dogs like to run

Some dogs like to swim

Some dogs look like their masters

If the first three statements are facts, which of the following statements must also be a fact?

I. All dogs who like to swim look like their masters.

II. Dogs who like to swim also like to run.

III. Dogs who like to run do not look like their masters.

A. I only
B. II only
C. II and III only
D. None of the statements is a known fact

60. There are four photocopying machines in a shop. A mechanic has been told that there are exactly two faulty machines. He wants to test them one by one in a random order (without replacement) until he can identify the two faulty machines. The probability that exactly two tests are needed to find the two faulty machines is:

A. $\dfrac{1}{6}$ B. $\dfrac{1}{2}$

C. $\dfrac{2}{3}$ D. $\dfrac{1}{3}$

61. The figure shows two ellipses whose major axis are perpendicular to each other. Each ellipse passes through the foci of the other ellipse that forms the vertices of a square. The shaded square encloses an area of 16 square units.

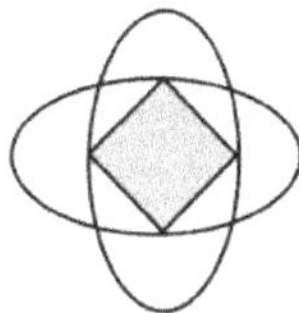

The equation of the ellipse with horizontal major axis is:

A. $\dfrac{x^2}{16} + \dfrac{y^2}{8} = 1$ B. $\dfrac{x^2}{8} + \dfrac{y^2}{4} = 1$

C. $\dfrac{x^2}{8} + y^2 = 1$ D. $\dfrac{x^2}{8} + \dfrac{y^2}{2} = 1$

62. The area of the triangle formed by the positive x-axis, the tangent and the normal to the circle $x^2 + y^2 = 9$ at $\left(2, \sqrt{5}\right)$ is:

A. $9\sqrt{5}$ sq. units   B. $\dfrac{9\sqrt{5}}{2}$ sq. units

C. $\dfrac{9\sqrt{5}}{4}$ sq. units   D. $\dfrac{3\sqrt{5}}{2}$ sq. units

63. The domain of $f(x)$ is (0, 1), therefore domain of $f(e^x) + f(\ln |x|)$ is:

A. $(-1, e)$ B. $(1, e)$
C. $(-e, -1)$ D. $(-e, 1)$

64. PABCD is a pyramid with a rectangular base ABCD. If $\overrightarrow{OP} = 3\hat{k}$, $\overrightarrow{OA} = \hat{i} + 2\hat{j}$ and $\overrightarrow{OC} = -\hat{i} - 2\hat{j}$, then $\overrightarrow{PB} =$

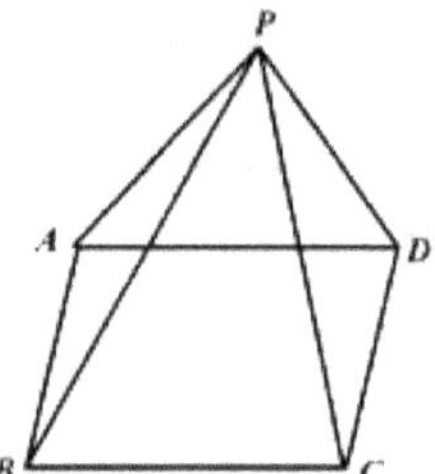

A. $\hat{i} - 2\hat{j} - 8\hat{k}$ B. $\hat{i} + 2\hat{j} + 8\hat{k}$

C. $-\hat{i} + 2\hat{j} - 8\hat{k}$ D. $-\hat{i} - 2\hat{j} - 8\hat{k}$

65. $\lim\limits_{x \to \infty} \left(\dfrac{\sum_{k=1}^{1000} (k+x)^m}{x^m + 10^{1000}} \right)$ for $m > 101$ is:

A. 10 B. 10^2

C. 10^3 D. 10^4

66. The graph gives the ratio of the export and import of a company. If the imports of the company in 2007 was increased by 40%, the ratio of exports to the increased import would be:

A. 0.25 B. 0.2

C. 1.25 D. 1.35

67. Mr. A wanted to visit Mr. B. The roads were laid out on a grid map, and Mr. B's house was 6 blocks north and 8 blocks east. Unfortunately, there was some rally, and that intersection (marked X) was blocked off so Mr. A could not go through it. If Mr. A were to travel only north and east, then the number of routes he can take to reach the house of Mr. B is:

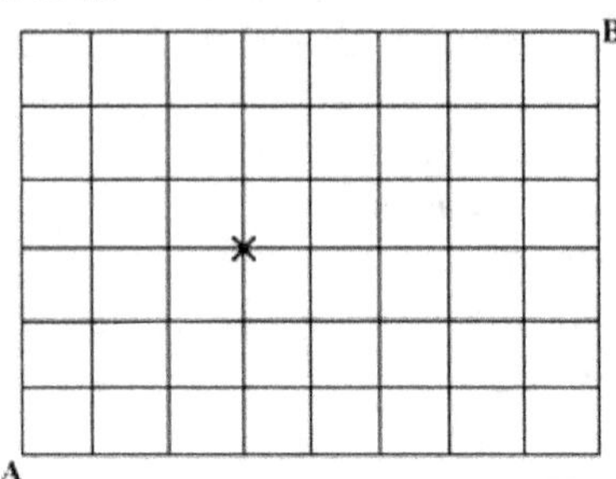

A. ${}^{8}C_6 - {}^{3}C_3$ B. ${}^{14}C_6 - {}^{6}C_3$

C. ${}^{14}C_6 - {}^{8}C_5$ D. ${}^{14}C_8 - {}^{6}C_3 \times {}^{8}C_5$

68. For two complex numbers z_1 and z_2, if $\dfrac{5z_2}{7z_1}$ is purely imaginary, then $\left| \dfrac{2z_1 + 3z_2}{2z_1 - 3z_2} \right|$ is equal to:

A. $\dfrac{5}{7}$ B. $\dfrac{2}{3}$

C. $\dfrac{25}{49}$ D. 1

69. Which of the answer figure best fits the missing portion of the question figure?

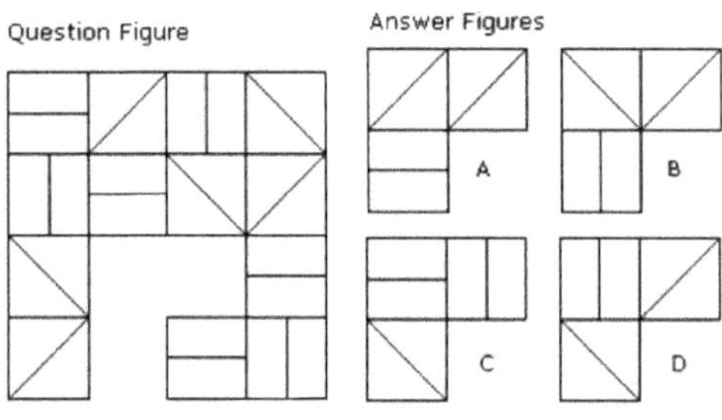

A. Figure A   B. Figure B

C. Figure C   D. Figure D

70. If a, b, c are complex numbers and $\bar{z}$ denotes the conjugate of a complex number z, then the determinant $\Delta = \begin{vmatrix} 0 & -b & -c \\ \bar{b} & 0 & -a \\ \bar{c} & \bar{a} & 0 \end{vmatrix}$ is:

A. a non-zero real number

B. purely imaginary

C. 0

D. a complex number with non-zero real part

71. If a function $f(x)$ satisfies the relation

$f(x + y) = f(x) + f(y) + xy(x + y), \forall\, x, y \in R.$
If $f'(0) = 1$, then
A. $f(X)$ is a polynomial function of degree 3
B. $f(X)$ is an exponential function
C. $f(X)$ is a polynomial function of degree 2
D. $f(3) = 6$

72. Let $\vec{a}, \vec{b}, \vec{c}$ be three vectors such that no two vectors are collinear.

If $\left(\vec{a} \times \vec{b}\right) \times \vec{c} = \dfrac{1}{3}|\vec{b}|\,|\vec{c}|\,\vec{a}$ and θ is the angle

between $\vec{b}$ and $\vec{c}$, then the value of $\sin\theta$ is:

A. $\dfrac{-2\sqrt{2}}{3}$ B. $\dfrac{2}{3}$

C. $\dfrac{2\sqrt{2}}{3}$ D. $\dfrac{\sqrt{2}}{3}$

73. In a code language 35796 is written as 44887. Find the code for 46823:
A. 55914   B. 57194
C. 55934   D. 55745

74. If for a complex number z, $|z| = \max\{|z - 1|, |z + 1|\}$, then

A. $|z + \bar{z}| = \dfrac{1}{2}$ B. $z + \bar{z} = 2$

C. $|z + \bar{z}| = 1$ D. $z - \bar{z} = 5$

75. Let $f(x) = \begin{cases} [x], & -2 \le x \le -\dfrac{1}{2} \\ 2x^2 - 1 & -\dfrac{1}{2} < x \le 2 \end{cases}$

where [.] represents the greatest integer function.
The number of points where $|f(x)|$ is non-differentiable, is:
A. 3   B. 4
C. 2   D. 5

76. Suppose that an oil well produces $P(t)$ thousands barrels of crude oil per month according to the formula

$P(t) = 100e^{-0.02t} - 100e^{-0.1t}$

where 't' is the number of months the well has been in production. The total amount of oil produced by the oil well in thousands of barrels will be:
A. 4000   B. 5000
C. 2000   D. 1000

77. A square is cut by two parallel lines at perpendicular distance 6 m apart such that the square is divide into three regions of equal areas. The area of the square is:

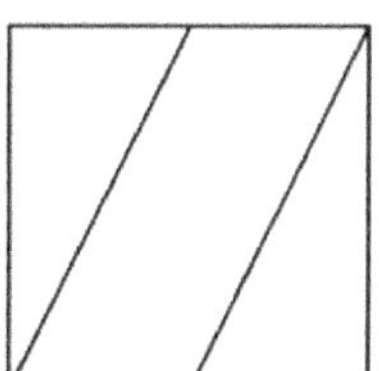

A. 468 sq. m   B. 486 sq. m
C. 684 sq. m   D. 648 sq. m

78. A point P(-1, 0) lies on the ellipse $4x^2 + y^2 = 4$. There are two points (a, b) and (a, c) on the ellipse at a maximum distance from P. The value of a is:
A. 1   B. 2

C. $\dfrac{1}{2}$ D. $\dfrac{1}{3}$

79. If $z = x + iy$, $z^{1/3} = a - ib$ and

$\dfrac{x}{a} - \dfrac{y}{b} = k(a^2 - b^2)$, then the value of k

equals:
A. 2   B. 4
C. 6   D. 1

80. Of the two men in a meeting, the guy sitting near the door is wearing a red tie and the guy sitting near the wall is wearing a blue tie. The two men are named X and Y, but we don't know who is X and who is Y. The person wearing the blue ties declares that he is X and the other person declares he is Y. If at least one of them is lying then:
A. X is wearing blue tie
B. Y is wearing red tie
C. X is wearing red tie
D. Information is not enough to decide

81. A particle starts at the origin with the velocity function $v(t)$ whose graph is as follows:

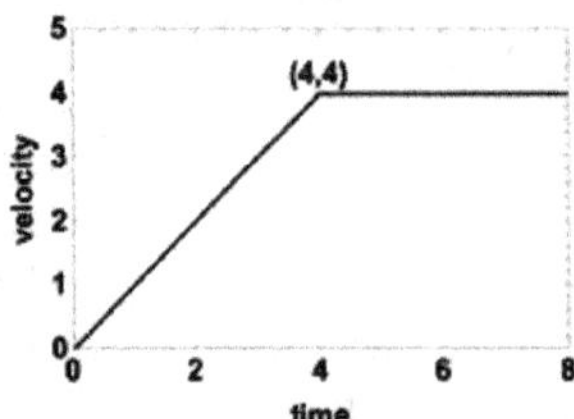

The displacement of the particle at $t = 5$ sec is:

A. 16 units
B. 8 units
C. 12 units
D. 4 units

82. Let $f(x)$ be a non-zero continuous function satisfying $f(x + y) = f(x)f(y)\ \forall x, y \in R$, if $f(2) = 9$. Then $f(3) =$

A. 1
B. 27
C. 9
D. 6

83. N characters of information are held on magnetic tape in batches of 'x' character each; the batch processing time is $\alpha + \beta x^2$ seconds, α and β are constants. The optimum value of x for fast processing is:

A. $\dfrac{\alpha}{\beta}$
B. $\dfrac{\beta}{\alpha}$
C. $\sqrt{\dfrac{\beta}{\alpha}}$
D. $\sqrt{\dfrac{\alpha}{\beta}}$

84. 12, 28, 92, _?_

A. 348
B. 100
C. 264
D. 184

85. What is the missing figure below?

$$\triangle\,\square\,\triangle\ |\ \square\,\bigcirc\,\bigcirc\ |\ \bigcirc\,\lozenge\,\bigcirc\ |\ \lozenge\,\square\ ?$$

$\lozenge$	$\square$	$\bigcirc$	$\triangle$
(1)	(2)	(3)	(4)

A. 1
B. 2
C. 3
D. 4

86. In the given grid each rectangle is labelled with its area in square units. The area of the shaded rectangle is (figure is not scaled):

2			▓
1	3		
	2	4	
		3	6

A. 2
B. 6
C. 18
D. 24

87. If $f(x) = \begin{vmatrix} 1 & x & x+1 \\ 2x & x(x-1) & (x+1)x \\ 3x(x-1) & x(x-1)(x-2) & (x+1)x(x-1) \end{vmatrix}$,

then $f(100)$ is equal to:

A. 0
B. 1
C. 100
D. -100

SECTION–B

Directions (Qs. No. 1 and 2): *Read the information carefully and answer these questions.*

If $f(x)$ is a differentiable function such that

$$f'(x) = f(x) + \int_0^2 f(x)\,dx.$$

If $f(0) = \dfrac{4 - e^2}{3}$, then:

1. $f(x)$ is equal to:

A. $e^x - \left(\dfrac{e^2 - 1}{3}\right)$

B. $e^x + \left(\dfrac{e^2 - 1}{3}\right)$

C. $e^x - \left(\dfrac{e^2 + 1}{3}\right)$

D. $e^x - \left(\dfrac{e^2 - 2}{3}\right)$

2. The number of solutions of $x + f(x) = 0$ is:

A. 0
B. 1
C. 2
D. 3

SECTION–C

Directions (Qs. No. 1 and 2): *Read the information carefully and answer these questions.*

The following graph represents the flow of traffic (number of vehicles) at intersections A, B and C in a city. x_1 and x_4 is the traffic coming at intersection A and x_2 is the traffic moving out of A. x_3 is the traffic moving out of B.

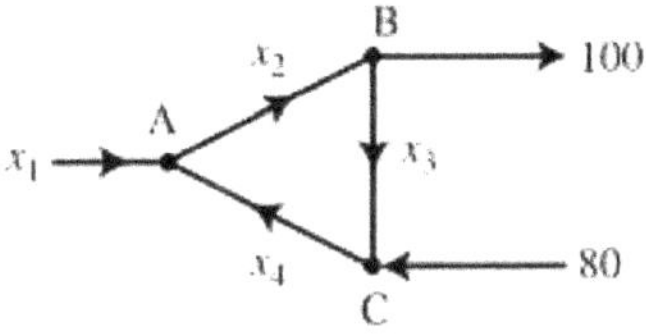

1. Assuming that the flows are all non-negative and the traffic moves smoothly with no traffic jams, then the general flow pattern of the network shown in the figure can be represented by the system of equations:

   A. $x_1 + x_4 = x_2$, $x_2 - x_3 = 100$, $x_3 - x_4 = -80$
   B. $x_1 - x_4 = x_2$, $x_2 - x_3 = 100$, $x_3 - x_4 = 80$
   C. $x_1 + x_4 = x_2$, $x_2 + x_3 = 100$, $x_3 - x_4 = -80$
   D. $x_1 + x_4 = x_2$, $x_2 - x_3 = 100$, $x_3 - x_4 = 80$

2. The system of equations obtained in previous question will have:
   A. no solution
   B. infinitely many solutions
   C. a unique solution with $x_1 = 29$
   D. a unique solution but x_1 will not be equal to 20.

SECTION–D

Directions (Qs. No. 1 and 2): *Read the information carefully and answer these questions.*

A disease is spreading in such a way that after 't' weeks, for $0 \le t \le 6$, it has affected $N(t) = 5 - t^2(t - 6)$ hundreds people.

1. The number of people infected when the rate at which the disease is spreading is maximum is:

   A. 3700
   B. 2300
   C. 2100
   D. 3000

2. The percentage rate at which the affected number of people change after week 5 is:
   A. 45% B. 32.3%
   C. 43.2% D. 50%

SECTION–E

Directions (Qs. No. 1 and 2): *Read the information carefully and answer these questions.*

Let (x, y) be a point on the perimeter of the triangle shown in the figure.

The vector $[x, y]^T$ is multiplied by the matrix

$$\begin{bmatrix} \cos\left(\dfrac{2\pi}{3}\right) & -\sin\left(\dfrac{2\pi}{3}\right) \\ \sin\left(\dfrac{2\pi}{3}\right) & \cos\left(\dfrac{2\pi}{3}\right) \end{bmatrix}$$

to get a new vector $[x'\ y']^T$.

1. The transformed triangle is

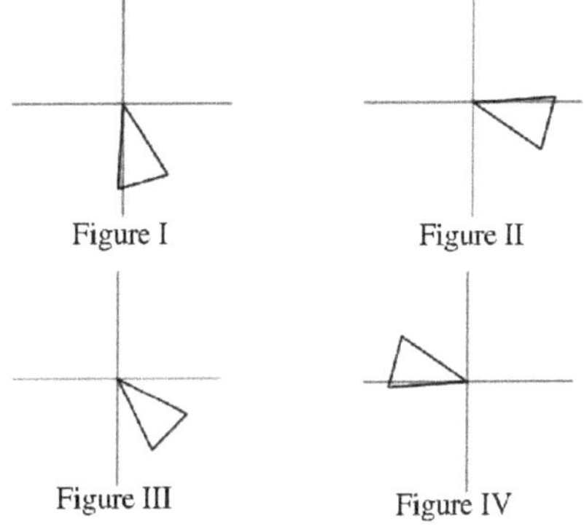

A. Figure I   B. Figure II
C. Figure III   D. Figure IV

2. The transformed triangle in previous question can also be obtained by:

A. Reflecting the original triangle about the line $y + \sqrt{3x} = 0$

B. Reflecting the original triangle about the x axis

C. Rotating the original triangle anticlockwise about the origin by an angle of $120°$

D. Rotating the original triangle clockwise about the origin by an angle of $120°$

SECTION–F

Directions (Qs. No. 1-5): *Read the information carefully and answer these questions.*

A survey of 100 people was conducted to find the popularity of Shahrukh Khan, Amir Khan and Salman Khan. 35 people liked watching the movies of Shahrukh Khan, 33 people liked watching the movies of Salman Khan and 43 people liked watching the movies of Amir Khan. 11 people said that they enjoyed watching movies of Shahrukh Khan and Amir Khan but not of Salman Khan, 7 people said that they enjoyed watching movies of Shahrukh Khan and Salman Khan but not of Amir Khan and 18 people said that they enjoyed watching movies of Salman Khan and Amir Khan. 5% of the respondents enjoyed watching the movies of all the three stars.

1. How many people did not enjoy watching the movies of any of the three given stars?
A. 11   B. 30
C. 23   D. 31

2. How many people enjoyed watching the movies of only one star?
A. 34   B. 11
C. 20   D. 30

3. How many people enjoyed watching the movies of at least two stars?
A. 31   B. 46
C. 80   D. 36

4. How many people do not enjoy watching the movies of Amir Khan?
A. 29   B. 57
C. 43   D. 46

5. How many people enjoy watching the movies of Shahrukh Khan but not Salman Khan?
A. 23   B. 12
C. 28   D. 33

ANSWERS

SECTION–A

1	2	3	4	5	6	7	8	9	10
D	C	A	B	B	A	C	D	A	C

11	12	13	14	15	16	17	18	19	20
B	C	A	C	D	A	C	C	B	D

21	22	23	24	25	26	27	28	29	30
D	A	D	A	B	C	A	A	A	B

31	32	33	34	35	36	37	38	39	40
A	A	A	A	B	B	*	A	B	A

41	42	43	44	45	46	47	48	49	50
C	A	C	A	B	C	C	A	B	C

51	52	53	54	55	56	57	58	59	60
A	C	C	D	B	A	A	B	B	D

61	62	63	64	65	66	67	68	69	70
A	C	C	A	C	C	D	D	D	B

71	72	73	74	75	76	77	78	79	80
A	C	A	C	A	A	A	D	B	C

81	82	83	84	85	86	87
C	B	D	A	A	D	A

SECTION–B		SECTION–C		SECTION–D		SECTION–E	
1	2	1	2	1	2	1	2
A	B	A	B	C	D	D	C

SECTION–F				
1	2	3	4	5
B	A	D	B	A

EXPLANATORY ANSWERS

1. Let,

$$z = \sqrt{3}\sin x + \cos x$$

$$= 2\left[\frac{\sqrt{3}}{2}.\sin x + \frac{1}{2}\cos x\right]$$

$$= 2\left[\sin x.\cos\frac{\pi}{6} + \sin\frac{\pi}{6}.\cos x\right]$$

$$= 2\sin\left(x+\frac{\pi}{6}\right)$$

Thus, for $-1 \le \sin\left(x+\frac{\pi}{6}\right) \le 1$

$$= -2 \le z \le 2$$

$$y = f(x) = [-2 + 4, 2 + 4]$$

$$\Rightarrow \qquad y = [2, 6]$$

3. We know that,

$$\lim_{(x,y)\to(\infty,\infty)} (f + g)(x,y)$$

$$= \lim_{(x,y)\to(\infty,\infty)} f(x,y) + \lim_{(x,y)\to(\infty,\infty)} g(x,y)$$

and $\lim_{(x,y)\to(\infty,\infty)} (f\,g)(x,y)$

$$= \lim_{(x,y)\to(x_0,y_0)} f(x,y) \, . \, \lim_{(x,y)\to(x_0,y_0)} g(x,y)$$

Based on that

$$\lim_{m\to\infty,n\to\infty}\left[1+\cos^{2m}(n!\pi x)\right]$$

$$= \lim_{m\to\infty,n\to\infty} 1 + \lim_{m,n\to\infty,\infty} \cos^{2m}(n!\pi x)$$

$= 1 + 1$ for $m \to \infty$, $n \to \infty$ and x is rational

$= 2$.

and for x is Irrational,

$$\lim_{m,n\to\infty,\infty} \cos^{2m}(n!\pi x) = 0$$

then, $\lim_{m,n\to\infty,\infty}\left[1+\cos^{2m}(n!\pi x)\right] = 1 + 0$

$$= 1.$$

4. We know that $|-x| = x$

Now, $\displaystyle\int_{-3}^{5} f(|x|).dx$

$$= \int_{-3}^{-2} f(|x|).dx + \int_{-2}^{-1} f(|x|).dx + \int_{-1}^{0} f(|x|).dx$$

$$+ \int_{0}^{1} f(|x|).dx + \int_{1}^{2} f(|x|).dx + \int_{2}^{3} f(|x|).dx$$

14

$$+\int_{3}^{4} f(|x|).dx + \int_{4}^{5} f(|x|).dx$$

Again from, $\displaystyle\int_{n}^{n+1} f(x).dx = \dfrac{n^2}{2}$

then, $\displaystyle\int_{-3}^{-2} f(|x|).dx = \dfrac{(|-2|^2)}{2}$

$$\int_{-2}^{-1} f(|x|).dx = \dfrac{(|-1|^2)}{2}$$

thus, $\displaystyle\int_{-3}^{5} f(|x|).dx$

$$= \dfrac{2^2}{2} + \dfrac{1^2}{2} + 0 + \dfrac{1^2}{2} + \dfrac{2^2}{2} + \dfrac{3^2}{2} + \dfrac{4^2}{2}$$

$$= \dfrac{4+1+1+4+9+16}{2} = \dfrac{35}{2}.$$

5. From question, only one statement is true and only one box contains a car. When the statement 3, "The car is not in box 1" true, then logically "The car is not in box 2" is false statement. And hence, the car is in box 2.

6. $\quad f(\sin 2x) = \sin x + \cos x$

Statement-I:

When, $\quad \sin 2x = \tan^2 x$

then, $f(\sin 2x) = f(\tan^2 x)$

$\qquad = \sin x + \cos x$

$\qquad = \sqrt{(\sin x + \cos x)^2}$

$\qquad = \sqrt{\sin^2 x + \cos^2 x + 2\sin x.\cos x}$

$\qquad = \sqrt{1 + \sin 2x}$

$\qquad = \sqrt{1 + \tan^2 x}$

$\qquad = \sqrt{\sec^2 x}$

$\qquad = \sec x$

$\therefore \quad f(\sin 2x) = f(\tan^2 x) = \sec x.$

Statement-II:

When, $\quad \sin 2x = x$

then, $f(\sin 2x) = f(x) = \sin x + \cos x$

$\qquad = \sqrt{(\sin x + \cos x)^2}$

$\qquad = \sqrt{\sin^2 x + \cos^2 x + 2\sin x.\cos x}$

$\qquad = \sqrt{1 + \sin 2x} = \sqrt{1 + x}$

$\therefore f(\sin 2x) = f(x) = \sqrt{1 + x}$

Hence, both statements I & II are true.

7. Let, $\qquad \vec{c} = x\hat{i} + y\hat{j} + z\hat{k}$

As, $\qquad |\vec{a}| = |\vec{b}| = |\vec{c}|$

$\therefore \quad \sqrt{x^2 + y^2 + z^2} = \sqrt{(1)^2 + (1)^2}$

$\qquad x^2 + y^2 + z^2 = 2 \qquad ...(i)$

Angle between $\vec{a}$ & $\vec{b}$

$$\cos\theta = \dfrac{\vec{a}.\vec{b}}{|\vec{a}|.|\vec{b}|}$$

$$= \dfrac{(\hat{i} + \hat{j}).(\hat{j} + \hat{k})}{\left|\sqrt{1^2 + 1^2}\right|.\left|\sqrt{1^2 + 1^2}\right|}$$

$$= \dfrac{1}{\sqrt{2}.\sqrt{2}}$$

$$\cos\theta = \dfrac{1}{2} \Rightarrow \theta = \dfrac{\pi}{3}$$

From question, angle between $\vec{b}$ & $\vec{c}$ $= \dfrac{\pi}{3}$

$$\cos\left(\dfrac{\pi}{3}\right) = \dfrac{\vec{b}.\vec{c}}{|\vec{b}|.|\vec{c}|}$$

$$= \dfrac{(\hat{j} + \hat{k}).(x\hat{i} + y\hat{j} + z\hat{k})}{\left|\sqrt{1^2 + 1^2}\right|.\left|\sqrt{x^2 + y^2 + z^2}\right|}$$

$$= \dfrac{y+z}{\sqrt{2}.\sqrt{2}} = \dfrac{y+z}{2}$$

$$\dfrac{1}{2} = \dfrac{y+z}{2}$$

$$y + z = 1 \qquad \qquad \qquad ...(ii)$$

Similarly, angle between $\vec{c}$ & $\vec{a}$ is $\dfrac{\pi}{3}$

then, $\cos\left(\dfrac{\pi}{3}\right) = \dfrac{\vec{c}.\vec{a}}{|\vec{c}|.|\vec{a}|}$

$$\dfrac{1}{2} = \dfrac{(x\hat{i} + y\hat{j} + z\hat{k}).(\hat{i} + \hat{j})}{\sqrt{x^2 + y^2 + z^2}.\sqrt{1^2 + 1^2}}$$

$$\dfrac{1}{2} = \dfrac{x+y}{\sqrt{2}.\sqrt{2}} \Rightarrow x + y = 1 \;...(iii)$$

From (ii) and (iii), we have,

$$x = z$$

Pluging $x = z$ into equation (i), we have,

$$x^2 + y^2 + x^2 = 2$$
$$2x^2 + y^2 = 2$$

From (iii) $x + y = 1 \Rightarrow y = 1 - x$

Then, $2x^2 + (1 - x)^2 = 2$

$$2x^2 + 1 + x^2 - 2x = 2$$
$$3x^2 - 2x - 1 = 0$$

$$x = \dfrac{2 \pm \sqrt{(-2)^2 - 4.3(-1)}}{2 \times 3}$$

$$= \dfrac{2 \pm 4}{6}$$

As, $\quad x^2 + y^2 + z^2 = 2$

then, $\qquad x = \dfrac{2-4}{6} = -\dfrac{1}{3}$

$$y = 1 - \left(-\dfrac{1}{3}\right) = 1 + \dfrac{1}{3} = \dfrac{4}{3}$$

$$z = x = -\dfrac{1}{3}$$

Hence, $\qquad \vec{c} = -\dfrac{1}{3}\hat{i} + \dfrac{4}{3}\hat{j} - \dfrac{1}{3}\hat{k}.$

8. We know that if $f(x)$ has period P

then period of $f\left(\dfrac{x}{k}\right) = k.P.$

Here, period of $f(x) = 7$

then period of $f\left(\dfrac{x}{3}\right) = 7 \times 3 = 21$

Again, Period of $g(x) = 11$

then, period of $g\left(\dfrac{x}{5}\right) = 11 \times 5 = 55$

Hence, period of $f(x).g\left(\dfrac{x}{5}\right) - g(x).f\left(\dfrac{x}{3}\right)$

$$= 21 \times 55 = 1155.$$

9. There are 3 members only

Suppose Radha is mother of Geeta and Geeta is mother of Sheela *i.e.,* Radha is grandmother of Sheela.

In this way, 1 grandmother is Radha

1 granddaughter is Sheela and 2 mothers are Radha & Geeta.

10. For $x = \left(-\dfrac{2}{5}, \dfrac{\pi-2}{5}\right)$

Domain of $f(x) = 5\left(\dfrac{-2}{5}\right) + 2 = 0$

to $\quad 5\left(\dfrac{\pi-2}{5}\right) + 2 = \pi$

For domain $(0, \pi)$,

Range of Cosine function $= [-1, 1]$

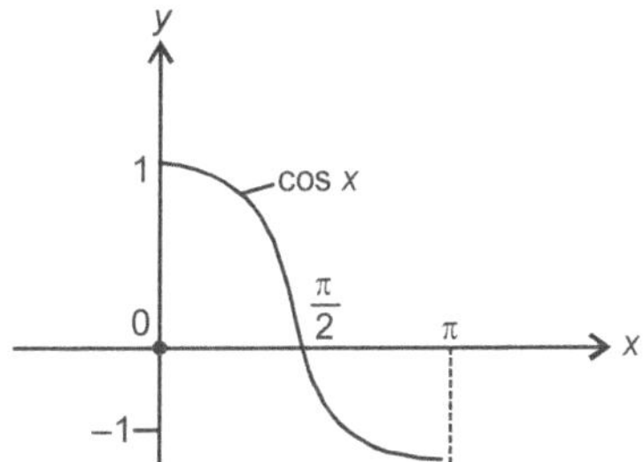

Hence, $f : A \to B$ is one-one and onto.

11. $\qquad f(x) = \displaystyle\int_{1}^{x} x(x^2 - 3x + 2).dx$

$$= \int_{1}^{x} (x^3 - 3x^2 + 2x).dx$$

$$= \left[\dfrac{x^4}{4} - \dfrac{3x^3}{3} + \dfrac{2x^2}{2}\right]_{1}^{x}$$

$$= \dfrac{x^4}{4} - x^3 + x^2 - \dfrac{1}{4}$$

Again, $\qquad f'(x) = x(x^2 - 3x + 2)$
$$= x(x - 2)(x - 1)$$
when, $\qquad f'(x) = 0,$
$$x(x - 2)(x - 1) = 0$$
$$x = 0, 1, 2$$
and $\qquad f''(x) = 3x^2 - 6x + 2$
Clearly, $f''(1) < 0$
Hence, $f(x)$ is local maximum at $x = 1$
$$f(1) = \frac{1}{4} - 1 + 1 - \frac{1}{4} = 0$$
And $f(x)$ has global maximum in $1 \le x \le 4$
at $x = 4$
$$f(4) = \frac{(4)^4}{4} - (4)^3 + (4)^2 - \frac{1}{4}$$
$$= \frac{64 - 1}{4} = \frac{63}{4}.$$

12. Given f is continuous and $f(x)$ is rational no. $\forall \in [1, 3]$ and $f(2) = 10$

$\Rightarrow f$ is a constant function in this interval thus $f(1.8) = 10.$

13.

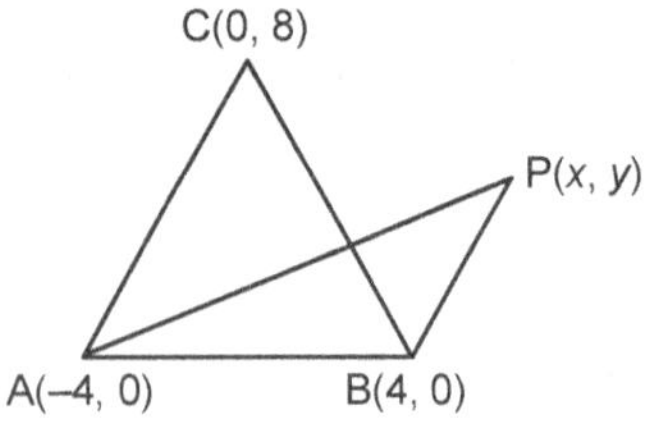

C(0, 8)

P(x, y)

A(–4, 0) $\qquad$ B(4, 0)

Length $AB = 4 - (-4) = 8$ unit
$$BC = AC = \sqrt{(4 - 0)^2 + (0 - 3)^2}$$
$$= \sqrt{25} = 5 \text{ units}$$
Let co-ordinate of point $P = (x, y)$

then, Area of $\triangle ABP = \frac{1}{2} \times AB \times y$

and, Area of $\triangle ABC = \frac{1}{2} \times AB \times 3$

From question,

$$\text{Area of } \triangle ABP = \frac{1}{2} \times \text{Area of } \triangle ABC$$

$$\frac{1}{2} \times AB \times y = \frac{1}{2} \times \frac{1}{2} \times AB \times 3$$

$\therefore \qquad\qquad y = \dfrac{3}{2}$

Again from question,
Perimeter of $\triangle ABC$ = Perimeter of $\triangle ABP$
So, AC + BC + AB = AP + BP + AB

$$5 + 5 = \sqrt{(x + 4)^2 + \left(\frac{3}{2}\right)^2} + \sqrt{(x - 4)^2 + \left(\frac{3}{2}\right)^2}$$

or, $\sqrt{(x + 4)^2 + \left(\dfrac{3}{2}\right)^2} + \sqrt{(x - 4)^2 + \left(\dfrac{3}{2}\right)^2} = 10$

On solving for x, we get, $x = 4.33$
Point P $(x, y) = (4.33, 1.5)$

Distance $CP = \sqrt{(4.33)^2 + (1.5 - 3)^2}$

$$= \sqrt{18.75 + 2.25} = \sqrt{21} \text{ units.}$$

15.

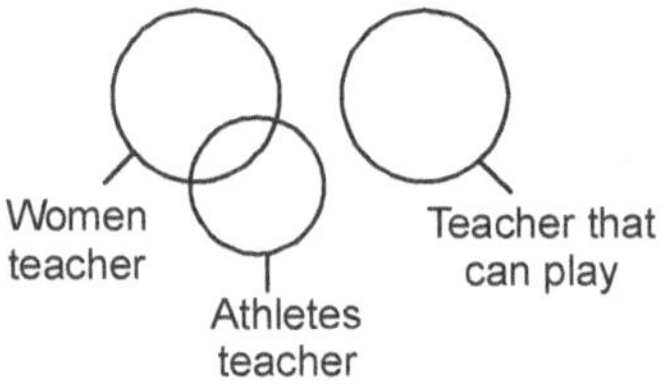

Women teacher

Teacher that can play

Athletes teacher

Thus, neither conclusion I nor conclusion II follows.

17. First we consider a set of three consecutive numbers *i.e.*, (1, 2, 3), (2, 3, 4)....(18, 19, 20)
Number of such sets = 18
Now, consider a set of two consecutive numbers
If the consecutive numbers are $(n - 1)$ and n
Then the remaining number can be $(n + 2)$, $(n + 3)$ 20
Since, the lowest n can be 2, we get

$$17 + 16 + 15 \dots + 1 = \frac{17 \times 18}{2} = 153$$

By symmetry we also have 153 subsets which have the non-consecutive element as the smallest.
Total number of consecutive elements set
= 18 + 153 + 153 = 324

Total number of subset

$$= {}^{20}C_3 = \frac{20 \times 19 \times 18}{6}$$
$$= 1140$$

So, total number of subsets with no consecutive elements

$$= 1140 - 324 = 816$$

Hence, required probability

$$= \frac{816}{1140} = \frac{68}{95}.$$

18.

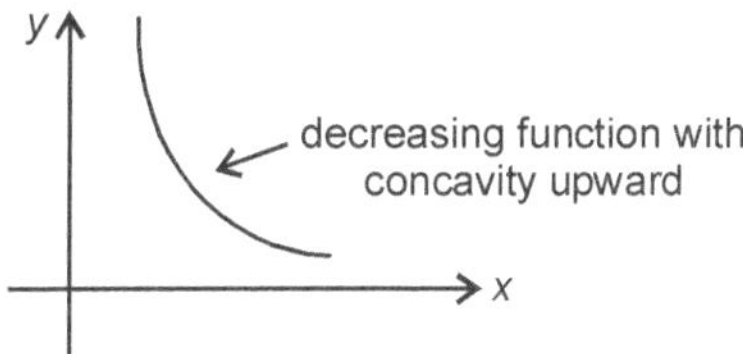

Code for 'wax' is 'bako'

Hence, code for 'wax statue' is 'wasibako'.

19. 30th September 1997 — Tuesday
30th September 1998 — Wednesday
30th September 1999 — Thursday
30th September 2000 — Saturday
30th September 2001 — Sunday
30th September 2002 — Monday
30th September 2003 — Tuesday

Hence, Wedding anniversary on 30th September, 2003 will be on same day Tuesday.

20. Graph of any function $f(x)$, a decreasing function with concavity upwards:

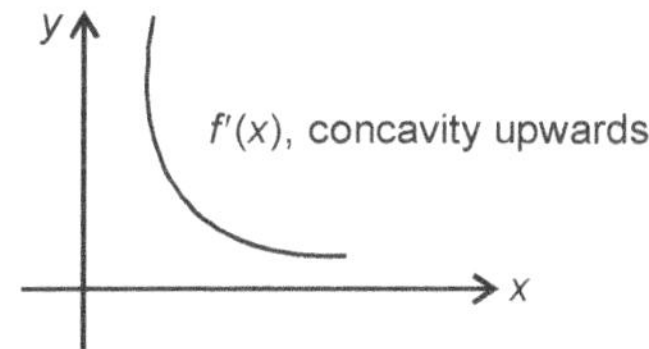

On drawing the $f'(x)$, we can see it's concavity is also upwards.

21. Let the equation of the circle is $x^2 + y^2 = r^2$ where r = radius of the circle.

From parabola equation

$$y = x^2 - 3 \Rightarrow x^2 = y + 3$$

Plug in $x^2 = y + 3$ into circle equation,

$$y + 3 + y^2 = r^2$$
$$y^2 + y + (3 - r^2) = 0$$

For real value of y, discriminant D $\geq$ 0

$$(-1)^2 - 4(3 - r^2) \geq 0$$
$$4r^2 \geq 12 - 1$$
$$4r^2 \geq 11$$
$$2r \geq \sqrt{11}$$

Here, circle is inscribed inside parabola,

$$\therefore \qquad 2r = \sqrt{11}$$

Perimeter of the circle = $2\pi r = \pi\sqrt{11}$ units.

22. Alpha : "Always tells truth"

Beta : "Always lies"

Gamma : "may be truth or lies".

Y says he is beta and X declares that he is not beta. So X may be gamma.

23.
$$f(x) = [x], \quad -2 \leq x \leq -\frac{1}{2}$$
$$f(x) = -2, \text{ from } -2 \leq x < -1$$
$$f(x) = -1, \text{ from } -1 \leq x < -\frac{1}{2}$$

and $\quad f(x) = 2x^2 - 1, \quad -\frac{1}{2} < x \leq 2$

$$f\left(-\frac{1}{2}\right) = 2\left(-\frac{1}{2}\right)^2 - 1 = -\frac{1}{2}$$

thus $f(x)$ is discontinuous at three points. Now graph of $f|x|$ would be:

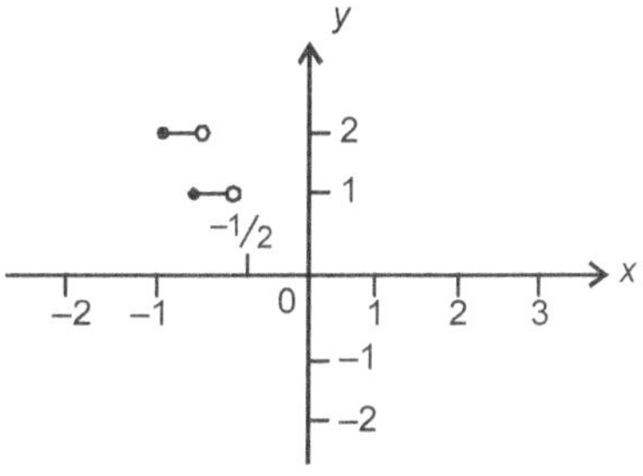

24. Given system of equation have non-trivial solution

then,
$$\begin{vmatrix} 1 & 4a & a \\ 1 & 3b & b \\ 1 & 2c & c \end{vmatrix} = 0$$

$$\begin{vmatrix} 1 & 4a & a \\ 0 & 3b-4a & b-a \\ 0 & 4a-2c & a-c \end{vmatrix} = 0$$

$\{$Applying $R_2 \to R_2 - R_1$ and $R_3 \to R_1 - R_3\}$

$(3b - 4a)(a - c) - (b - a)(4a - 2c) = 0$

$3ab - 4a^2 - 3bc + 4ac - 4ab + 4a^2 + 2bc - 2ac = 0$

$$-ab - bc + 2ac = 0$$

$$-\frac{1}{c} - \frac{1}{a} + \frac{2}{b} = 0$$

$$\frac{2}{b} = \frac{1}{a} + \frac{1}{c}$$

Hence, a, b and c are in H.P.

25. $|z_1 - z_2| \geq |z_1| - |z_2|$

For minimum value of

$$|z_1 - z_2| = |z_1| - |z_2|$$
$$|z_2 - (3 + i4)| = 5$$
$$|z_2| - |5| = 5$$
$$|z_2| = 5 + 5 = 10$$

Thus, minimum values of

$$|z_1 - z_2| = 12 - 10 = 2.$$

27. $1 \blacksquare 2 \blacksquare 3 \blacksquare 4 \blacksquare 5 \blacksquare 6 \blacksquare 7 \blacksquare 8 = 9$

By put in '+' or '–' sign in place of square boxes we can't get required number 9 in any way.

28. Halting a bus at three station out of 10 stations on a circular road of a city is same as sitting at three position among 10 sitting positions in circular sitting arrangement.

$$= \frac{1}{2} \times {}^{10}C_3 = \frac{1}{2} \times \frac{10 \times 9 \times 8}{3 \times 2} = 60$$

Now, three are total 10 positions in which all three stops are continuous.

Hence, required number of possible bus routes

$$= 60 - 10 = 50.$$

29. Point P_i (α_i, β_i) are lies on the circle

$$x^2 + y^2 = a^2$$

Such that magnitude of product is maximum

then,
$$\alpha_i^2 + \beta_i^2 = a^2$$
$$\alpha_i^2 = a^2 - \beta_i^2$$
$$\alpha_i = \sqrt{a^2 - \beta_i^2}$$

Now,   Let $Z = \alpha_i.\beta_i$

$$Z = \sqrt{a^2 - \beta_i^2} \cdot \beta_i$$

Differentiating both sides with respect to β_i, we have,

$$\frac{dz}{d\beta_i} = \sqrt{a^2 - \beta_i^2} + \frac{\beta_i(-2\beta_i)}{2\sqrt{a^2 - \beta_i^2}}$$

$$= \sqrt{a^2 - \beta_i^2} - \frac{\beta_i^2}{\sqrt{a^2 - \beta_i^2}}$$

$$= \frac{a^2 - \beta_i^2 - \beta_i^2}{\sqrt{a^2 - \beta_i^2}} = \frac{a^2 - 2\beta_i^2}{\sqrt{a^2 - \beta_i^2}}$$

For maximum value, $\dfrac{dz}{d\beta_i} = 0$,

then, $\dfrac{a^2 - 2\beta_i^2}{\sqrt{a^2 - \beta_i^2}} = 0 \Rightarrow a^2 - 2\beta_i^2$

$$\Rightarrow \quad \beta_i = \frac{a}{\sqrt{2}}$$

From, $\alpha_i = \sqrt{a^2 - \beta_i^2}$

$$= \sqrt{a^2 - \frac{a^2}{2}} = \frac{a}{\sqrt{2}}$$

Thus, $(\alpha_i, \beta_i) = \left(\dfrac{a}{\sqrt{2}}, \dfrac{a}{\sqrt{2}} \right)$

Hence, Point P_i lies on a square inscribed in the circle $x^2 + y^2 = a^2$.

30. Number of ways of selecting 4 students out of 8 students $= {}^8C_4$

$$= \frac{8 \times 7 \times 6 \times 5}{4 \times 3 \times 2 \times 1} = 70$$

Now, these 4 students can go one of the two teams in $^2C_1$ ways.

Hence, required number of ways of forming a team

$$= \frac{70}{^2C_1} = \frac{70}{2} = 35.$$

31. For worker performing most efficiently,

$$Q'(t) = 0$$
$$Q'(t) = -3t^2 + 6t + 9$$
$$= -3(t^2 - 2t - 3)$$

For
$$Q'(t) = 0$$
$$-3(t^2 - 2t - 3) = 0$$
$$(t - 3)(t + 1) = 0$$
$$t = 3$$

Hence, worker is performing most efficiently at $8 + 3 = 11{:}00$ A.M.

32. $|z + 4| \le 3 \Rightarrow$ Maximum of $|z + 4| = 3$

Now,
$$= |z + 1|$$
$$= |z + 1 + 3 - 3|$$
$$= |z + 4 - 3|$$
$$= |z + 4| + |-3|$$
$$= |z + 4| + 3$$
$$\Rightarrow \qquad 3 + 3 = 6$$

Thus, $\qquad |z + 1| \le 6$

Hence, maximum value of $|z + 1| = 6$.

33. $f(x) = \cos ax + \sin x$

$\sin x$ is periodic with period $= 2\pi$

$\cos ax$ is periodic with period $= \dfrac{2\pi}{a}$

In order to the given function

$f(x) = \cos ax + \sin x$ be periodic, it is necessary that some integer number n of periods of $\cos ax$ must be equal to some integer number m of periods $\sin x$.

Thus, we have

$$n \cdot \frac{2\pi}{a} = m \cdot 2\pi$$
$$\Rightarrow \qquad a = \frac{n}{m}$$

Hence, a must be a rational number.

Thus $a \ne \pi$.

34. Number of diagonals in a hexagon

$$= {}^6C_2 - 6 = 9$$

We can choose any 2 out of these 9 in

$$^9C_2 = 36$$
$$\therefore \qquad n(S) = 36$$

Now, number of intersection points inside the hexagon, $\qquad n(A) = {}^6C_4 = 15$

We can choose any 1 out of these 15 points in 15 ways

$$\therefore \qquad n(E) = 15$$

Hence, required probability $= \dfrac{15}{36} = \dfrac{5}{12}$.

35. B_2CD, BC_3D, BCD_4, B_5CD, BC_6D

In each next term, number position shifted on place right and also it is increases by 1.

39. Number of ways of arrangement of these 6 numbers $\qquad = 6! = 720$

Number of ways of arrangement in which 4 and 5 together $\qquad = 5! \times 2! = 240$

Number of ways of arrangement in which 5 and 6 together $\qquad = 5! \times 2! = 240$

Number of ways of arrangement in which number are '456' or '654' pattern

$$= 2! \times 4! = 48$$

$\therefore$ Number of ways of arrangement in which 5 is neither adjacent to 4 or 6

$$= 720 - 240 - 240 + 48$$
$$= 288.$$

40. In first weighing, we put 40 balls in weighing balance, and take out those 40 balls which measure less weight.

Again we put 20 balls in weighing balance each time and take out those 20 balls which measure less weight.

Again we put 10 balls in each weighing balance and take out those 10 balls which measure, less weight.

Again, we put 5 balls in each weighing balance and take out those 5 balls which measure less weight.

Now, we are left with 5 balls which contains one ball of indifferent weight.

In those 5 balls we put 2 balls on each balance and try to get balance. In due cases we would get 5th ball which is not on the balance is the indifferent ball among all the 80 balls.

41.

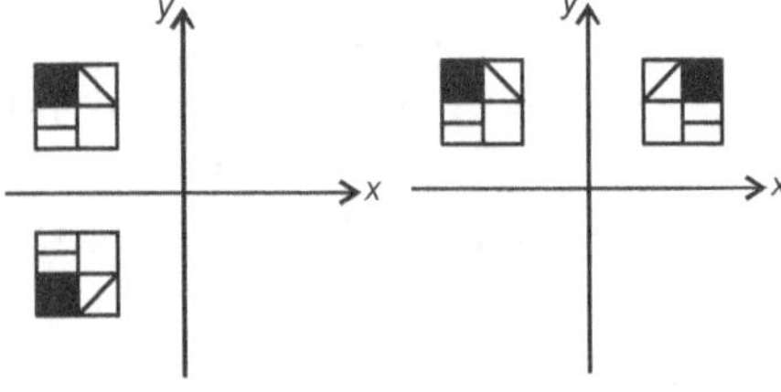

Symmetry about x-axis   Symmetry about y-axis

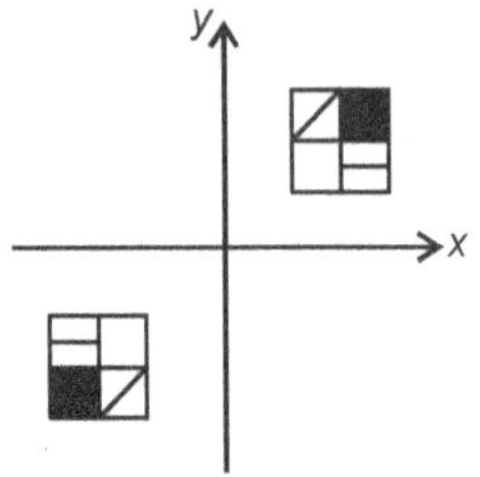

Symmetry about origin.

42. We know that for a third order matrix P

$$|\text{Adj P}| = |\text{P}^2|$$

Where,

$$|\text{Adj P}| = 1(3-7) - 4(6-7) + 4(2-1) = 4$$
$$|\text{P}^2| = 4$$
$$|\text{P}| = \pm 2.$$

43.

$$n(E) = n\left[\frac{x}{2}\right]$$

$$\left[\frac{x}{2}\right] = 0;\ 1 \le x < 2$$
$$= 1;\ 2 \le x < 4$$
$$= 2;\ 4 \le x < 6$$
$$= 3;\ 6 \le x < 8$$
$$= 4;\ 8 \le x < 10$$
$$= 5;\ 10 \le x < 12$$
$$= 6;\ x = 12$$

$\left[\dfrac{x}{2}\right]$ is even for 0, 2, 4, 6 $\therefore n\left[\dfrac{x}{2}\right] = 4$

$$n(S) = n[x] = 11$$

Hence, required probability

$$= \frac{n(E)}{n(S)} = \frac{4}{11}.$$

44.

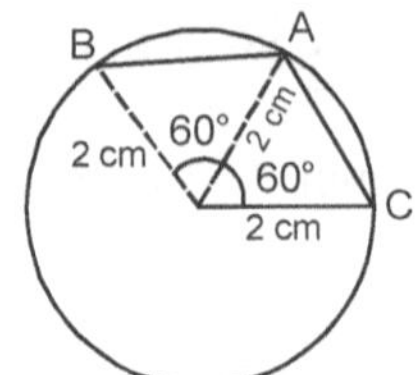

Let, A be any point on the circumference of a circle of radius 2 cm.

Any other points which lies less than 2 cm from point A is shown here.

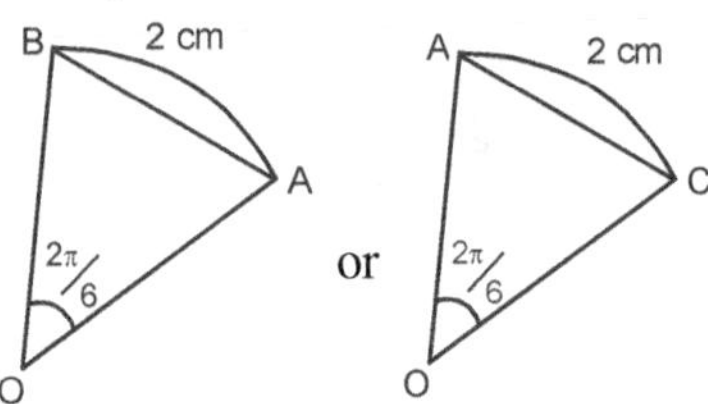

Circumference on that two points are less than 2 cm aparts

$$= 2 \times \frac{60°}{360°} \times 2\pi \times 2 = \frac{1}{3} \times 2\pi \times 2$$

Circumference of the circle $= 2\pi \times 2$

Probability that 2 points are less than 2 cm apart

$$= \frac{\dfrac{1}{3} \times 2\pi \times 2}{2\pi \times 2} = \frac{1}{3}$$

Hence, required probability

$$= 1 - \frac{1}{3} = \frac{2}{3}.$$

45. $f(x) = y = 2^{x(x-1)}$

Taking log on both sides, we have

$$\log y = x(x-1) \log 2$$
$$x(x-1) = \log_2 y$$
$$x^2 - x - \log_2 y = 0$$
$$x = \frac{1 \pm \sqrt{1 + 4\log_2 y}}{2}$$

For, $f : [1, \infty) \to [1, \infty)$

$$x = \frac{1 + \sqrt{1 + 4\log_2 y}}{2}$$

$$\therefore \quad f^{-1}(x) = \frac{1 + \sqrt{1 + 4\log_2 x}}{2}.$$

46. Given equation $9|x|^2 - 18|x| + 5 = 0$

Let, $\qquad |x| = z$

Then, $\quad 9z^2 - 18z + 5 = 0$

$$9z^2 - 3z - 15z + 5 = 0$$
$$(3z - 5)(3z - 1) = 0$$
$$z = \frac{1}{3} \text{ or } \frac{5}{3}$$
$$|x| = \frac{1}{3} \text{ or } \frac{5}{3}$$
$$x = \pm\frac{1}{3} \text{ or } \pm\frac{5}{3}$$

Domain of $\log_e(x + 1)(x + 2)$ is

$$(x + 1)(x + 2) \geq 0$$

$x \in (-\infty, -2] \cup [-1, \infty)$

Hence, value of x in the domain of

$x \in (-\infty, -2] \cup [-1, \infty)$ are $\dfrac{-1}{3}, \dfrac{1}{3}$ and $\dfrac{5}{3}$.

47. $\qquad\qquad f'(x) = 0$

then, $\qquad \dfrac{d}{dx}(x.\sin \pi x) = 0$

$$\pi x \cos(\pi x) + \sin \pi x = 0$$
$$\pi x = -\tan \pi x$$

The existence of a solution is ensured by the fact that on each interval $\tan(\pi x)$ go from $-\infty$ to ∞ and πx is finite.

The uniqueness is given by the strict monotony of $\pi x + \tan(\pi x)$ in the interval $\left(n, \ n+\dfrac{1}{2}\right)$.

48. 17 : 19 :: 47 : $\boxed{53}$

$(\times 3)-4$

$(\times 3)-4$

49. Weight of one rectangle $\square$: x kg

Weight of one circle $\bigcirc$: y kg

Weight of one triangle $\triangle$: a kg

Weight of one pentagon $\pentagon$: b kg.

From figure in the question:

$$x + y = a + b$$

and $\qquad 2(x + b) = 2a \Rightarrow x + b = a$

Plug in $a = x + b$ in above equation,

$$x + y = x + b + b$$
$$y = 2b \Rightarrow 2y = 4b$$

Thus, weight of two circles is equal to weight of four pentagons.

50. Area of the enclosed square = 16 sq. units

Side of the square = $\sqrt{16}$ = 4 units

Diagonal of the square

$= \sqrt{4^2 + 4^2} = 4\sqrt{2}$ units

From fig. diagonal of the square

= Distance between foci

= Length of the minor axis = $4\sqrt{2}$

Thus, semi-minor axis, $b = \dfrac{4\sqrt{2}}{2} = 2\sqrt{2}$

and the distance from the centre to one of the foci is $c = 2\sqrt{2}$

Using the formula:

$$a^2 - b^2 = c^2$$
$$a^2 = b^2 + c^2$$
$$= \left(2\sqrt{2}\right)^2 + \left(2\sqrt{2}\right)^2 = 16$$
$$a = 4$$

Again, Area of the ellipse

$$= \pi.a.b.$$
$$= \pi.4.\left(2\sqrt{2}\right) = 8\pi\sqrt{2}.$$

51. For mapping $y = x + 1$

For $x = [-1, 1]$; $\quad y = -1 + 1 = 0$

and $\qquad\qquad\quad y = 1 + 1 = 2$

$\qquad\qquad\qquad\quad y = [0, 2]$

This is onto mapping

Again for $y = -x + 1$ mapping

For $x = [-1, 1]$; $\quad y = -(-1) + 1 = 2$

$\qquad\qquad\qquad\quad y = -1 + 1 = 0$

$\qquad\qquad\qquad\quad y = [0, 2]$

This is onto mapping.

52. Given curve $y = \cos(x + y)$
$$y' = -\sin(x + y)(1 + y')$$
$$(1 + \sin(x + y))y' = -\sin(x + y)$$
$$y' = \frac{-\sin(x+y)}{(1+\sin(x+y))}$$

As the tangent is parallel to the line
$$x + 2y = 0$$
So, slope of the tangent
$$y' = \frac{-\sin(x+y)}{1+\sin(x+y)} = -\frac{1}{2}$$
$$\frac{\sin(x+y)}{1+\sin(x+y)} = \frac{1}{2}$$
$$2\sin(x + y) = 1 + \sin(x + y)$$
$$\sin(x + y) = 1$$
$$\Rightarrow \quad (x + y) = n\pi + (-1)^n . \frac{\pi}{2}$$

Possible values in the given range of x will be $\dfrac{\pi}{2}, \dfrac{3\pi}{2}$ and $\dfrac{5\pi}{2}$.

54. The price of crude oil remains unchange when its prices in international market remains unchange. With change in price of crude oil in the international market, its price in domestic market also changes.

Hence, both the statements are effects of two independent causes.

55. On Thursday first person will lie honest and on friday he tells lies

So, first person says "I will lie tomorrow" on Thursday.

On Thursday second person lie that "I will lie tomorrow" because on Friday second person will be honest. Hence, that particular day is "Thursday".

57. Let, $t = \tan \theta$
$$x = \frac{1 - \tan^2 \theta}{1 + \tan^2 \theta}$$
$$\Rightarrow \quad x = \cos 2\theta$$
$$y = \frac{2 \tan \theta}{1 + \tan^2 \theta}$$
$$\Rightarrow \quad y = \sin 2\theta$$

Area enclosed by the curve
$$A = \frac{\pi}{2} \sqrt{\left(\frac{dx}{d\theta}\right)^2 + \left(\frac{dy}{d\theta}\right)^2} . d\theta$$
$$= \frac{\pi}{2} \sqrt{\left\{\frac{d(\cos 2\theta)}{d\theta}\right\}^2 + \left\{\frac{d(\sin 2\theta)}{d\theta}\right\}^2} . d\theta$$
$$= \frac{\pi}{2} \sqrt{(-2\sin 2\theta)^2 + (2\cos 2\theta)^2} = \frac{\pi}{2} \times 2$$
$$= \pi \text{ sq. units.}$$

58. Eight digits positive integers, the sum of whose digits is 4:

Consist of '0' and '1' only:

One of such number is:

1	0	1	0	1	0	1	0

Number of such numbers $= 1 \times \dfrac{7!}{4!3!} = 35$

When number consists of 0, 1 and 2 only one of such number is:

1	0	1	0	2	0	0	0

Number of numbers with first digit '1'
$$= \frac{7!}{5!} = 7 \times 6 = 42$$

Number of numbers with first digit '2'
$$= \frac{7!}{2!5!} = 21$$

Number of numbers consists of '0' and '2'; one of such number is

2	0	0	0	2	0	0	0

Number of such number,
$$= \frac{7!}{6!} = 7$$

Number of numbers consists of '0', '1' and '3'; only one of such number is

3	0	0	1	0	0	0	0

Number of such numbers
$$= \frac{7! \, 2!}{6!} = 7 \times 2 = 14$$

Number of numbers consists of '0' and '4'; only one and that number is $= 1$

4	0	0	0	0	0	0	0

Hence, total numbers of such number is

$= 35 + 42 + 21 + 7 + 14 + 1$

$= 120.$

59. 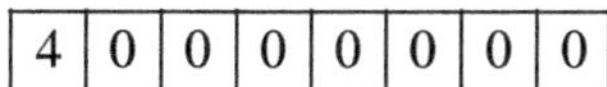
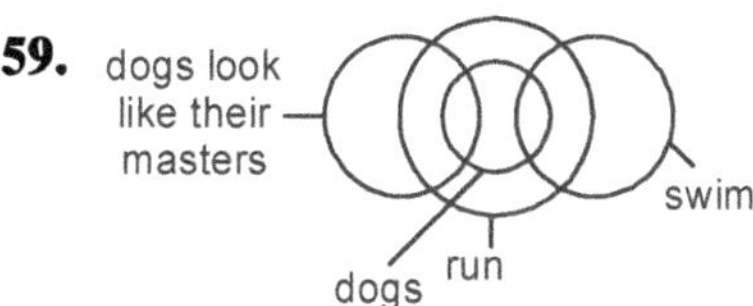

Thus, dogs who like to swim also like to run.

60. Number of ways of find a faulty machines,

$$x = \frac{{}^2C_1}{{}^4C_1} = \frac{1}{2}$$

Number of ways of find a non-faulty machine

$$y = \frac{{}^2C_1}{{}^4C_1} = \frac{1}{2}$$

Number of trial $n = 4$

So, $(x + y)^4 = {}^4C_0(x)^4 + {}^4C_1 x^3 y + {}^4C_2 x^2 y^2$
$\qquad\qquad + {}^4C_3 xy^3 + {}^4C_4 y^4$

Hence, required probability

$$= \frac{{}^2C_1}{{}^4C_2} = \frac{2}{\dfrac{4 \times 3}{2}} = \frac{1}{3}.$$

61. Area of the square $= 16$ sq. units.

Side of the square $= \sqrt{16} = 4$ units

Diagonal of the square

$$= \sqrt{4^2 + 4^2} = 4\sqrt{2} \text{ units}$$

Distance between two foci

$$= \text{Length of minor axis}$$
$$= \text{Distance between two foci}$$
$$= 4\sqrt{2}$$

Semi-minor axis,

$$b = \frac{4\sqrt{2}}{2} = 2\sqrt{2}$$

Also, distance between centre and focus

$$c = 2\sqrt{2}$$

From formula,

$$a^2 - b^2 = c^2$$

$$a^2 = b^2 + c^2$$

$$= \left(2\sqrt{2}\right)^2 + \left(2\sqrt{2}\right)^2 = 16$$

$$a = 4$$

Thus, equation of the ellipse:

$$\frac{x^2}{a^2} + \frac{y^2}{b^2} = 1$$

$$\frac{x^2}{4^2} + \frac{y^2}{\left(2\sqrt{2}\right)^2} = 1 \Rightarrow \frac{x^2}{16} + \frac{y^2}{8} = 1$$

62.

Given, equation of circle: $x^2 + y^2 = 9$

Slope of tangent at $\left(2, \sqrt{5}\right)$

$$2x + 2y \cdot \frac{dy}{dx} = 0$$

$$x + y \cdot \frac{dy}{dx} = 0$$

$$2 + \sqrt{5}\frac{dy}{dx} = 0$$

$$\Rightarrow \qquad \frac{dy}{dx} = \frac{-2}{\sqrt{5}}$$

Equation of tangent at $\left(2, \sqrt{5}\right)$:

$$\left(y - \sqrt{5}\right) = \frac{-2}{\sqrt{5}}(x - 2)$$

$$\sqrt{5}y - 5 = -2x + 4$$

$$2x + \sqrt{5}y = 9$$

This tangent cut the x-axis at print $y = 0$

$$2x = 9 \Rightarrow x = \frac{9}{2}$$

Point on x-axis, where tangent cut $= \left(\frac{9}{2}, 0\right)$

Now, Area of right triangle with vertices:

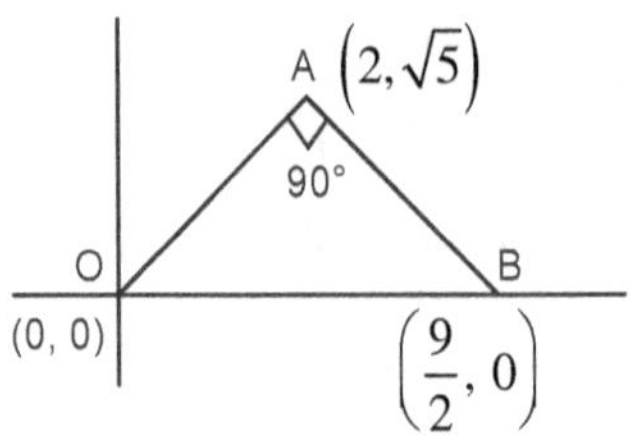

Length $OA = \sqrt{2^2 + \sqrt{5}^2} = 3$

Base $AB = \sqrt{\left(\dfrac{9}{2} - 2\right)^2 + \left(0 - \sqrt{5}\right)^2} = \sqrt{\dfrac{45}{4}}$

Area of right triangle OAB

$$= \frac{1}{2} \times OA \times AB$$

$$= \frac{1}{2} \times 3 \times \sqrt{\frac{45}{4}} = \frac{9\sqrt{5}}{4} \text{ sq. units.}$$

64.

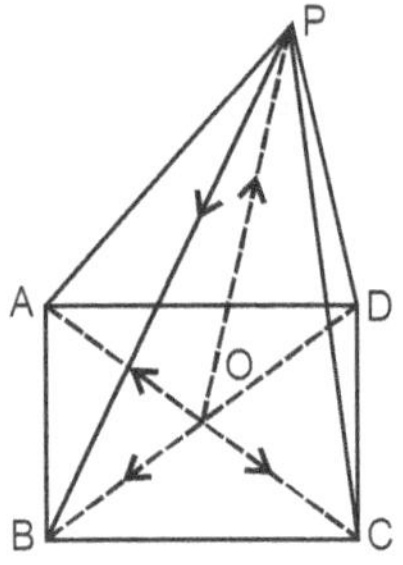

Given, that $\quad \overrightarrow{OP} = 8\hat{k}$

$$\overrightarrow{OA} = \hat{i} + 2\hat{j}$$

and $\quad \overrightarrow{OC} = -\hat{i} - 2\hat{j}$

And, $\overrightarrow{OA} \perp \overrightarrow{OB}$

{In a rectangle diagonals are $\perp$}

Let, $\quad \overrightarrow{OB} = x\hat{i} + y\hat{j}$

then, $\left(x\hat{i} + y\hat{j}\right)\left(\hat{i} + 2\hat{j}\right) = 0$

$$x + 2y = 0$$

$\Rightarrow \quad x = -2y$

Also, $\quad |\overrightarrow{OA}| = |\overrightarrow{OB}|$

then, $\quad \overrightarrow{OB} = \hat{i} - 2\hat{j}$

Now, from $\triangle OBP$,

$$\overrightarrow{OP} + \overrightarrow{PB} = \overrightarrow{OB}$$

$$8\hat{k} + \overrightarrow{PB} = \hat{i} - 2\hat{j}$$

$\Rightarrow \quad \overrightarrow{PB} = \hat{i} - 2\hat{j} - 8\hat{k}.$

65. $\displaystyle \lim_{x \to \infty} \left(\dfrac{\sum_{k=1}^{1000} (k + x)^m}{x^m + 10^{1000}} \right)$

$$= \lim_{x \to \infty} \left(\frac{\sum_{k=1}^{1000} \left(\dfrac{k}{x} + 1\right)^m}{1 + \dfrac{10^{1000}}{x^m}} \right)$$

$= 1 + 1 + 1 \,\ldots\, 1000 \text{ times} = 1000 = 10^3.$

67. Due to rally, marked X route is blocked and mark X is three blocks north and 3 blocks east.

Then, A has go to the route with 'X' marks in ${}^6C_3 \times {}^8C_3$

or $\quad {}^6C_3 \times {}^8C_{(8-3)} = {}^6C_3 \times {}^8C_5$

Total number of blocks in row + column

$$= 6 + 8 = 14$$

Total number of routes to go to Mr. B

$$= {}^{14}C_6 \text{ or } {}^{14}C_{14-6} = {}^{14}C_8$$

Thus, number of routes to go to Mr. B, without X mark

$$= {}^{14}C_6 - {}^6C_3 \times {}^8C_3$$

or $\qquad = {}^{14}C_8 - {}^6C_3 \times {}^8C_5.$

68. Let, $\qquad \dfrac{5z_2}{7z_1} = k\hat{i}$

$$\frac{z_2}{z_1} = \frac{7}{5} k\hat{i}$$

$$\left| \frac{2z_1 + 3z_2}{2z_1 - 3z_2} \right| = \left| \frac{2 + 3 \cdot \dfrac{z_2}{z_1}}{2 - 3\dfrac{z_2}{z_1}} \right| = \left| \frac{2 + 3 \times \dfrac{7}{5} k\hat{i}}{2 - 3 \times \dfrac{7}{5} k\hat{i}} \right|$$

$$= \left| \frac{2 + \dfrac{21}{5} k\hat{i}}{2 - \dfrac{21}{5} k\hat{i}} \right| = \left| \frac{10 + 21k\hat{i}}{10 - 21k\hat{i}} \right|$$

$$= \left| \frac{(10 + 21k\hat{i})^2}{(100 + 441k^2)^{1/2}} \right|$$

$$= \frac{(100 + 441k^2)^{\frac{1}{2} \times 2}}{(100 + 441k^2)} = 1.$$

77.

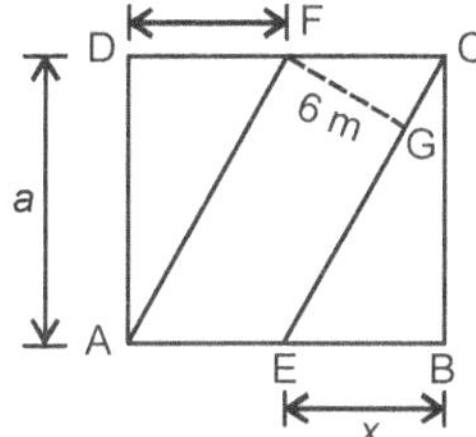

Let, ABCD is a square with side length $= a$ m
and DF = BE = x m

From question,

Area of $\triangle$ADF = Area of parallelogram AECF

$$= \text{Area of } \triangle BCE$$

$$= \frac{a^2}{3}$$

$$\frac{1}{2} a \times x = \frac{a^2}{3}$$

$$\Rightarrow \qquad x = \frac{2}{3}a$$

Now, area of $||$ gm AECF = CE × FG

From, $\triangle$BCE,   CE $= \sqrt{a^2 + x^2}$

$$x \qquad = \sqrt{a^2 + \left(\frac{2}{3}a\right)^2} = \frac{\sqrt{13}}{3}a$$

Area of $||$ gm AECF

$$= \frac{\sqrt{13}}{3} a \times 6 = \frac{a^2}{3}$$

$$x \, a = 6\sqrt{13}$$

$\therefore$ Area of square $a^2 = \left(6\sqrt{13}\right)^2$

$$= 468 \text{ sq. m.}$$

78.

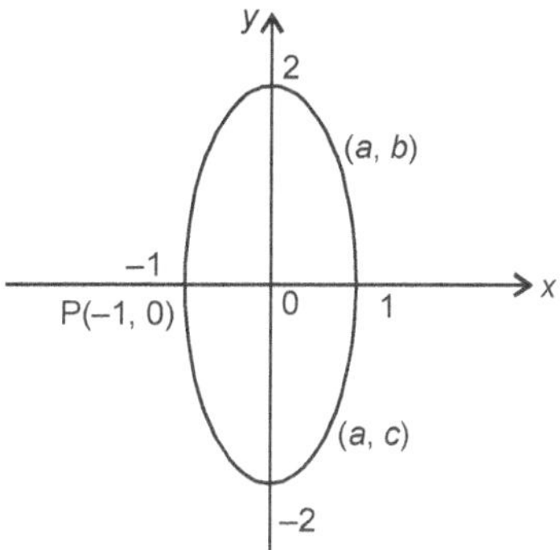

As point (a, b) and (a, c) lies on the ellipse, then,

$$4a^2 + b^2 = 4 \qquad \qquad ...(i)$$

and $\qquad 4a^2 + c^2 = 4 \qquad \qquad ...(ii)$

$$b^2 - c^2 = 0 \Rightarrow b = \pm \, c$$

Again, from $4a^2 + b^2 = 4$

$$b^2 = 4 - 4a^2$$

Distance of point (a, b) from point $(-1, 0)$

$$y^2 = (a + 1)^2 + (b - 0)^2$$

$$y^2 = (a + 1)^2 + 4 - 4a^2$$

Differentiating both sides, with respect to a,

$$2y \cdot \frac{dy}{da} = 2(a + 1) - 8a$$

$$y \cdot \frac{dy}{da} = 1 - 3a$$

For maximum values,

$$\frac{dy}{da} = 0$$

$$1 - 3a = 0$$

$$a = \frac{1}{3}.$$

79. $z = x + iy$

$$z^{1/3} = a - ib$$

$$\Rightarrow \qquad z = (a - ib)^3$$

$$= a^3 + ib^3 - 3ab^2 - 3ia^2 b$$

$$= a(a^2 - 3b^2) + ib(b^2 - 3a^2)$$

So, $\qquad x = a(a^2 - 3b^2)$

$$y = b(b^2 - 3a^2)$$

$$\frac{x}{a} - \frac{y}{b} = \frac{a(a^2 - 3b^2)}{a} - \frac{b(b^2 - 3a^2)}{b}$$

$$= a^2 - 3b^2 - b^2 + 3a^2$$

$$= 4(a^2 - b^2)$$

Hence, $\quad K = 4$.

80. The person X is wearing red tie and he is lying. The other person Y is wearing blue tie.

81. From graph particle is moving linearly from $t = 0$ to $t = 4$ sec

and velocity v becomes constant since $t = 4$ sec onward

Acceleration of the particle during $t = 0$ to $t = 4$ sec

$$a = \frac{4-0}{4-0} = 1 \text{ m/sec}$$

Now, the displacement of the particle at $t = 5$ sec

$$S = 4 \times (5-4) + \frac{1}{2} \times 1 \times (4-0)^2$$

$$= 4 + \frac{1}{2} \times 16$$

$$= 4 + 8 = 12 \text{ units.}$$

82.
$$f(1 + 1) = f(1) \cdot f(1)$$
$$f(2) = 3 \times 3 = 9$$
$$\therefore \quad f(1) = 3, \ f(2) = 9$$
$$f(3) = f(2 + 1) = f(2) \cdot f(1)$$
$$= 9 \times 3 = 27.$$

83.

yy ---- y	yy ---- y

$\qquad x \qquad\qquad x$

Characters $\quad \dfrac{N}{x}$ batches

Let total time taken in processing all batches is T.

then, $\quad T = \dfrac{N}{x}(\alpha + \beta x^2) = \dfrac{N\alpha}{x} + N\beta.x$

Differentiating both sides with respect to x, we get

$$\frac{dT}{dx} = \frac{-N\alpha}{x^2} + N\beta$$

For extremum values,

$$\frac{dT}{dx} = 0 \Rightarrow \frac{-N\alpha}{x^2} + N\beta = 0$$

$$x^2 = \frac{\alpha}{\beta}$$

$$x = \sqrt{\frac{\alpha}{\beta}}$$

Again, $\quad \dfrac{d^2T}{dx^2} = \dfrac{+2N\alpha}{x^3}$

at $\qquad x = \sqrt{\dfrac{\alpha}{\beta}}$

$$\Rightarrow \quad \frac{d^2T}{dx^2} = 2N\beta.\sqrt{\frac{\beta}{\alpha}} > 0$$

So, optimum values of x for past processing is

$$x = \sqrt{\frac{\alpha}{\beta}} \ .$$

86.

	1	3	6	12
2	2			▓
1	1	3		
2/3		2	4	
1/2			3	6

Grid Area	Length	Width
Row 2 : 1 = 1 × 1	1	1
Row 1 : 2 = 2 × 1	2	1
Row 2 : 3 = 3 × 1	3	1
Row 3 : 4 = 6 × $\dfrac{2}{3}$	6	$\dfrac{2}{3}$
Row 3 : 2 = 3 × $\dfrac{2}{3}$	3	$\dfrac{2}{3}$
Row 4 : 3 = 6 × $\dfrac{1}{2}$	6	$\dfrac{1}{2}$
Row 4 : 6 = 12 × $\dfrac{1}{2}$	12	$\dfrac{1}{2}$

Hence, Area of shaded grid

$$= 12 \times 2 = 24 \text{ units.}$$

87. $f(x) = \begin{vmatrix} 1 & x & x+1 \\ 2x & x(x-1) & x(x+1) \\ 3x(x-1) & x(x-1)(x-2) & (x+1)x(x-1) \end{vmatrix}$

$= \begin{vmatrix} 1 & x & 0 \\ 2x & x(x-1) & 0 \\ 3x(x-1) & x(x-1)(x-2) & 0 \end{vmatrix}$

{Applying $C_3 \to C_3 - C_1 - C_2$}

$= 0$

$\therefore f(100) = 0.$

SECTION-B

1. $f(0) = \dfrac{4 - s^2}{3} = \dfrac{3 + 1 - s^2}{3}$

$= 1 + \dfrac{1 - s^2}{3} = 1 - \dfrac{(s^2 - 1)}{3}$

$= e^0 - \left(\dfrac{s^2 - 1}{3}\right)$

$\therefore f(x) = \boxed{e^x - \left(\dfrac{s^2 - 1}{3}\right)}$

SECTION-C

1.

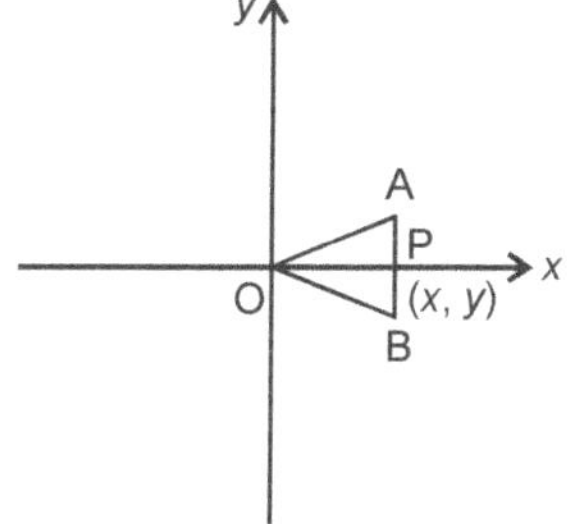

At junction A: traffic coming are x_1 and x_4 and traffic going is x_2

then, $\qquad x_1 + x_4 = x_2$

At junction B: traffic coming is x_2 and traffic going are x_3 and 100

then, $\qquad x_2 = x_3 + 100$

$\qquad x_2 - x_3 = 100$

At junction C: traffic coming are x_3 and 80 and traffic going is x_4

then, $\qquad x_4 = x_3 + 80$

$\qquad x_3 - x_4 = -80.$

2. From previous explanation, three equations, We obtained are

$\qquad x_1 + x_4 = x_2 \qquad \qquad ...(i)$

$\qquad x_2 - x_3 = 100 \qquad \qquad ...(ii)$

$\qquad x_4 - x_3 = 80 \qquad \qquad ...(iii)$

From these three equations, we get

$\qquad x_1 = 20$

and $\qquad x_2 - x_4 = 20$

and $\qquad x_4 - x_3 = 80$

Thus, we get infinite many solution for x_2, x_3 and x_4.

SECTION-E

1.

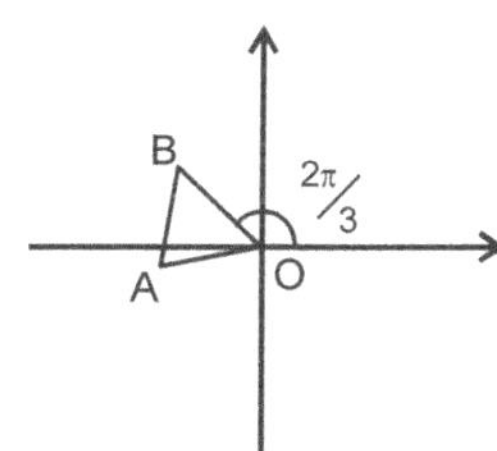

Let Point $P(x, y)$ lies on the Perimeter of $\triangle AOB$

When, this is multiplied by the matrix

$\begin{vmatrix} \cos\left(\dfrac{2\pi}{3}\right) & -\sin\left(\dfrac{2\pi}{3}\right) \\ \sin\left(\dfrac{2\pi}{3}\right) & \cos\left(\dfrac{2\pi}{3}\right) \end{vmatrix}$

then, the new vector $[x', y']^T$ is shown by:

2. Thus, the transformed triangle can also be obtained by rotating the original triangle anticlockwise about the origin by an angle of $\dfrac{2\pi}{3}$ radian.

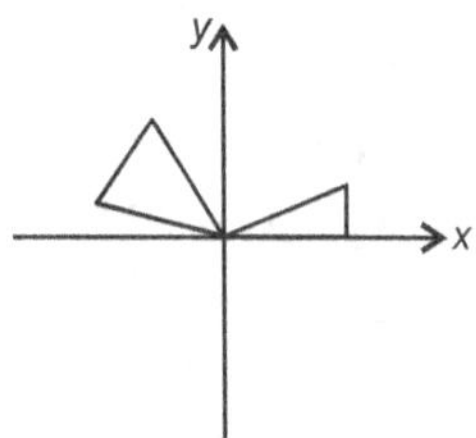

SECTION-F

1. Let Number of people likes Shahrukh Khan movies are $n(x) = 35$

Number of people likes Salman Khan movies are $n(y) = 33$

Number of people likes Amir Khan movies are $n(z) = 43$

Number of people likes Shahrukh Khan & Amir Khan but not Salman Khan movies are $= n(x \cap y' \cap z) = 11$

Number of people likes Shahrukh Khan & Salman Khan but not Amir's movies are $n(x \cap y \cap z') = 7$

Number of people likes Salman Khan & Amir Khan moives $n(y \cap z) = 18$

Number of people likes movies of all the three stars $n(x \cap y \cap z) = 5$

$\therefore\ n(x \cup y \cup z)$

$= n(x) + n(y) + n(z) - n(x \cap y \cap z')$

$\qquad - n(x \cap y' \cap z) - n(y \cap z) - n(x \cap y \cap z)$

$= 35 + 33 + 43 - 11 - 7 - 18 - 5 = 70$

$\therefore$ Number of people does not like movies of any Khan's $= 100 - 70 = 30$.

2. Number of people likes only Shahrukh Khan movies

$= n(x) - n(x \cap y \cap z') - n(x \cap y' \cap z)$

$\qquad\qquad\qquad\qquad - n(x \cap y \cap z)$

$= 35 - 11 - 5 - 7 = 12$

People, likes only Salman's movies

$= n(y) - n(x \cap y \cap z') - n(y \cap z)$

$= 33 - 7 - 18 = 8$

People, likes only Amir's movies

$= n(z) - n(x \cap y' \cap z) - n(y \cap z)$

$= 43 - 11 - 18 = 14$

Number of people, likes only one Khan's movies $= 8 + 12 + 14 = 34$.

3. Number of person likes at least two stars

$= n(x \cap y \cap z') + n(x \cap y' \cap z) + n(y \cap z)$

$= 7 + 11 + 18 = 36$.

4. Number of people's likes at least one Khan's movies $= 70$

Number of people's likes Amir Khan movies $= 43$

Number of people's does not likes any movies $= 100 - 70 = 30$

Number of people's does not like Amir Khan movies

$= 70 + 30 - 43 = 57$.

5. Number of people's likes Shahrukh Khan's movies $= 35$

Number of people's likes both Shahrukh & Salman Khan movies

$= 7 + 5 = 12$

Thus, Number of people's likes Shahrukh Khan but not Salman Khan's movies

$= 35 - 12 = 23$.

REASONING ABILITY

Series

1

LETTER SERIES

In letter series, the letters follow a definite order. The given series of letters can be in natural order or in reverse order or combination of both. The letters may be skipped or repeated or consecutive. The given series may be single or may comprise two different series merged at alternate positions. While attempting questions on letter series one should note the pattern of alphabet series.

Alphabets in natural series

A B C D E F G H I J K L M N O P Q R S T U V W X Y Z
1st   5th   10th   15th   20th   25th

are:

Alphabets in reverse series

Z Y X W V U T S R O P O N M L K J I H G F E D C B A
1st   5th   10th   15th   20th   25th

    Note: On reaching Z, the series restarts from A and on reaching A, it restarts from Z.

Example

  1. A Z B Y C ?
- A. D
- B. X
- C. U
- D. E

Ans.: (B) There are two alternate series.

    Series I : A B C (Consecutive letters in natural series)

    Series II : Z Y X (Consecutive letters in reverse series)

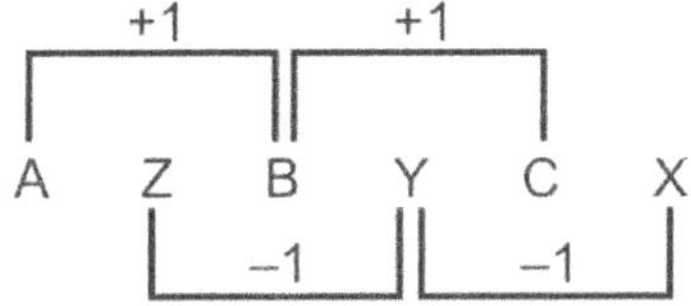

REPEAT SERIES

In this type of series small letters of the alphabet are used to make a set of letters which are repeated. The candidate has to find the set of letters which will fit the blanks left in the given series in such a manner that one section of the series is further repeated in the same manner.

Example

  2. Which of the following groups of letters will complete the given series?

ba-b-aab-a-b

- A. baab
- B. abba
- C. abaa
- D. babb

Ans.: (B) The series is baab, baab, baab. Here the section 'baab' is repeated in the series. Solving steps : The candidate has to look for clues to solve such series pattern. 'aab' in the series indicates that 'b' in this series is preceded by two 'a' so, the first blank and the last blank will be filled by 'a'. Now the first set is formed, *i.e.*, 'baab' in the beginning. This set is repeated, so the second and third blanks will have 'b' filling them.

NUMBER SERIES

In this type of series, the set of given numbers in a series are related to one another in a particular pattern or manner. The relationship between the numbers may be (i) consecutive odd/even numbers; (ii) consecutive prime numbers; (iii) squares/cubes of some numbers with/without variation of addition or subtraction of some number; (iv) sum/product/difference of preceding numbers; (v) addition/subtraction/multiplication/division by some number; and (vi) many more combinations of the relationships given above.

Example

3. Complete the given series. 2, 14, 98, 686, ?
A. 1976   B. 2548
C. 980   D. 4802

Ans.: (D) The numbers are multiplied by 7 to obtain the next numbers.

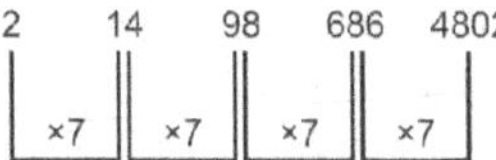

The given series may also comprise of two alternate series merged as one.

MIXED SERIES

Mixed series comprises of the combinations of letters and numbers. In this type of series, the letters and numbers may have a common sequence pattern or may have separate sequence patterns.

Example

4. What should come in the place of question mark in the following letter-number combination?

F6, H8, J10, L12, ?

A. N15
B. O14
C. N14
D. O13

Ans.: (C) The letters are moved two steps forward and the number indicates the position of the letter in the alphabet series.

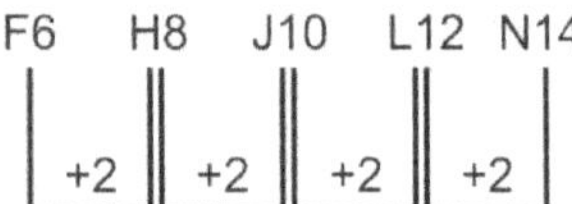

EXERCISE

Directions (Qs. 1 to 8): *In each of the following series determine the order of the letters. Then from the given options select the one which will complete the given series.*

1. GH, JL, NQ, SW, YD, ?
A. EJ   B. FJ
C. EL   D. FL

2. AI, BJ, CK, ?
A. DL   B. DM
C. GH   D. LM

3. b e d f ? h j ? l
A. i m   B. m i
C. i n   D. j m

4. ADVENTURE, DVENTURE, DVENTUR, ?, VENTU
A. DVENT   B. VENTURE
C. VENTUR   D. DVENTU
E. None of these

5. PERPENDICULAR, ERPENDICULA, RPENDICUL, ?
A. PENDICUL   B. PENDIC
C. ENDIC   D. ENDICU
E. None of these

6. ATTRIBUTION, TTRIBUTIO, RIBUTIO, IBUTI, ?
A. IBU   B. UT
C. UTI   D. BUT
E. None of these

7. M, N, O, L, R, I, V, ?
A. A   B. E
C. F   D. H
E. Z

8. A, CD, GHI, ?, UVWXY
A. LMNO   B. MNO
C. MNOP   D. NOPQ

Directions (Qs. 9 to 15): *Which letter(s) in each of the following series is wrong or is misfit in the series?*

9. Z A W B X C
A. D   B. C
C. X   D. W

10. M L O N Q P T R
A. T   B. O
C. Q   D. L

11. D K R Y F L

A. L   B. D

C. R   D. Y

12. L N Q T W Z C F

A. C   B. Q

C. L   D. F

13. XW, DC, CB, NM, PQ, QP

A. NM   B. CB

C. PQ   D. XW

14. B E I N S A I

A. A   B. E

C. S   D. I

15. Z T P K H F

A. Z   B. P

C. T   D. F

Directions (Qs. Nos. 16 to 20): *In each of the following letter series, some of the letters are missing which are given in that order as one of the alternatives below it. Choose the correct alternative.*

16. ba _ cb _ b _ bab _

A. acbb   B. bacc

C. bcaa   D. cabb

17. c _ bba _ cab _ ac _ ab _ ac

A. abebe   B. acbcb

C. babec   D. bcacb

18. ab _ _ baa _ _ ab _

A. aaaaa   B. aabaa

C. aabab   D. baabb

19. _ bc _ ca _ aba _ c _ ca

A. abcbb   B. bbbec

C. bacba   D. abbec

20. ab _ aa _ bbb _ aaa _ bbba

A. abba   B. baab

C. aaab   D. abab

Directions (Qs. 21 to 25): *Choose the correct alternative that will continue the same pattern and replace the question mark in the given series.*

21. 3, 9, 27, 81, 243, ?

A. 486   B. 729

C. 972   D. 359

22. 1, 6, 12, 19, 27 ?

A. 38   B. 35

C. 36   D. 54

23. 125, 80, 45, 20, ?

A. 5   B. 8

C. 10   D. 12

24. 120, 99, 80, 63, 48, ?

A. 35   B. 38

C. 39   D. 40

25. 589654237, 89654237, 8965423, 965423, ?

A. 58965   B. 65423

C. 89654   D. 96542

Directions (Qs. 26–33): *In each series given below, what would come in place of the question-mark?*

26. 2B, 4C, 8E, 14H, ?

A. 20L   B. 22L

C. 21I   D. 16K

27. C(1)L, F(4)O, I(9)R, L(16)U, ?

A. P(27)W   B. N(24)Y

C. M(23)X   D. O(25)X

28. 3F, 6G, 11I, 18L, ?

A. 27P   B. 21O

C. 27Q   D. 25N

29. W(1)A, X(4)Z, Y9Y, ?, A(25)W

A. X(11)Z   B. Z(21)A

C. Z(16)X   D. Z(14)X

30. 81Y, 27S, 9N, 3J, ?

A. 0H   B. IG

C. 0F   D. IE

31. E5, K11, Q17, ?

A. X20   B. Y24

C. V22   D. W25

32. D2, I3, N6, S18, ?

A. V72   B. W36

C. Y90   D. X108

33. 3J, 6M, 12L, ?, 48N

A. 24O   B. 8M

C. 26M   D. 22O

Directions (Qs. Nos. 34 and 35) : *Which of the following does not fit in the letter number series given below?*

34. G4T, J10R, M20P, P43N, S90L

A. J10R   B. S90L

C. M20P   D. G4T

35. B0R, G3U, E3P, J7S, H9N

A. E3P   B. J7S

C. H9N   D. G3U

ANSWERS

1	2	3	4	5	6	7	8	9	10
D	A	A	C	E	C	B	C	D	A
11	12	13	14	15	16	17	18	19	20
A	C	C	C	B	B	B	B	A	B
21	22	23	24	25	26	27	28	29	30
B	C	A	A	D	B	D	A	C	B
31	32	33	34	35					
C	D	A	A	B					

EXPLANATORY ANSWERS

1. 1st letter:

$$G \xrightarrow{+3} J \xrightarrow{+4} N \xrightarrow{+5} S \xrightarrow{+6} Y \xrightarrow{+7} \boxed{F}$$

2nd letter:

$$H \xrightarrow{+4} L \xrightarrow{+5} Q \xrightarrow{+6} W \xrightarrow{+7} D \xrightarrow{+8} \boxed{L}$$

2. 1st letter: $A \xrightarrow{+1} B \xrightarrow{+1} C \xrightarrow{+1} \boxed{D}$

2nd letter: $I \xrightarrow{+1} J \xrightarrow{+1} K \xrightarrow{+1} \boxed{L}$

3. The series may be divided into groups as shown: b e d / f ? h / j ? l
Clearly in the first group, the second and third letters are respectively three and two steps ahead of the first letter. A similar pattern would follow in the second and third groups.

4. One letter from the beginning and one from the end of a term are removed, one by one, in alternate steps.

5. Each term of the series is obtained by removing two letters from the preceding term one from the beginning and one from the end. So, the missing term is PENDICU.

6. In the first step, one letter from the beginning and one from the end of a term are removed to give the next term. In the second step, two letters from the beginning of a term are removed. These two steps are repeated alternately.

7. The given sequence is a combination of two series: I. M, O, R, V and II. N, L, I, ?

The pattern in I is: $M \xrightarrow{+2} O \xrightarrow{+3} R \xrightarrow{+4} V$

The pattern in II is: $N \xrightarrow{-2} L \xrightarrow{-3} I \xrightarrow{-4} \boxed{E}$

8. Each term consists of consecutive letters in order. The number of letters in the terms goes on increasing by one at each step. Also, there is a gap of one letter between the last letter of the first term and the first letter of the second term; a gap of two letters between the last letter of the second term and the first letter of the third term; and so on. So, there should be a gap of three letters between the last letter of the third term and the first letter of the desired term.

9. There are two alternate series I. Z, Y, X and II. A, B, C

The pattern in I is : $Z \xrightarrow{-1} \boxed{Y} \xrightarrow{-1} X$

The pattern in II is : $A \xrightarrow{+1} B \xrightarrow{+1} C$

10. Two consecutive letters are written backwards.
$\overset{ML}{\leftarrow} \overset{ON}{\leftarrow} \overset{OP}{\leftarrow} \overset{SR}{\leftarrow}$
S should be in place of T.

11. The pattern in this series is moving the letters seven steps forward.

$$D \underset{+7}{\quad} K \underset{+7}{\quad} R \underset{+7}{\quad} Y \underset{+7}{\quad} F \underset{+7}{\quad} \boxed{M}$$

M should be in place of L.

12. The pattern in the series is +3

Ⓚ N Q T W Z C F
+3 +3 +3 +3 +3 +3 +3

K should be in place of L.

13. The series is made with any two consecutive letters written backwards.

XW DC CB NM QP
← ← ← ← ←

Q should come before P in the series.

14. The difference between the letters is increased by one at each step.

B E I N Ⓣ A I
+3 +4 +5 +6 +7 +8

T should be in place of S.

15. The difference between the letters is decreased by one at each step.

Z T O K H F
-6 -5 -4 -3 -2

O should be in place of P.

16. The series is babc/babc/babc. Thus, the pattern 'babc' is repeated.

17. The series is cabbac/cabbac/cabbac. Thus, the pattern 'cabbac' is repeated.

18. The series is aba/aba/aba/aba. Thus, the pattern 'aba' is repeated.

19. The series is abc/bca/cab/abc/bca. Thus, the letters change places in a cyclic order.

20. The series is abb/aaabbb/aaaabbbb/a. Thus, the letters are repeated twice, then thrice, then four times and so on.

21. The numbers in the series are multiplied by 3 to get the next numbers.

22. The difference between the numbers in the series increases by 1, after beginning from 5,

1 6 12 19 27 36
i.e.,
+5 +6 +7 +8 +9

23. The pattern is –45, –35, –25, ...
So, missing term = 20 – 15 = 5.

24. The pattern is –21, –19, –17, –15,.....
So, missing term = 48 – 13 = 35.

25. The digits are removed one-by-one from the beginning and the end in order alternately, so as to obtain the subsequent terms of the series.

26. The sequence of numbers is +2, +4, +6, +8 and sequence of letters is +1, +2, +3, +4.

27. The corresponding letters are moved 3 steps forward and the sequence of numbers is +3, +5, +7, +9.

28. The sequence of numbers is +3, +5, +7, +9 and the letters are moved 1, 2, 3, 4 steps forward.

29. The letters on the left are in reverse series, the letters on the right are in natural series, and the numbers are squares of numbers in natural order starting from 1.

30. The numbers are divided by 3 at each step and the letters are moved 6, 5, 4, 3 steps backward.

31. The series comprises of random letters and numbers indicate the position of the letter in alphabet series.

32. The letters are moved five steps forward and every third number is the product of two preceding numbers.

33. Every number is double the previous number and the sequence of letters is +3, –1 (3 steps forward, 1 step backward) which is repeated.

34. The letters on the left are moved 3 steps forward, the letters on the right are moved 2 steps backward and the sequence of numbers is (4 × 2) +1, (9 × 2) +2, (20 × 2) +3, (43 × 2) +4. So, J9R should be in place of J10R.

35. The sequence of letters on the left is +5, –2 (5 steps forward, 2 steps backward) which is repeated, the sequence of letters on the right is +3, –5 (3 steps forward, 5 steps backward) which is repeated, and the numbers are the sum of two preceeding numbers. So, J6S should be in place of J7S.

❀ ❀ ❀

2 | Coding-Decoding

Coding is a secretive language which is used to change the representation of the actual term/word/value. This coded language can be framed by

(*i*) moving the letters one or more steps forward or backward;

(*ii*) substituting numbers for letters and vice-versa;

(*iii*) writing the letters of the given word in reverse order in part or in whole; and

(*iv*) replacing the letters in their natural series by the same positioned letters in their reverse series.

Alphabet in natural series are :

A B C D E F G H I J K L M N O P Q R S T U V W X Y Z

1st   5th   10th   15th   20th   25th

Alphabet in reverse series are :

Z Y X W V U T S R Q P O N M L K J I H G F E D C B A

1st   5th   10th   15th   20th   25th

> **Note :** On reaching Z, the series restarts from A and on reaching A, it restarts from Z

Example

1. If FACE is coded as GBDF, then BADE will be coded as :

A. CBEF   B. CEBF

C. CFBE   D. CBFE

Ans.: (A) The word is coded by moving the letters one step forward

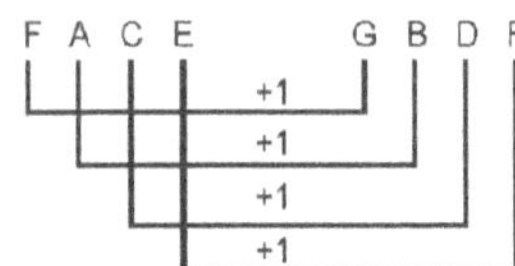

Similarly,

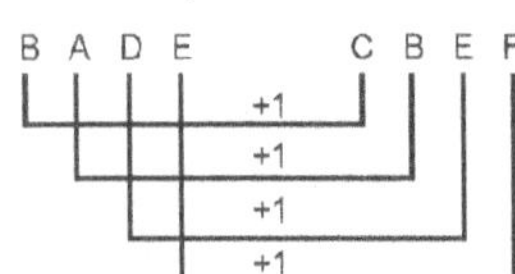

2. In a certain code 'ra mei ket' means 'he is rich'; 'rui pha jeu' means 'run for money'; and 'pha rui ket' means 'money for rich'. Which of the following is the code for 'rich'?

A. ra   B. pha

C. ket   D. jeu

Ans.: (C) The given information is :

Code	Sentence
1. ra mei ket	he is rich
2. rui pha jeu	run for money
3. pha rui ket	money for rich

After comparing codes and sentences 1 and 3, it is clear that word 'rich' is common and so is the code 'ket'.

3. If 'banana' is called 'jelly', 'jelly' is called 'green', 'green' is called 'apple'. 'apple' is called 'mango', what is the colour of leaf?

A. green B.   mango

C. apple D.   banana

Ans.: (C) Leaf is green in colour and according to the codes in the question 'green' is called 'apple'.

In another form of coding, the Digits and its coded Letters or vice versa are already given. One has to find out the answers to the given questions just by tallying the given codes.

EXERCISE

Directions (Qs. Nos. 1 to 8): *In the following questions select the right option which indicates the correct code for the word or letter given in the question.*

1. If PHILOSOPHY is coded as HPLISOPOYH, ornamental will be coded as :
   A. ROANEMNTLA   B. ONRAMNEALT
   C. ROANEMTNLA   D. ROANEMNATL

2. If OPFGBCST stands for NEAR, in the same manner IJVWHI will stand for :
   A. HAG   B. HUG
   C. HUT   D. KEG

3. If m is coded as g, g as o, a as *i* and *i* as y, then 'imagination' will be written as :
   A. ygagynatyin   B. ygioynityog
   C. ygioynityon   D. ygioyintyon

4. If OUT is coded as 152120, IN will be coded as :
   A. 1015   B. 819
   C. 1813   D. 914

5. If BAD is coded as 7. HIS as 9, LOW will be coded as :
   A. 50   B. 8
   C. 23   D. 5

6. In a certain code ABCD is written as 2468 and EFGH as 1357. How will CAGE be written in that code?
   A. 6453   B. 6251
   C. 6521   D. 6215

7. If HARD is coded as 1357 and SOFT as 2468, what will 21448 stand for?
   A. SHAFT   B. SHORT
   C. SHOOT   D. SHART

8. If FACE is coded as 6135, BIG as 297, HAD as 814 and BADGE as 21475, then what is the code for 'A'?
   A. 3   B. 1
   C. 2   D. 4

Directions (Qs. 9 to 13): *In the following questions study the coded patterns and then select the right option from the given alternatives.*

9. In a certain language, A. 'FOR' stands for 'old is gold'; B. 'ROT' stands for 'gold is pure'; C. 'ROM' stands for 'gold is costly'. How will 'pure old gold is costly' be written?
   A. TFROM   B. FOTRM
   C. FTORM   D. TOMRF

10. In a certain code '643' means 'she is beautiful', '593' means 'he is handsome', and '567' means 'handsome meets beautiful'. What number will indicate the word 'meets'?
    A. 5   B. 3
    C. 7   D. 6

11. In a certain code language, A. 'pic vic nic' stands for 'winter is cold'; B. 'to nic re' for 'summer is hot'; C. 're pic boo' for 'winter and summer' and D. 'vic tho pa' for nights are cold'. Which of the following word is the code for 'summer'?
    A. nic   B. boo
    C. to   D. re

12. In a certain language 'mu mit es' means 'who is she' and 'elb mu es' means 'where is she'. What is the code for 'where' in this language?
    A. es   B. elb
    C. mu   D. mit

13. In a certain code language 'roi ja kyo twa' means ' Moody is writing letters', 'pok ju ja twa' means 'Woody is writing cards', 'trn kyo pos un' means 'they are writing letters', and 'koi rus pok' means 'gifts and cards'. What is the code word for 'Moody'?
    A. ja   B. twa
    C. roi   D. kyo

Directions (Qs. 14 to 18): *Read the given coded information and choose the correct answer from the given options.*

14. If 'red' is called 'air', 'air' is called 'black', 'black' is called 'sky', 'sky' is called 'blue', 'blue' is called 'wind' and 'wind' is called 'white', where to birds fly?
    A. air   B. sky
    C. blue   D. wind
    E. black

15. If 'green' is called 'pink', 'pink' is called 'blue', 'blue' is called 'purple', 'purple' is called 'white', 'white' is called 'orange' and 'orange' is called 'peach', what is the colour of snow?

A. peach   B. orange
C. purple   D. blue
E. white

16. If 'colour' is called 'blue', 'blue' is called 'light', 'light' is called 'showy', 'showy' is called 'dark' and 'dark' is called 'colour', what is the colour of ink?

A. blue   B. showy
C. dark   D. colour
E. light

17. If 'yellow', is called 'pale', 'pale' is called 'blue', 'blue' is called 'orange', 'orange' is called 'dull', 'dull' is called 'green' and 'green' is called 'yellow', what is the colour of grass in a lawn?

A. pale   B. yellow
C. blue   D. green
E. orange

18. If 'black' is called 'pink', 'pink' is called 'blue', 'blue' is called 'brown', 'brown' is called 'orange', 'orange' is called 'violet', 'violet' is called 'red' and 'red' is called 'black', what is the colour of blood?

A. black   B. brown
C. pink   D. orange
E. red

Directions (Qs 19 to 23): *The following questions are based on the code pattern given below :*

Letters : T R A H U X C I B L
Numbers : 3 0 1 7 4 9 6 8 2 5

Which of the given options has the correct coded form of the given letters?

19. RACIXT
A. 016823   B. 016873
C. 016843   D. 016893

20. BUHLAI
A. 247018   B. 247508
C. 247538   D. 247518

21. LBIHAR
A. 528471   B. 528710
C. 528947   D. 528103

22. UBAXTC
A. 421736   B. 421956
C. 421936   D. 421906

23. HULBRT
A. 745203   B. 723045
C. 752340   D. 732145

ANSWERS

1	2	3	4	5	6	7	8	9	10
C	B	C	D	D	B	B	B	A	C

11	12	13	14	15	16	17	18	19	20
D	B	C	C	B	E	B	A	D	D

21	22	23
B	C	A

EXPLANATORY ANSWERS

1. The places of two consecutive letters in the word are interchanged to form the coded word.

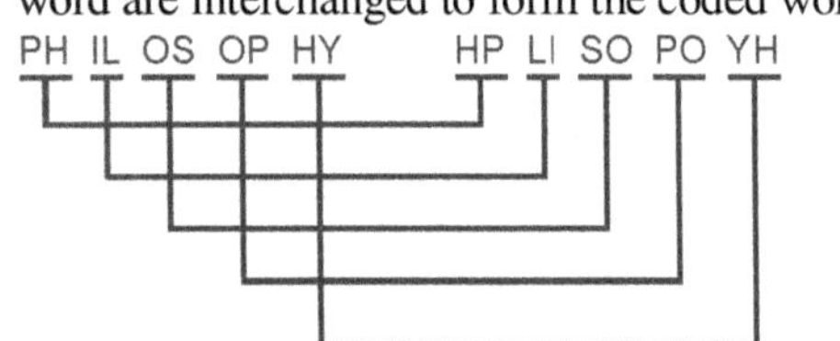

Similarly,

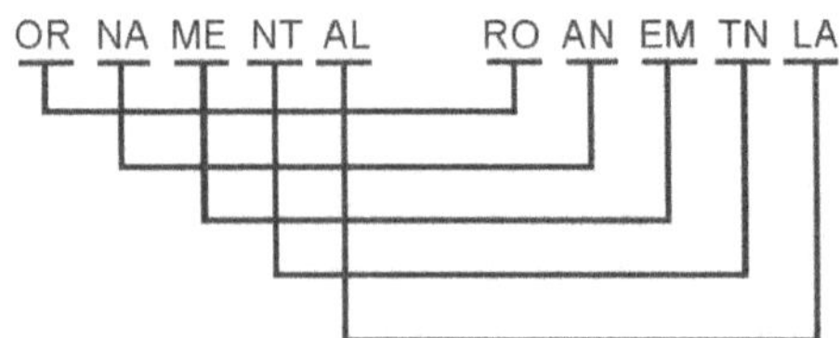

2. The manner of decoding is

$\downarrow$ OP $\downarrow$ FG $\downarrow$ BC $\downarrow$ ST $\;\rightarrow\;$ codes

N   E   A   R $\rightarrow$ given word

The letters preceeding two consecutive letters in the alphabetical series are picked to depict the words.

Similarly,

$\downarrow$ IJ $\downarrow$ VW $\downarrow$ HI $\;\rightarrow\;$ given codes

H   U   G $\rightarrow$ answer word

3. Alphabet whose codes are given

m $\rightarrow$ g

g $\rightarrow$ o

a $\rightarrow$ i

i $\rightarrow$ y

All other alphabet will remain unchanged so, 'imagination' will be coded as :

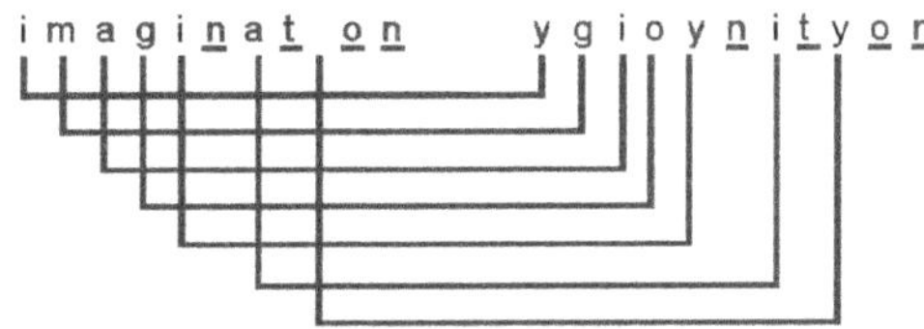

4. The coded number signifies the position of the alphabet in its natural alphabetical series (ABCD...)

O   U   T $\rightarrow$ OUT

15th 21st 20th→ 152120

Similarly,

I   N $\rightarrow$ IN

9th   14th $\rightarrow$ 914

5. The coded number is the sum of number digits signifying the position of the alphabet in the natural order.

B   A   D

$\downarrow$ $\downarrow$ $\downarrow$

2nd 1st 4th

i.e., 2 + 1 + 4 = 7

Similarly,

H   I   S

$\downarrow$ $\downarrow$ $\downarrow$

8th 9th 19th

i.e., 8 + 9 + 19 = 36, further 3 + 6 = 9

Also,

L   O   W

$\downarrow$ $\downarrow$ $\downarrow$

12th 15th 23rd

i.e., 12 + 15 + 23 = 50,

further, 5 + 0 = 5

6. The letters of the given groups are coded by numbers and the word CAGE is formed by letters from the given words. So, to find the answer, select the respective numbers.

A B C D E F G H $\rightarrow$ letters

2 4 6 8 1 3 5 7 $\rightarrow$ codes

So,

C A G E $\rightarrow$ letters

6 2 5 1 $\rightarrow$ answer codes

7. The numbers represent letters and to find the answer, select the respective letters.

1 3 5 7   2 4 6 8 $\rightarrow$ codes

H A R D   S O F T $\rightarrow$ letters

So,

2 1 4 4 8 $\rightarrow$ codes

S H O O T $\rightarrow$ answer letters

8. The letter 'A' is present in three words and so is the number '1' in all the three words.

FACE   HAD   BADGE

6135   814   21475

9.   *Code*   *Sentence*

1. F O R   old is gold

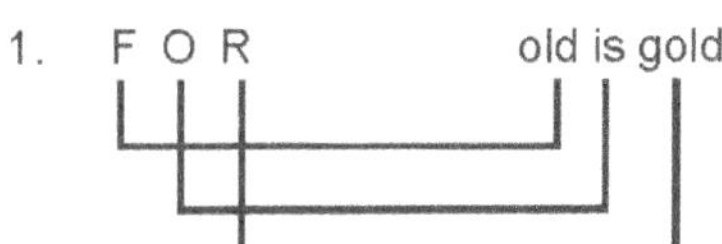

2. R O T   gold is pure

3. R O M   gold is costly

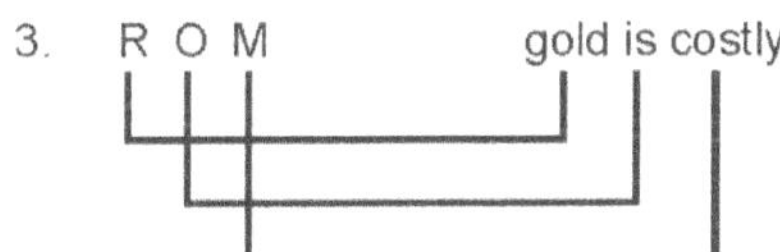

Therefore,

F	stands	for old
O	stands	for is
R	stands	for gold
T	stands	for pure
M	stands	for costly

So, 'pure old gold is costly' will be written as 'TFROM'.

10. *Code*   *Sentence*

1. 643   she is beautiful
2. 593   he is handsome
3. 567   handsome meets beautiful

From 3rd code and its sentence, neither number '7' nor the word 'meets' is repeated.

11. *Code*   *Sentence*

1. pic vic nic   winter is cold
2. to nic re   summer is hot
3. re pic boo   winter and summer
4. vic tho pa   nights are cold

The word 'summer' is common in 2nd and 3rd sentences and so is the code 're'

12. *Code*   *Sentence*

1. mu mite es   who is she
2. **elb** mu es   **where** is she

The code words 'mu' and 'es' are repeated in Ist sentence. The only code left is 'elb' which means 'where'

13. *Code Sentence*

1. **roi** *ja kyo twa*   **Moody** is *writing letters*
2. pok ju *ja twa*   Woody is *writing* cards
3. trn *kyo* pos un   they are writing *letters*
4. koi rus pok   gifts and cards

'Moody' is in 1st sentence only. The code words 'ja' and 'twa' are repeated in 2nd sentence and 'kyo' in 3rd sentence. Only code 'roi' remains which stands for 'Moody'.

14. Birds fly in the 'sky' and 'sky' is called 'blue'.

15. Colour of snow is 'white' and 'white' is called 'orange'.

16. Colour of ink is 'blue' and 'blue' is called 'light'.

17. The colour of grass in a lawn is 'green' and 'green' is called 'yellow'.

18. Colour of blood is 'red' and 'red' is called 'black'.

Questions in these category are easy to attempt. Candidates must be quick in substituting symbols and calculations. The common pattern of questions asked are given below.

Example

1. If '+' stands for '×'; '×' stands for '÷'; '÷' stands for '−' and '−' stands for '+' then

$2 − 8 × 2 + 6 ÷ 7 = ?$

   A. 32   B. 19
   C. 23   D. 9
   E. 15

Ans. After substituting the symbols in the given expression the new expression will be :

$2 + 8 ÷ 2 × 6 − 7$

The solving steps will be :

$2 + 4 × 6 − 7$

$2 + 24 − 7$

$26 − 7 = 19$

2. If ▲ stands for '+'
      ■ stands for '−'
      ● stands for '÷'
      ∗ stands for '×' then

$13 ▲ 5 ∗ 20 ● 10 ■ 9 = ?$

   A. 26   B. 37
   C. 14   D. 55
   E. 20

Ans. After substituting the symbols the new expression will be :

$13 + 5 × 20 ÷ 10 − 9$

The solving steps will be :

$13 + 5 × 2 − 9$

$13 + 10 − 9$

$23 − 9 = 14$

EXERCISE

1. If × stand for addition, ÷ stands for subtraction, + stands for multiplication and − stands for division, then $(20 × 6 ÷ 6 × 4)$ is equal to

   A. 5   B. 24
   C. 25   D. 80
   E. None of these

2. If "+" means "×"; "÷" means "−"; "×"means "÷" and "−" means "+", what will be the value of the following expression?

$4 + 11 ÷ 5 − 50 = ?$

   A. 79   B. − 11
   C. 91   D. − 48.5
   E. None of these

3. If P = 6, J = 4, L = 8, M = 24, then which of the given values can replace the question mark (?) in the following?

$M × J ÷ L + J = ?$

   A. 8   B. 36
   C. 52   D. 0
   E. 16

4. If A + B > C + D, B + E = 2 C and C + D > B + E, it necessarily follows that

   A. A > C   B. A + B > 2D
   C. A + B > 2C   D. A + B > 2E
   E. D + B < 2C

5. If A + D > C + E, C + D = 2B and B + E > C + D, it necessarily follows that

   A. A + D > B + E
   B. A + D > B + C
   C. A + B > 2D
   D. B + D > C + E
   E. A + D < B + C

6. What will be the correct mathematical signs that can be inserted in the following equation?

9 . . . 8 . . . 8 . . . 4 . . . 9 = 65

A. − + × ÷   B. ÷ × + −
C. ÷ + × −   D. × + ÷ −
E. + × ÷ −

7. If "÷" means "+"; "−" means "÷"; "×"means "−" and "+" means "×", then

32 ÷ 8 − 4 × 12 + 4 = ?

A. 40   B. 1/12
C. 16   D. 12
E. None of these

8. If "*x*" stands for "+"; "*y*" stands for "−"; "*z*"stands for "÷" and "*w*" stands for "×", then

10*w* 2*x* 5*y* 5 = ?

A. 15   B. 12

C. 20   D. 10
E. 25

9. If "−" stands for "×"; "×" stands for "+"; "+"stands for "÷" and "÷" stands for "−", then what will be the value of the following equation?

8 − 4 + 16 × 8 − 10 = ?

A. 54   B. 82
C. 15   D. 10
E. 110

10. If Δ denotes =; + denotes >, − denotes <, $\square$ denotes ≠, × denotes > and ÷ denotes < then a + b − c denotes

A. b Δ c $\square$ a   B. b $\square$ a ÷ c
C. a ÷ b × c   D. b − a + c
E. none of these

ANSWERS

1	2	3	4	5	6	7	8	9	10
B	E	E	C	B	D	E	C	B	D

EXPLANATORY ANSWERS

1. 20 + 6 − 6 + 4 = 24

2. 4 × 11 − 5 + 50
44 − 5 + 50 = 89

3. 24 × 4 ÷ 8 + 4
12 + 4 = 16

4. A + B > C + D > B + E or 2 C
∴ A + B > 2C

5. 1. A + D > C + E
2. B + E > C + D or 2 B
Since, the relation between 1 and 2 is not clear it is however certain that A + D > B + C (combination with C is < A + D).

6. A. 9 − 8 + 8 × 4 ÷ 9 = 65
(8 × 4 ÷ 9 gives the result in fractions. So, there is no need for further calculation as the result 65 is a whole number.)
B. 9 ÷ 8 × 8 + 4 − 9 = 65
9 + 4 − 9 *ie* 4 = 65

C. 9 ÷ 8 + 8 × 4 − 9 = 65
(9 ÷ 8 gives the result in fraction)
D. 9 × 8 + 8 ÷ 4 − 9 = 65
72 + 2 − 9 *ie* 65 = 65
E. 9 + 8 × 8 ÷ 4 − 9
9 + 16 − 9 *ie* 16 = 65

7. 32 + 8 ÷ 4 − 12 × 4
32 + 2 − 48 = − 14

8. 10 × 2 + 5 − 5
20 + 5 − 5 = 20

9. 8 × 4 ÷ 16 + 8 × 10
2 + 80 = 82

10. What is given is a > b < c
The equations are :
A. b = c ≠ a   which is wrong
B. b ≠ a < c   which is wrong
C. a < b > c   which is wrong
D. b < a > c   which is correct
Therefore, '*d*' is the answer.

❀ ❀ ❀

Blood Relation

Coded relationships problem involves interpreting a given relationship—string which is coded in a particular way and then matching it with the relationship mentioned in the questions. The process of decoding each and every relation and then interpreting from the given relationship—string the final relationship is a cumbersome process and doing it for all the choices makes it very time consuming. However systematic representation and some clever common sense observations may give a speedy solution.

BLOOD RELATIONSHIPS

While attempting questions on blood relations, one should be clear of all the relation patterns that can exist between any two individuals. Very well-known relations are:

Mother	Father	Son
Daughter	Brother	Sister
Niece	Nephew	Uncle
Aunt	Husband	Wife
Grandmother	Grandfather	Grandson
Granddaughter	Brother-in-law	Sister-in-law
Father-in-law	Mother-in-law	Son-in-law
Daughter-in-law	Cousin	

The patterns of some relationships which help in solving questions in these tests are :

Father's or Mother's Father	– Grandfather (Paternal or Maternal)
Father's or Mother's Mother	– Grandmother (Paternal or Maternal)
Father's or Mother's Son	– Brother
Father's or Mother's Daughter	– Sister
Father's Brother	– Paternal Uncle
Father's Sister	– Paternal Aunt
Mother's Brother	– Maternal Uncle
Mother's Sister	– Maternal Aunt
Uncle or Aunt's Son or Daughter	– Cousin
Son's Wife	– Daughter-in-law
Daughter's Husband	– Son-in-law
Husband's or Wife's Brother	– Brother-in-law
Husband's or Wife's Sister	– Sister-in-law
Brother's Wife	– Sister-in-law
Sister's Husband	– Brother-in-law
Brother's Son	– Nephew
Brother's Daughter	– Niece

Example

1. R is the daughter of Q. M is the sister of B, who is the son of Q. How is M related to R?
   A. Cousin B. Niece
   C. Sister D. Aunt
   E. None of these

Ans. C. B is the son of Q and R is the daughter of Q. This means M is sister of B and R.

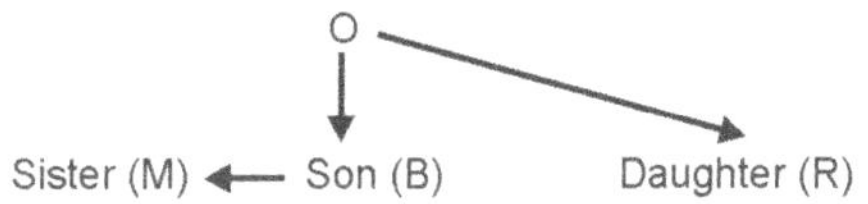

2. M is father of N. L is brother of M. P is mother of L. How is N related to P?
   A. Grandson
   B. Nephew
   C. Granddaughter
   D. Can't be determined
   E. None of these

Ans. D. P is mother of L and M. N is child of M. Therefore, N is grandson or granddaughter of P.

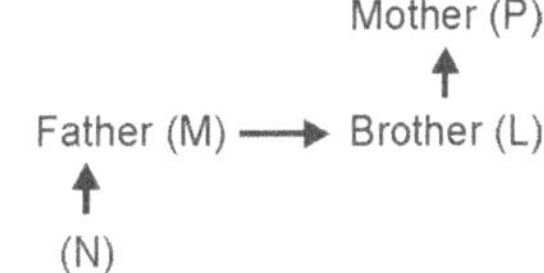

EXERCISE

1. Introducing a boy, a girl said, "He is the son of the daughter of the father of my uncle." How is the boy related to the girl?
A. Brother   B. Nephew
C. Uncle   D. Son-in-law

2. Pointing to a photograph of a boy Suresh said, "He is the son of the only son of my mother." How is Suresh related to that boy?
A. Brother   B. Uncle
C. Cousin   D. Father

3. If A + B means A is the brother of B; A – B means A is the sister of B and A × B means A is the father of B. Which of the following means that C is the son of M?
A. M – N × C + F   B. F – C + N × M
C. N + M – F × C   D. M × N – C + F

4. If A is the brother of B; B is the sister of C; and C is the father of D, how D is related to A?
A. Brother
B. Sister
C. Nephew
D. Cannot be determined

5. If A + B means A is the mother of B; A – B means A is the brother of B; A % B means A is the father of B and A × B means A is the sister of B, which of the following shows that P is the maternal uncle of Q?
A. Q – N + M × P   B. P + S × N – Q
C. P – M + N × Q   D. Q – S % P

6. Pointing to a photograph Lata says, "He is the son of the only son of my grandfather." How is the man in the photograph related to Lata?
A. Brother   B. Uncle
C. Cousin   D. Data is inadequate

7. If D is the brother of B, how B is related to C? To answer this question which of the statements is/are necessary?
1. The son of D is the grandson of C.
2. B is the sister of D.
A. Only 1
B. Only 2
C. Either 1 or 2
D. 1 and 2 both are required

8. Pointing to a photograph. Balram said, "He is the son of the only daughter of the father of my brother." How Balram is related to the man in the photograph?
A. Nephew   B. Brother
C. Father   D. Maternal Uncle

9. Pointing to a woman, Abhay said, "Her granddaughter is the only daughter of my brother." How is the woman related to Abhay?
A. Sister   B. Grandmother
C. Mother-in-law   D. Mother

10. If A + B means A is the sister of B; A × B means A is the wife of B, A % B means A is the father of B and A – B means A is the brother of B. Which of the following means T is the daughter of P?
A. P × Q % R + S – T
B. P × Q % R – T + S
C. P × Q % R + T – S
D. P × Q % R + S + T

11. Deepak said to Naresh, "That boy playing with the football is the younger of the two brothers of the daughter of my father's wife." How is the boy playing football related to Deepak?
A. Son   B. Brother
C. Cousin   D. Brother-in-law

12. Reena who is the sister-in-law of Ashok, is the daughter-in-law of Kalyani. Dheeraj is the father of Suresh who is the only brother of Ashok. How Kalyani is related to Ashok?
A. Mother-in-law   B. Aunt
C. Wife   D. None of these

13. A and B are children of M. Who is the father of A? To answer this question which of the statements 1 and 2 is necessary?
1. C is the brother of A and the son of E.
2. F is the mother B.
A. Only 1   B. Only 2
C. Either 1 or 2   D. 1 and 2 both

14. Anil said, "This girl is the wife of the grandson of my mother". How is Anil related to the girl?
A. Brother
B. Grandfather
C. Husband
D. Father-in-law

15. Pointing towards a man, a woman said, "His mother is the only daughter of my mother." How is the woman related to the man?
A. Mother B. Grandmother
C. Sister D. Daughter

16. If P $ Q means P is the brother of Q; P # Q means P is the mother of Q; P * Q means P is the daughter of Q in A # B $ C * D, who is the father?
A. D
B. B
C. C
D. Data is inadequate

17. Introducing Shalu, Aamir says, "She is the wife of only nephew of only brother of my mother." How Shalu is related to Aamir?
A. Wife
B. Sister
C. Sister-in-law
D. Data is inadequate

Directions (Qs. Nos. 18 and 19): *Read the following information to answer the questions:*
A + B means A is the father of B
A – B means A is the sister of B
A × B means A is the husband of B
A % B means A is the wife of B

18. Which of the following means 'T is the nephew of Q'?
A. Q × R – S + T
B. Q + R % S + T
C. Q – R % S + T
D. None of these

19. Which of the following means S is granddaughter of R?
A. R + P % Q + S
B. K % R + P × Q – L + S
C. K % R + P % Q + S – L
D. K % R + P % Q + S + L

20. If 'A + B' means 'A is brother of B', 'A – B' means 'A is sister of B', 'A × B' means 'A is wife of B' and 'A % B' means 'A is father of B', then which of the following indicates 'S is the son of P'?
A. P × Q % R + S – T
B. P × Q % S – R + T
C. P × Q % R – T + S
D. P × Q % R – S + T

ANSWERS

1	2	3	4	5	6	7	8	9	10
A	D	D	D	C	A	D	D	D	B

11	12	13	14	15	16	17	18	19	20
B	D	B	D	A	A	A	D	C	D

EXPLANATORY ANSWERS

1. 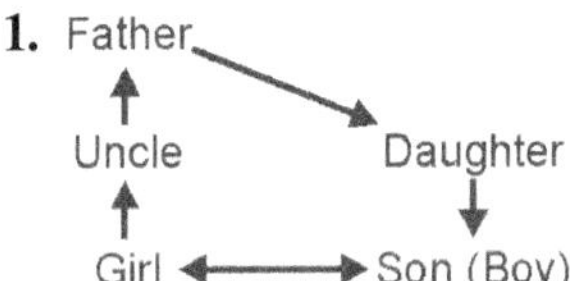

The father of the boy's uncle → the grandfather of the boy and daughter of the grandfather → sister of father.

2. 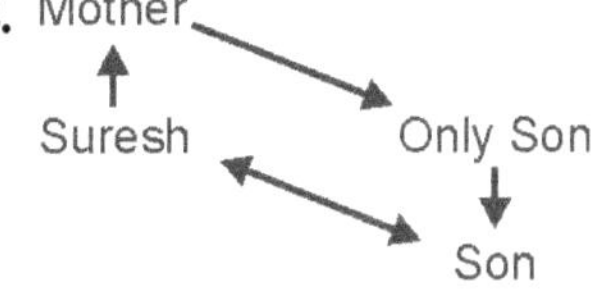

The boy in the photograph is the only son of the son of Suresh's mother *i.e.*, the son of Suresh. Hence, Suresh is the father of boy.

3. 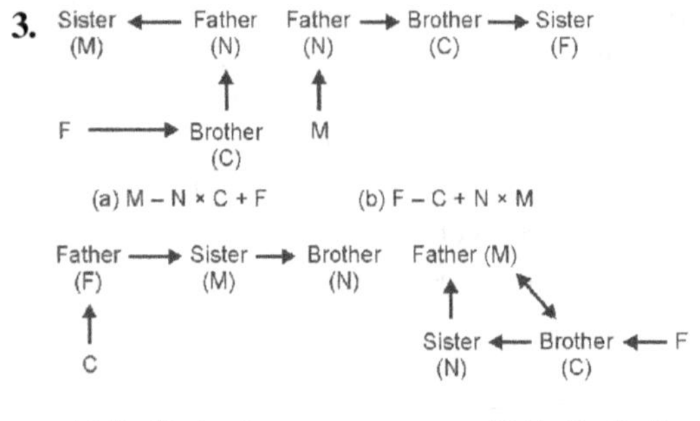

(a) M – N × C + F   (b) F – C + N × M

(c) N + M – F × C   (d) M × N – C + F

$M \times N \to$ M is the father of N

$N - C \to$ N is the sister of C

and $C + F \to$ C is the brother of F.

Hence, M is the father of C or C is the son of M.

4. Father (C) $\longrightarrow$ Sister (B) $\longrightarrow$ Brother (A)

     ↑

     D

If D is Male, the answer is Nephew.

If D is Female, the answer is Niece.

As the sex of D is not known, hence, the relation between D and A cannot be determined.

Note: Niece - A daughter of one's brother or sister, or of one's brother-in-law or sister-in-law. Nephew - A son of one's brother or sister, or of one's brother-in-law or sister-in-law.

5. 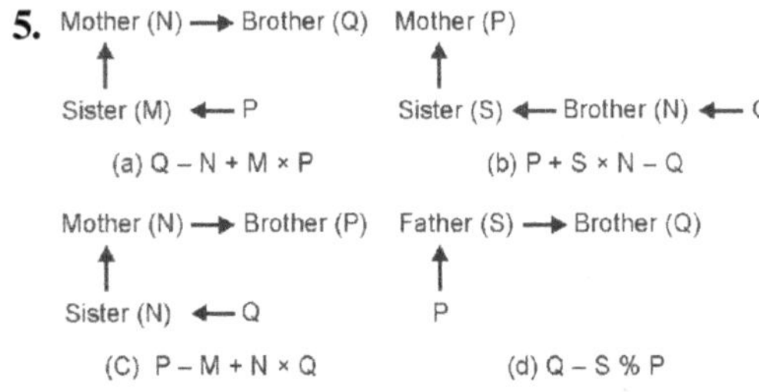

(a) Q – N + M × P   (b) P + S × N – Q

(C) P – M + N × Q   (d) Q – S % P

6. 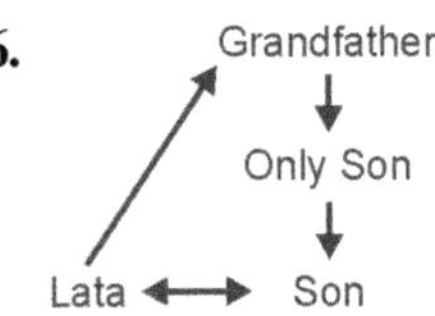

The man in the photograph is the son of the only son of Lata's grandfather *i.e.*, the man is the son of Lata's father. Hence, the man is the brother of Lata.

7. 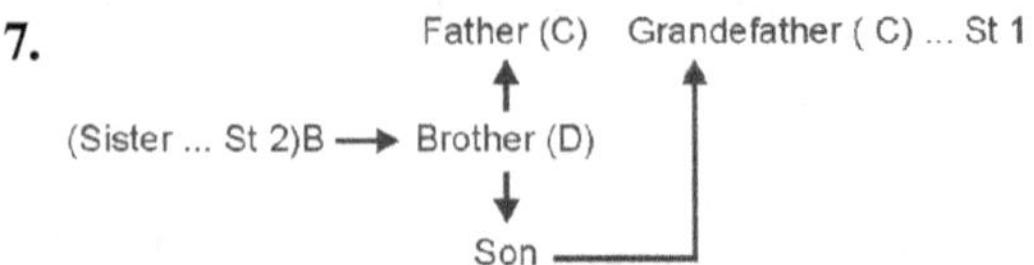

Given: D is the brother of B.

From statement 1, we can detect that D is son of C (son of D is the grandson of C).

From statement 2, we can detect that B is 'Female' (sister of D).

Therefore, B is daughter of C.

8. 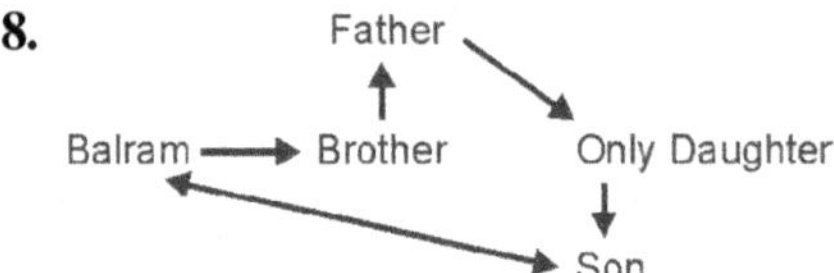

The man in the photograph is the son of the sister of Balram. Hence, Balram is the maternal uncle of the man in the photograph.

9. 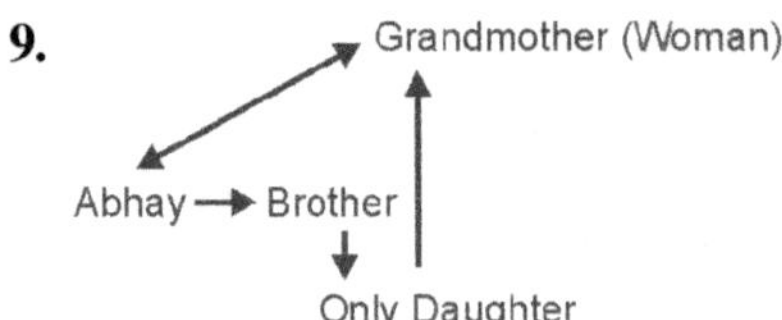

Daughter of Abhay's brother → niece of Abhay. Thus the granddaughter of the woman is Abhay's niece. Hence, the woman is the mother of Abhay.

10. We can note that sex of last person in each option will be unknown. Since T should be daughter of P so T will be definitely female in correct option. So options A and D are straightaway ruled out. Also in the correct option only '+' or '×' will follow T as T is definitely a female so option C is also ruled out.

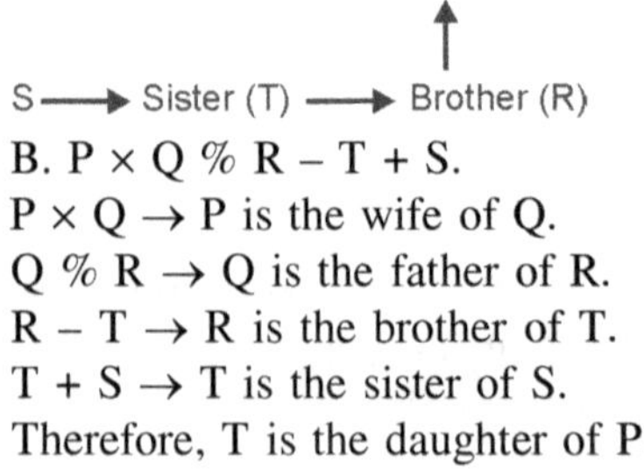

B. P × Q % R – T + S.

$P \times Q \to$ P is the wife of Q.

$Q \% R \to$ Q is the father of R.

$R - T \to$ R is the brother of T.

$T + S \to$ T is the sister of S.

Therefore, T is the daughter of P.

11.

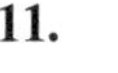

Father's wife → mother.

Hence, the daughter of the mother means sister and sister's younger brother means brother. Therefore, the boy is the brother of Deepak.

12.

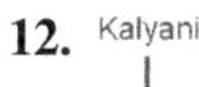

Ashok is the only brother of Suresh and Reena is the sister-in-law of Ashok. Hence, Reena is the wife of Suresh. Kalyani is the mother-in-law of Reena. Kalyani is the mother of Ashok.

13.

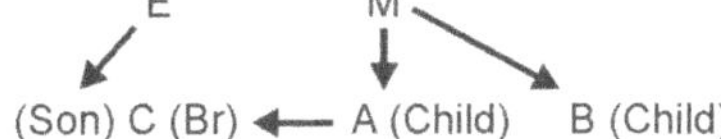

From main st. & st. 1

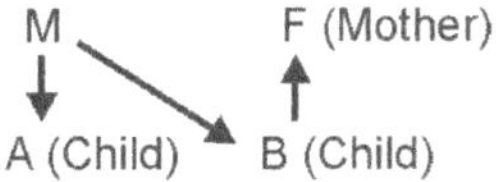

From main st. & st. 2

A and B are children of M. From 1, C is the brother B and son of E. Since, the sex of M and E are not known. Hence 1 is not sufficient to answer the question.

From 2. F is the mother of B. Hence, F is also the mother of A. Hence M is the father of A. Thus, 2 is sufficient to answer the question.

14.

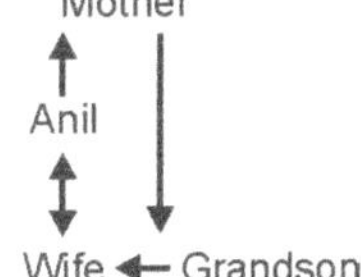

The girl is the wife of grandson of Anil's mother *i.e.*, the girl is the wife of son of Anil. Hence, Anil is the father-in-law of the girl.

15.

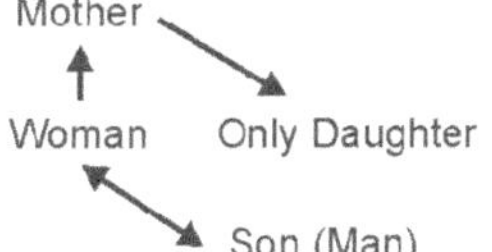

Only daughter of my mother → myself. Hence, the woman is the mother of the man.

16.

A is the mother of B, B is the brother of C and C is the daughter of D. Hence, D is the father.

17.

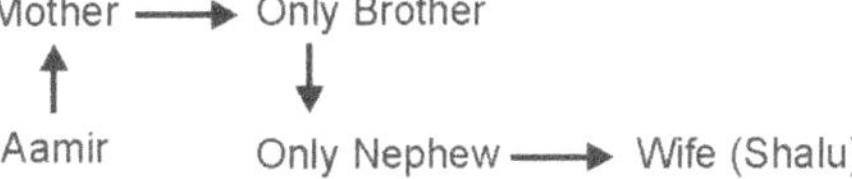

Brother of mother means maternal uncle. Hence only nephew of Aamir's maternal uncle means Aamir himself. Therefore Shalu is the wife of Aamir.

18. Since 'T is the nephew of Q' so 'T' must be a male but sex of 'T' cannot be established in any of the option.

19. Choice A, B is not correct as sex of S is not known. D is ruled out because S is a male here. Representation for choice C is as follows:

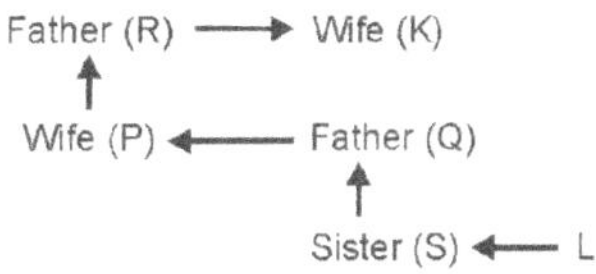

So, S is granddaughter of R is correct here.

20. As 'S' is female in option A and B, both are rejected directly. The sex of 'S' in option C is not known, hence it is also eliminated. Now, check option D.

Clearly, S is son of P.

❀ ❀ ❀

In these type of tests, the directions in questions needs to be perceived, Such questions are based on the direction chart.

N = North, S = South, E = East, W = West

The sense of the different directions are guided by the left and righ turns or angular turns.

Example

1. Shobha was facing East. She walked 20 metres. Turning left she moved 15 metres and then turning right moved 25 metres. Finally, she turned right and moved 15 metres more. How far is she from her starting point?

(a) 25 metres
(b) 35 metres
(c) 50 metres
(d) 45 metres

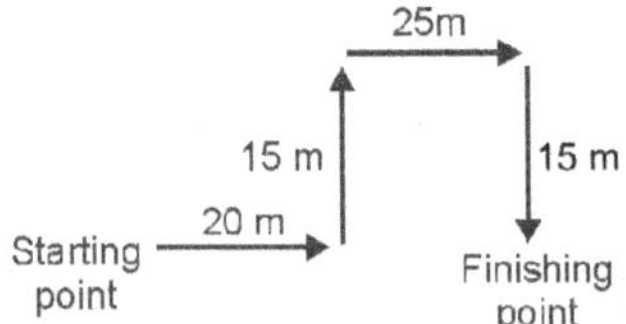

Ans.: Shobha turns left after walking 20 metres towards East. Now she walks 15 metres towards North. She turns right towards East again and walks 25 metres further. Finally turning right towards South, she walks 15 metres. The distance moved towards North and towards South is same, i.e., 15 metres. So, Shobha is 20 + 25 metres = 45 metres away from her starting point.

EXERCISE

1. One morning Urmilla and Vishal were talking to each other face to face at a crossing. If Vishal's shadow was exactly to the left of Urmilla, which direction was Urmilla facing?
   A. East   B. West
   C. North   D. South

2. If South-East becomes North, North-East becomes West and so on. What will West become?
   A. North - East   B. North - West
   C. South - East   D. South - West

3. Ravi put his timepiece on the table in such a way that at 6 P.M. hour hand points to North. In which direction the minute hand will point at 9.15 P.M. ?

A. South - East   B. South
C. North   D. West

4. Rakesh walked 20 m towards north. Then he turned right and walks 30 m. Then he turns right and walks 35 m. Then he turns left and walks 15 m. Finally he turns left and walks 15 m. In which direction and how many metres is he from the starting position?
   A. 15 m West   B. 30 m East
   C. 30 m West   D. 45 m East

5. Starting from the point X, John walked 15 m towards west. He turned left and walked 20 m. He then turned left and walked 15 m. After this he turned to his right and walked 12 m.

How far and in which directions is now John from X?

A. 32 m, South   B. 47 m, East
C. 42 m, North   D. 27 m, South

6. Suman is 40 metres South – West of Ashok, Prakash is 40 metres South – East of Ashok. Prakash is in which direction of Suman?

A. South   B. West
C. East   D. North – East

7. Vijayan started walking towards South. After walking 15 metres he turned to the left and walked 15 metres. He again turned to his left and walked 15 metres. How far is he from his original position and in which direction?

A. 15 metres, North
B. 15 metres, East
C. 30 metres, South
D. 15 metres, West

Directions (8 to 10): *Each of the following questions is based on the following information:*

1. P # Q means B is at 1 metre to the right of P.
2. P $ Q means B is at 1 metre to the North of P.
3. P * Q means B is at 1 metre to the left of P.
4. P @ Q means B is at 1 metre to the south of P.
5. In each question first person from the left is facing North.

8. According to X @ B * P, P is in which direction with respect to X?

A. North   B. South
C. North - East   D. South-West

9. According to M # N $ T, T is in which direction with respect to M?

A. North-West   B. North-East
C. South-West   D. South-East

10. According to P # R $ A * U, in which direction is U with respect to P?

A. East   B. West
C. North   D. South

Directions (Qs. 11 to 15): *P, Q, R and S are standing on four corners of a square piece of plot as shown in the given figure. They start moving, and the movements are explained in each of the questions. Read the question and select the right alternative.*

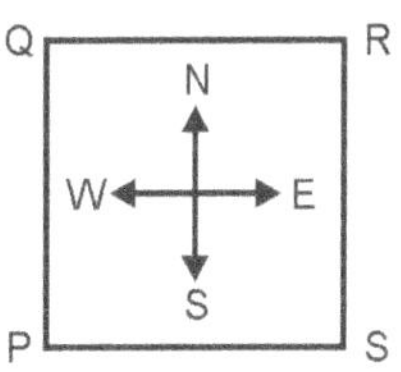

11. P, Q , R and S walk diagonally to opposite corners and from there Q and R walk one and a half sides anti-clockwise while P and S walk one side clockwise along the sides. Where is S now?

A. At the North – West corner
B. At the North -East
C. At the South – West corner
D. None of these

12. Q travelled straight to R, a distance of 10 m. He turned right and walked 7 m towards S, again he turned right and walked 8 m, and then finally turned right and walked 7m. How far is he from his original position?

A. 7 m   B. 8 m
C. 2m   D. 3m

13. From the original position, S starts crossing the field diagonally. After walking half the distance he turns right; walks some distance and turns left. Which direction is S facing now?

A. South - East   B. North - West
C. South - West   D. North

14. P and S walk one and a half length of the side clockwise and anti-clockwise respectively. Which one of the following statements is true?

A. P is at midpoint between Q and R and S at the corner originally occupied by P
B. P and S are both at the midpoint between R and S
C. P and S are both at the midpoint between Q and R.
D. S is at midpoint between Q and R and P is at the midpoint between original side of R and S

15. P, Q, R and S walk one and a half sides clockwise. Who is on the left of Q if he is facing West?

A. P   B. R
C. S   D. No one

ANSWERS

1	2	3	4	5	6	7	8	9	10
C	C	D	D	A	C	B	D	B	C

11	12	13	14	15
B	C	B	C	B

EXPLANATORY ANSWERS

1. 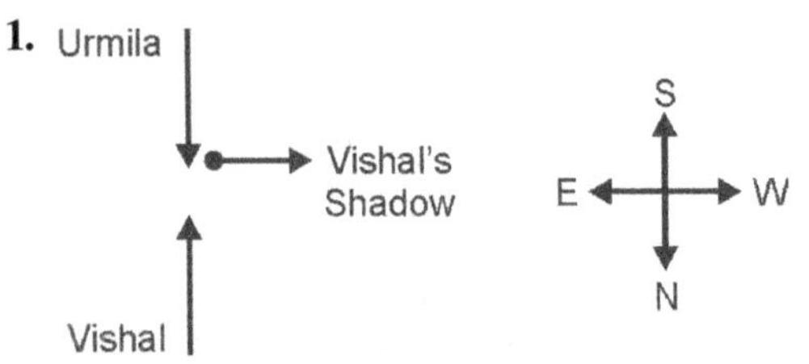

2. 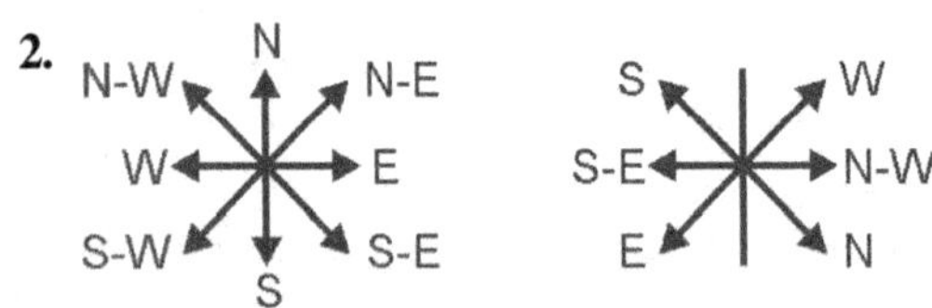

It is clear from the diagrams that new name of West will become South-East.

3. 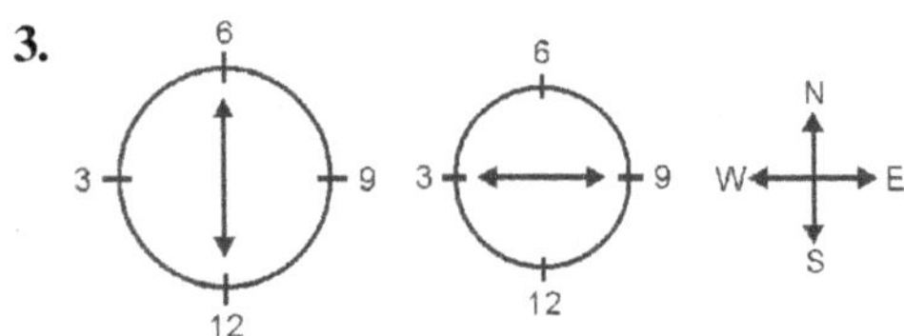

At 9.15 P.M., the minute hand will point towards west.

4. 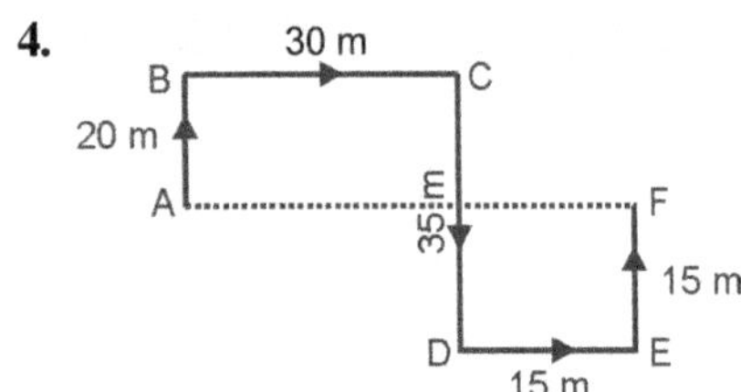

Required distance = AF = 30 + 15 = 45 m. From the above figure, F is in East direction from A. So the answer is '45 m East'.

5. 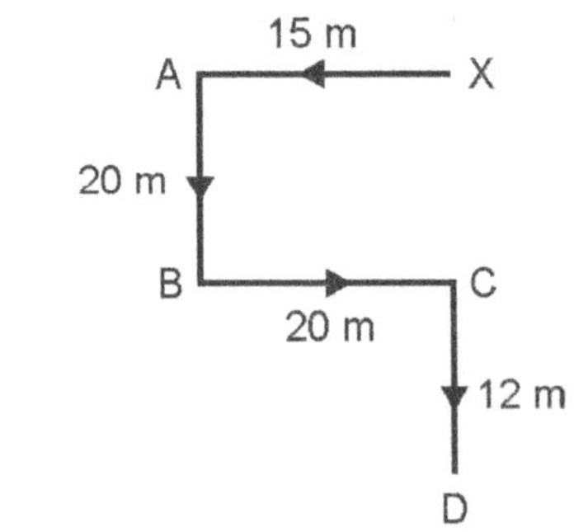

Required distance = 20 + 12 = 32 m South.

6. 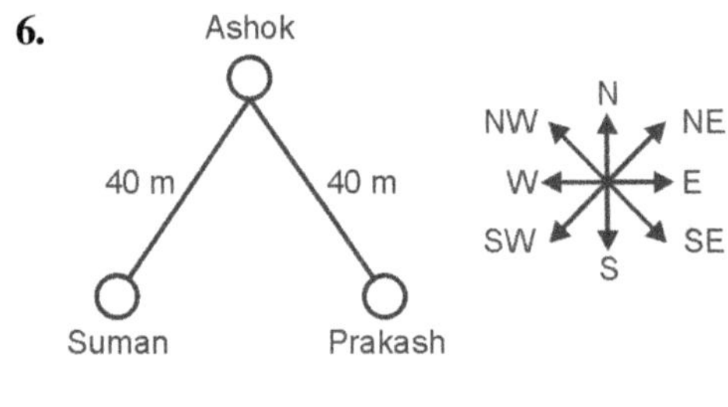

7. 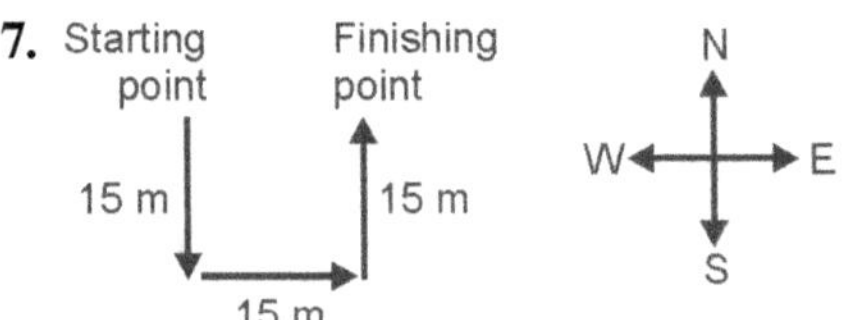

8. According to X @ B * Y

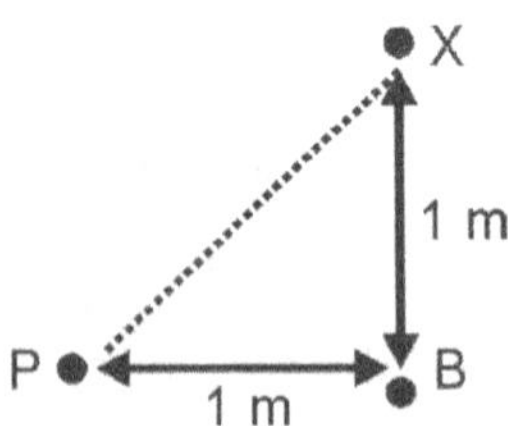

Hence, P is in South-West of X.

9. According to M # N $ T

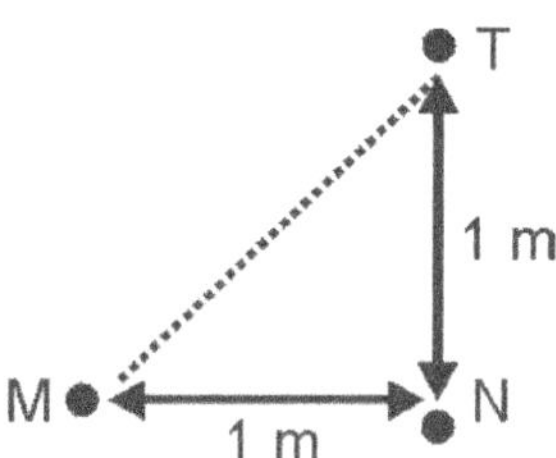

Hence, T is in the North-East of M.

10. According to P # R $ A * U

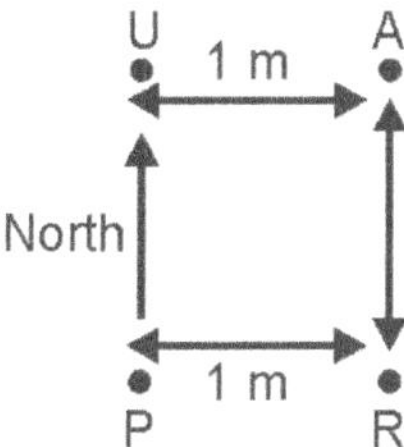

Hence, U is in North direction with respect to P.

11.

(1) (2) (3)

12. (10 m – 8 m = 2 m)

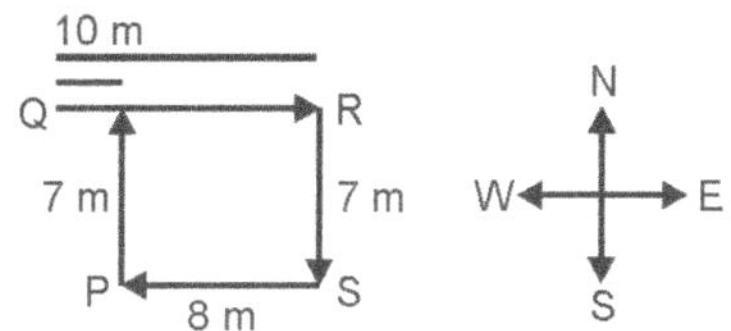

13.

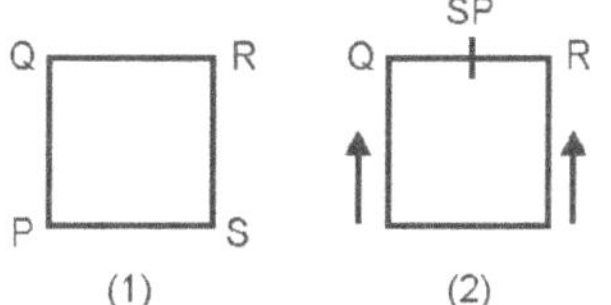

14. The movements are :

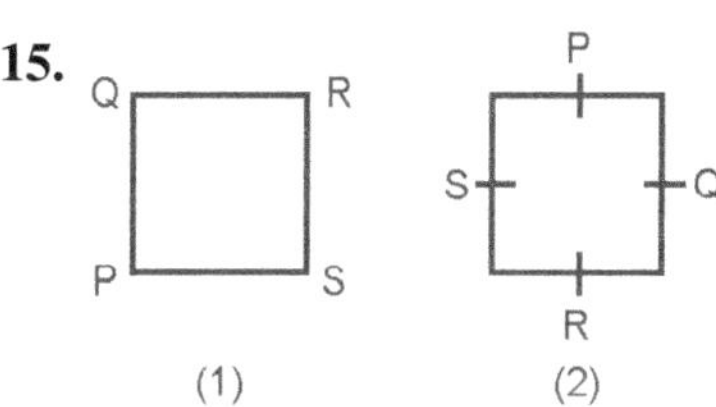

(1) (2)

15.

(1) (2)

❀ ❀ ❀

Statement Analysis

In these questions, a series of interlinked information or data is given. Quantitatively analysis of given information or data provides certain conclusions.

In Statement Analysis (Problem Solving) questions, all given information has to be interpreted and arranged step-by-step. One should be careful that no given data is left incorporated. A brief glimpse to all questions asked on given data is helpful in preparing the solution format.

Directions: *Read the following information carefully and answer the questions given below:*

In a family of six persons—A, B, C, D, E and F—there are three males and three females. There are two married couples and two persons are unmarried. Each one of them reads different newspapers, viz. Times of India, Indian Express, Hindustan Times, Financial Times, Navbharat Times and Business Standard. E, who reads Indian Express, is mother-in-law of A, who is wife of C. D is the father of F and he does not read Times of India or Business Standard. B reads Navbharat Times and is the sister of F, who reads Hindustan Times. C does not read Business Standard.

1. Who among the following reads the Times of India?
   A. C
   B. D
   C. A
   D. Data inadequate
   E. None of these

2. How is F related to E?
   A. Daughter
   B. Brother
   C. Son
   D. Data inadequate
   E. None of these

3. Which of the following is one of the married couples?
   A. D-B
   B. D-E
   C. B-F
   D. E-F
   E. None of these

4. Which of the following newspapers is read by 'A'?
   A. Times of India
   B. Navbharat Times
   C. Financial Times
   D. Data inadequate
   E. None of these

5. How many sons does E have?
   A. Four
   B. Three
   C. Two
   D. One
   E. None of these

Following is the detail presentation of mental approach for solution of the given problem. In practice these questions are solved briefly.

E, who reads Indian Express, is mother-in-law of A, who is the wife of C

Person	Newspaper read	Sex	Information/Reasons
A		Fe	A-C Couple
B			
C		M	A is the wife of C
D			
E	I.E	Fe	mother-in-law of A
F			

D is the father of F and he does not read TOI or B.S

Person	Newspaper read	Sex	Information/Reasons
A		Fe	A-C Couple
B			
C		M	A is the wife of C
D	H.T or F.T or N.T	M	father of F, (TOI, B.S,I.E- not)
E	I.E	Fe	mother-in-law of A

As there are two married couples. This implies that D and E are couples. B reads N.T and is the sister of F, who reads H.T. C does not read B.S

Person	Newspaper read	Sex	Information/Reasons
A	B.S	Fe	A-C Couple
B	N.T	Fe	Sister of F
C	TOI	M	B.S -no
D	F.T	M	father of F
E	I.E	Fe	D-E, Couple
F	H.T	M	There are 3 males- 3 females

E is mother in law of A and A is wife of C implies C is Son of E. D is father of F and D-E are couples implies F is Son of E.

    1. A   **2.** C   **3.** B   **4.** E   **5.** C

EXERCISE

Directions (Qs. Nos. 1 to 4): *Read the following information carefully and answer the questions given below:*

1. There are five types of cards viz. A, B, C, D and E. There are three cards of each type. These are to be inserted in envelopes of three colours—red, yellow and brown. There are five envelopes of each colour.
2. B, D and E type cards are to be inserted in red envelopes; A, B and C type cards are to be inserted in yellow envelopes; and C, D and E type cards are to be inserted in brown envelopes.
3. Two cards each of B and D type are inserted in red envelopes.

1. How many cards of E type are inserted in brown envelopes?
A. Nil
B. One
C. Two
D. Three
E. Data inadequate

2. Which of the following combinations of the type of cards and the number of cards is **definitely correct** in respect of yellow-coloured envelopes?
A. A-2, B-1, C-2
B. B-1, C-2, D-2
C. A-2, E-1, D-2
D. A-3, B-1, C-1
E. None of these

3. Which of the following combinations of types of cards and the number of cards and colour of envelope is **definitely correct**?
A. C-2, D-1, E-2, Brown
B. C-1, D-2, E-2, Brown
C. B-2, D-2, A-1, Red
D. A-2, B-2, C-1, Yellow
E. None of these

4. Which of the following combinations of colour of the envelope and the number of cards is **definitely correct** in respect of E type cards?

A. Red-2, Brown-1
B. Red-1, Yellow-2
C. Red-2, Yellow-1
D. Yellow-1, Brown-2
E. None of these

Directions (Qs. Nos. 5 to 7): *Read the following information carefully and answer the questions given below:*

Six persons A, B, C, D, E and F took up a job with a firm in a week from Monday to Saturday. Each of them joined for different posts on different days. The posts were of–Clerk, Officer, Technician, Manager, Supervisor, and Sales Executive, though not respectively. F joined as a Manager on the first day. B joined as a Supervisor but neither on Wednesday nor Friday. D joined as a Technician on Thursday. Officer joined the firm on Wednesday. E joined as a clerk on Tuesday. A joined as a Sales Executive.

5. Who joined the firm on Wednesday?
A. B
B. C
C. B or C
D. Data inadequate
E. None of these

6. Who was the last person to join the firm?
A. E
B. F
C. A
D. B
E. None of these

7. On which of the following days did the Sales Executive join?
A. Tuesday
B. Thursday
C. Saturday
D. Wednesday
E. None of these

Directions (Qs. Nos. 8 to 11): *Read the following information carefully and answer the questions given below:*

(*a*) An examination board has organised examination for ten s ubjects viz. A, B, C, D, E, F, G, H, I and J on six days of the week with a holiday on Sunday, not having more than two papers on any of the days.

(*b*) Exam begins on Wednesday with subject F.

(*c*) D is accompained by some other subject but not on Thursday. A and G are on the same day immediately after holiday.

(*d*) There is only one paper on last day and Saturday. B is immediately followed by H, which is immediately followed by I.

(*e*) C is on Saturday. H is not on the same day as J.

8. Examination for which of the following pairs of subjects is on Thursday?
A. HE
B. DB
C. FD
D. Data inadequate
E. None of these

9. Examination for which of the following subjects is on the next day of D?
A. B
(2) C
C. I
D. H
E. None of these

10. Examination for which of the following subjects is on the last day?
A. B
B. E
C. J
D. Data inadequate
E. None of these

11. Examination for subject F is on the same day as which of the following subjects?
A. E
(2) D
C. I
D. B
E. None of these

Directions (Qs. Nos. 12 to 16): *Study the following information to answer the given questions:*

P, Q, R, S, T, V, W and Z are travelling to three destinations Delhi, Chennai and Hyderabad in three different vehicles Honda City, Swift D'Zire and Ford Ikon. There are three females among them one in each car. There are atleast two persons in each car. R is not travelling with Q and W. T , a male, is travelling with only Z and they are not travelling to Chennai. P is travelling in Honda City to Hyderabad. S is sister of P and travels by Ford Ikon. V and R travel together. W does not travel to Chennai.

12. Who is travelling with W?
A. Only Q
B. Only P
C. Both P and Q
D. Cannot be determined
E. None of these

13. Members in which of the following combinations are travelling in Honda City?

A. PRS B. PQW
C. PWS D. Data inadequate
E. None of these

14. In which car are four members travelling?

A. None
B. Honda City
C. Swift D'zire
D. Ford Ikon
E. Honda City or Ford Ikon

15. Which of the following combinations represents the three female members?

A. QSZ
B. WSZ
C. PSZ
D. Cannot be determined
E. None of these

16. Members in which car are travelling To Chennai?

A. Honda City
B. Swift D'Zire
C. Ford Ikon
D. Either Swift D'Zire or Ford Ikon
E. None of the above

Directions (Qs. 17-23): *Each problem consists of three statements. Based on the first two statements, the third statement may be true, false, or uncertain.*

17. (i) Tanya is older than Easha.
(ii) Celina is older than Tanya.
(iii) Easha is older than Celina.

If the first two statements are true, the third statement is

A. True B. False
C. Uncertain D. None of these

18. (i) Blueberries cost more than strawberries.
(ii) Blueberries cost less than raspberries.
(iii) Raspberries cost more than both strawberries and blueberries.

If the first two statements are true, the third statement is

A. True B. False
C. Uncertain D. None of these

19. (i) Maria runs faster than Gail.
(ii) Lily runs faster than Maria.
(iii) Gail runs faster than Lily.

If the first two statements are true, the third statement is

A. True B. False
C. Uncertain D. None of these

20. (i) A fruit basket contains more apples than mangoes.
(ii) There are more mangoes in the basket than there are oranges.
(iii) The basket contains more apples than oranges.

If the first two statements are true, the third statement is

A. True B. False
C. Uncertain D. None of these

21. (i) Jullie is younger than Katrina.
(ii) Maya was born after Jullie.
(iii) Katrina is older than Maya.

If the first two statements are true, the third statement is

A. True B. False
C. Uncertain D. None of these

22. (i) The temperature on Monday was lower than on Tuesday.
(ii) The temperature on Wednesday was lower than on Tuesday.
(iii) The temperature on Monday was higher than on Wednesday.

If the first two statements are true, the third statement is

A. True B. False
C. Uncertain D. None of these

23. (i) All Lamels are Signots with buttons.
(ii) No blue Signots have buttons.
(iii) No Lamels are blue.

If the first two statements are true, the third statement is

A. True
B. False
C. Uncertain
D. None of these

ANSWERS

1	2	3	4	5	6	7	8	9	10
C	D	A	E	B	D	E	A	B	C

11	12	13	14	15	16	17	18	19	20
D	C	B	A	D	C	B	A	B	C

21	22	23
A	C	A

EXPLANATORY ANSWERS

Solution (1-4): From (2), Out of fifteen cards nine cards will be inserted as following:

Red envelope	Yellow envelope	Brown envelope
B	A	C
D	B	D
E	C	E

From (3) and using the above table, we get

Red envelope	Yellow envelope	Brown envelope
B(2)	A	C
D(2)	B(1)	D(1)
E(1)	C	E(2)

The digits in brackets shows the no. of cards. Now, From (1), it is clear that each colour of envelope contains five cards, so there are two cards of C-type in brown envelope. Hence the remaining one card of C-type is in yellow envelope. Hence all the three A-type are in yellow envelope.

4. Brown-2, Red-1.

Solution (5-7): Summarising the given information in tabular form, we get

Person	Posts	Days
F	Manager	Monday
B	Supervisor	*Saturday*
D	Technician	Thursday
C	Officer	Wednesday
E	Clerk	Tuesday
A	Sales Executive	*Friday*

The places of italized letter/words is the last left one and can be filled easily by fulfilling all other given conditions.

Solution (8-11):

Wed	Thu	Fri	Sat	Sun	Mon	Tue
F, B	H, E	I, D	C	Hol	A, G	J

12-16: T(m) Z(f) Swift D'Zire Delhi
QWP Honda City Hyderabad
V(m)R(m)S(f) Ford Ikon Chennai.

17. Because the first two statements are true, Easha is the youngest of the three, so the third statement must be false.

18. Because the first two statements are true, raspberries are the most expensive of the three.

19. We know from the first two statements that Lily runs fastest. Therefore, the third statement must be false.

20. There are fewer oranges than either apples or mangoes, so the statement is true. (another approach)
  1. A fruit basket contains more apples than mangoes = App > Mang.
  2. There are more mangoes in the basket than there are oranges = Mang > Org Now, Combine the above two results: App > Mang > Org.
  3. The basket contains more apples than oranges (App > ... > Org) = Yes.
  Therefore, the given 3rd statement is true.

21. Jullie is younger than Katrina and older than Maya, so Maya must be younger than Katrina.

22. We know from the first two statements that Tuesday had the highest temperature, but we cannot know whether Monday's temperature was higher than Tuesday's.

23. We know that there are Signots with buttons, or Lamels, and that there are blue Signots, which have no buttons. Therefore, Lamels do not have buttons and cannot be blue.

❀ ❀ ❀

Sitting Arrangement

Sitting arrangement around circle: Nowadays in some competitive exams problems based on sitting arrangement around circle is frequently asked. These questions appear very simple but are not a cakewalk and are often solved wrongly. Main confusing point is deciding between left hand side and right hand side of a person when all persons are sitting around a circle facing centre. Because the left hand side of a person in lower semicircle is right hand side of a person in upper semicircle. This confusion is not met when these problems are solved by numbered line method. In numbered line method all members are first placed on a numbered line numbered up to total number of persons starting from one. For extreme end members line is assumed to be continued with other extreme member as immediate neighbour. Right hand side or left hand side confusion is by passed in this method. Following solved problems will make the method very clear.

Example

Directions (Qs. Nos. 1 to 6): *Study the following information carefully and answer the questions given below:*

P, Q, R, S, T, V, W and Z are sitting around a circle facing at the centre. R is fourth to the left of P who is second to the right of S. V is fourth to the right of S. Q is fourth to the left of W who is not an immediate neighbour of P or S. Z is not an immediate neighbour of R.

1. Who is to the immediate right of V?
   A. R   B. W
   C. Z   D. Data inadequate
   E. None of these

2. Who is to the immediate right of R?
   A. T   B. S
   C. W   D. Data inadequate
   E. None of these

3. Who is second to the left of Z?
   A. Q   B. V
   C. S   D. W
   E. None of these

4. In which of the following pairs is the first person sitting to the immediate right of the second person?
   A. VW   B. RT
   C. WR   D. QP
   E. ZP

5. Which of the following pairs are the immediate neighbours of Z?
   A. WQ   B. VQ
   C. WP   D. VP
   E. None of these

6. Who is third to the right of R?
   A. P   B. S
   C. Q   D. Data inadequate
   E. None of these

Solution (1-6):

(a) R is fourth to the left of P who is second to the right of S.
(b) V is fourth to the right of S.
(c) Q is fourh to the left of W who is not an immediate neighbour of P or S.
(d) Z is not an immediate neighbour of R.

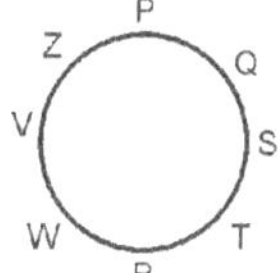

1. B   2. A   3. A   4. E   5. D   6. C

EXERCISE

Directions (Qs. Nos. 1 to 5): *Study the following information carefully and answer the questions given below:*

M, P, J, B, R, T and F are sitting around a circle facing at the centre. B is third to the left of J who is second to the left of M. P is third to the left of B and second to the right of R. T is not an immediate neighbour of M.

1. Who is fourth to the right of M?
   A. B
   B. T
   C. J
   D. Data inadequate
   E. None of these

2. Who is second to the left of T?
   A. F
   B. M
   C. P
   D. J
   E. Data inadequate

3. In which of the following pairs the second person is sitting to the immediate right of the first person?
   A. JR
   B. PJ
   C. TR
   D. MP
   E. None of these

4. What is F's position with respect to R?
   A. Third to the left
   B. Fourth to the right
   C. Third to the right
   D. Both A and B
   E. None of these

5. Who is third to the right of B?
   A. R
   B. J
   C. M
   D. Data inadequate
   E. None of these

Directions (Qs. Nos. 6 to 10): *Study the following information to answer the given questions:*

Representatives from eight different Banks viz. A, B, C, D, E, F, G and H are sitting around a circular table facing the centre but not necessarily in the same order. Each one of them is from a different Bank viz. UCO Bank, Oriental Bank of Commerce, Bank of Maharashtra, Canara Bank, Syndicate Bank, Punjab National Bank, Bank of India and Dena Bank. F sits second to right of the representative from Canara Bank. Representative from Bank of India is an immediate neighbour of the representative from Canara Bank. Two people sit between the representative of Bank of India and B. C and E are immediate neighbours of each other. Neither C nor E is an immediate neighbour of either B or the representative from Canara Bank. Representative from Bank of Maharashtra sits second to right of D. D is neither the representative of Canara Bank nor Bank of India. G and the representative from UCO Bank are immediate neighbours of each other. B is not the representative of UCO Bank. Only one person sits between C and the representative from Oriental Bank of Commerce. H sits third to left of the representative from Dena Bank. Representative from Punjab National Bank sits second to left of the representative from Syndicate Bank.

6. Who amongst the following sit exactly between B and the representative from Bank of India?
   A. A and the representative from UCO Bank
   B. F and G
   C. H and the representative from Bank of Maharashtra
   D. H and G
   E. Representatives from Syndicate Bank and Oriental Bank of Commerce

7. Who amongst the following is the representative from Oriental Bank of Commerce?
   A. A
   B. C
   C. H
   D. G
   E. D

8. Four of the following five are alike in a certain way based on the given arrangement and thus form a group. Which is the one that does not belong to that group?
   A. H – UCO Bank
   B. A – Canara Bank
   C. D – Bank of Maharashtra
   D. E – Syndicate Bank
   E. F – Punjab National Bank

9. Who amongst the following sits second to left of B?
  A. C
  B. H
  C. The representative from Canara Bank
  D. The representative from Punjab National Bank
  E. G

10. Which of the following is true with respect to the given sitting arrangement?
  A. B is the representative from Bank of Maharashtra
  B. C sits second to right of H
  C. The representative from Dena Bank sits to the immediate left of the representative from UCO Bank
  D. A sits second to right of the representative from Bank of India
  E. The representatives from Bank of Maharashtra and Syndicate Bank are immediate neighbours of each other

Directions (Qs. Nos. 11 to 14): *Six friends P, Q, R, S, T and U are sitting around the hexagonal table each at one corner and are facing the centre of the hexagonal. P is second to the left of U. Q is neighbour of R and S. T is second to the left of S.*

11. Which one is sitting opposite to P?
  A. R
  B. Q
  C. T
  D. S

12. Who is the fourth person to the left of Q?
  A. P
  B. U
  C. R
  D. Data inadequate

13. Which of the following are the neighbours of P?
  A. U and P
  B. T and R
  C. U and R
  D. Data inadequate

14. Which one is sitting opposite to T?
  A. R
  B. Q
  C. Cannot be determined
  D. S

Direction (Qs. Nos. 15 and 16): *Five girls are sitting on a bench to be photographed. Seema is to the left of Rani and to the right of Bindu. Mary is to the right of Rani. Reeta is between Rani and Mary.*

15. Who is sitting immediate right to Reeta?
  A. Bindu
  B. Rani
  C. Mary
  D. Seema

16. Who is in the middle of the photograph?
  A. Seema
  B. Rani
  C. Reeta
  D. Seema

Directions (Qs. Nos. 17 to 20) : *In a class there are seven students (including boys and girls) A, B, C, D, E, F and G. They sit on three benches I, II and III. Such that at least two students on each bench and at least one girl on each bench. C who is a girl student, does not sit with A, E and D. F a boy student sits with only B. A boyfriend of D sits on the bench I with his best friends. G sits on the bench III. E is the brother of C.*

17. How many girls are there out of these 7 students?
  A. 3
  B. 3 or 4
  C. 4
  D. Data inadequate

18. Which of the following is the group of girls?
  A. BAC
  B. BFC
  C. BCD
  D. CDF

19. Who sits with C?
  A. B
  B. D
  C. G
  D. E

20. On which bench there are three students?
  A. Bench I
  B. Bench II
  C. Bench III
  D. Bench I or II

Directions (Qs. Nos. 21 to 25): *In an Exhibition seven cars of different companies—Tata, Ambassador, Fiat, Maruti, Mercedes, Bedford and Fargo are standing facing to east in the following order.*

  I. Tata is next to right of Fargo.
  II. Fargo is fourth to the right of Fiat.
  III. Maruti car is between Ambassador and Bedford.
  IV. Fiat which is third to the left of Ambassador, is at one end.

21. Which of the cars are on both the sides of Tata car?
   A. Ambassador and Maruti
   B. Maruti and Fiat
   C. Fargo and Mercedes
   D. Ambassador and Fargo

22. Which of the following statement is correct?
   A. Maruti is next left of Ambassador.
   B. Bedford is next left of Fiat.
   C. Bedford is at one end.
   D. Fiat is next second to the right of Maruti.

23. Which one of the following statements is correct?
   A. Fargo car is in between Ambassador and Fiat.
   B. Tata is next left to Mercedes car.
   C. Fargo is next right of Tata.
   D. Maruti is fourth right of Mercedes.

24. Which of the following groups of cars is to the right of Ambassador?
   A. Tata, Fargo and Maruti
   B. Mercedes, Tata and Fargo
   C. Maruti, Bedford and Fiat
   D. Bedford, Tata and Fargo

25. Which one of the following is the correct position of Mercedes?
   A. Next to the left of Tata
   B. Next to the left of Bedford
   C. Fourth to the right of Maruti
   D. Fourth to the right of Maruti

ANSWERS

1	2	3	4	5	6	7	8	9	10
E	A	C	D	B	C	E	B	D	E

11	12	13	14	15	16	17	18	19	20
D	A	B	B	C	B	A	C	C	A

21	22	23	24	25
C	A	B	B	D

EXPLANATORY ANSWERS

1-5: (a) B is third to the left of J who is second to the left of M.
(b) P is third to the left of B and second to the right of R.
(c) T is not an immediate neighbour of M.

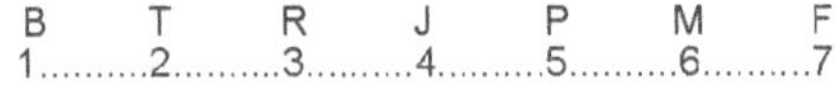

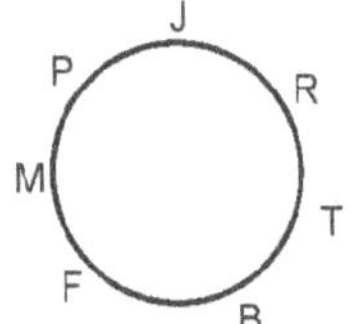

6-10:

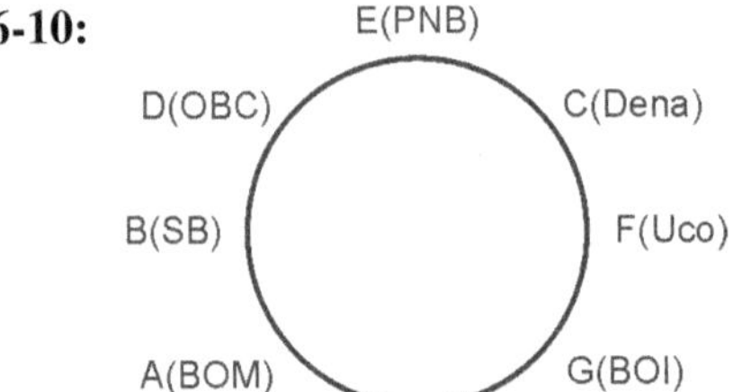

11-14:

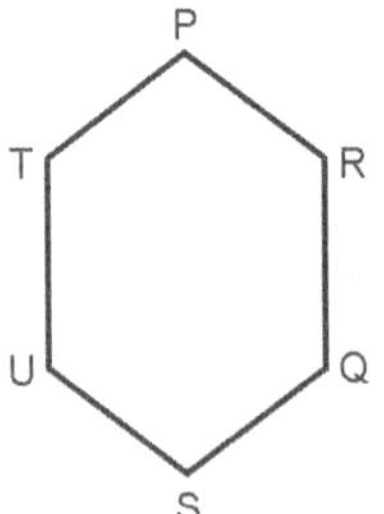

15-16:

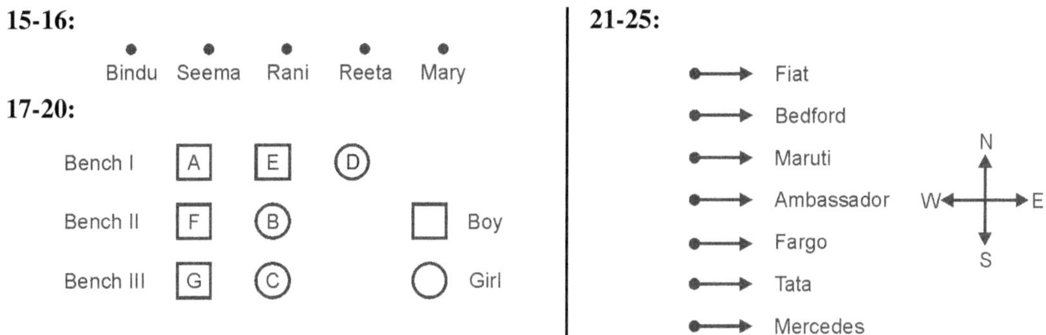

17-20:

21-25:

❀ ❀ ❀

Data Sufficiency

In these questions, all one have to do is to analyse the given data and see if the answer to the problem can be given by all the data provided or by few of the data provided or cannot be answered with the data provided. Sometimes questions are qualitative in nature, wherein one has to apply his own value-judgement in order to reach a conclusion.

Example

Directions: *In the question below consists of a question and two or three statements given below it. You have to decide whether the data provided in the statements are sufficient to answer the question.*

2. Who is the North-East of R?
   1. S is to the South-East of N, who is to the South-West of P, who is to the North of Q.
   2. T is to the North-West of Q, who is to the South of P.
   3. R, who is to the North of S, is midway between N and Q, N being to the West of R.
   A. All 1, 2, 3 together are required
   B. Only 1 and 3 together are sufficient
   C. Only 2 and 3 together are sufficient
   D. Either 1 and 3 together or 2 and 3 together are sufficient
   E. None of these

Ans. D

EXERCISE

Directions (Qs. Nos. 1 to 30): *In each of the questions below consists of a question and two statements numbered I and II given below it. You have to decide whether the data provided in the statements are sufficient to answer the question. Read both the statements and* give answer:
   A. If the data in statement I alone are sufficient to answer the question, while the data in statement II alone are not sufficient to answer the question.
   B. If the data in statement II alone are sufficient to answer the question, while the data in statement I alone are not sufficient to answer the question.
   C. If the data either in statement I alone or in statement II alone are sufficient to answer the question.
   D. If the data given in both statements I and II together are not sufficient to answer the question and

   E. If the data in both statements I and II together are necessary to answer the question.

1. The last Sunday of March, 2006 fell on which date?
   Statements:
   I. The first Sunday of that month fell on 5th.
   II. The last day of that month was Friday.

2. In which year was Raju born?
   Statements:
   I. Raju at present is 25 years younger to his mother.
   II. Raju's brother, who was born in 1964, is 35 years younger to his mother.

3. How many children does M have?
   Statements:
   I. H is the only daughter of X who is wife of M.
   II. K and J are brothers of M.

4. How much was the total sale of the company?
Statements:
  I. The company sold 8000 units of product A each costing ₹ 25.
  II. This company has no other product line.

5. What will be the total weight of 10 rods, each of the same weight?
Statements:
  I. One-fourth of the weight of each rod is 5 kg.
  II. The total weight of three rods is 20 kilograms more than the total weight of two rods.

6. How is J related to Y?
Statements:
  I. Y and Z are children of D who is wife of J.
  II. R's sister J is married to Y's father.

7. How is T related to F?
Statements:
  I. R's sister J has married T's brother L, who is the only son of his parents.
  II. F is the only daughter of L and J.

8. What is the code for 'sky' in the code language?
Statements:
  I. In the code language, 'sky is clear' is written as 'de ra fa'.
  II. In the same code language, 'make it clear' is written as 'de ga jo'.

9. How is J related to P?
Statements:
  I. M is brother of P and T is sister of P.
  II. P's mother is married to J's husband who has one son and two daughters.

10. How many children are there between P and V in a row of children?
Statements:
  I. P is fifteenth from the left in the row.
  II. V is exactly in the middle and there are ten children towards his right.

11. B is the brother of A. How is A related to B?
Statements:
  I. A is the sister of C.
  II. E is the husband of A.

12. Who is to the immediate right of P among five persons P, Q, R, S and T facing North?
Statements:
  I. R is third to the left of Q and P is second to the right of R.
  II. Q is to the immediate left of T who is second to the right of P.

13. How is X related to Y?
Statements:
  I. Y says, "I have only one brother".
  II. X says, "I have only one sister".

14. How many children are there in the row of children facing North?
Statements:
  I. Vibha who is fifth from the left end is eighth to the left of Ashish who is twelfth from the right end.
  II. Rohit is fifth to the left of Nisha who is seventh from the right end and eighteenth from the left end.

15. How is Tannu related to the man in the photograph?
Statements:
  I. Man in the photograph is the only son of Tannu's grandfather.
  II. The man in the photograph has no brothers or sisters and his father is Tannu's grandfather.

16. On which day of the week was birthday of Salim?
Statements:
  I. Salim celebrated his birthday the very next day on which Arun celebrated his birthday.
  II. The sister of Salim was born on the third day of the week and two days after Salim was born.

17. How many doctors are practicing in this town?
Statements:
  I. There is one doctor per seven hundred residents.
  II. There are 16 wards with each ward having as many doctors as the number of wards.

18. How many pages of book C did Robert read on Sunday?
Statements:
  I. The book has 300 pages out of which two-thirds were read by him before Sunday.
  II. Robert read the last 40 pages of the book on the morning of Monday.

19. Among F, V, B, E and C, who is the third from the top when arranged in the descending order of their weights?
Statements:
  I. B is heavier than F and C and is less heavier than V who is not the heaviest.
  II. C is heavier than only F.

20. On a T.V. channel, four films A, B, C and D were screened, one on each day, on four consecutive days but not necessarily in that order. On which day was the film C screened?
Statements:
  I. The first film was screened on 23rd, Tuesday and was followed by film D.
  II. Film A was not screened on 25th and one serial was screened between films A and B.

21. Which word in the code language means 'flower'?
Statements:
  I. 'de fu la pane' means 'rose flower is beautiful' and 'la quiz' means 'beautiful tree'.
  II. 'de la chin' means 'red rose flower' and 'pa chin' means 'red tea'.

22. Who is C's partner in a game of cards involving four players A, B, C and D?
Statements:
  I. D is sitting opposite to A.
  II. B is sitting right of A and left of D.

23. How many students in a class play football?
Statements:
  I. Only boys play football.
  II. There are forty boys and thirty girls in the class.

24. Can Ramesh retire from office X in January 2020, with full pension benefits?
Statements:
  I. Ramesh will complete 30 years of service in office X in April 2014 and desires to retire.
  II. As per office X rules, an employee has to complete minimum 30 years of service and attain age of 60. Ramesh has 3 years to complete age of 60.

25. On which date in August was Kunal born?
Statements:
  I. Kunal's mother remembers that Kunal was born before nineteenth but after fifteenth.
  II. Kunal's brother remembers that Kunal was born before seventeenth but after twelfth.

26. Madan is elder than Kamal and Sharad is younger than Alok. Who among them is the youngest?
Statements:
  I. Sharad is younger than Madan.
  II. Alok is younger than Kamal.

27. What is the code for 'or' in the code language?
Statements:
  I. 'nik sa te' means 'right or wrong', 'ro da nik' means 'he is right' and 'fe te ro' means 'that is wrong'.
  II. 'pa nik la' means 'that right man', 'sa ne pa' means 'this or that' and 'ne ka re' means 'tell this there'.

28. What is Gagan's age?
Statements:
  I. Gagan, Vimal and Kusum are all of the same age.
  II. Total age of Vimal, Kusum and Anil is 32 years and Anil is as old as Vimal and Kusum together.

29. How much money do Vivek and Sunny have together?
Statements:
  I. Sunny has 20 rupees less than what Tarun has.
  II. Vivek has 30 rupees more than what Tarun has.

30. Who among P, Q, R, S and T is the lightest?
Statements:
  I. R is heavier than Q and T but lighter than S.
  II. S is not the heaviest.

ANSWERS

1	2	3	4	5	6	7	8	9	10
C	E	D	E	C	C	E	D	B	E

11	12	13	14	15	16	17	18	19	20
C	C	D	C	C	B	B	E	A	E

21	22	23	24	25	26	27	28	29	30
D	C	D	E	E	B	C	E	D	D

EXPLANATORY ANSWERS

1. From I, we conclude that 5th, 12th, 19th and 26th of March, 2006 were Sundays.

So, the last Sunday fell on 26th.

From II, we conclude that 31st March, 2006 was Friday. Thus, 26th March, 2006 was the last Sunday of the month.

2. From both I and II, we find that Raju is $(35 - 25) = 10$ years older than his brother, who was born in 1964. So, Raju was born in 1954.

3. From I, we conclude that H is the only daughter of M. But this does not indicate that M has no son. The information given in II is immaterial.

4. From I, total sale of product A = ₹ (8000×25) = ₹ 200000.

From II, we know that the company deals only in product A.

This implies that sale of product A is the total sale of the company, which is ₹ 200000.

5. From I, we conclude that weight of each rod = (4×5) kg = 20 kg.

So, total weight of 10 rods = (20×10) kg = 200 kg.

From II, we conclude that:

Weight of each rod = (weight of 3 rods) – (weight of 2 rods) = 20 kg.

So, total weight of 10 rods = (20×10) kg = 200 kg.

6. From I, we conclude that Y is the child of D who is wife of J i.e. J is Y's father.

From II, J is married to Y's father. This implies that J is Y's mother.

7. From I, we know that L is T's brother and J's husband. Since L is the only son of his parents, T is L's sister.

From II, we know that F is L's daughter. Thus, from I and II, we conclude that T is the sister of F's father i.e. T is F's aunt.

8. The only word common to I and II is 'clear' and as such, only the code for 'clear' can be ascertained from the given information.

9. From II, we know that P's mother is married to J's husband, which means that J is P's mother.

10. From II, V being in the middle, there are 10 children to his right as well as to his left. So, V is 11th from the left. From I, P is 15th from the left. Thus, from both I and II, we conclude that there are 3 children between P and V.

11. B is A's brother means A is either brother or sister of B. Now, each one of I and II individually indicates that A is a female, which means that A is B's sister.

12. From I, we have the order: R, –, P, Q.

From II, we have the order: P, Q, T. Clearly, each one of the above two orders indicates that Q is to the immediate right of P.

13. The statements in I and II do not provide any clue regarding relation between X and Y.

14. Since 8th to the left of 12th from the right is 20th from the right, so from I, we know that Vibha is 5th from left and 20th from right *i.e.* there are 4 children to the left and 19 to the right of Vibha.

So, there are (4 + 1 + 19) *i.e.* 24 children in the row.

From II, Nisha is 7th from right and 18th from left end of the row.

So, there are (6 + 1 + 17) = 24 children in the row.

15. From I, we conclude that the man is the only son of Tannu's grandfather *i.e.* he is Tannu's father or Tannu is the man's daughter.

From II, we conclude that the man's father is Tannu's grandfather. Since the man has no brothers or sisters, so he is Tannu's father or Tannu is the man's daughter.

16. I does not mention the day of the week on the birthday of either Arun or Salim. According to II, Salim's sister was born on Wednesday and Salim was born two days before Wednesday *i.e.* on Monday.

17. From I, total number of doctors in town = (1/700 × N), where N = total number of residents in town. But, the value of N is not known.

From II, total number of doctors in town
= (Number of wards in town) × (Number of doctors in each ward)
= 16 × 16 = 256.

18. From I and II, we find that Robert read (300 × 2/3) *i.e.* 200 pages before Sunday and the last 40 pages on Monday. This means that he read [300 – (200 + 40)] *i.e.* 60 pages on Sunday.

19. From I, we have: B > F, B > C, V > B. Thus, V is heavier than each one of B, F and C. But V is not the heaviest. So, E is the heaviest.

Thus, we have the order:

E > V > B > T > C or E > V > B > C > F.

Clearly, B is third from the top.

20. From I, we know that the films were screened on 23rd, 24th, 25th and 26th. Clearly, D was screened second *i.e.* on 24th, Wednesday.

From II, we know that one film was screened between A and B.

So, A and B were screened first and third, *i.e.*

on 23rd and 25th. But, A was not screened on 25th.

So, A was screened on 23rd and B on 25th. Thus, C was screened on 26th, Friday.

21. From the given two statements in I, the code for the only common word 'beautiful' can be determined.

From the given two statements in II, the code for the only common word 'red' can be determined.

In I and II, the common words are 'rose and 'flower' and the common code words are 'de' and 'la'. So, the code for 'flower' is either 'de' or 'la'.

22. Clearly, each of the given statements shows that B is sitting opposite to C or B is the partner of C.

23. It is not mentioned whether all the boys or a proportion of them play football.

24. Clearly, the facts given in I and II contain two conditions to be fulfilled to get retirement and also indicate that Ramesh fulfils only one condition out of them.

25. From I, we conclude that Kunal was born on any one of the dates among 16th, 17th and 18th.

From II, we conclude that Kunal was born on any one of the dates among 13th, 14th, 15th and 16th.

Thus, from both I and II, we conclude that Kunal was born on 16th August.

26. As given, we have: M > K, A > S.

From II, K > A.

Thus, we have: M > K > A > S.

So, Sharad is the youngest. From I, M > S. Thus, we have: M > K > A > S or M > A > K > S or M > A > S > K.

27. I. In 'right or wrong' and 'he is right', the common word is 'right' and the common code word is 'nik'. So 'nik' means 'right'. In 'right or wrong' and 'that is wrong', the common word is 'wrong' and the common code word is 'te'. So, 'te' means 'wrong'. Thus, in 'right or wrong', 'sa' is the code for 'or'. II. In 'that right man' and 'this or that', the common word is 'that' and the common code word is 'pa'. So, 'pa' means 'that'. In 'this or that' and 'tell this there', the common word is 'this' and the common code word is 'ne'. So, 'ne' means 'this'. Thus, in 'this or that', 'sa' is the code for 'or'.

28. As given in I and II, we have: G = V = K, V + K + A = 32 and A = V + K.
Putting V + K = A in V + K + A = 32, we have: 2A = 32 or A = 16.
Thus, V + K = 16 and V = K. So, V = K = 8.
Thus, G = 8.

29. From I, we have: S = T – 20.
From II, we have: V = T + 30.
Thus, from both I and II, we have:
V + S = (T + 30) + (T – 20) = (2 T + 10).
So, to get the required amount, we need to know the amount that Tarun has.

30. From I, we have: R > Q, R > T, S > R *i.e.*
S > R > Q > T or S > R > T > Q.
From II, S is not the heaviest. So, P is the heaviest.
Thus, we have: P > S > R > Q > T or P > S > R > T > Q.
Hence, either T or Q is the lightest.

9

Coded Inequalities

To solve coded inequalities problem one's primarily task is to combine (visualise) two or more inequalities in to one combined notation.

Rule-Carry one directional lightest inequality to deduce conclusion from combined inequality Whenever inequalities are combined together in one combined notation writing common terms only once then conclusion will follow between any two terms if and only if all the inequalities between these two terms points in one same direction and conclusion will carry lightest ('<' is lighter than '≤' and '>'is lighter than '≥') inequality sign present between these two terms.

Basics of above rule

1. Two inequalities can be combined if and only if they have a common term.

2. Two inequalities can be combined (to give valid conclusion) if and only if the common term is greater than (or 'greater than or equal to') one and less than (or 'less than or equal to') the other.

3. The conclusion –inequality will have an '≥' sign (or a '≤' sign) if and only if both the signs in the combined inequality were '≥'(or '≤',as the case may be).

EXERCISE

Directions (Qs. Nos. 1 to 6): *In the following questions, the symbols @, ©, •, % and $ are used with the following meaning as illustrated below:*

'P © Q' means 'P is neither greater than nor smaller than Q'.

'P @ Q' means 'P is smaller than Q'.

'P $ Q' means 'P is greater than Q'.

'P • Q' means 'P is either smaller than or equal to Q'.

'P % Q' means 'P is either greater than or equal to Q'.

Now in each of the following questions assuming the given statements to be true, find which of the two conclusions I and II given below them is/are Definitely true?

> **Give answer :**
> A. if only conclusion I is true
> B. if only conclusion II is true
> C. if either conclusion I or II is true
> D. if neither conclusion I nor II is true
> E. if both conclusions I and II are true

1. **Statements:** J $ N, N % F, F • D
   Conclusions: I. F @ J   II. D % N

2. **Statements:** J % N, N © D, D @ K
   Conclusions : I. D © J   II. D @ J

3. **Statements:** R © M, M @ V, V $ F
   Conclusions: I. F @ M   II. V $ R

4. **Statements:** N @ K, K • F, F $ W
   Conclusions: I. F % N   II. W @ K

5. **Statements:** B •K, K $ R, R % E
   Conclusions: I. E @ K   II. E @ B

6. **Statements:** M• T, T @ R, R © K
   Conclusions: I. K $ T   II. R % M

Directions (Qs. Nos. 7 to 11): *In the following questions, the symbols @, ©, %, $ and β are used with the following meaning as illustrated below:*

> 'P © Q' means 'P is smaller than Q'.
> 'P @ Q' means 'P is either smaller than or equal to Q'.
> 'P % Q' means 'P is greater than Q'.
> 'P $ Q' means 'P is either greater than or equal to Q'.
> 'P β Q' means 'P is equal to Q'.

Now in each of the following questions

assuming the given statements to be true, find which of the two conclusions I and II given below them is/are Definitely true?

Give answer:

A. if only conclusion I is true
B. if only conclusion II is true
C. if either conclusion I or II is true
D. if neither conclusion I nor II is true
E. if both conclusions I and II are true

7. Statements: B © T, T β M, M % F
   Conclusions: I. B © M   II. B © F

8. Statements: M β R, R % T, T $ K
   Conclusions: I. K @ M   II. K © M

9. Statements: W © D, D @ H, H β N
   Conclusions: I. N $ D   II. W © N

10. Statements: W @ D, D $ R, R © K
   Conclusions: I. R β W   II. R % W

11. Statements : F $ J, J % V, V © N
   Conclusions: I. N $ F   II. N % J

Directions (Qs. Nos. 12 to 16): *In the following questions, certain symbols have been used to indicate relationships between elements as follows:*
A % B means A is neither smaller than nor greater than B.
A $ B means A is greater than B.
A & B means A is either greater than or equal to B.
A @ B means A is smaller than B.
A # B means A is either smaller than or equal to B.

In each question, three statements showing relationships have been given, which are followed by two conclusions I and II. Assuming that the given statements are true, find out which conclusion(s) is/are definitely true.

Mark answer :

A. if only conclusion I is true
B. if only conclusion II is true
C. if either conclusion I or II is true
D. if neither conclusion I nor II is true
E. if both conclusions I and II are true

12. Statements: P & Q, Q $ R, Q % S
   Conclusions: I. P @ S   II. R @ P

13. Statements: F & G, G % H, H $ K
   Conclusions: I. H @ F   II. F % H

14. Statements: T # V, V $ X, X & Y
   Conclusions: I. V $ Y   II. X # T

15. Statements: C % E, E # W, W @ Z
   Conclusions: I. W & C   II. C @ Z

16. Statements : L # M, M @ N, N $ P
   Conclusions: I. L # N   II. M & P

Directions (Qs. Nos. 17 to 22): *In the following questions, the symbols @, ©, %, $ and ? are used with the following meaning as illustrated below :*
'P © Q' means 'P is either smaller than or equal to Q.
'P Ω Q' means 'P is either greater than or equal to Q'.
'P % Q' means 'P is smaller than Q'.
'P $ Q' means 'P is greater than Q'.
'P @ Q' means 'P is equal to Q'

Now in each of the following questions assuming the given statements to be true, find which of the two conclusions I and II given below them is/are Definitely true?

Give answer:

A. if only conclusion I is true
B. if only conclusion II is true
C. if either conclusion I or II is true
D. if neither conclusion I nor II is true
E. if both conclusions I and II are true

17. Statements: M % T, T $ K, K © D
   Conclusions: I. T $ D   II. D $ M

18. Statements: F @ B, B % N, N $ H
   Conclusions: I. N $ F   II. H $ F

19. Statements: R Ω M, M @ K, K © J
   Conclusions: I. J $ M   II. J @ M

20. Statements: B $ N, N Ω R, R @ K
   Conclusions: I. K © N   II. B $ K

21. Statements: J © K, K $ N, N Ω D
   Conclusions: I. J % N   II. D % K

22. Statements: R @ D, D © M, M $ T
   Conclusions: I. T % D   II. M Ω R

Directions (Qs. Nos. 23 to 27): *In the following questions, the symbols $, •, %, Ω and @ are used with the following meaning as illustrated below :*
'P • Q' means ' P is neither greater than nor equal to Q'.
'P @ Q' means ' P is neither smaller than nor equal to Q,.
'P Ω Q' means ' P is not greater than Q'.
'P % Q' means 'P is not smaller than Q'.
'P $ Q' means 'P is neither greater than nor smaller than Q'.

Now in each of the following questions assuming the given statements to be true, find which of the two conclusions I and II given below them is/are Definitely true?

Give answer:

A. if only conclusion I is true
B. if only conclusion II is true
C. if either conclusion I or II is true
D. if neither conclusion I nor II is true
E. if both conclusions I and II are true

23. Statements: R % W, W @ F, F $ Z
   Conclusions: I. F • R   II. Z • W

24. Statements: B @ K, K % J, J • M
   Conclusions: I. J • B   II. M @ B

25. Statements: D $ T, T Ω H, H @ N
   Conclusions: I. H $ D   II. H @ D

26. Statements: H Ω N, N • K, K Ω D
   Conclusions: I. D @ N   II. H • K

27. Statements : W % E, E @ K, K $ J
   Conclusions: I. J Ω E   II. W % K

Directions (Qs. Nos. 28 to 30): *Read the information/statement given in each question carefully and answer the questions.*

28. Which of the following expressions will be true if the expression' A > B ≥ C < D is definitely true?
   A. A > D   B. C ≤ A
   C. D > B   D. D ≥ A
   E. None is true

29. Which of the following expressions will not be true if the expression ' F ≤ G = H < K' is definitely true?
   A. K ≥ F   B. H ≥ F
   C. G < K   D. F < K
   E. None of these

30. In which of the following expressions will the expression 'P < Q' be definitely true?
   A. P ≥ R > N = Q   B. Q < R ≥ N > P
   C. P < R ≤ Q > N   D. P ≥ N ≥ M > Q
   E. None is true

ANSWERS

21	22	23	24	25	26	27	28	29	30
A	C	B	D	A	A	A	B	E	D
31	**32**	**33**	**34**	**35**	**36**	**37**	**38**	**39**	**40**
D	B	C	A	E	D	D	A	C	E
41	**42**	**43**	**44**	**45**	**46**	**47**	**48**	**49**	**50**
D	B	E	A	C	E	D	E	A	C

EXPLANATORY ANSWERS

(1-6): © → =   • → ≤   @ → < $ → >   % → ≥

1. J $ N → J > N, N % F → N ≥ F,
   F • D → F ≤ D
   Therefore, J > N ≥ F ≤ D
   Conclusions:
   I. F @ J → F < J : True
   II. D % N → D ≥ N: False

2. J % N → J ≥ N, N © D → N = D,
   D @ K → D < K
   Therefore, J ≥ N = D < K
   Conclusions:
   I. D © J → D = J : False
   II. D @ J → D < J : False
   Either I or II is true

3. R © M → R = M, M @ V → M < V,
   V $ F → V > F
   Therefore, R = M < V > F
   Conclusions:
   I. F @ M → F < M : False
   II. V $ R → V > R : True

4. N @ K → N < K,
   K • F → K ≤ F,
   F $ W → F > W
   Therefore, N < K ≤ F > W
   Conclusions:
   I. F % N → F ≥ N : False
   II. W @ K → W < K : False

5. B • K → B ≤ K,
K $ R → K > R,
R % E → R ≥ E
Therefore, B ≤ K > R ≥ E
Conclusions:
  I. E @ K → E < K : True
  II. E @ B → E < B : False

6. M • T → M ≤ T,
T @ R → T < R,
R © K → R = K
Therefore, M ≤ T < R = K
Conclusions:
  I. K $ T → K > T : True
  II. R % M → R ≥ M : False

(7- 11): © → < @ → ≤ % → > $ → ≥ β → =

7. B © T → B < T,
T β M → T = M,
M % F → M > F
Therefore, B < T = M > F
Conclusions:
  I. B © M → B < M : True
  II. B © F → B < F : False

8. M β R → M = R,
R % T → R > T,
T $ K → T ≥ K
Therefore, M = R > T ≥ K
Conclusions:
  I. K @ M → K ≤ M : False
  II. K © M → K < M : True

9. W © D → W < D,
D @ H → D ≤ H,
H β N → H = N
Therefore, W< D ≤ H = N
Conclusions:
  I. N $ D → N ≥ D : True
  II. W © N → W < N : True

10. W @ D → W ≤ D,
D $ R → D ≥ R,
R © K → R < K
Therefore, W ≤ D ≥ R < K
Conclusions:
  I. R β W → R = W : False
  II. R % W → R > W : False

11. F $ J → F ≥ J,
J % V → J > V,
V © N → V < N
Therefore, F ≥ J > V< N
Conclusions:
  I. N $ F → N ≥ F : False
  II. N % J → N > J : False

(12- 16): A % B → A = B, A $ B → A > B,
A & B → A ≥ B, A @ B → A < B, A # B → A ≤ B

12. P & Q → P ≥ Q,
Q $ R → Q > R,
Q % S → Q = S
Therefore, P ≥ Q = S > R
Conclusions:
  I. P @ S → P < S : False
  II. R @ P → R < P : True

13. F & G → F ≥ G,
G % H → G = H,
H $ K → H > K
Therefore, F ≥ G = H > K
Conclusions:
  I. H @ F → H < F : False
  II. F % H → F = H : False
H is either smaller than or equal to F.

14. T # V → T ≤ V,
V $ X → V > X,
X & Y → X ≥ Y
Therefore, T ≤ V > X ≥ Y
Conclusions:
  I. V $ Y → V > Y : True
  II. X # T → X ≤ T : False

15. C % E → C = E,
E # W → E ≤ W,
W @ Z → W < Z
Therefore, C = E ≤ W < Z
Conclusions:
  I. W & C → W ≥ C : True
  II. C @ Z → C < Z : True

16. L # M → L ≤ M,   M @ N → M < N,
N $ P → N > P
Therefore, L ≤ M < N > P
Conclusions:
  I. L # N → L ≤ N : False
  II. M & P → M ≥ P : False

(17-22): @ → =, © → ≤, % → <, \$ → >, Ω → ≥

17. M % T → M < T,
T \$ K → T > K,
K © D → K ≤ D
Therefore, M < T > K ≤ D
Conclusions:
 I. T \$ D → T > D : False
 II. D \$ M → D > M : False

18. F @ B → F = B,
B % N → B < N,
N \$ H → N > H
Therefore, F = B < N > H
Conclusions:
 I. N \$ F → N > F : True
 II. H \$ F → H > F : False

19. R Ω M → R ≥ M,
M @ K → M = K,
K © J → K ≤ J
Therefore, R ≥ M = K ≤ J
Conclusions:
 I. J \$ M → J > M : False
 II. J @ M → J = M : False
J is either greater than M or equal to M.

20. B \$ N → B > N,
N Ω R → N ≥ R,
R @ K → R = K
Therefore, B > N ≥ R = K
Conclusions:
 I. K © N → K ≤ N : True
 II. B \$ K → B > K : True

21. J © K → J ≤ K,
K \$ N → K > N,
N Ω D → N ≥ D
Therefore, J ≤ K > N ≥ D
Conclusions:
 I. J % N → J < N : False
 II. D % K → D < K: False

22. R @ D → R = D, D © M → D ≤ M,
M \$ T → M > T
Therefore, R = D ≤ M > T
Conclusions:
 I. T % D → T < D : False
 II. M Ω R → M ≥ R : True

(23 – 27): • → <, @ → >, Ω → ≤, % → ≥, \$ → =

23. Statements: R % W → R ≥ W,
W @ F → W > F,
F \$ Z → F = Z
Therefore, R ≥ W > F = Z
Conclusions:
 I. F • R → F < R : True
 II. Z • W → Z < W: True

24. Statements: B @ K → B > K,
K % J → K ≥ J,
J • M → J < M
Therefore,   B > K ≥ J < M
Conclusions:
 I. J • B → J < B : True
 II. M @ B → M > B : False

25. Statements: D \$ T → D = T,
T Ω H → T ≤ H,
H @ N → H > N
Therefore, D = T ≤ H > N
Conclusions:
 I. H \$ D → H = D : False
 II. H @ D → H > D: False
H is greater than or equal to D.
So either I or II is true

26. Statements: H Ω N → H ≤ N,
N • K → N < K,
K Ω D → K ≤ D
Therefore, H ≤ N < K ≤ D
Conclusions:
 I. D @ N → D > N : True
 II. H • K → H < K : True

27. Statements: W % E → W ≥ E,
E @ K → E > K,
K \$ J → K = J
Therefore, W ≥ E > K = J
Conclusions:
 I. J Ω E → J ≤ E : False
 II. W % K → W ≥ K : False

28. A > B ≥ C < D None is true.

29. F ≤ G = H < K, we have K > F.
Therefore, K ≥ F is not true.

30. In P < R ≤ Q > N , P < Q is true.

❀ ❀ ❀

Input Interpretations

In input-output problems one is asked to imagine that there is some computer or a word-processing machine and it performs some operation on a given input. These operations are performed repeatedly as per a pre-fixed pattern and subsequently one has different output in different steps. One's primarily job is to deduce the rule followed by computer/machine in arranging numbers and words. One should analyze final arranged step while deducing rule applied.

Example

Directions (Qs. Nos. 1 to 4): *Study the following information to answer the given questions:*
A word rearrangement machine when given an input line of words, rearranges them, following a particular rule, in each step. The following is an illustration of input and the steps of rearrangement.
Input: over you pat me crow easy to.
Steps: (I) pat over you crow easy to me
    (II) crow pat over you to me easy
    (III) over crow pat to me easy you
    (IV) to over crow pat easy you me, and so on.
As per the rule followed in the above steps, find out the appropriate step for the given input in the following questions.

1. If step V of an input is 'put down col in as much sa', what would be the VIIIth step?
   A. down in put much sa as col
   B. in put down col much sa as
   C. much in put down sa as col
   D. col put down as much sa in
   E. None of these

Ans. E. The steps followed are :
   Step V : put down col in as much sa
   Step VI : in put down col much sa as
   Step VII : down in put much sa as col
   Step VIII : much down in put as col sa

2. **Input:** but calm free are so not eat. Which of the following will be the IIIrd step for this input?
   A. so free but calm eat are not
   B. but calm are free not so eat
   C. are but calm free not eat so
   D. but so free eat are not calm
   E. None of these

Ans. D. The step followed are :
   Input : but calm free are so not eat
   Step I : free but calm so not eat are
   Step II : so free but calm eat are not
   Step III : but so free eat are not calm

3. **Input :** rim bye eat klin fe to low. Which of the following steps would be 'fe low rim to bye klin eat'?
   A. VIth   B. Vth
   C. IVth   D. IIIrd
   E. None of these

Ans. B. The step followed are :
   Input : rim bye eat klin fe to low
   Step I : eat rim bye fe to low klin
   Step II : fe eat rim bye low klin to
   Step III : rim fe eat low klin to bye
   Step IV : low rim fe eat to bye klin
   Step V : fe low rim to bye klin eat

4. If step II of an input is 'ge su he for game free but', what would be the step VI?
   A. ge for but free he game su
   B. for free ge game su he but
   C. free ge for but game su he
   D. he ge su but game free for
   E. None of these

Ans. E. The step followed are :
   Step II : ge su he for game free but
   Step III : he ge su game free but for
   Step IV : game he ge su but for free
   Step V : ge game he but for free su
   Step VI : but ge game he free su for

EXERCISE

Directions (Qs. Nos. 1 to 5): *Study the following information carefully and answer the questions given below:*

When an input line of words is given to a word arrangement machine, it rearranges them following a particular rule in each step.

> **Input:** car some pour tie more tin bee goat
> **Step I :** goat car some pour tie more tin bee
> **Step II :** goat more car some pour tie tin bee
> **Step III :** goat more pour car some tie tin bee
> **Step IV :** goat more pour some car tie tin bee
> **Step V :** goat more pour some bee car tie tin

and step V is the last output.

1. If the 3rd step of an input is:
   bend take vide nut zeal pot car tin.
   Which of the following will be the last step?
   A. 6th   B. 5th
   C. 7th   D. 4th
   E. None of these

2. If the 2nd step of an input is:
   coat some for die song kill bit son.
   Which is certainly the input?
   A. for come die song kill coat bit son
   B. for die come song kill coat bit son
   C. for die song come kill coat bit son
   D. Can't be determined
   E. None of these

3. **Input :** door site may for you mean now goal
   Which of the following is the 3rd step of the above input?
   A. door goal mean site for may now you
   B. door goal mean site may for you now
   C. door site goal mean may for you now
   D. Can't be determined
   E. None of these

4. **Input:** mute deal sit cut coat day long for
   Which of the following will be the 4th step?
   A. coat deal mute sit cut day long for
   B. coat deal long mute sit cut day for
   C. coat deal long mute cut sit day for
   D. coat deal long mute cut day for sit
   E. None of these

5. **Input :** ask not feel task opt sale dark den
   Which of the following will be the last step?
   A. 5th   B. 6th
   C. 4th   D. 7th
   E. None of these

Directions (Qs. Nos. 6 to 10): *Study the following information to answer the questions given below:*

A number arrangement machine when given an input of numbers, rearranges them following a particular rule in each step. The following is an illustration of input and steps of rearrangement.

Input:	48	245	182	26	99	542	378	297
Step I	542	48	245	182	26	99	378	297
Step II	542	26	48	245	182	99	378	297
Step III	542	26	378	48	245	182	99	297
Step IV	542	26	378	48	297	245	182	99
Step V	542	26	378	48	297	99	245	182

This is the final arrangement and step V is the last step for this input.

6. What will be the fourth step for an input whose second step is given below?
   Step II: 765 42 183 289 542 65 110 350
   A. 765 42 542 350 183 289 65 110
   B. 765 42 542 65 110 183 289 350
   C. 765 42 542 65 183 289 110 350
   D. Cannot be determined
   E. None of these

7. What should be the third step of the following input?
   Input: 239 123 58 361 495 37
   A. 495 37 361 123 239 58
   B. 495 37 58 361 123 239
   C. 495 37 58 123 361 239
   D. 495 37 361 239 123 58
   E. None of these

8. How many steps will be required to get the final output from the following input?
   Input: 39 88 162 450 386 72 29
   A. Two   B. Three
   C. Four   D. Six
   E. None of these

9. What should be the last step of the following input?
Input: 158 279 348 28 326 236
A. 348 28 326 158 279 236
B. 348 28 326 236 158 279
C. 348 28 236 158 279 326
D. 348 28 158 326 236 279
E. None of these

10. If the first step of an input is "785 198 32 426 373 96 49", then which of the following steps will be "785 32 426 49 198 373 96"?
A. Third   B. Fourth
C. Fifth   D. Second
E. None of these

Directions (Qs. Nos. 11 to 15): *A word-number arrangement machine, when given an input as a set of words and numbers, rearranges them following a particular rule and generates stepwise outputs till the rearrangement is complete following that rule.*

Followings is an illustration of input and steps of rearrangement till the last step.
Input: pour ask 57 dear 39 fight 17 28
Step I : ask pour 57 dear 39 fight 17 28
Step II : ask 57 pour dear 39 fight 17 28
Step III : ask 57 dear pour 39 fight 17 28
Step IV : ask 57 dear 39 pour fight 17 28
Step V : ask 57 dear 39 fight pour 17 28
Step VI : ask 57 dear 39 fight 28 pour 17
and Step VI is the last output.

As per the rule followed in the above steps find out the answer to each of the following questions:

11. If step II of an input is "cut 97 38 end for 29 46 down", which of the following will be the last step?
A. Fifth   B. Fourth
C. Sixth 4   D. Seventh
E. None of these

12. If the 4th step of an input is "ago 85 elite 79 exile fat 26 41", which of the following will definitely be the 2nd step of the input?
A. ago 85 79 elite fat 41 26 exile
B. ago 85 exile elite 41 26 fat 79
C. ago 85 26 exile 41 elite 79 fat
D. Cannot be determined
E. None of these

13. If the 1st step of an input is "car 17 vas tiger 92 87 like 52", which of the following will be the 4th step?
A. car 92 like 87 tiger 52 17 vas
B. car 92 like 87 17 vas tiger 52
C. car 92 like 87 tiger 17 vas 52
D. car 92 like 17 vas tiger 87 52
E. None of these

14. **Input:** zeal for 49 31 high 22 track 12
Which of the following will be the 3rd step?
A. for 49 high 31 track 22 zeal 12
B. for 49 high 31 zeal 22 track 12
C. for 49 high zeal 31 22 track 12
D. for 49 high 31 track zeal 22 12
E. None of these

15. **Input :** 19 feat 34 28 dog bag take 43
Which of the following steps would be "bag 43 dog 19 feat 34 28 take"?
A. Second
B. Fourth
C. First
D. Cannot be determined
E. None of these

Directions (Qs. Nos. 16 to 20): *A word-number arrangement machine, when given an input as a set of words and numbers, rearranges them following a particular rule and generates stepwise outputs till the rearrangement is complete following that rule.*

Followings is an illustration of input and steps of rearrangement till the last step.
Input: sine 88 71 cos theta 14 56 gamma delta 26
Step I: cos sine 71 theta 14 56 gamma delta 26 88
Step II: delta cos sine theta 14 56 gamma 26 88 71
Step III: gamma delta cos sine theta 14 26 88 71 56
Step IV: sine gamma delta cos theta 14 88 71 56 26
Step V: theta sine gamma delta cos 88 71 56 26 14

And Step V is the last Step of the arrangement of the above input as the intended arrangement is obtained.

As per the rules followed in the above steps, find out in each of the following questions the appropriate steps for the given input, Input for the questions

Input : for 52 all 96 25 jam road 15 hut 73 bus stop 38 46
(all numbers are in two digits)

16. Which word/number would be at the 6th position from the left in Step V?

   A. 25   B. stop

   C. jam   D. all

   E. road

17. Which of the following would be the Step III?

   A. hut for bus all 25 jam road 15 stop 38 96 73 52 46

   B. for us all 25 jam road 15 hut 38 stop 96 46 73 52

   C. hut for bus all jam road 15 stop 38 96 73 52 46 25

   D. for bus all 25 jam road 15 hut stop 38 46 96 73 52

   E. None of the above

18. Which word/number would be at the 8th position from the right in Step IV?

   A. 15   B. road

   C. hut   D. jam

   E. stop

19. Which of the following would be Step VII?

   A. stop road jam hut for bus all 15 96 73 52 46 38 25

   B. road jam hut for bus all stop 15 25 38 46 52 73 96

   C. stop road jam hut for bus all 96 73 52 46 38 25 15

   D. jam hut for bus all 25 road stop 15 96 73 52 46 38

   E. There will be no such step as the arrangement gets established at Step VI

20. Which step number would be the following output?

bus all for 52 25 jam road 15 hut stop 38 46 96 73

   A. There will be no such step

   B. III   C. II

   D. V   E. VI

Directions (Qs 21 to 24.): *A word-number arrangement machine, when given an input as a set of words and numbers, rearranges them following a particular rule and generates stepwise outputs till the rearrangement is complete following that rule.*

Input : tall 48 13 rise alt 99 76 32 wise jar high 28 56 barn

Followings is an illustration of input and steps of rearrangement till the last step.

Input : tall 48 13 rise alt 99 76 32 wise jar high 28 56 barn

Step I: 13 tall 48 rise 99 76 32 wise jar high 28 56 barn alt

Step II: 28 13 tall 48 rise 99 76 32 wise jar high 56 alt barn

Step III: 32 28 13 tall 48 rise 99 76 wise jar 56 alt barn high

Step IV: 48 32 28 13 tall rise 99 76 wise 56 alt barn high jar

Step V: 56 48 32 28 13 tall 99 76 wise alt barn high jar rise

Step VI: 76 56 48 32 28 13 99 wise alt barn high jar rise tall

Step VII: 99 76 56 48 32 28 13 alt barn high jar rise tall wise

Step VII is the last step of the above input, as desired arrangement is obtained.

As per the rules followed in the above steps, find out in each of the following questions the appropriate steps for the given input.

Input: 84 why sit 14 32 not best ink feet 51 27 vain 68 92 (All the numbers are two digit numbers)

21. Which step number is the following output? 32 27 14 84 why sit not 51 vain 92 68 feet best ink

   A. Step V   B. Step VI

   C. Step IV   D. Step III

   E. There is no such step

22. Which word/number would be at 5th position from the right in Step V?

   A. 14   B. 92

   C. feet   D. best

   E. why

23. How many elements (words or numbers) are there between 'feet' and '32' as they appear in the last step of the output?

A. One   B. Three
C. Four   D. Five
E. Seven

24. Which of the following represents the position of 'why' in the fourth step?
   A. Eighth from the left
   B. Fifth from the right
   C. Sixth from the left
   D. Fifth from the left
   E. Seventh from the left

Directions (Qs. Nos. 25 to 30): *A word-number arrangement machine, when given an input as a set of words and numbers, rearranges them following a particular rule and generates stepwise outputs till the rearrangement is complete following that rule.*

Followings is an illustration of input and steps of rearrangement till the last step.

Input :   rose girl 13 petal 16 go 35 ate 71 wild 22 87

Step I :   go rose girl 13 petal 16 35 ate 71 wild 22 87

Step II :   go 13 rose girl petal 16 35 ate 71 wild 22 87

Step III : go 13 ate rose girl petal 16 35 71 wild 22 87

Step IV : go 13 ate 16 rose girl petal 35 71 wild 22 87

Step V :   go 13 ate 16 girl rose petal 35 71 wild 22 87

Step VI : go 13 ate 16 girl 22 rose petal 35 71 wild 87

Step VII: go 13 ate 16 girl 22 rose 35 petal 71 wild 87

Step VIII: go 13 ate 16 girl 22 rose 35 wild petal 71 87

Step IX : go 13 ate 16 girl 22 rose 35 wild 71 petal 87

and Step IX is the last step of the rearrangement.

25. **Input:** man 79 over 63 like 43 joy 15 never climbed 21 56
   How many steps will be required to complete the arrangement?

A. Eight   B. Nine
C. Ten   D. Eleven
E. None of these

26. Step II of an input: to 13 world news 73 29 win 52.
   How many more steps will be required to complete the arrangement?
   A. Six   B. Four
   C. Five   D. Two
   E. None of these

27. **Input :** no 11 19 94 join for 81 style 37 matched.
   Which of the following steps will be the last?
   A. VI   B. VII
   C. VIII   D. IX
   E. None of these

28. Step III of an input is : we 12 you 19 meet 17 discuss 15 result 16.
   Which of the following will be step II?
   A. we 12 you 17 meet 19 discuss 15 result 16
   B. we 12 17 you meet 19 discuss 15 result 16
   C. we 12 you 15 17 meet 19 discuss result 16
   D. Cannot be determined
   E. None of these

29. Which of the following cannot be definitely Step V of an input?
   A. be 13 did 27 eye 43 soon 34 39 wonder
   B. be 13 did 27 eye 43 soon 39 34 wonder
   C. be 13 did 27 soon 43 eye 39 wonder 34
   D. Cannot be determined
   E. None of these

30. If two given inputs gives identically same output, which of the following is definitely true?
   A. Both require same number of steps for final arrangement.
   B. Two inputs are identically same
   C. Both contains same elements which may or may not be in same sequence
   D. 2nd last step for both arrangements will be same
   E. None of these

ANSWERS

1	2	3	4	5	6	7	8	9	10
B	D	E	C	A	C	D	E	A	B

11	12	13	14	15	16	17	18	19	20
A	D	B	C	E	A	D	B	C	A

21	22	23	24	25	26	27	28	29	30
E	D	B	C	C	B	A	D	C	C

EXPLANATORY ANSWERS

Solution (1 to 5): Following rule is followed here: Words are arranged according to their no. of letters. Words with largest no. of letters are arranged first. If two words have equal no. of letters then the word which comes first in English Dictionary is arranged first. In each step only one word is arranged and the rest shift one position rightwards. The process goes on until all the words are arranged.

1.
Step III: bend take vide nut zeal pot car tin
           ⑥   4   ⑥   5   ⑥

Step III : bend take vide nut zeal pot car tin
Step IV : bend take vide zeal nut pot car tin
Step V : bend take vide zeal car nut pot tin

2. Previous step can't be determined

3.
Input: door site may for you mean now goal
      ①   ③   3   2   1

Input : door site may for you mean now goal
Step I : door goal site may for you mean now
Step II : door goal mean site may for you now
Step III : door goal mean site for may you now

4.
Input: mute deal sit cut coat day long for
      ④   2   4   1   3

Input: mute deal sit cut coat day long for
Step I : coat mute deal sit cut day long for
Step II: coat deal mute sit cut day long for
Step III: coat deal long mute sit cut day for
Step IV: coat deal long mute cut sit day for

5.
Input: ask not feel task opt sale dark den
      ⑤   ⑥   2   4   ⑥   3   4   5

Input : ask not feel task opt sale dark den
Step I : dark ask not feel task opt sale den
Step II : dark feel ask not task opt sale den
Step III : dark feel sale ask not task opt den
Step IV : dark feel sale task ask not opt den
Step V : dark feel sale task den ask not opt

Solution(6 to 10): On observing last step it is clear that there are two alternating series of numbers: one in descending order and the other in ascending order. When we reach step 1 through input, we find that the largest no. becomes the first and remaining numbers shift rightward. In the next step, the smallest no. becomes the second and the rest shift rightward. These two steps continue alternately until the two alternate series are formed.

6.
Step II: <u>765</u> <u>42</u> 183 289 542 65 110 350
                3   4

Step II : 765 42 183 289 542 65 110 350
Step III : 765 42 542 183 289 65 110 350
Step IV : 765 42 542 65 183 289 110 350

7.
Input: 239 123 58 361 495 37
           3   1   2

Input: 239 123 58 361 495 37
Step I : 495 239 123 58 361 37
Step II : 495 37 239 123 58 361
Step III : 495 37 361 239 123 58

8.
Input: 39 88 162 450 386 72 29
     ④   4   1   3   5   2

Input: 39 88 162 450 386 72 29
Step I : 450 39 88 162 386 72 29

Step II :	450	29	39	88	162	386	72
Step III :	450	29	386	39	88	162	72
Step IV :	450	29	386	39	162	88	72
Step V :	450	29	386	39	162	72	88

9.

Input: 158 279 348 28 326 236
④ 4 1 2 3

Last step can be known directly.

10.

Step I : 785 198 32 426 373 96 49
1 2 3 4

Step I :	785	198	32	426	373	96	49
Step II :	785	32	198	426	373	96	49
Step III :	785	32	426	198	373	96	49
Step IV :	785	32	426	49	198	373	96

Solution (11 to 15): Following rule is followed here: Words are arranged in alphabetical order and nos. are arranged in decreasing order alternately. In output the word, which comes first in dictionary, comes to the first place and the rest shift one place rightwards. In the next step, the largest no. comes to the second place and the rest shift one place rightwards. These two steps occur alternately until the last step is obtained.

11.

Step II : <u>cut</u> <u>97</u> 38 end for 29 46 down
⑥ 5 ⑥ ⑥ 4 3

Step II :	cut	97	38	end	for	29	46	down
Step III :	cut	97	down	38	end	for	29	46
Step IV :	cut	97	down	46	38	end	for	29
Step V :	cut	97	down	46	end	38	for	29

13.

Step I : <u>car</u> 17 vas tiger 92 87 like 52
2 4 3

Step I :	car	17	vas	tiger	92	87	like	52
Step II :	car	92	17	vas	tiger	87	like	52
Step III :	car	92	like	17	vas	tiger	87	52
Step IV :	car	92	like	87	17	vas	tiger	52

14.

Input: zeal for 49 31 high 22 track 12
1 2 3

Step I:	for	zeal	49	31	high	22	track	12
Step II:	for	49	zeal	31	high	22	track	12
Step III:	for	49	high	zeal	31	22	track	12

15.

Input : 19 feat 34 28 dog bag take 43
3 1 2

Input :	19	feat	34	28	dog	bag	take	43
Step I :	bag	19	feat	34	28	dog	take	43
Step II :	bag	43	19	feat	34	28	dog	take
Step III :	bag	43	dog	19	feat	34	28	take

Solution (16 to 20) : Here in Step I word which come first in dictionary takes first position from left and rest elements shifts one position rightwards and in the same step largest number takes first position from right and other elements shifts one step leftwards. In next step, same methodology is applied to only unarranged ones. Process continues until all words are arranged fzrom left to right in reverse dictionary order and numbers are arranged in increasing sequence from right to left.

Input: sine 88 71 cos theta 14 56 gamma delta 26
4 1B 2B 1 5 5B 3B 3 2 4B

Here, to get final arrangement sequence will be : 5 4 3 2 1 1B 2B 3B 4B 5B

(Note here first unnumbered from left or right will not be circled as no element could arrive at arranged position)

Input: for 52 all 96 25 jam road 15 hut 73 bus stop 38 46
3 3B 1 1B 6B 5 6 7B 4 2B 2 7 5B 4B

Input :	for 52 all 96 25 jam road 15 hut 73 bus stop 38 46
Step I :	all for 52 25 jam road 15 hut 73 bus stop 38 46 96
Step II :	bus all for 52 25 jam road 15 hut stop 38 46 96 73
Step III :	for bus all 25 jam road 15 hut stop 38 46 96 73 52
Step IV :	hut for bus all 25 jam road 15 stop 38 96 73 52 46
Step V :	jam hut for bus all 25 road 15 stop 96 73 52 46 38
Step VI :	road jam hut for bus all 15 stop 96 73 52 46 38 25
Step VII :	stop road jam hut for bus all 96 73 52 46 38 25 15

Solution (21 to 24) : Here in Step I smallest number takes first position from left and rest elements shifts one position rightwards and in the same step word which comes first in dictionary takes first position from right and rest elements shifts one position leftwards. In next step, same methodology is applied to only unarranged ones. Process continues until all numbers are arranged in decreasing sequence from left to right and all words are arranged in reverse dictionary order from right to left.

Input: 84 why sit 14 32 not best ink feet 51 27 vain 68 92
   6 7B 5B 1 3 4B 1B 3B 2B 4 2 6B 5 7

Here, to get final arrangement sequence will be:

7 6 5 4 3 2 1 1B 2B 3B 4B 5B 6B 7B

(Note here first unnumbered from left or right will not be circled as no element could arrive at arranged position)

Input :	84 why sit 14 32 not best ink feet 51 27 vain 68 92
Step I :	14 84 why sit 32 not best ink feet 51 27 vain 68 92 best
Step II :	27 14 84 why sit 32 not ink 51 vain 68 92 best feet
Step III :	32 27 14 84 why sit not 51 vain 68 92 best feet ink
Step IV :	51 32 27 14 84 why sit vain 68 92 best feet ink not
Step V :	68 51 32 27 14 84 why vain 92 best feet ink not sit
Step VI :	84 68 51 32 27 14 why 92 best feet ink not sit vain
Step VII :	92 84 68 51 32 27 14 best feet ink not sit vain why

Solution (25 to 30) : Here numbers and words are arranged alternately. Numbers are arranged in increasing order while words are arranged in decreasing order of their dictionary placements. If a number or word is already arranged, then next member is arranged in the same step.

25.

Input : man 79 over 63 like 43 joy 15 never climbed 21 56
   ③   6   9 4 5 1 2   8   10   3   7

Input :	man 79 over 63 like 43 joy 15 never climbed 21 56
Step I :	joy man 79 over 63 like 43 15 never climbed 21 56
Step II :	joy 15 man 79 over 63 like 43 never climbed 21 56
Step III :	joy 15 man 21 79 over 63 like 43 never climbed 56
Step IV :	joy 15 man 21 like 79 over 63 43 never climbed 56
Step V :	joy 15 man 21 like 43 79 over 63 never climbed 56
Step VI :	joy 15 man 21 like 43 over 79 63 never climbed 56
Step VII :	joy 15 man 21 like 43 over 56 79 63 never climbed
Step VIII :	joy 15 man 21 like 43 over 56 never 79 63 climbed
Step IX :	joy 15 man 21 like 43 over 56 never 63 79 climbed
Step X :	joy 15 man 21 like 43 over 56 never 63 climbed 79

26.

Step II:	to 13	world	news	73	29	win	52
	⑦	5	⑦	4	3		6

Step II:	to 13 world news 73 29 win 52
Step III :	to 13 win world news 73 29 52
Step IV :	to 13 win 29 world news 73 52
Step V :	to 13 win 29 news world 73 52
Step VI :	to 13 win 29 news 52 world 73

This is the final arrangement.

27.

Input : no 11 19 94 join for 81 style 37 matched
   ① ① ② ⑦ 2 1 5 4 3 6

Input :	no 11 19 94 join for 81 style 37 matched
Step I :	no 11 for 19 94 join 81 style 37 matched
Step II :	no 11 for 19 join 94 81 style 37 matched
Step III :	no 11 for 19 join 37 94 81 style matched
Step IV :	no 11 for 19 join 37 style 94 81 matched
Step V :	no 11 for 19 join 37 style 81 94 matched
Step VI :	no 11 for 19 join 37 style 81 matched 94

This is the final arrangement.

28. Previous steps cannot be determined.

29. Step V of any input should have at least five elements arranged.

❀ ❀ ❀

11. Drawing Inference

In evaluating inferences problems a passage is followed by some inferences and the job is to decide whether a given inference follows or not in the context of the given passage. The most vital aspect of this question is intensity of probability of a particular inference. Some of the inferences can be easily and quickly judged because they are directly based on the facts given in the passage. But in some cases, an inference is indirect. Here the interference appears to be overlapping *i.e.* one may be confused between definitely true or probably true, probably true or data inadequate, data inadequate or probably false and probably false or data inadequate

The inference can

(1) directly follow from the passage

(2) be inferred from the passage

(3) be inferred with the help of some key words.

While evaluating inferences, first of all check whether it can be evaluated with the help of the passage directly. Check if the given inference is directly supported (or contradicted) by something in the passage. More or less direct inference is a restatement of something already stated in the passage.

EXERCISE

Directions (Qs. 1 to 20): *Below are given some passages followed by several possible inferences which can be drawn from the facts stated in the passage. You have to examine each inference separately in the context of the passage and decide upon its degree of truth or falsity.*

Mark answer

A. if the inference is definitely true, *i.e.* properly follows from the statement of facts given.

B. if the inference is probably true, though not 'definitely true' in the light of facts given.

C. if the data are inadequate, *i.e.* from the facts given you cannot say whether the inference is likely to be true or false.

D. if the inference is probably false, *i.e.* though not 'definitely false' in the light of the facts given.

E. if the inference is 'definitely false', *i.e.* it cannot possibly be drawn from the facts given or it contradicts the given facts.

PASSAGE 1

The immediate challenge is on the food front. Shortfalls in production have been allowed to affect supplies and hence prices. The government is planning to focus on investment in irrigation and strategy. It appears that the Green Revolution instruments to encourage farmers to invest are no longer effective. The Green Revolution strategy was based on the state taking out the risk of collapse in prices. Farmers were offered remunerative prices and a guaranteed procurement of their produce in case the open market could not absorb it. Farmers could then borrow from banks, acquire the Green Revolution Technology and produce as much as they could. The pressure on the food subsidy was manageable as long as there was a food shortage. Prices in the open market then tended to be above the procurement prices. But with the food surpluses the situation has changed. The situation was unsustainable not merely because of the magnitude of this subsidy. It was also inefficient. It meant farmers were being led to produce crops based just on the prices Government fixed and not in relation to any legal demand. In these circumstances, the Government was reluctant to keep increasing procurement prices at the pace that used to be the norm in earlier years.

1. The Government is planning to make crucial changes in the Green Revolution strategies.
2. The Government is no longer in a position to provide subsidy to farmers.
3. As the open market prices are lower, all the burden of procurement of crops is on the Government.
4. Demand is much higher than the quantity of crops produced by the farmers.
5. The farmers tend to produce the crops as per their convenience and not constant with the demand.

PASSAGE 2

Long term economic progress comes mainly from the invention and spread of improved technologies. The scientific revolution was made possible by the printing press, the industrial revolution by the steam engine and India's escape from famine by increased farm yields the so called 'Green Revolution'. Right now rich countries are changing the world's climate by emitting billions of tones of carbon dioxide each year from the use of coal, oil and natural gas. In future years, China and India will make massive contributions to increase carbon dioxide in the atmosphere. Yet no country rich or poor, is keen to cut its energy use, owing to concern that to do so would threaten jobs, incomes and economic growth. New technologies will provide a key part of the solution. Already, 'hybrid' automobiles, which combine gasoline and battery power, can roughly double fuel efficiency cutting carbon dioxide emission by half. Similarly, engineers have developed ways to capture the carbon dioxide that results from burning coal in power plants and store it safely underground. The new technology called "carbon capture and sequestration" can cut 80%, of the carbon dioxide emitted during the production of electricity.

6. It may not be practically possible to switch over to the new hybrid technologies from the present ones.

7. In the forthcoming years, India and China are going to be at the top of the list of world's developed countries.
8. The more developed is a country; less is the contribution to increase in air pollution.
9. The new technologies can control emission of carbon dioxide caused only during electricity generation.
10. The developing countries in the world are trying to evolve new technologies to reduce the emission of carbon dioxide.

PASSAGE 3

In the overall economy of India, agriculture is the largest sector of economic activity. It plays a crucial role in the country's economic development by providing food to its people and raw materials to industry. It accounts for the largest share to the national income. The share of the various agricultural commodities, animal husbandry and ancillary activities has been more than 40 per cent since independence. During the decade of the fifties, it actually contributed about half of the national output.

11. Agriculture is the mainstay of Indian economy.
12. The contribution of agricultural sector has decreased in recent years.
13. Agriculture is the only source of income in India.
14. The contribution of agriculture to Indian economy rose substantially after independence.
15. Agriculture contributes to national income more than all other activities put together.

PASSAGE 4

Gujarat has hardly 8.5 per cent of its total area under forest. Of this a considerable portion is covered by wild grass and marshes. Denuded of thick forests, fauna have disappeared from many places. Mandvi, for instance, had its share of panthers once. The state government has imposed a total ban on cutting of trees for five years from this year. The imminent destruction of over 40000 hectares of forest land by the Narmada project has led to nationwide strong protest.

16. People in Gujarat are quite conscious of the need of conservation of forests.

17. There is thick forest in 8.5 per cent of the total area of Gujarat.

18. Gujarat is the first state in India to impose a total ban on cutting of trees.

19. A dam on the Narmada river is planned.

20. Once there was thick forest in Mandvi.

ANSWERS

1	2	3	4	5	6	7	8	9	10
A	B	E	E	E	E	E	E	E	A

11	12	13	14	15	16	17	18	19	20
A	C	E	A	A	A	E	C	A	A

SOME SELECTED EXPLANATORY ANSWERS

6. A new technology is developed in view of its viability and acceptance. So, the inference is false.

7. A developed country does not emit huge quantity of carbon dioxide.

9. It is clear from the passage that the technologies are being developed to decrease the emission of carbon dioxide from automobiles as well as from the production of electricity.

❈ ❈ ❈

Syllogism was introduced by Aristotle (a reasoning consisting two premises and a conclusion). Aristotle gives the following definition of syllogism in his fundamental treatise Organon.

"A syllogism is discourse, in which, certain things being stated, something other than what is stated follows of necessity from their being so". Things that have stated are known as premises and the one that follows from the premises is known as the conclusion of the syllogism.

A categorical syllogism is a type of argument with two premises and one conclusion. Each of these three propositions is one of four forms of categorical proposition.

Type	Form	Example
A	All S are P	All monkeys are mammals
E	No S is P	No monkeys are birds
I	Some S are P	Some philosophers are logicians
O	Some S are not P	Some logicians are not philosophers

These four type of proposition are called A, E, I and O type propositions, the variables S and P are place-holders for terms which represent out a class or category of thing, hence the name "categorical" proposition.

Example

Directions (Qs. 1 to 3): *Below are given three or four statements followed by three or four conclusions. You have to take the given statements to be true even if they appear to be at variance with commonly known facts, and then decide which of the conclusions logically follow(s) from the given statements. For each question, mark out an appropriate answer choice that you think is correct.*

1. Statements: **Solution:**
- (*a*) All locks are keys   (*a*) LL – K
- (*b*) All keys are bats   (*b*) KK – B
- (*c*) Some clocks are bats   (*c*) C – B

Conclusions:
1. Some bats are locks.   1. B – L
2. Some clocks are keys.   2. C – K ×
3. All keys are locks.   3. KK – LL ×
- A. Only 1 and 2 follow
- B. Only 2 and 3 follow
- C. Only 1 follows
- D. Only 2 follows
- E. 1, 2 and 3 follow

C. Only 1 follows

2. Statements: **Solution:**
- (*a*) Some cups are pots   (*a*) C – P
- (*b*) All pots are tubes   (*b*) PP – T
- (*c*) All cups are bottles   (*c*) CC – B

Conclusions:
1. Some bottles are tubes. 1. B – T
2. Some pots are bottles 2. P – B
3. Some tubes are cups 3. T – C
- A. Only 1 and 2 follow
- B. Only 2 and 3 follow
- C. Only 1 and 3 follow
- D. 1, 2 and 3 follow
- E. None follows

D. 1, 2 and 3 follow

3. Statements: **Solution:**
- (*a*) All papers are books.   PP – B
- (*b*) All bags are books.   BaBa – B
- (*c*) Some purses are bags   Pu – Ba

Conclusions:
1. Some papers are bags. P – Ba ×
2. Some books are papers.   B – P
3. Some books are purses. B – Pu
- A. Only 1 follow
- B. Only 2 and 3 follow
- C. Only 1 and 3 follow
- D. Only 1 and 2 follow
- E. 1, 2 and 3 follow

D. Only 2 and 3 follow

EXERCISE

Directions (Qs. Nos. 1 to 10): *In each question below are given two statements followed by two conclusions numbered I and II. You have to take the given two statements to be true even if they seem to be at variance from commonly known facts. Read the conclusion and then decide which of the given conclusions logically follows from the two given statements, disregarding commonly known facts.*

Give answer:

A. If only conclusion I follows
B. If only conclusion II follows
C. If either I or II follows
D. If neither I nor II follows and
E. If both I and II follow.

1. **Statements:** I. All tables are chalks.
      II. All chalks are chairs.

  Conclusions: I. All chairs are tables.
       II. All tables are chairs.

2. **Statements:** I. Some radios are stones.
      II. All stones are rods.

3. **Statements:** I. Some birds are flowers.
      II. Some flowers are books.

  Conclusions: I. Some birds are books.
       II. No book is a flower.

4. **Statements:** I. Some cows are jackals.
      II. No fox is a cow.

  Conclusions: I. Some jackals are foxes.
       II. Some jackals are not foxes.

5. **Statements:** I. Only cats are animals.
      II. No dog is an animal.

  Conclusions: I. Some cats are not dogs.
       II. Some dogs are cats.

6. **Statements :** I. All shoes are carpets.
      II. No carpet is a pullover.

  Conclusions: I. No shoes are pullovers.
       II. All carpets are shoes.

7. **Statements:** I. No window is a wall.
      II. No wall is a door.

  Conclusions: I. No window is a door.
       II. No door is a window.

8. **Statements:** I. All players are tall.
      II. Johan is tall.

  Conclusions: I. Johan is a player.
       II. Johan is not a player.

9. **Statements:** I. All dogs are wolves.
      II. Some wolves are tigers.

  Conclusions: I. Some dogs are tigers.
       II. Tigers which are wolves are not dogs.

10. **Statements:** I. All cars fly.
      II. Some cycles fly.

  Conclusions: I. All cars are cycles.
       II. Some cycles do not fly.

Directions (Qs. Nos. 11 to 20): *In each question below are given three statements followed by two conclusions numbered I and II. You have to take the given two statements to be true even if they seem to be at variance from commonly known facts. Read the conclusion and then decide which of the given conclusions logically follows from the two given statements, disregarding commonly known facts.*

Give answer:

A. If only conclusion I follows
B. If only conclusion II follows
C. If either I or II follows
D. If neither I nor II follows and
E. If both I and II follow.

11. **Statements:** I. Some spoons are pots.
      II. All pots are cups.
      III. Some cups are cards.

  Conclusions: I. Some cards are spoons.
       II. Some cups are spoons.

12. **Statements:** I. Some keys are locks.
      II. Some locks are doors.
      III. Some doors are windows.

  Conclusions: I. Some windows are locks.
       II. Some doors are keys.

13. **Statements:** I. Some boys are flowers.
      II. All flowers are jungles.
      III. All jungles are houses

Conclusions: I. Some houses are flowers.
II. Some houses are boys.

14. Statements: I. All bottles are tanks.
II. All tanks are drums.
III. All drums are pipes.

Conclusions: I. Some pipes are tanks.
II. Some drums are bottles.

15. Statements: I. All sticks are brushes.
II. No brush is a fruit.
III. Some fruits are trees.

Conclusions: I. Some trees are sticks.
II. No tree is stick.

16. Statements: I. Some shirts are pants.
II. All pants are clothes.
III. Some clothes are napkins.

Conclusions: I. Some napkins are shirts.
II. Some clothes are shirts.

17. Statements: I. All packets are tents.
II. All tents are houses.
III. Some boxes are houses.

Conclusions: I. Some houses are packets.
II. Some boxes are tents.

18. Statements: I. Some nuts are bolts.
II. Some bolts are hammers.
III. Some hammers are nails.

Conclusions: I. Some nails are bolts.
II. No nail is a bolt.

19. Statements: I. All windows are doors.
II. No door is mountain.
III. Some mountains are roads.

Conclusions: I. Some roads are windows.
II. Some roads are doors.

20. Statements: I. Some phones are bangles.
II. Some bangles are rings.
III. All rings are sticks.

Conclusions: I. Some rings are phones.
II. Some sticks are bangles.

Directions (Qs. Nos. 21 to 25): *In each question below are given four statements followed by four conclusions numbered I, II, III and IV. You have to take the given two statements to be true even if they seem to be at variance from commonly known facts. Read the conclusion and then decide which of the given conclusions logically follows from the two given statements, disregarding commonly known facts.*

21. Statements: I. All silver are metals.
II. All metals are steel.
III. Some steel are stones.
IV. All stones are stands.

Conclusions: I. Some stands are metals.
II. Some stones are silver.
III. Some stands are steel.
IV. Some stones are steel.

A. Only conclusions III and IV follow
B. Only conclusion I follows
C. Only conclusion II follows
D. Only conclusion III follows
E. None of these

22. Statements: I. All chairs are tables.
II. All tables are songs.
III. Some songs are rhythms.
IV. Some rhythms are pillows.

Conclusions: I. Some tables are chairs.
II. All tables are rhythms.
III. All chairs are songs.
IV. Some pillows are songs.

A. Only conclusions I and III follow
B. Only conclusions I and IV follow
C. Only conclusion I follows
D. Only conclusion III follows
E. None of these

23. Statements: I. Some mobiles are pens.
II. Some pens are covers.
III. Some covers are plates.
IV. All plates are papers.

Conclusions: I. All mobiles are covers.
II. Some pens are papers.
III. All plates are pens.
IV. Some papers are mobiles.

A. Only conclusion I follows
B. Only conclusion II follows
C. Only conclusions I and IV follow
D. Only conclusions II and IV follow
E. None follows

24. Statements: I. All shoes are tables.
II. Some tables are lanes.
III. All caps are lanes.
IV. Some lanes are row.

Conclusions: I. Some tables are rows.
II. Some tables are shoes.
III. Some rows are caps.
IV. Some lanes are shoes.

A. Only conclusions I and II follow
B. Only conclusion II follows
C. Only conclusion III follows
D. Only conclusion I either or conclusion IV follows
E. None of these

25. Statements: I. Some symbols are numbers.
II. Some numbers are letters.
III. All alphabets are symbols.
IV. All pianos are letters.

Conclusions: I. Some symbols are letters.
II. Some numbers are pianos.
III. No letter is symbol.
IV. Some symbols are alphabets.

A. Only conclusion I follows
B. Only conclusion II follows
C. Only conclusions III and IV follow
D. Only conclusion IV follows
E. Only either I or III and IV follow

ANSWERS

1	2	3	4	5	6	7	8	9	10
B	E	D	B	A	A	D	C	D	D

11	12	13	14	15	16	17	18	19	20
B	D	E	E	C	B	A	C	D	B

21	22	23	24	25
A	A	E	B	E

EXPLANATORY ANSWERS

1. [A + A = A, All tables are chairs]

2. [I + A = I, Some radios are rods. Also, some radios are stones *conversion* Some stones are radios.]

3. [I + I = no conclusion]

4. [Change order of the statements to align. Now, No fox is a cow + Some cows are jackals = E + I = O*, Some jackals are not foxes.]

5. [Change order first. Now, No dog is an animal + Only cats are animals *implies* No dog is an animal + All animals are cats = E + A = O*, Some cats are not dogs.]

6. [A + E = E]

7. [E + E = no conclusion]

8. [Align: Johan is tall + Some tall are players = A + I = no conclusion. But, Johan should either be a player or a non-player. Hence either of the two choices follows.

9. [A + I = no conclusion]

10. [After alignment, All cars fly + Some fly are cycles = no conclusion]

11. [Some spoons are *pots,* + *All pots* are cups. I + A = I type of conclusion "Some spoons are cups". Conclusion II is converse of it.]

12. [All the three premises are I type. No conclusion follows from two I premises.]

13. Some boys are *flowers.* + *All flowers* are jungles. I + A = I type conclusion, "Some boys are jungles". Some boys are flowers + *All jungles* are houses.

I + A = I type conclusion, "Some boys are houses". Conclusion II is converse of it.

14. All bottles are tanks. + All tanks are drums. A + A = A – type of conclusion *i.e.* "all bottles are drums'. Conclusion II is converse of it. All tanks are drums + All drums are pipes A + A implies A-type of conclusion "All tanks are pipes". Conclusion I is converse of it.

15. All sticks are brushes + No brush is fruit. *i.e.* A + E = E type of conclusion. "No stick is fruit". No brush is fruit + Some fruits are trees. *i.e.* E + I = O*,"Some trees are not brushes". Conclusions I and II forms a complementary pair. Therefore, either I or II follows.

16. Some shirts are pants + All pants are clothes = Some shirts are clothes. Conclusion II is converse of it.

17. All packets are tents + All tents are houses = All packets are houses. Conclusion I is the converse of it.

18. All the three premises are particular affirmative. No conclusion can be reached from two particular premises (I type).

19. All windows are doors + No door is mountain = No window is mountain. No door is mountain + Some mountains are roads = Some roads are not doors.

20. Some bangles are rings + All rings are sticks = Some bangles are sticks. Conclusion II is converse of the third premise.

21. All silver are metals + All metals are steel = All silver are steel. Some steel are stones + All stones are stands = Some steel are stands conversion Conclusion III. Conclusion IV is converse of the third premise.

22. All chairs are tables + All tables are songs = All chairs are songs (Conclusion III) Conclusion I is converse of first premise.

23. Some covers are plates + All plates are papers = Some covers are papers.

24. All shoes are tables + Some tables are lanes = no conclusion.

Conclusion II is the converse of the first premise.

25. All alphabets are symbols + Some symbols are numbers = no conclusion.

Conclusion IV follows from the conversion of the third premise. Conclusion I and III form complementary pair.

❁ ❁ ❁

Cause & Effect

In these questions, the job is to determine whether a given event is the cause or the effect of some other event. Events do not just happen without any cause behind them. These causes are the conditions under which these events (or results or effects) happen. Cause is an event which leads to a said effect and this fact is either scientifically proven or logically expected. An immediate cause means a cause that immediately precedes the effect and a principal cause means a cause that immediately precedes the effect and a principal cause means a cause that was the most important reason behind the effect. Obviously cause must occur before the effect, we can merely look at the given two events first and by analyzing the time of occurrence, we can find which event can't be a cause.

Example

Directions (Qs. Nos. 1-4): *In each of the following questions, two statements numbered I and II are given. There may be cause and effect relationship between the two statements. These two statements may be the effect of the same cause or independent causes. These statements may be independent causes without having any relationship. Read both the statements in each question and mark your answer as*

A. If statement I is the cause and statement II is its effect;

B. If statement II is the cause and statement I is its effect;

C. If both the statements I and II are independent causes;

D. If both the statements I and II are effects of independent causes; and

E. If both the statements I and II are effects of some common cause.

1. **Statements:**
   I. Police had resorted to lathi-charge to disperse the unruly mob from the civic headquarters.
   II. The civic administration has recently hiked the property tax of the residential buildings by about 30 per cent.

Ans. D: Both the statements I and II are the effects of independent causes.

2. **Statements:**
   I. The government has allowed private airline companies in India to operate to overseas destinations.
   II. The national air carrier has increased its flights to overseas destinations.

Ans. A: Since the Government has allowed private airline companies in India to operate to overseas, so the national air carrier has increased its flights to overseas destinations.

3. **Statements:**
   I. Many people visited the religious place during the week-end.
   II. Few people visited the religious place during the week days.

Ans. E: Both the statements I and II are the effects of some common cause.

4. **Statements:**
   I. The performance of Indian sports persons in the recently held Olympics could not reach the level of expectation the country had on them.
   II. The performance of Indian sports person in the last Asian games was far better than any previous games.

Ans. E: Both the statements are effects of some common cause.

EXERCISE

Directions (Qs. Nos. 1 to 12): *In each of the following questions, two statements numbered I and II are given. There may be cause and effect relationship between the two statements. These two statements may be the effect of the same cause or independent causes. These statements may be independent causes without having any relationship. Read both the statements in each question and mark your answer as*

    A. If statement I is the cause and statement II is its effect;

    B. If statement II is the cause and statement I is its effect;

    C. If both the statements I and II are independent causes;

    D. If both the statements I and II are effects of independent causes; and

    E. If both the statements I and II are effects of some common cause.

1. Statements:
   I. The prices of petrol and diesel in the domestic market have remained unchanged for the past few months.
   II. The crude oil prices in the international market have gone up substantially in the last few months.

2. Statements:
   I. India has surpassed the value of tea exports this year over all the earlier years due to an increase in demand for quality tea in the European market.
   II. There is an increase in demand of coffee in the domestic market during the last two years.

3. Statements:
   I. The government has recently fixed the fees for professional courses offered by the unaided institutions which are much lower than the fees charged last year.
   II. The parents of the aspiring students launched a severe agitation last year protesting against the high fees charged by the unaided institutions.

4. Statements:
   I. The Reserve Bank of India has recently put restrictions on few small banks in the country.
   II. The small banks in the private and co-operative sector in India are not in a position to withstand the competitions of the bigger in the public sector.

5. Statements:
   I. All the schools in the area had to be kept closed for most part of the week.
   II. Many parents have withdrawn their children from the local schools.

6. Statements:
   I. There is unprecedented increase in the number of young unemployed in comparison to the previous year.
   II. A large number of candidates submitted applications against an advertisement for the post of manager issued by a bank.

7. Statements:
   I. The school authority has asked the X Std. students to attend special classes to be conducted on Sundays.
   II. The parents of the X Std. students have withdrawn their wards from attending private tuitions conducted on Sundays.

8. Statements:
   I. Majority of the students in the college expressed their opinion against the college authority's decision to break away from the university and become autonomous.
   II. The university authorities have expressed their inability to provide grants to its constituent colleges.

9. Statements:
   I. The police authority has recently caught a group of house breakers.
   II. The citizens group in the locality have started night vigil in the area.

10. Statements:

    I. The Government has imported large quantities of sugar as per trade agreement with other countries.

    II. The prices of sugar in the domestic market have fallen sharply in the recent months.

11. Statements:

    I. It is the aim of the city's civic authority to get the air pollution reduced by 20% in the next two months.

    II. The number of asthma cases in the city is constantly increasing.

12. Statements:

    I. The private medical colleges have increased the tuition fees in the current year by 200 per cent over the last year's fees to meet the expenses.

    II. The Government medical colleges have not increased their fees in spite of price escalation.

ANSWERS

1	2	3	4	5	6	7	8	9	10
D	C	B	B	D	A	A	B	E	A

11	12
B	C

EXPLANATORY ANSWERS

1. The prices of petrol and diesel being stagnant in the domestic market and the increase in the same in the international market must be backed by independent causes.

2. The two statements discuss two separate statistical and generalised results.

3. The parents' protest against high fees being charged by the institutions led the government to interfere and fix the fees at a more affordable level.

4. The inability of the small banks to compete with the bigger ones shall not ensure security and good service to the customers, which is an essential concomitant that has to be looked into by the Reserve Bank. I seems to be a remedial step for the same.

5. Closing the schools for a week and the parents withdrawing their wards from the local schools are independent issues, which must have been triggered by different individual causes.

6. An increase in the number of unemployed youth is bound to draw in huge crowds for a single vacancy.

7. It seems quite evident that the parents have instructed their wards to abstain from private tuitions on Sundays and attend special classes organised by the school.

8. Clearly, the university's decision to refuse grant to the colleges must have triggered the college authority to become autonomous.

9. Both the statements are clearly backed by a common cause, which is clearly an increase in the number of thefts in the locality.

10. Since the Government has imported large quantities of sugar as per trade agreement with other countries, therefore, the prices of the sugar in the domestic market have fallen sharply in the recent months.

11. The increase in number of asthma cases must have alerted the authorities to take action to control air pollution that triggers the disease.

12. The increase in the fees of the private colleges and there being no increase in the same in Government colleges seem to be policy matters undertaken by the individual decisive boards at the two levels.

❀ ❀ ❀

In these questions, a situation is presented and some courses of action are suggested in the context of that situation. Job is to determine which of them should be followed. Such questions tests one's ability to judge a problem correctly, to determine the root cause of the problem and then to prescribe a suitable course of action.

Basically there are two broad types of patterns in such questions, it is a 'problem-solution' or 'fact-follow-up action' type.

To solve questions on 'course of action' first of all, determine whether it is a 'problem-solution' or 'fact-follow-up action' type.

Example

Directions (Qs. Nos. 1 and 2): *In each question given below a statement is followed by three courses of action denoted 1, 2 and 3. A course of action is a step or administrative decision to be taken for improvement, follow-up for further action in regard to the problem, policy etc. on the basis of the information given in the statement. You have to assume everything in the statement to be true, then decide which of the three given/suggested courses of action logically follows for pursuing and decide the answer.*

1. Statement: The chairman of the car company announced in the meeting that all trial of its first product of the new car model 'M' are over and company plans to launch its car in the market after six months.

Courses of action:

1. The network of dealers is to be finalised and all legal, financial and other matters in this connection will have to be finalised shortly.
2. The company will have to make plan for product other than car.
3. Material, managerial and other resources will have to be in fine tune to maintain production schedule.

A. 1 and 3 only   B. Only 1
C. All the three   D. Only 2
E. None of these

Ans. A: After trials, the best availability of material, managerial and other resources is necessary to maintain production schedule. Hence 3 follows. As stated 'model M is its first product', so it is necessary to finalise the network of dealers and all matters regarding the sale of the product. Hence 1 follows. 2 has no connection with the statement.

2. Statement: The Company 'X' has rejected first lot of valves supplied by company"Y' and has cancelled its entire huge order quoting use of inferior-quality material and poor crafts-manship.

Courses of action:

1. The Company 'Y' needs to investigate functioning of its purchase, production and quality control departments.
2. The Company 'Y' should inspect all the valves rejected by Company 'X'.
3. The Company 'Y' should inform Company 'X' that steps have been taken for improvement and renegotiate schedule of supply.

A. Only 1 and 2   B. Only 2
C. All 1, 2 and 3   D. 2 and either 1 or 3
E. None of these

Ans. 3: As stated 'rejection due to inferior-quality material and poor craftsmanship', since purchase deptt is responsible for purchasing the inferior quality material and for improper inspection. Hence investigation is compulsory for all the departments. Hence 1 follows. 2 follows because claim of company 'X' may not be true. 3 follows because relationships with a previous client should always be kept out.

EXERCISE

Directions (Qs. Nos. 1 to 15): *In each question below is given a statement followed by two courses of action numbered I and II. You have to assume everything in the statement to be true and on the basis of the information given in the statement, decide which of the suggested courses of action logically follow(s) for pursuing.*

- A. If only I follows
- B. If only II follows
- C. If either I or II follows
- D. If neither I nor II follows
- E. If both I and II follow

1. Statement: Severe drought is reported to have set in several parts of the state.

Courses of Action:
- I. Government should immediately make arrangement for providing financial assistance to those affected.
- II. Food, water and fodder should immediately be sent to all these areas to save the people and cattle.

2. Statement: A large number of people in ward J of the city are diagnosed to be suffering from a fatal dengue type fever.

Courses of Action:
- I. The city municipal authority should take immediate steps to carry out extensive fumigation in ward J.
- II. The people in the area should be advised to take steps to avoid mosquito bites.

3. Statement: Since its launching in 2001, Kingfisher Airlines has so far accumulated losses amounting to ₹ 8000 crore.

Courses of Action:
- I. Kingfisher Airlines should be directed to reduce wasteful expenditure and to increase passenger fare.
- II. An amount of about ₹ 300 crore should be provided to Kingfisher Airlines to make the airliner economically viable.

4. Statement: Exporters in the town are alleging that commercial banks are violating a Reserve Bank of India directive to operate a post shipment export credit denominated in foreign currency at international rates from March this year.

Courses of Action:
- I. The officers concerned in the commercial banks are to be suspended.
- II. The RBI should be asked to stop giving such directives to commercial banks.

5. Statement: A large number of people suffer illness every year due to drinking polluted water during the rainy season.

Courses of Action:
- I. The government should make adequate arrangements to provide safe drinking water to all its citizens.
- II. The people should be educated about the dangers of drinking polluted water.

6. Statement: Most of those who study in premier government engineering colleges in India migrate to developed nations for better prospects in their professional pursuits.

Courses of Action:
- I. All the students joining these colleges should be asked to sign a bond at the time of admission to the effect that they will remain in India at least for ten years after they complete education.
- II. All those students who desire to settle in the developed nations should be asked to pay entire cost of their education which the government subsidies.

7. Statement: As stated in the last census report the female to male ratio is alarmingly low in most of the states.

Courses of Action:
- I. The government should conduct another census to verify the results.
- II. The government should immediately issue orders to all the departments to encourage people to improve the ratio.

8. Statement: The retired Professors of the S Institute should also be invited to deliberate on restructuring of the organization, as their contribution may be beneficial to the Institute.

Courses of Action:
- I. Management may seek opinion of the employees before calling retired professors.

II. Management should involve experienced people for the systematic restructuring of the organization.

9. Statement: Three districts in State F have been experiencing severe drought for the last four years resulting into exodus of people from these districts.

Courses of Action:

I. The government should immediately start food for work programme in these districts to put a halt to the exodus.

II. The government should make sincere efforts to provide drinking/potable water to these districts.

10. Statement: The sale of a particular product has gone down considerably causing great concern to the company.

Courses of Action:

I. The company should make a proper study of rival products in the market.

II. The price of the product should be reduced and quality improved.

11. Statement: A recent study revals that children below five die in the cities of the developing countries mainly from diarrhoea and parasitic intestinal worms.

Courses of Action:

I. Governments of the developing countries should take adequate measures to improve the hygienic conditions in the cities.

II. Children below five years in the cities of the developing countries need to be kept under periodic medical check-up.

12. Statement: A recent survey shows that the teachers are still not familiarised with the need, importance and meaning of population education in the higher education system. They are not even clearly aware about their role and responsibilities in the population education programme.

Courses of Action:

I. Population education programme should be included in the college curriculum.

II. Orientation programme should be conducted for teachers on population education.

13. Statement: STAR TV is concerned about the quality of its programmes particularly in view of stiff competition it is facing from SAB and other satellite TV channels and is contemplating various measures to attract talent for its programmes.

Courses of Action:

I. In an effort to attract talent, the STAR TV should revise its fee structure for the artists.

II. The fee structure should not be revised until other electronic media also revise it.

14. Statement: The Asian Development Bank has approved a $285 million loan to finance a project to construct coal ports by Coal India Limited in Kerala.

Courses of Action:

I. India should use financial assistance from other international financial organisations to develop such ports in other places.

II. India should not seek such financial assistance from the international financial agencies.

15. Statement: The Rabi crops have been affected by the insects for consecutive three years in the district and the farmers on average harvested less than fifty percent of produce during these years.

Courses of Action:

I. The farmers should seek measures to control the attack of insects to protect their crops next year.

II. The Government should increase the support price of Rabi crops considerably to protect the economic interests of farmers.

ANSWERS

1	2	3	4	5	6	7	8	9	10
B	E	A	D	E	B	B	B	E	A

11	12	13	14	15
E	B	A	A	E

EXPLANATORY ANSWERS

1. In the break-out of a natural calamity, the basic duty of the government becomes to provide the basic amenities essential to save the lives of people and cattle. Providing financial assistance to all would put undue burden on the country's resources. So, only II follows.

2. Clearly, prevention from mosquitoes and elimination of mosquitoes are two ways to prevent dengue. So, both the courses follow.

3. Clearly, for better economic gain, losses should be reduced and income increased. So, only course I follows.

4. The statement mentions that the commercial banks violate a directive issued by the RBI. The remedy is only to make the banks implement the Act. So, none of the courses follows.

5. The situation demands creating awareness among people about the dangers of drinking polluted water so that they themselves refrain from the same, and at the same time taking steps to provide safe drinking water. So, both the courses follow.

6. Clearly, no student can be bound to live and work in the country against his wish. So, I does not follow. However, it is quite right to recover the extra benefits awarded to students if they do not serve their own country. So, II follows.

7. A census is always conducted with the utmost precision, leaving negligible chances of differences. So, I does not follow. Further, the ratio can be improved by creating awareness among the masses and abolishing female foeticide. Thus, only course II follows.

8. The statement stresses that the contribution of retired Professors shall be beneficial. This means that these people's experience regarding working of the organisation is helpful. So, only course II follows.

9. The exodus can be checked by providing the people conditions conducive to living. So, both the courses follow.

10. Clearly, a study of rival products in the market will help assess the cause for the lowering down of sales and then a suitable action can be taken. Thus, I follows. The second course may not be implementable.

11. Clearly, the two diseases mentioned are caused by unhygienic conditions. So, improving the hygienic conditions will check the spread of disease. Also, periodic medical check-up will help timely detection of the disease and hence a proper treatment. So, both I and II follow.

12. The statement stresses on teachers' lack of awareness and knowledge in population education and as such the best remedy would be to guide them in this field through orientation programmes. So, only course II follows.

13. Revised its fee structure for artists will attract talent and enchance quality of STAR TV programmes. It cannot wait till other media take action. So, only course I follows.

14. Clearly, such projects will provide employment and shall be an asset and a source of income to the country later on. So, course I shall follows. Course II will slowdown country's economic growth.

15. Clearly, the problem demands taking extra care and adequate precautions to protect crops from insects and extending help to farmers to prevent them from incurring huge losses. Thus, both the courses follow.

❀ ❀ ❀

Distinguishing Argument

Arguments are the fundamentals unit of logic. An argument contains two explict constituents: supporting premises and conclusion. Some supporting premises make strong arguments while some make weak arguments. The question statement is (usually) in the form of a suggested course of action. Followed by the statement are two arguments, one argument advocates the suggested course of action by stating out the positive features or positive results of that action and the other argues against the suggested course of action by stating out the negative features or harmful results of that action.

To determine forcefulness of argument it should be preliminary screened first to reject an argument on the basis of preliminary observations. An argument can be rejected if it is ambiguous or if it is 'half-hearted' or if it is too simple to be acceptable or if it is in the form of a question. If a argument is not rejected in preliminary screening then argument is subjected to three steps to ascertain its strength.

Thus, solution consists of four stages: 1. Preliminary screening 2. Check, whether the result really follows or not 3. Check, whether the result really desirable or not (or harmful, in case of negative arguments)? 4. Check, whether the argument and the suggested course of action are properly related or not?

If an argument passes all the four checks, it is a strong argument, otherwise it is weak.

Example

Directions (Qs. Nos. 1 and 2): *In making decisions about important questions, it is desirable to be able to distinguish between "strong" arguments and "weak" arguments insofar as they relate to the question. "Strong" arguments are those which are both important and directly related to the question. "Weak" arguments are those which are of minor importance and also may not be directly related to the question or may be related to a trivial aspect of the question.*

Instructions: Each statement below is followed by two arguments denoted by I and II. you have to decide which of the arguments is a "strong" argument and which is a "weak" argument.

Give answer:
- A. if only argument I is "strong".
- B. if only argument II is "strong".
- C. if either I or II is "strong".
- D. if neither I nor II is "strong".
- E. if both I and II are "strong".

1. **Statement:** Should one close relative of a retiring government employee be given a job in government services in India?

   Arguments:
   - I. Yes, where else relative get a job like this?
   - II. No, it will close doors of government service to competent and needy youth.

   Ans. B: I is weak because that relative may not be suitable for the job. II is strong. As the seats will be filled by close relatives of retiring government employees, deserving and other needy youths won't get entry for government services.

2. **Statement:** Should purchase of gold by individuals be restricted in India to improve its foreign exchange position?

Arguments:

I. Yes, interference on customer's right and freedom is desirable.

II. No, business interest has to be guarded first.

Ans. D: I is weak because such interference is not desirable in a democracy. II is weak because it gives priority to business interest on foreign exchange position, which is undesirable.

EXERCISE

Directions (Qs. 1 to 10): *Each question given below consists of a statement, followed by two arguments numbered I and II. You have to decide which of the arguments is a 'strong' argument and which is a 'weak' argument.*

1. Statement: Should there be a restriction on the migration of people from one state to another state in India?

Arguments:

I. No. Any Indian citizen has a basic right to stay at any place of his/her choice and hence they cannot be stopped.

II. Yes. This is the way to effect an equitable distribution of resources across the states in India.

2. Statement: Should there be a complete ban on use of all types of chemical pesticides in India?

Arguments:

I. No. The pests will destroy all the crops and the farmers will have nothing to harvest.

II. Yes. The chemical pesticides used in agriculture pollute the water underground and this has become a serious health hazard.

3. Statement: Should officers accepting bribe be punished?

Arguments:

I. No. Certain circumstances may have compelled them to take bribe.

II. Yes. They should do the job they are entrusted with, honestly.

4. Statement: Should cutting of trees be banned altogether?

Arguments:

I. Yes. It is very much necessary to do so to restore ecological balance.

II. No. A total ban would harm timber based industries.

5. Statement: Should all refugees, who make unauthorized entry into a country, be forced to go back to their homeland?

Arguments:

I. Yes. They make their colonies and occupy a lot of land.

II. No. They leave their homes because of hunger or some terror and on human grounds, should not be forced to go back.

6. Statement: Should all the practising doctors be brought under Government control so that they get salary from the Government and treat patients free of cost?

Arguments:

I. No. How can any country do such an undemocratic thing?

II. Yes. Despite many problems, it will certainly help minimize, if not eradicate, unethical medical practices.

7. Statement: Should there be a ban on product advertising?

Arguments:

I. No. It is an age of advertising. Unless your advertisement is better than your other competitors, the product will not be sold.

II. Yes. The money spent on advertising is very huge and it inflates the cost of the product.

8. Statement: Are nuclear families better than joint families?

Arguments:

I. No. Joint families ensure security and also reduce the burden of work.

II. Yes. Nuclear families ensure greater freedom.

9. Statement: Should there be compulsory medical examination of both the man and the woman before they marry each other?

Arguments:

I. No. This is an intrusion to the privacy of an individual and hence cannot be tolerated.

II. Yes. This will substantially reduce the risk of giving birth to children with serious ailments.

10. Statement: Should government stop spending huge amounts of money on international sports?

Arguments:

I. Yes. This money can be utilized for upliftment of the poor.

II. No. Sports persons will be frustrated and will not get international exposure.

ANSWERS

1	2	3	4	5	6	7	8	9	10
A	E	B	E	B	B	E	E	B	B

EXPLANATORY ANSWERS

1. Clearly, argument I holds strong, while argument II is vague.

2. Obviously, pesticides are meant to prevent the crops from harmful pests. But at the same time, they get washed away with water and contaminate the groundwater. Thus, both the arguments hold strong.

3. Obviously, officers are paid duly for the jobs they do. So, they must do it honestly. Thus, argument II alone holds.

4. Definitely, trees play a vital role in maintaining ecological balance and so must be preserved. So, argument I holds. Also, trees form the basic source of timber and a complete ban on cutting of trees would harm timber based industries. So, only a controlled cutting of trees should be allowed and the loss replenished by planting more trees. So, argument II is also valid.

5. Obviously, refugees are people forced out of their homeland by some misery and need shelter desperately. So, argument II holds. Argument I against the statement is vague.

6. A doctor treating a patient individually can mislead the patient into wrong and unnecessary treatment for his personal gain. So, argument II holds strong. Also, a policy benefiting common people cannot be termed 'undemocratic'. So, I is vague.

7. Obviously, it is the advertisement which makes the customer aware of the qualities of the product and leads him to buy it. So, argument I is valid. But at the same time, advertising nowadays has become a costly affair and the expenses on it add to the price of the product. So, argument II also holds strong.

8. Obviously, with so many people around in a joint family, there is more security. Also, work is shared. So, argument I holds. In nuclear families, there are lesser number of people and so lesser responsibilities and more freedom. Thus, II also holds.

9. Definitely, such a step would help to prevent the growth of diseases like AIDS. So, only argument II is strong.

10. Obviously, spending money on sports should not be avoided merely because it can be spent on socio-economic problems. So, argument I does not hold. Also, if the expenses on sports are curtailed, the sports persons would face lack of facilities and training and our country will lag behind in the international sports competitions. So, II holds.

❀ ❀ ❀

16 Drawing Conclusions

In this reasoning pattern, a statement is given followed by two conclusions. The statement is to be taken as the fact. Then based on it one has to decide which of the conclusion(s) definitely follows or does not follow from the given statement.

Example

In the questions below the answer is given as:
A. If only conclusion I follows
B. If only conclusion II follows
C. If either I or II follows
D. If neither I nor II follows and
E. If both I and II follow.

1. **Statement:** It is said that teachers should not go on strike. Why should they not? Strike is an inherent right.

    Conclusions:
    I. Teachers cannot get justice unless they go on strike.
    II. Every teacher should go on strike.

Ans. A: Only conclusion I follows from the given statements, *i.e.*, as an inherent right the teachers can get justice in appropriate cases if they go on strike. Conclusion II does not follow.

2. **Statement:** The government of country 'X' has recently announced several concessions and offered attractive package tours for foreign visitors.

    Conclusions:
    I. Now, more numbers of foreign tourists will visit the country.
    II. The government of country 'X' seems to be serious in attracting foreign tourists.

Ans. E: Concessions and attractive package tours will encourage tourists and country 'X' has taken the step only because it seems to be serious about foreign visitors. So both conclusion I and conclusion II follow from the given statement.

EXERCISE

Directions (Qs. Nos. 1 to 10): *In each question below is given a statement followed by two conclusions numbered I and II. You have to assume everything in the statement to be true, then consider the two conclusions together and decide which of them logically follows beyond a reasonable doubt from the information given in the statement*

Give answer:
A. If only conclusion I follows
B. If only conclusion II follows
C. If either I or II follows
D. If neither I nor II follows and
E. If both I and II follow.

1. **Statement:** In a one day cricket match, the total runs made by a team were 200. Out of these 160 runs were made by spinners.

    Conclusions:
    I. 80% of the team consists of spinners.
    II. The opening batsmen were spinners.

2. **Statement:** The old order changed yielding place to new.

    Conclusions:
    I. Change is the law of nature.
    II. Discard old ideas because they are old.

3. Statement: Government has spoiled many top ranking financial institutions by appointing bureaucrats as Directors of these institutions.

Conclusions:
 I. Government should appoint Directors of the financial institutes taking into consideration the expertise of the person in the area of finance.
 II. The Director of the financial institute should have expertise commensurate with the financial work carried out by the institute.

4. Statement: Population increase coupled with depleting resources is going to be the scenario of many developing countries in days to come.

Conclusions:
 I. The population of developing countries will not continue to increase in future.
 II. It will be very difficult for the governments of developing countries to provide its people decent quality of life.

5. Statement: Prime age school-going children in urban India have now become avid as well as more regular viewers of television, even in households without a TV. As a result, there has been an alarming decline in the extent of readership of newspapers.

Conclusions:
 I. Method of increasing the readership of newspapers should be devised.
 II. A team of experts should be sent to other countries to study the impact of TV. On the readership of newspapers.

6. Statement: The Government run company had asked its employees to declare their income and assets but it has been strongly resisted by employees union and no employee is going to declare his income.

Conclusions:
 I. The employees of this company do not seem to have any additional undisclosed income besides their salary.
 II. The employees union wants all senior officers to declare their income first.

7. Statement: The distance of 900 km by road between Bombay and Jafra will be reduced to 280 km by sea. This will lead to a saving of ₹ 7.92 crores per annum on fuel.

Conclusions:
 I. Transportation by sea is cheaper than that by road.
 II. Fuel must be saved to the greatest extent.

8. Statement: The manager humiliated Sachin in the presence of his colleagues.

Conclusion:
 I. The manager did not like Sachin.
 II. Sachin was not popular with his colleagues.

9. Statements: Nation X faced growing international opposition for its decision to explode eight nuclear weapons at its test site.

Conclusions:
 I. The citizens of the nation favoured the decision.
 II. Some powerful countries do not want other nations to become as powerful as they are.

10. Statement: National Aluminium Company has moved India from a position of shortage to self-sufficiency in the metal.

Conclusions:
 I. Previously, India had to import aluminium.
 II. With this speed, it can soon become a foreign exchange earner.

ANSWERS

1	2	3	4	5	6	7	8	9	10
D	A	E	B	D	D	B	D	D	E

EXPLANATORY ANSWERS

1. According to the statement, 80% of the total runs were made by spinners. So, I does not follow. Nothing about the opening batsmen is mentioned in the statement. So, II also does not follow.

2. Clearly, I directly follows from the given statement. Also, it is mentioned that old ideas are replaced by new ones, as thinking changes with the progressing time. So, II does not follow.

3. According to the statement, Government has spoiled financial institutions by appointing bureaucrats as Directors. This means that only those persons should be appointed as Directors who are experts in finance and are acquainted with the financial work of the institute. So, both I and II follow.

4. The fact given in I is quite contrary to the given statement. So, I does not follow. II mentions the direct implications of the state discussed in the statement. Thus, II follows.

5. The statement concentrates on the increasing viewership of TV. and does not stress either on increasing the readership of newspapers or making studies regarding the same. So, neither I nor II follows.

6. Nothing about the details of the employees' income or the cause of their refusal to declare their income and assets, can be deduced from the given statement. So, neither I nor II follows.

7. According to the statement, sea transport is cheaper than road transport in the case of route from Bombay to Jafra, not in all the cases. So, conclusion I does not follow. The statement stresses on the saving of fuel. So, conclusion II follows.

8. The manager might have humiliated Sachin not because of his dislike but on account of certain negligence or mistake on his part. So, I does not follow. Also, nothing about Sachin's rapport with his colleagues can be deduced from the statement. So, II also does not follow.

9. Neither the citizens response to the decision nor the reason for opposition by other nations can be deduced from the statement. So, neither I nor II follows.

10. According to the statement, National Aluminium Company has moved India from a position of shortage in the past to self-sufficiency in the present. This means that previously, India had to import aluminium. So, I follows. Also, it can be deduced that if production increases at the same rate, India can export it in future. So, II also follows.

The mental recognition of cause-and-effect relationship is called reasoning. It may be the prediction of an event from an observed cause or the inference of a cause from an observed event. Logical reasoning is a process of passing from the known to the unknown. It is the process of deriving a logical inference from a hypothesis through reasoning.

Argumentation is fundamental to all logic. In logic, we advocate a certain point of view with the help of some evidences and certain assumptions. The whole thing is known as "argumentation". An argument contains two explict constituents: supporting premises and conclusion. There is also an implict (hidden) constituent called assumption. Conclusion is arrived at with the help of one or more than one statement, which may be called premise or proposition. In an argument, the number of premises can be more than one and it is not necessary that every argument have an assumption *i.e.* if an argument is complete in itself and does not have the hidden links, it will not have any assumptions. An assumption is something which is assumed, supposed and taken for granted.

Example

Directions: *In each question below is given a statement followed by two assumptions numbered 1 and 2. An assumption is something supposed or taken for granted. You have to consider the statement and the following assumptions and to decide which of the assumptions is implict in the statement.*

Give answer

  A. if only assumption 1 is implict.
  B. if only assumption 2 is implict.
  C. if either 1 or 2 is implict.
  D. if neither 1 nor 2 is implict.
  E. if both 1 and 2 are implict.

1. Statement: The 'X' group of employees' association have opposed Voluntary Retirement Scheme to the employees of some organisations.

Assumptions:

1. Only those employees who are not efficient may opt for the scheme.
2. The response of the employees may be lukewarm towards the scheme and it may not the benefit the organisation to the desired level.

Ans. A: The employees association is generally concerned with the welfare of employees and not with benefit of the organisation, hence 2 is not implict. 1 is not related with the statement.

    Alter: If assumptions 1 and 2 are considered wrong then too main statement is valid one so none of them follows.

2. Statement: In view of the statement on the ongoing strike of work by the employees, the government has agreed to work out an effective social security programme.

Assumptions:

1. The striking employees may not be satisfied with the announcement and continue the agitation.
2. The striking employees may withdraw their agitation with immediate effect and start working.

Ans. B: Assuming 2 only, the government has agreed to work out an effective social security programme.

    Alter: If 1 is considered correct than the main statement is absurd so 1 does not follow. Main statement is meaningful only when 2 is considered correct, so 2 follows.

EXERCISE

Directions (Qs. Nos. 1-10): *In each question below is given a statement followed by two assumptions numbered I and II. You have to consider the statement and the following assumptions and decide which of the assumptions is implicit in the statement.*

Give answer

A. if only assumption I is implict.
B. if only assumption II is implict.
C. if either I or II is implict.
D. if neither I nor II is implict.
E. if both I and II are implict.

1. **Statement:** Many historians have done more harm than good by distorting truth.
   Assumptions:
   I. People believe what is reported by the historians.
   II. Historians are seldom expected to depict the truth.

2. **Statement:** "As there is a great demand, every person seeking tickets of the programme will be given only five tickets."
   Assumptions:
   I. The organizers are not keen on selling the tickets.
   II. No one is interested in getting more than five tickets.

3. **Statement:** "Computer education should start at schools itself."
   Assumptions:
   I. Learning computers is easy.
   II. Computer educated is hardly unemployed.

4. **Statement:** "The programme will start at 6 p.m. but you can come there up to 7 p.m. or so and still there is no problem."
   Assumptions:
   I. The programme will continue even after 7 p.m.
   II. The programme may not even start by that time.

5. **Statement:** The organization should promote employees on the basis of merit alone and not on the basis of length of service or seniority.

Assumptions:
   I. Length of service or seniority do not alone reflect merit of an employee.
   II. It is possible to determine and measure merit of an employee.

6. **Statement:** The higher echelons of any organization are expected to be models of observational learning and should not be considered as merely sources of reward and punishments.
   Assumptions:
   I. Employees are likely to be sensitive enough to learn by observing the behaviour of their bosses.
   II. Normally bosses are considered as sources of reward and punishment.

7. **Statement:** "If you want to give any advertisement, give it in the newspaper X." — A tells B.
   Assumptions:
   I. B wants to publicise his products.
   II. Newspaper X has a wide circulation.

8. **Statement:** Kundan left for Delhi on Tuesday by train to attend a function to be held on Friday at his uncle's house in Delhi.
   Assumptions:
   I. Kundan may reach Delhi on Wednesday.
   II. Kundan may reach Delhi before Friday.

9. **Statement:** "Get rid of your past for future, get our new generation fridge at a discount in exchange of old".—An advertisement.
   Assumptions:
   I. The sales of the new fridge may increase in the coming months.
   II. People prefer to exchange future with past.

10. **Statement:** "Ensure a good night's sleeps for your family with safe and effective X mosquito coil."—An advertisement.
    Assumptions:
    I. X mosquito coil is better than any other mosquito coil.
    II. A good night's sleep is desirable.

ANSWERS

1	2	3	4	5	6	7	8	9	10
A	D	A	A	E	E	B	B	E	B

EXPLANATORY ANSWERS

1. The view that historians have done harm by distorting truth means that people believe what is reported by the historians. So, I is implicit. II does not follow from the statement and so is not implicit.

2. Clearly, the organizers are adopting this policy not to reduce the sale but to cope up with great demand so that maximum can get the ticket. So, I is not implicit. Also, due to great demand, the maximum number of tickets one person can get has been reduced to five. So, II is also not implicit.

3. Computer education can be started at the school level only if it is easy. So, I is implicit. Statement does not talk about the link between jobs and computer education. So, II is not implicit.

4. The statement tells that there is no problem if one comes up to 7 p.m. also. This means that the programme will continue even after 7 p.m. So, I is implicit. Also, it is clearly mentioned that the programme will start at 6 p.m. So, II is not implicit.

5. The statement advocates to award promotion to a person who has been displaying remarkable talent and performing extraordinarily for the organization rather than the one who has been working steadily for the organization since long. Thus, length of service does not alone prove a man worthy. His talent and his performance are the criteria to be considered. So, both I and II are implicit.

6. The statement advises people not to consider their bosses as mere 'instruments' to control and assess their acts, but as 'models' to imitate in their working. So, both I and II are implicit.

7. The statement speaks for any advertisement and it may not be restricted to promotion of products only. So I is not implicit. It is advised that advertisements be given in newspaper X. This means that X will help advertise better *i.e.*, it has wider circulation. So, II is implicit.

8. Clearly, it cannot be deduced as to which day Kundan would reach Delhi. But Kundan has left for Delhi to attend a function to be held on Friday. So, he must have planned his journey to reach Delhi before Friday. Thus, only II is implicit.

9. Obviously, the scheme is aimed to encourage those owning an old fridge to go for a new one at a reasonable price without the hassles of disposing off the old one. So, I is implicit. An advertisement highlights that which appeals to masses and which customers desire for. So, II is also implicit.

10. The statement mentions the good qualities of X coil but this does not necessitate it is the best. So, I is not implicit. Besides, an advertisement highlights the feature which is desirable by customers and can lure them. So, II is implicit.

❀ ❀ ❀

Cubes and Dice

The questions related to problems on cubes and dice are aimed to check the imaginative power of the candidate. The candidate must have the ability to visualise quickly in three-dimensional object for what is asked of it. To attempt such questions some basic facts should be kept in mind and the visualisation ability should be combined with fast and accurate calculations.

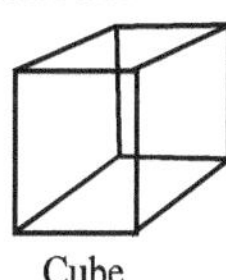

Cube

- Cube has six faces/sides and eight corners.
- Problems are based on the same or different coloured faces.
- Dice has six faces/sides.
- Problems are based only on the value occurring on the six faces.
- Problems are based on cutting the squares into specified number of smaller equal parts.

Dice

Diagrammatically, the explanation of a cube which is painted green on all sides can be understood easily taking one side of the cube.

a	b	a
b	c	b
a	b	a

This cube is divided into $3 \times 3 \times 3 = 27$ equal small cubes.

There are four corner pieces 'a', so 4×2, *i.e.*, 8 pieces will be painted on 3 sides.

There are four middle pieces 'b', so 4×3, *i.e.*, 12 pieces will be painted on 2 sides

There is one middle piece 'c', so 1×6, *i.e.*, 6 pieces will be painted only on 1 side.

There will be one piece right in the centre of this cube, *i.e.*, piece will not have paint at all.

So, this cube has $8 + 12 + 6 + 1$, *i.e.*, 27 smaller cubes.

EXERCISE

1. Two positions of a dice are shown below. When there are two circles at the bottom, the number of circles at the top will be :

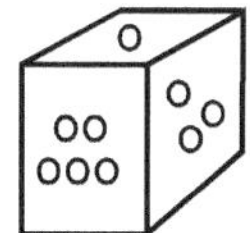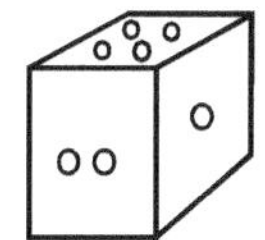

   A. 5
   B. 2
   C. 3
   D. 6
   E. None of these

2. Two positions of a dice are shown below. When 4 is at the bottom, what number will be on the top?

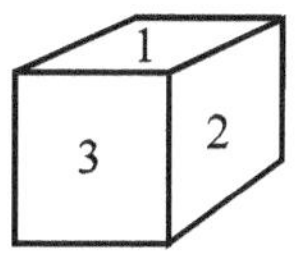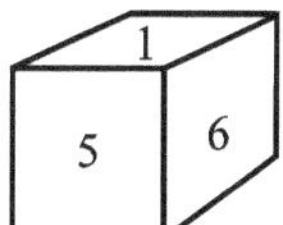

   A. 1
   B. 2
   C. 5
   D. 6
   E. None of these

3. A cube is painted red on two adjacent faces and on one opposite face, yellow on two adjacent faces and green on the remaining face. It is then cut into 64 equal cubes. How many cubes have only one red and one green face?

A. 4   B. 8
C. 12   D. 16
E. None of these

4. A cube, on whose sides letters have been written, is shown below in different positions as can be seen from different directions. Find the missing letter?

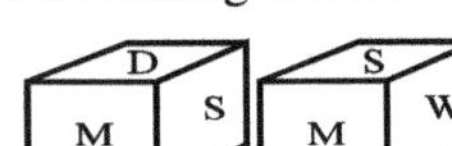

A. S   B. D
C. Y   D. W
E. None of these

5. In a dice a, b, c and d, are written on the adjacent faces, in a clockwise order and e and f at the top and bottom. When c is at the top, what will be at the bottom?

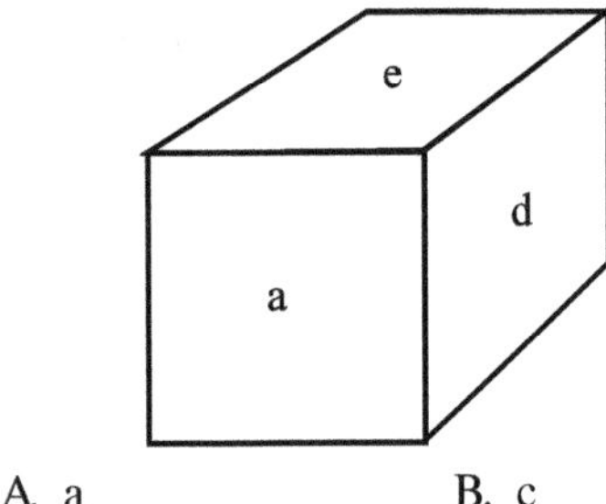

A. a   B. c
C. e   D. b
E. None of these

6. The number of cubes arranged one over the other in this figure will be :

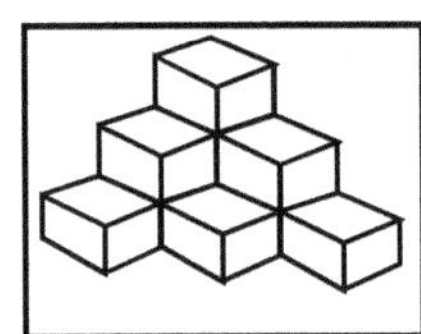

A. 8   B. 6
C. 5   D. 10
E. None of these

7. Two positions of a dice are shown below. When 2 is at the bottom, which number will be at the top?

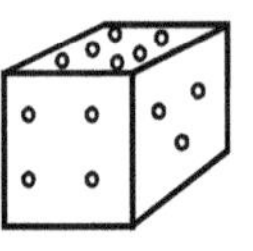

A. 1   B. 2
C. 3   D. 4
E. None of these

8. The sides of a cube are painted in different colours. Black side is opposite to red. White side is between black and red. Green side is adjacent to grey and blue side is adjacent to green. What colour will be on the side opposite to the white side of the cube?

A. Blue   B. Green
C. Grey   D. Data is insufficient
E. None of these

9. A cube is painted black on two adjacent faces and on one opposite face, red on two opposite faces and green on the remaining face. If it is cut into 64 equal cubes, then how many cubes will have only one black coloured face?

A. 32   B. 16
C. 12   D. 8
E. None of these

10. Six sides of a cube are coloured in the following manner

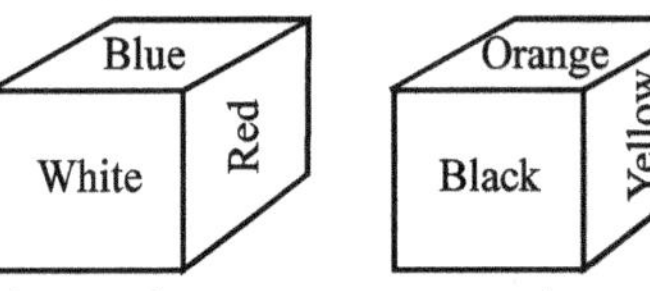

If blue and orange are opposite and red is on the top, which colour will be at the bottom?

A. Orange   B. Purple
C. Black   D. Yellow
E. None of these

11. A toy cube is painted orange on all sides. It is cut into 64 smaller cubes of equal size. How many smaller cubes are not painted at all?

A. 4   B. 8
C. 16   D. 20
E. None of these

Directions (Qs. 12-13) : *A die is thrown 4 times and its four different positions are given below :*

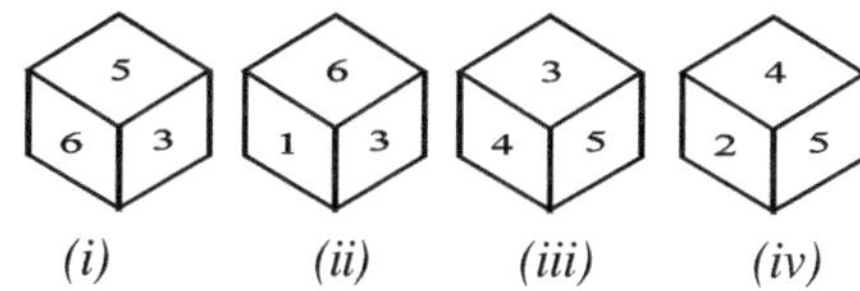

(i) (ii) (iii) (iv)

12. Find the number on the face opposite the face showing 3.
A. 2   B. 1
C. 5   D. 4
E. None of these

13. Find the number on the face opposite the face showing 6.
A. 5   B. 3
C. 4   D. 1
E. None of these

Directions (Qs. 14 to 16): *Study the information given below :*

The six faces of a cube are coloured black, brown, green, red, white and blue.
(*i*) Red is opposite of black
(*ii*) Green is between red and black
(*iii*) Blue is adjacent to white
(*iv*) Brown is adjacent to blue
(*v*) Red is at the bottom

14. Which colour is opposite of brown?
A. White   B. Red
C. Green   D. Blue
E. None of these

15. Which of the following can be deduced from (*i*) and (*v*)?
A. Black is on the top
B. Blue is on the top
C. Brown is on the top
D. Brown is opposite of black
E. None of these

16. The four adjacent colours are :
A. black, blue, brown, red
B. black, blue, brown, white
C. black, blue, red, white
D. black, blue, red, white
E. None of these

Directions (Qs. 17 to 19): *In each question below a dice has been marked with some letters or nu-merals and placed in three different positions. Answer the questions that follow :*

17. Which letter is opposite to Q?

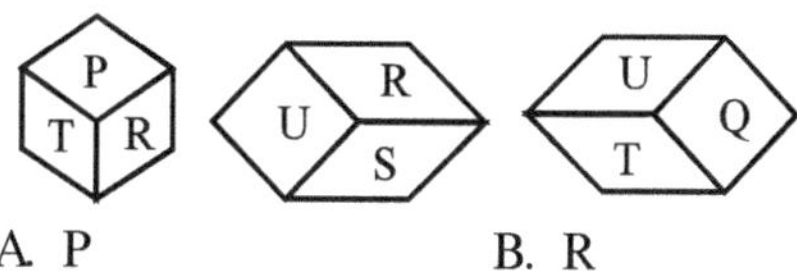

A. P   B. R
C. S   D. T
E. None of these

18. Which letter/numeral is opposite to 3?

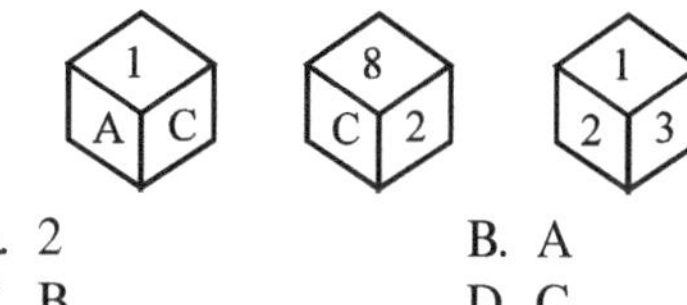

A. 2   B. A
C. B   D. C
E. None of these

19. If one of the 3 visible faces of the cube is hidden, which letter is opposite to O?

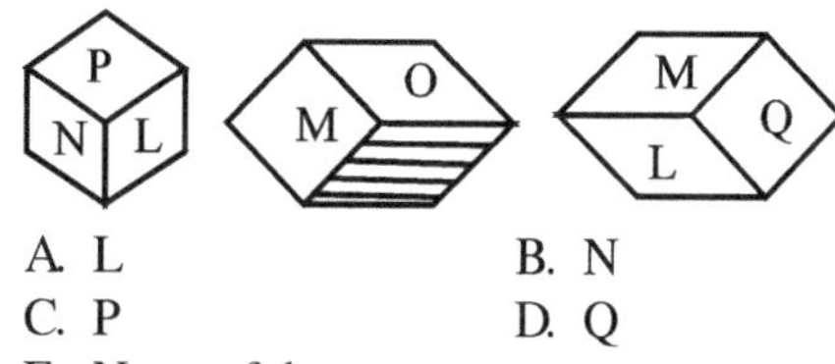

A. L   B. N
C. P   D. Q
E. None of these

Directions (Qs. 20 to 22): *Given below are the three positions of the same dice. Answer the questions that follow :*

20. What is the number on the face opposite of face 2?
A. 1
B. 6
C. 5
D. Cannot be determined
E. None of these

21. In the third position of the dice which number lies on the face on the bottom?
A. 2   B. 3
C. 4   D. 5
E. None of these

22. When value 5 is on the face on the top, which value lies on the face on the bottom?

A. 3   B. 4
C. 1   D. 2
E. None of these

Directions (Qs. 23 to 25): *A solid cube with each side 3 cm has been painted red, blue and green on pairs of opposite faces. It is then cut into small cubes with each side 1 cm. Answer the questions that follow :*

23. How many cubes have one face painted red and one face painted green?

A. 12   B. 8
C. 6   D. 14
E. None of these

24. How many cubes have only one face painted?

A. 6   B. 4
C. 12   D. 9
E. None of these

25. How many cubes are painted blue on one face and either red or green on another face?

A. 4   B. 6
C. 8   D. 12
E. None of these

Directions (Qs. 26 to 29): *The questions are based on the following statement :*

A cube is painted red on two adjacent faces, yellow on two opposite faces and green on the remaining faces. It is cut into 64 smaller cubes of equal size.

26. How many cubes are painted on two faces only and that too with the same colour?

A. 0   B. 4
C. 8   D. 16
E. None of these

27. How many cubes have three faces painted?

A. 4   B. 8
C. 16   D. 32
E. None of these

28. How many cubes are painted on one face only and are yellow?

A. 32   B. 16
C. 8   D. 4
E. None of these

29. How many cubes are painted on all faces?

A. 0   B. 4
C. 8   D. 64
E. None of these

ANSWERS

1	2	3	4	5	6	7	8	9	10
A	A	B	C	A	D	D	B	C	D
11	12	13	14	15	16	17	18	19	20
B	A	C	A	A	D	B	D	A	B
21	22	23	24	25	26	27	28	29	
C	A	A	A	C	B	B	C	A	

SOME SELECTED EXPLANATORY ANSWERS

1. After observing the views of the same dice, the faces that can be clearly understood to be the opposites are :

2 – 5, 4 – 3 and 1 – 6.

3.

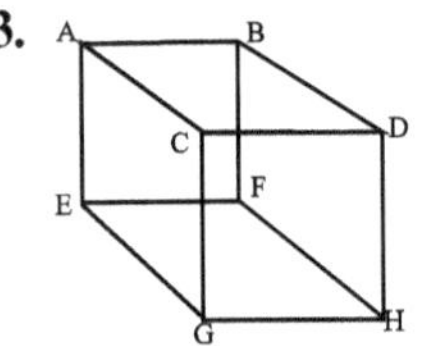

The red sides are EGAC, ABCD and BDFH.
The yellow sides are ABEF and EFGH
The green side is CDGH.

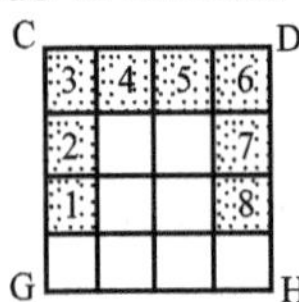

Sides GC, CD and DH are adjacent to red sides and side GH is adjacent to yellow side.

So, only 8 cubes will have one side red and one green.

4. The letters on the top and bottom sides are W and D respectively and the letters on the sides are U, Y, M and S clockwise.

5. The two positions of dice will be :

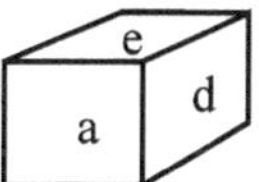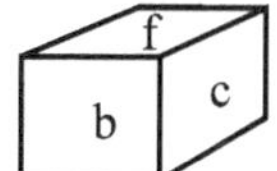

and the opposite sides will be a – c, b – d.

6.

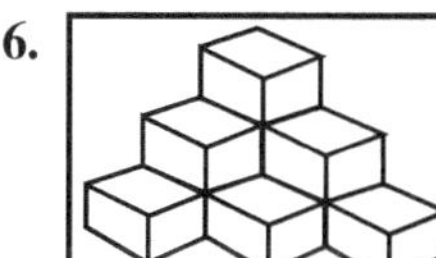

There are three columns containing 1 cube each. There are two columns containing 2 cubes each. There is one column containing 3 cubes. So, the total number of cubes is : $(3 \times 1) + (2 \times 2) + (1 \times 3)$, *i.e.*, $3 + 4 + 3 = 10$.

9.

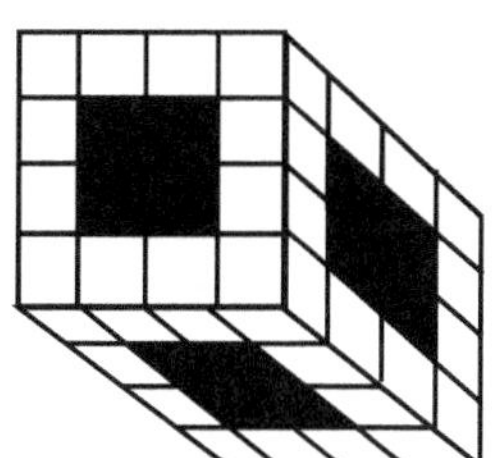

Three faces of the cube are painted black and the rest are in different colours. If this cube is cut into 64 equal cubes, then only the 4 cubes in centre of one face will come out with only one black coloured face. So, the total number of one black coloured face small cubes will be $4 \times 3 = 12$.

10.

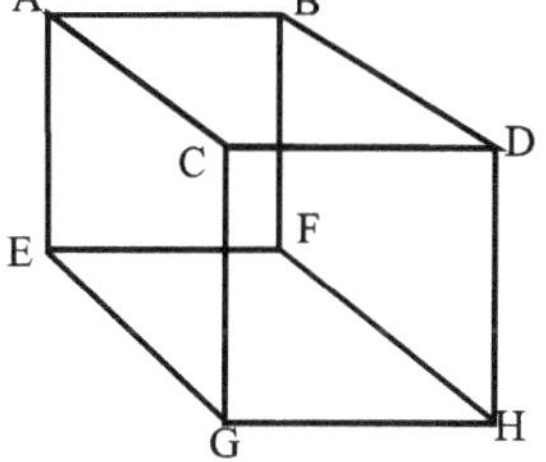

If side ABCD is red; then ABEF will be white; and ACEG will be blue. If side BDFH is orange (opposite to blue); then CDGH will be black; and EFGH will be yellow (opposite to red and at the bottom).

11. The smaller 64 pieces will be cut in the manner that :
1. 8 pieces will be painted on 3 sides,
2. 24 pieces on 2 sides.
3. 24 pieces on 1 side, and
4. 8 will not have paint at all.

Diagrammatically, the explanation taking one side of the cube will be :

a	b	b	a
b	c	c	b
b	c	c	b
a	b	b	a

1. 'a' are the corner pieces [4 × 2 = 8]
2. 'b' are the centre pieces of the cornered sides [8 × 3 = 24]
3. 'c' are the centre pieces [4 × 6 = 24]
4. Remaining interior pieces
   = 64 – (8 + 24 + 24)
   = 64 – 56 = 8.

12. From figures (*i*), (*ii*) and (*iii*) it is clear that the faces adjacent to 3 have numbers 6, 5, 1 and 4. So, the number on face opposite of face 3 will be 2.

13. From figures (*i*), (*iii*) and (*iv*) it is clear that the faces adjacent to 5 have numbers 6, 3, 4 and 2. So, the number on face opposite of face 5 is 1. In earlier question the face opposite 3 was 2. Now the opposite faces are 3 – 2, 5 – 1 and 4 – 6.

14. A, 15. A, 16. D :

According to the given information the two positions of the cube will be :

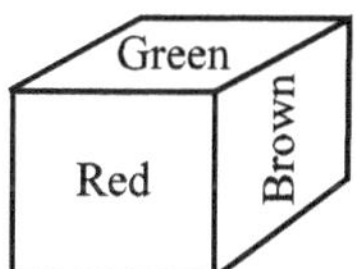

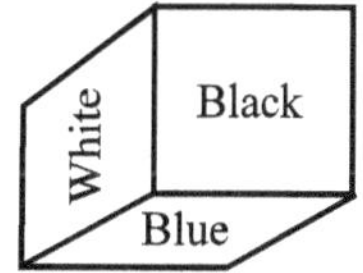

The whole cube will be :

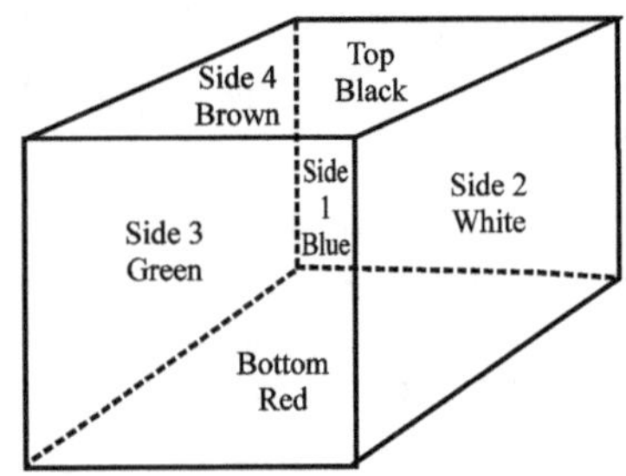

The colours on opposite faces will be : Red—Black, Green—Blue and Brown—White.

20. B, 21. C, 22. A,

The following observations can be made from the three positions of the same dice.

(*i*) Letters adjacent to 5 are 4, 2, 6 and 1. So, 3 is opposite 5.

(*ii*) Letters adjacent to 6 are 5, 4, 1 and necessarily 4. So, 2 is opposite 6.

(*iii*) When opposite numbers are 3–5 and 2–6 then 1 and 4 must be opposites.

23. A, 24. A, 25. C :

The whole cube is :

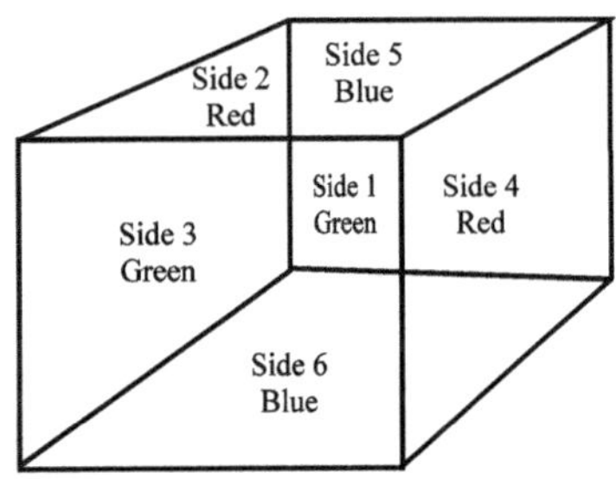

The divided cube is :

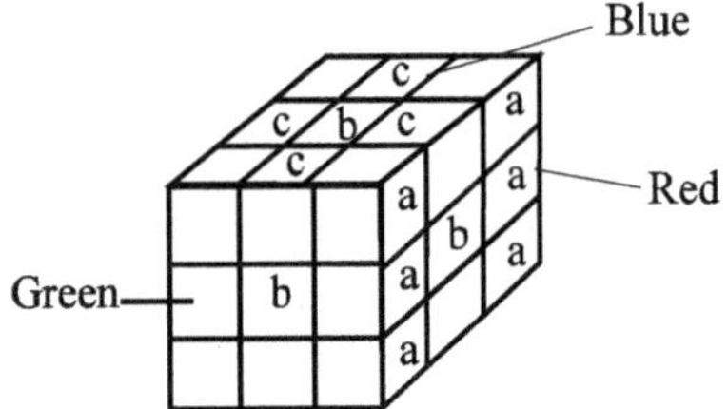

'a'— 12 cubes (6 each on opposite sides) have one face painted red and the other painted green.

'b'— 6 cubes (1 on each side) have only one face painted).

'c'— 8 cubes (4 each on opposite side) have one face painted blue and either red or green on the other.

26. B, 27. B, 28. C, 29. A :

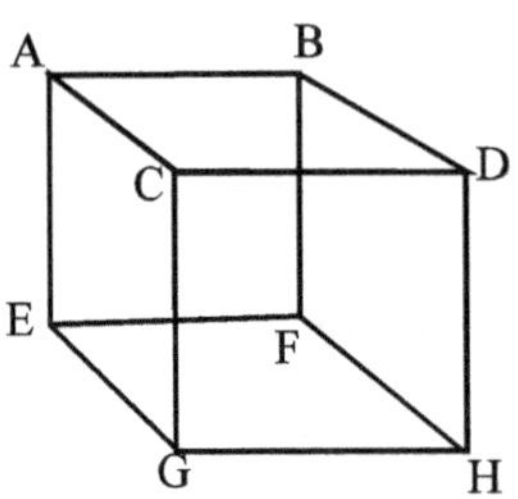

Red faces are ABCD and ABEF

Yellow faces are ACEG and BDFH

Green faces are EFGH and CDGH.

Note that Red and Green colours are on two adjacent faces. So, 2 corner cubical pieces of Red and 2 of Green (*i.e.*, total 4 cubes) will be painted on two faces only and that too with the same colour.

All the corners pieces of the cube will have three faces painted, *i.e.*, 8 cubes.

Yellow sides are on the opposites. Diagrammatically, the explanation taking one side will be :

a	b	b	a
b	c	c	b
b	c	c	b
a	b	b	a

'c' are the centered pieces and are painted on one face only in yellow. So, 4 × 2 (sides) *i.e.*, 8 cubes will have one side painted and in yellow.

Also, note that when a painted cube is cut into smaller cubes like this, not all pieces are coloured. The maximum number of sides painted in a small cube will be 3. No cube will be painted on all faces.

❀ ❀ ❀

19 Figure Series

In this form of non-verbal series, which are the most common, four or five consecutive problem figures form a definite sequence and one is required to select the one figure from the given set of Answer Figures that will continue the same sequence.

One has to try different set of moves, changes, replacements, rotations, repetitions and a lot more variations to arrive at the logical pattern making the series. Practising alone will sharpen one's skill of solving such sequences.

Example

1. Problem Figures   **Answer Figures**

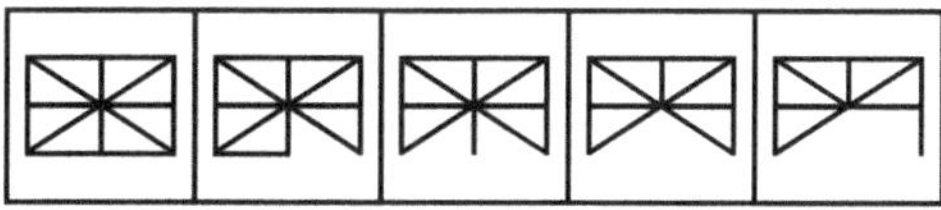

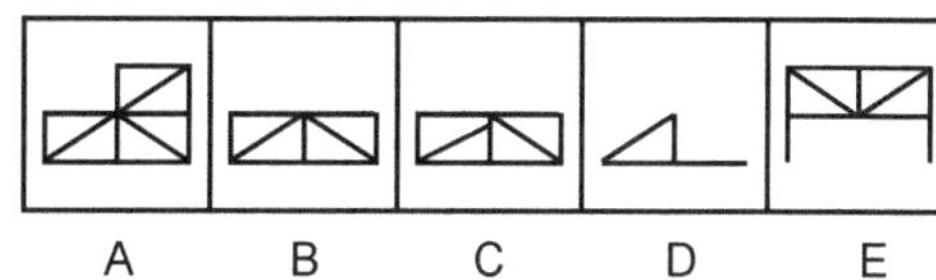

Answer E : Problem Figures consist of a rectangle divided into sections. At each step one of the lines is removed. First from the right, then left and then the centre. To continue this pattern, a right diagonal line is removed. In the answer figure a left diagonal line should be removed. Answer Figure 'E' continues the series.

EXERCISE

Directions : *Each of the following questions consist of problem figures followed by answer figures. Select a figure from amongst the answer figures which will continue the same series or pattern as established by the problem figures.*

1. Problem Figures

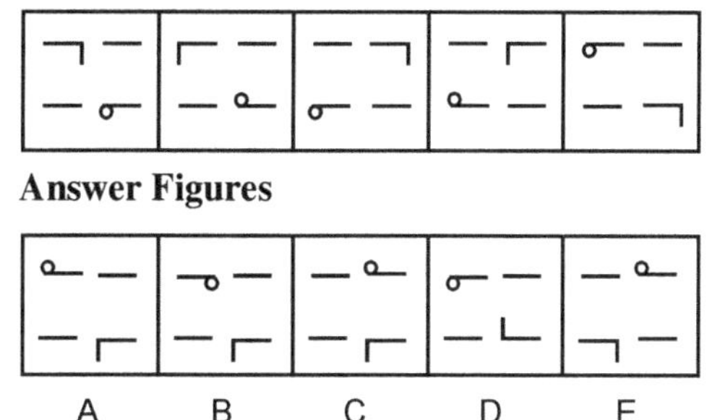

Answer Figures

2. Problem Figures

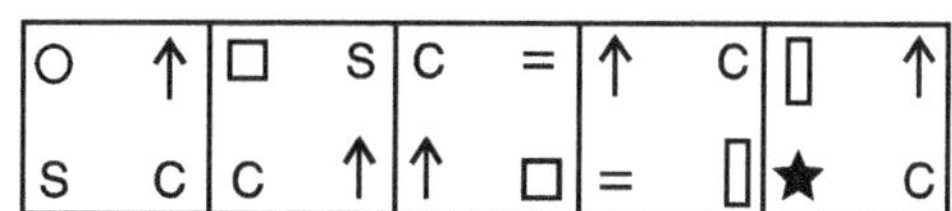

Answer Figures

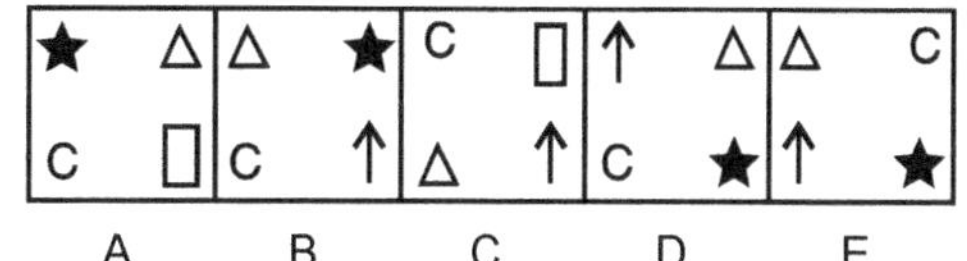

3. Problem Figures

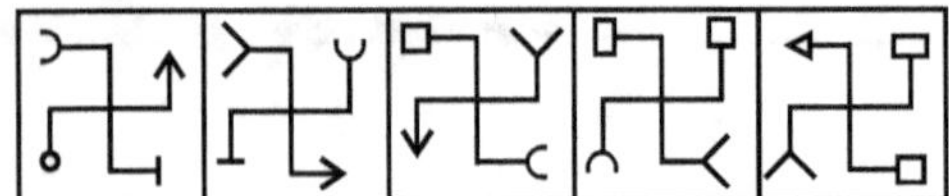

Answer Figures

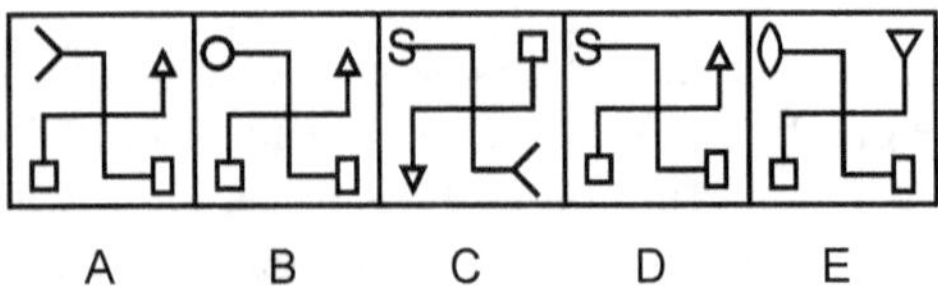

A B C D E

4. Problem Figures

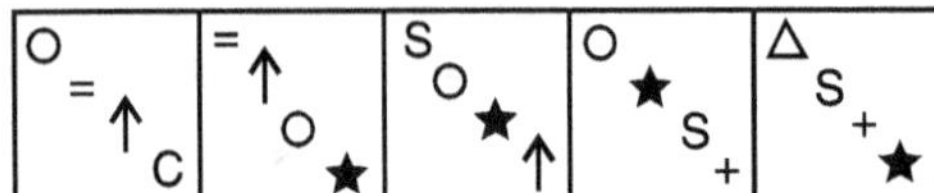

Answer Figures

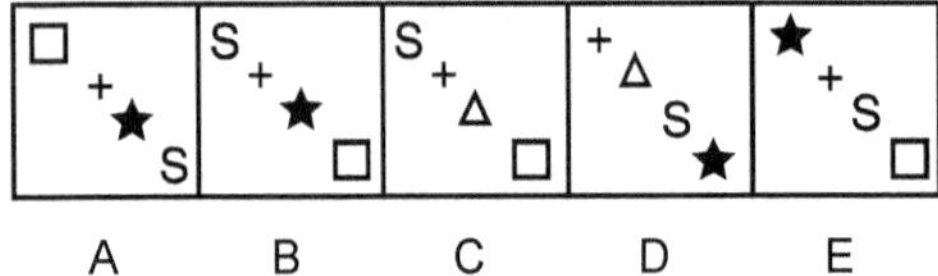

A B C D E

5. Problem Figures

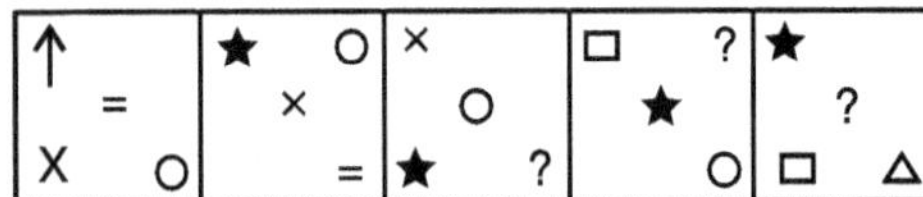

Answer Figures

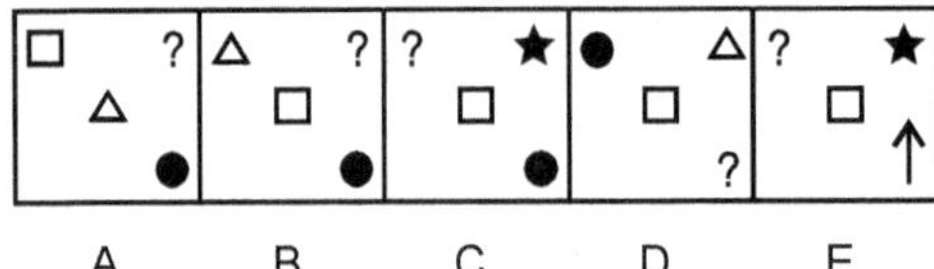

A B C D E

6. Problem Figures

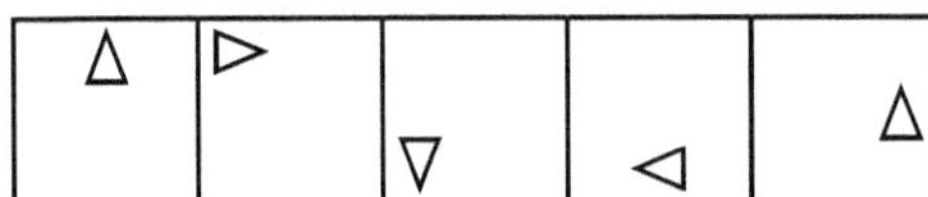

Answer Figures

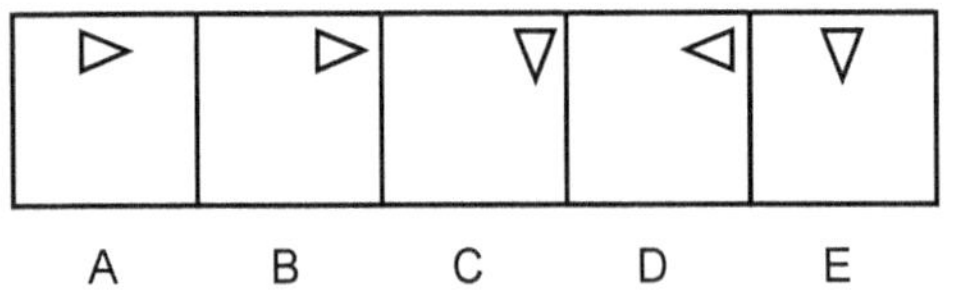

A B C D E

7. Problem Figures

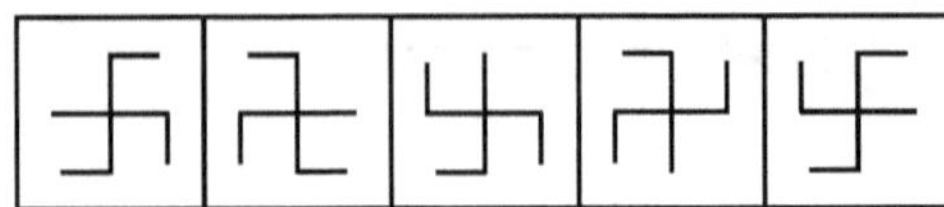

Answer Figures

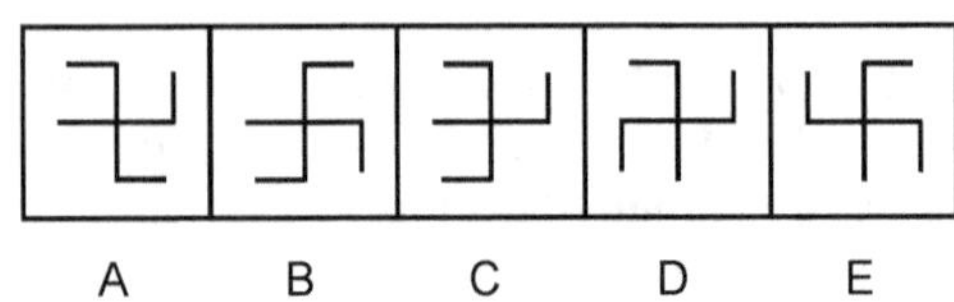

A B C D E

8. Problem Figures

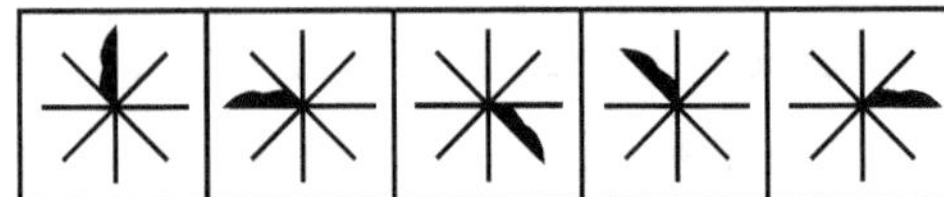

Answer Figures

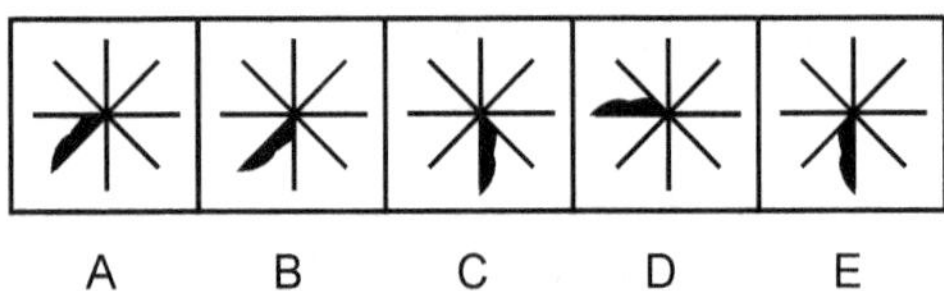

A B C D E

9. Problem Figures

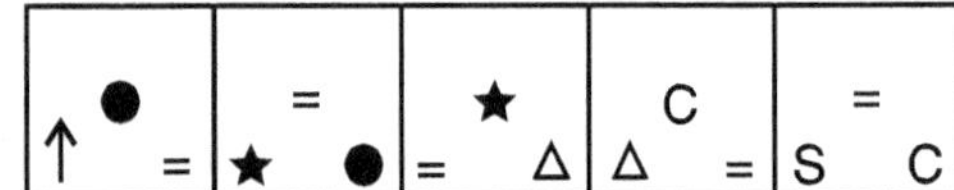

Answer Figures

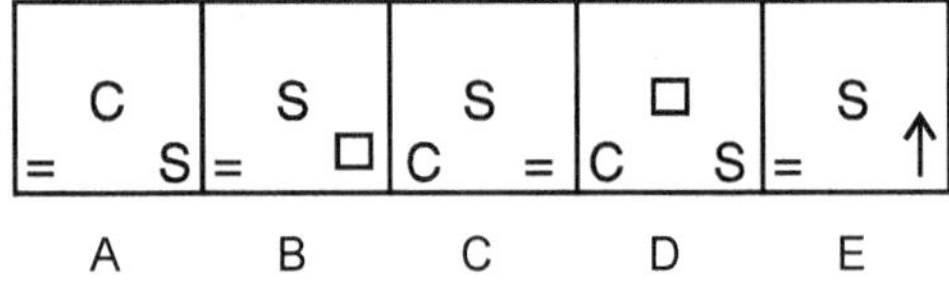

A B C D E

10. Problem Figures

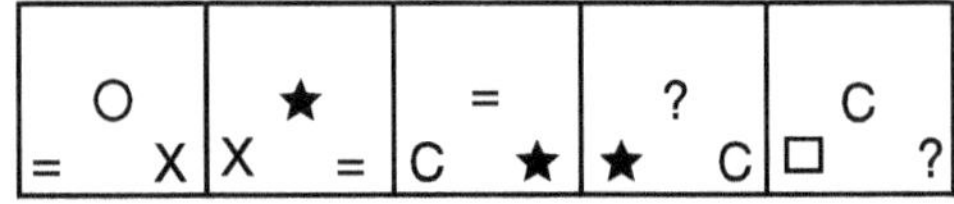

Answer Figures

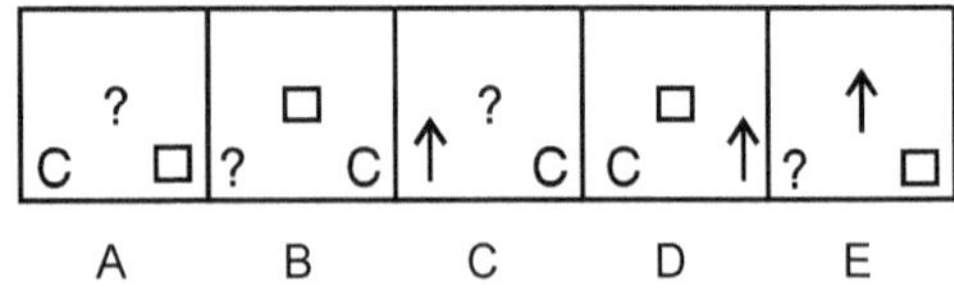

A B C D E

85

11. Problem Figures

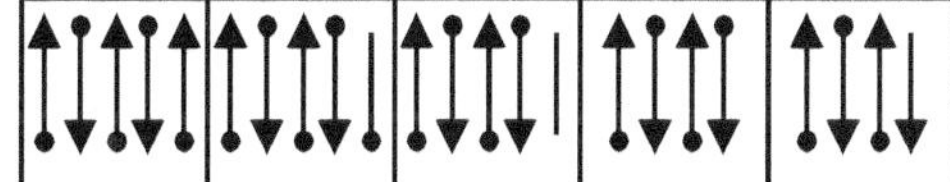

Answer Figures

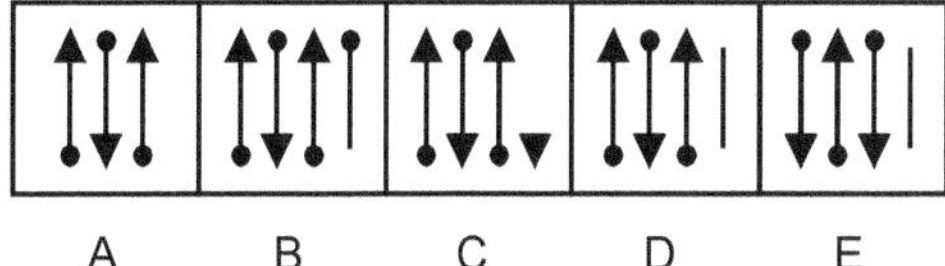

A B C D E

12. Problem Figures

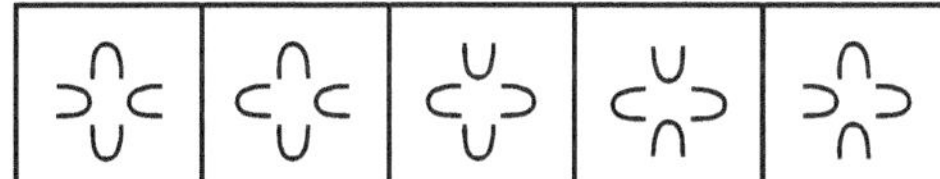

Answer Figures

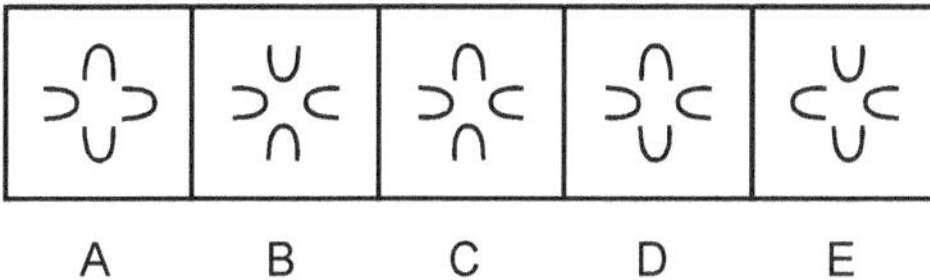

A B C D E

13. Problem Figures

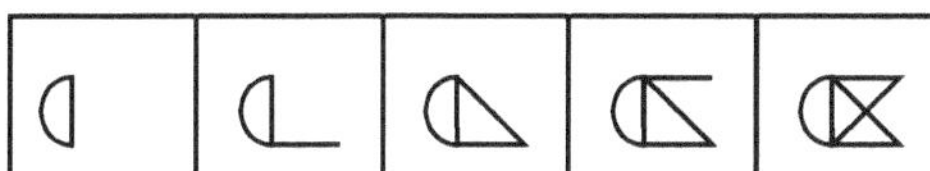

Answer Figures

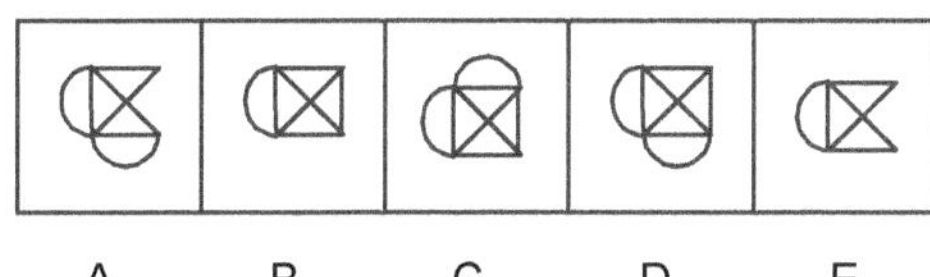

A B C D E

14. Problem Figures

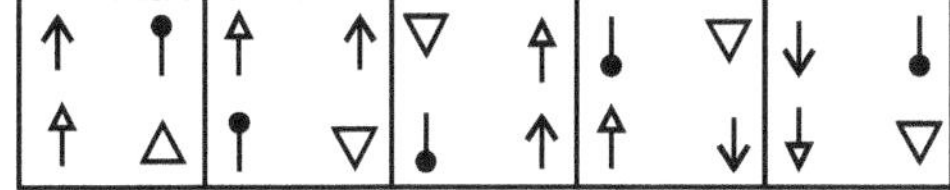

Answer Figures

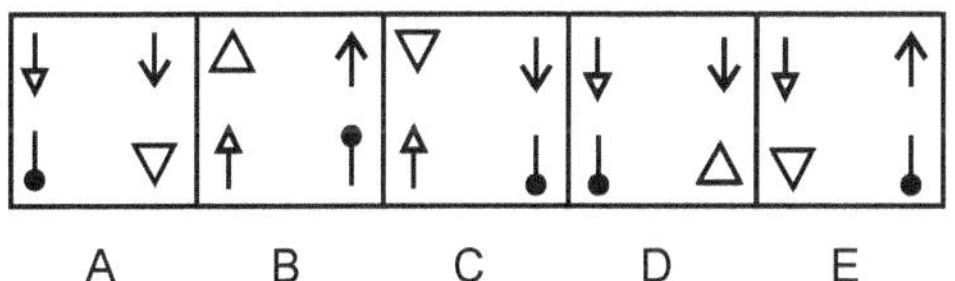

A B C D E

15. Problem Figures

Answer Figures

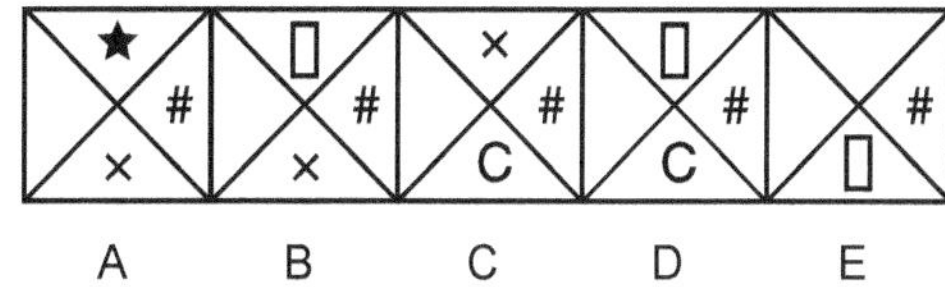

A B C D E

16. Problem Figures

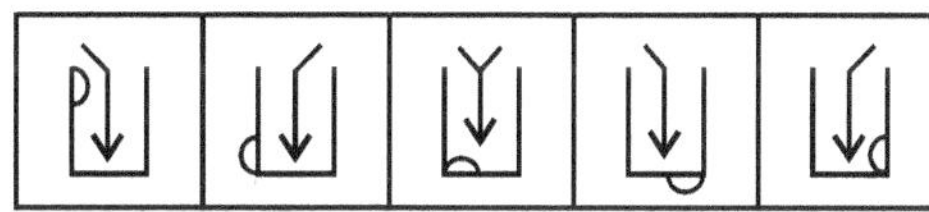

Answer Figures

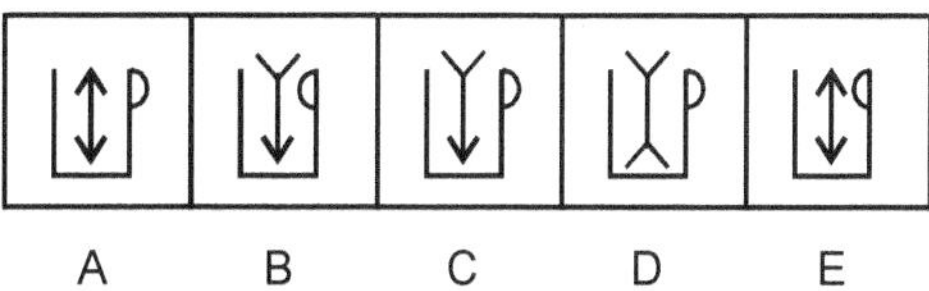

A B C D E

17. Problem Figures

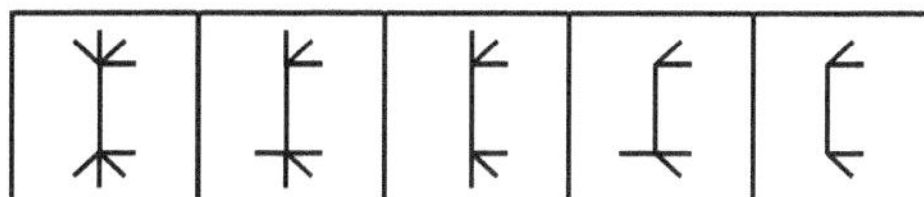

Answer Figures

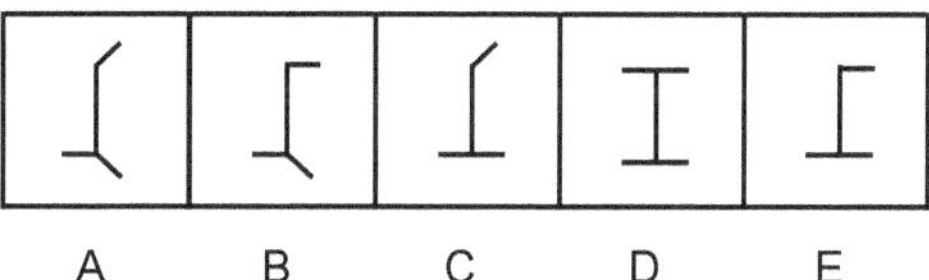

A B C D E

18. Problem Figures

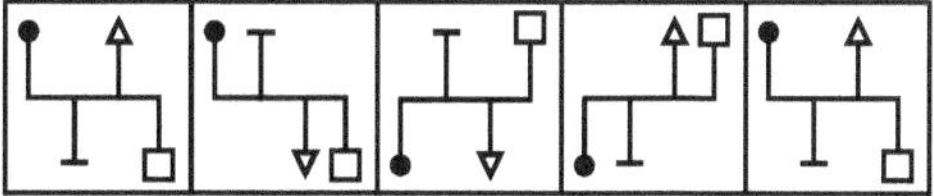

Answer Figures

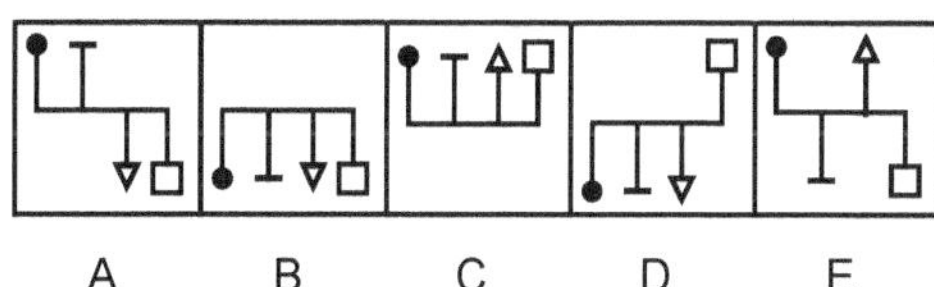

A B C D E

19. Problem Figures

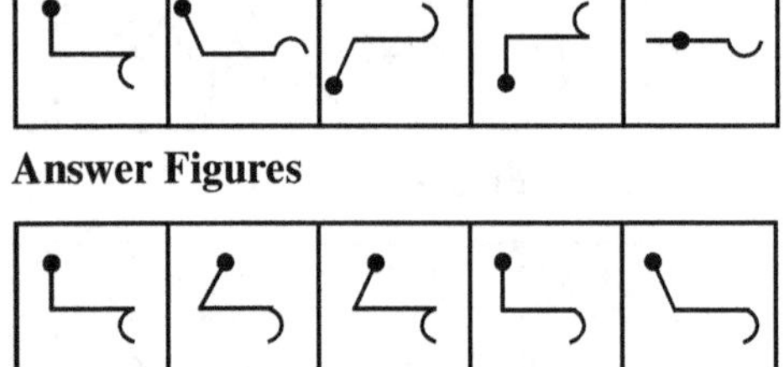

Answer Figures

A B C D E

20. Problem Figures

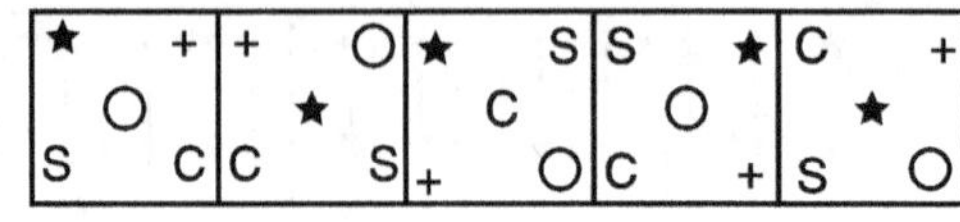

Answer Figures

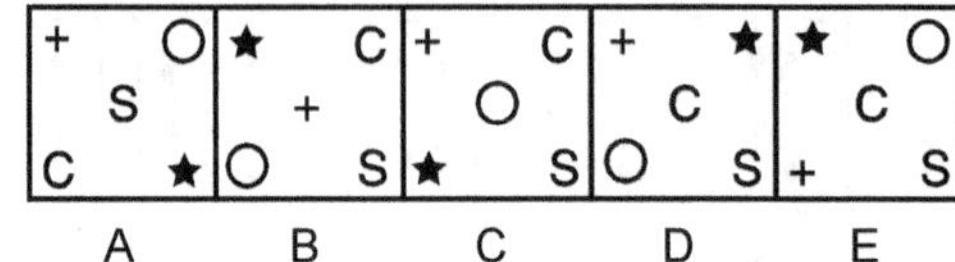

A B C D E

ANSWERS

1	2	3	4	5	6	7	8	9	10
A	B	D	C	D	B	A	E	B	E

11	12	13	14	15	16	17	18	19	20
D	C	A	D	B	C	E	A	B	D

SOME SELECTED EXPLANATORY ANSWERS

1. In alternate figures the four elements are moved clockwise.

3. The shape is turned 90° clockwise and the element attached to its top left side is replaced by an entirely new element.

6. The triangle is moved half and one steps anticlockwise alternately and turned 90° anticlockwise at each step.

7. In alternate figures the design is turned 90° clockwise.

8. The number of spikes the shade is moved anticlockwise, is increased by one at each step and the placement of the shade is same in alternate figures.

11. Starting from the extreme right element, at a time one part is removed in a set order. Answer Figure D continues the series.

12. Clockwise, starting from the left first one 'u' shape and then two 'u' shapes are turned by 180°. Option C fits the series.

13. Without lifting the pen one part is added to the figure at each step.

16. In alternate figures the semicircle is moved one step clockwise. The three stages of the arrow are repeated from the fourth figure.

18. First the two middle elements are turned to the other side of the horizontal line, then the two corner elements are turned. Also note, this series is repeated from the fifth figure.

20. Starting from the two bottom elements, anticlockwise, their places are interchanged, while the places of other three elements are changed one step anticlockwise.

❀ ❀ ❀

20 | Analogies or Relationships

Analogy is a process of reasoning between two parallel cases. It relates to agreement or correspon-dence in certain respects between two things. It is a process whereby the underlying relationship that exists between two figures, designs or patterns is determined. Under the process, one has to discover the features common to the two figures or designs. This common feature is a model or base. The question seeks solution on the basis of this model or base.

EXERCISE

Directions : *The second figure in the first unit of the Problem Figures bears a certain relationship to the first figure. Similarly, one of the figures in the Answer Figures bears the same relationship to the first figure in the second unit of the Problem Figures. Locate the figure which would fit the question mark.*

1. Problem Figures

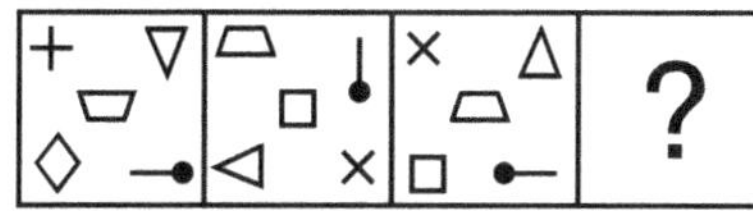

Answer Figures

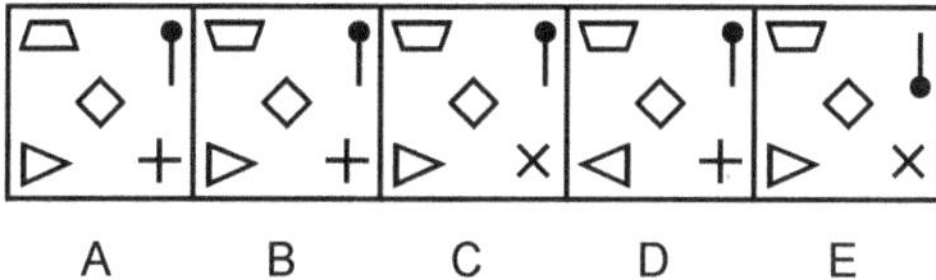

A   B   C   D   E

2. Problem Figures

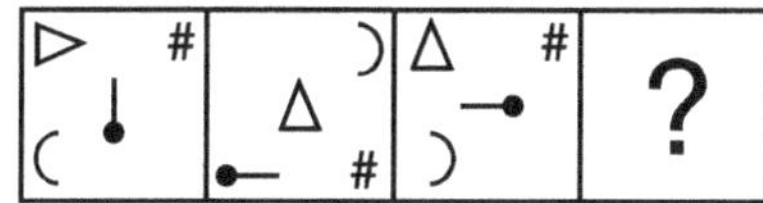

Answer Figures

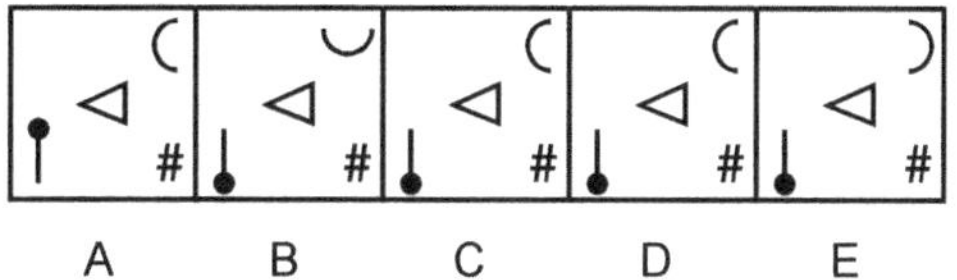

A   B   C   D   E

3. Problem Figures

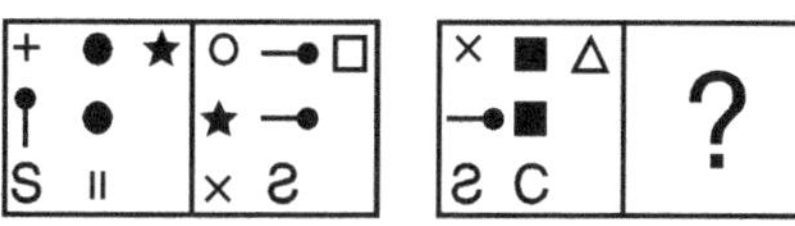

Answer Figures

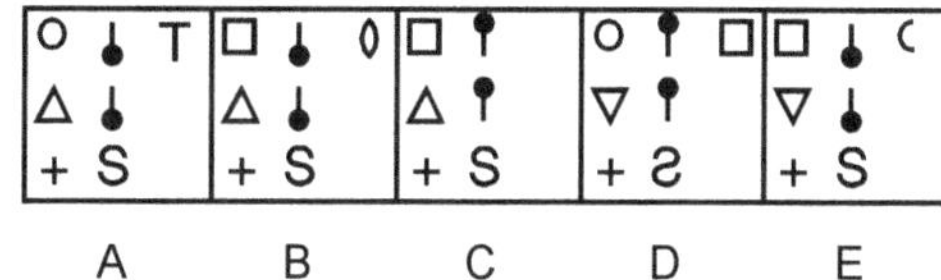

A   B   C   D   E

4. Problem Figures

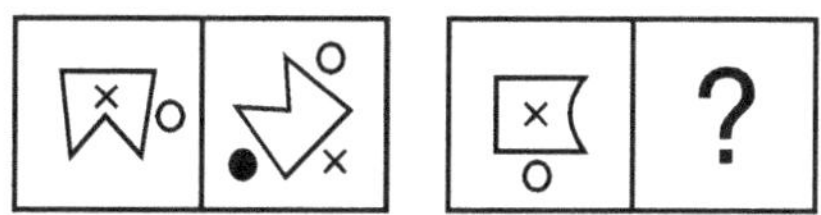

Answer Figures

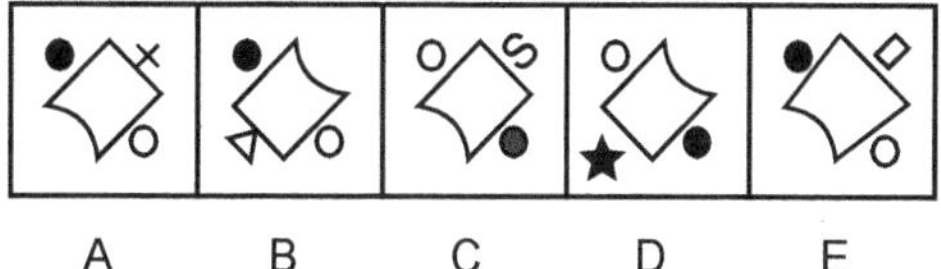

A   B   C   D   E

5. Problem Figures

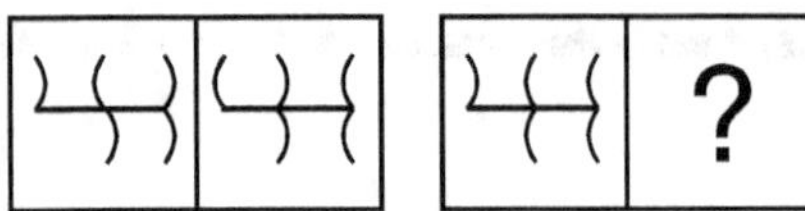

Answer Figures

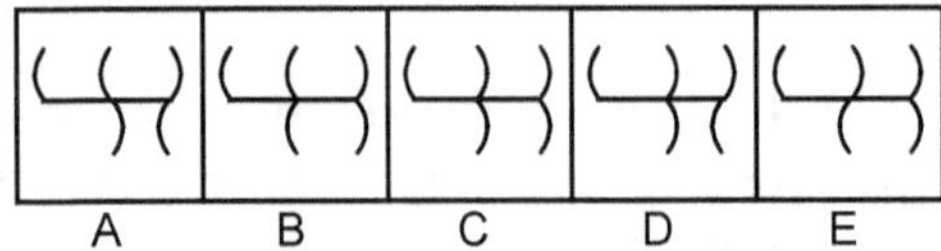

6. Problem Figures

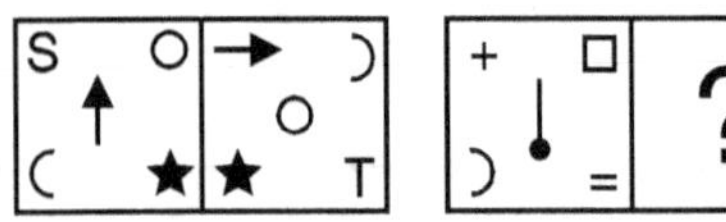

Answer Figures

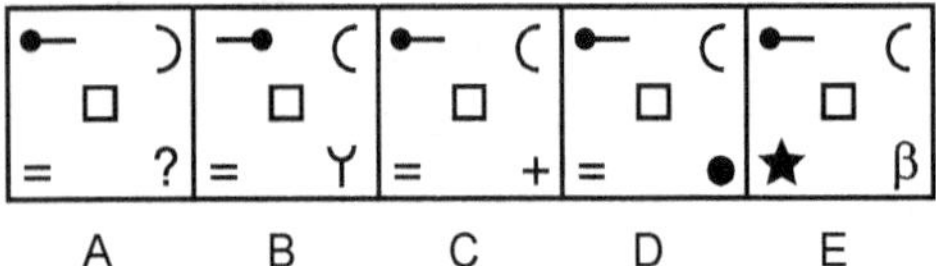

7. Problem Figures

Answer Figures

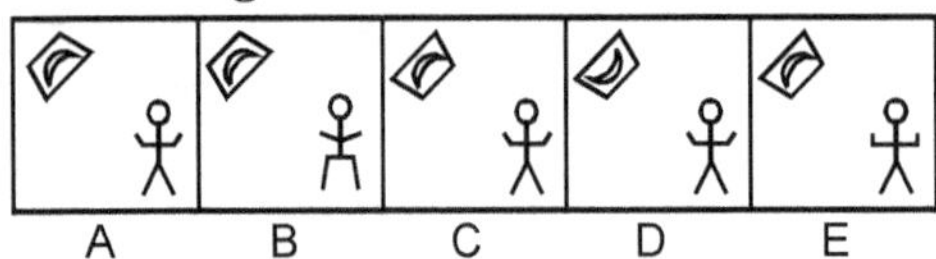

8. Problem Figures

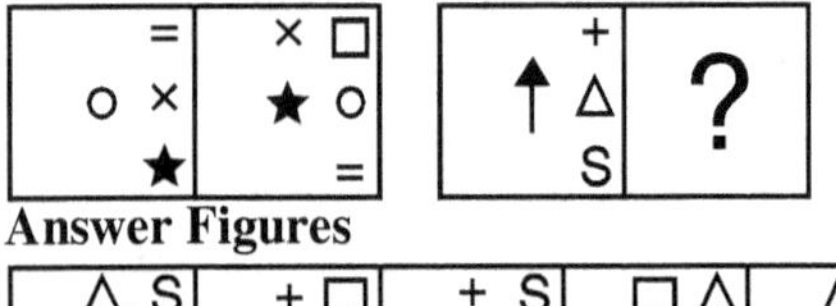

9. Problem Figures

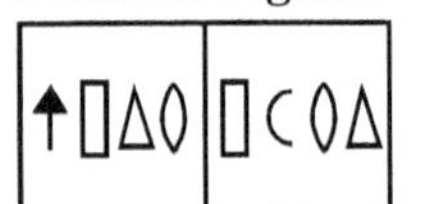

Answer Figures

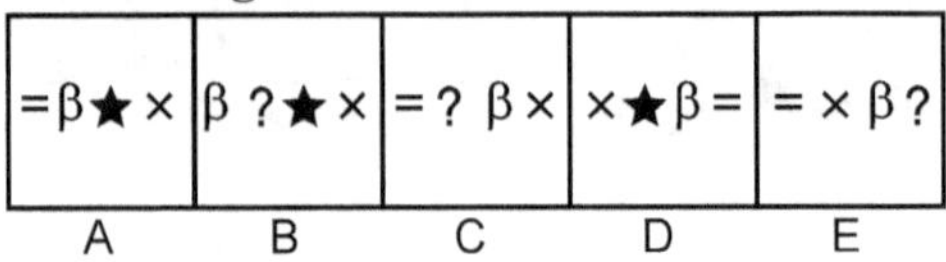

10. Problem Figures

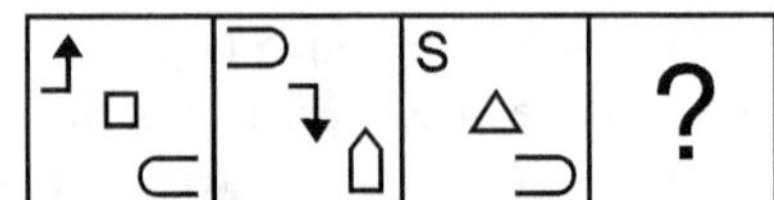

Answer Figures

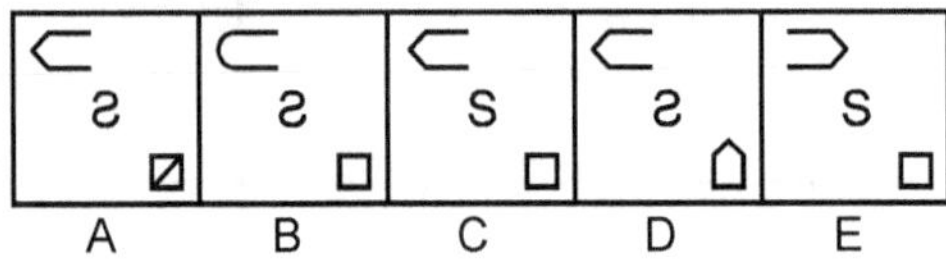

11. Problem Figures

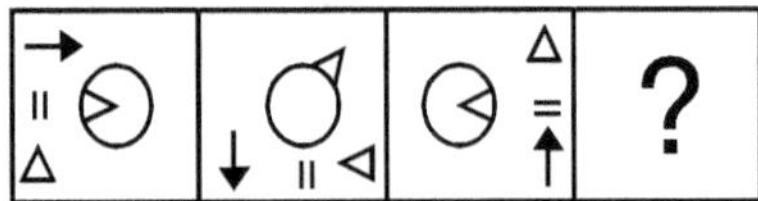

Answer Figures

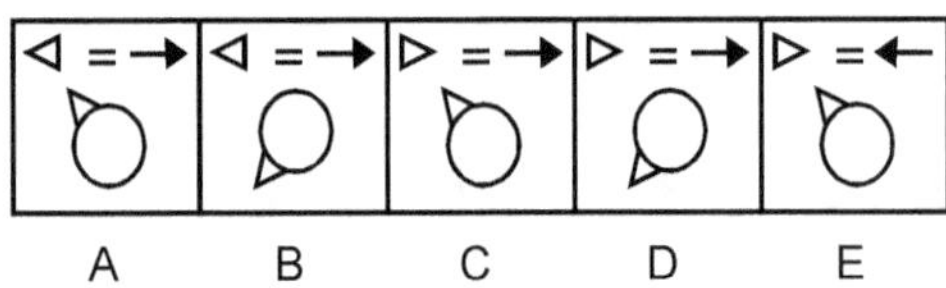

12. Problem Figures

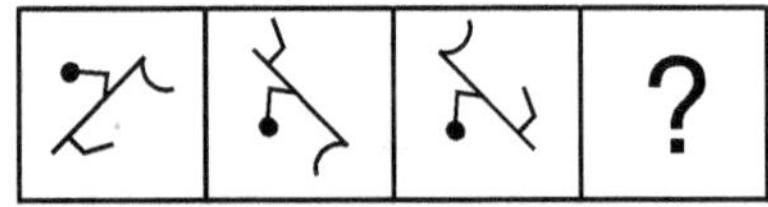

Answer Figures

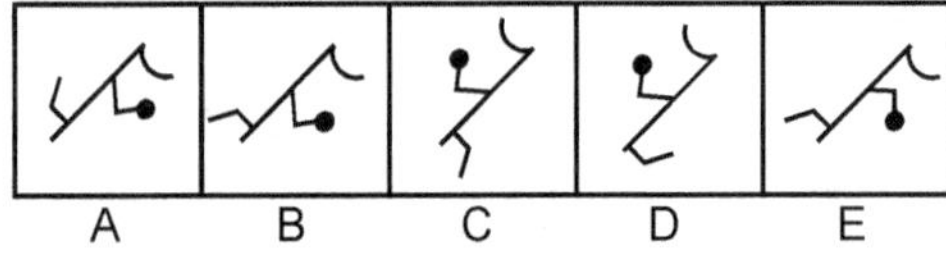

13. Problem Figures

Answer Figures

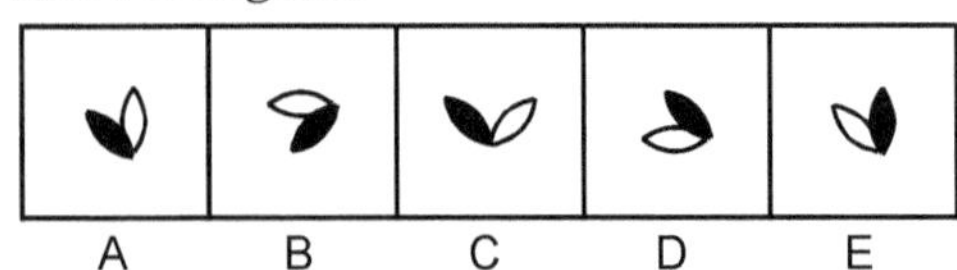

14. Problem Figures

Answer Figures

A   B   C   D   E

15. Problem Figures

Answer Figures

A   B   C   D   E

Directions (Q. 16–20): *In each of the following questions, a related pair of figures is followed by five numbered pairs of figures. Select the pair that has a relationship similar to that in the unnumbered pair.*

Problem Figure   **Answer Figures**

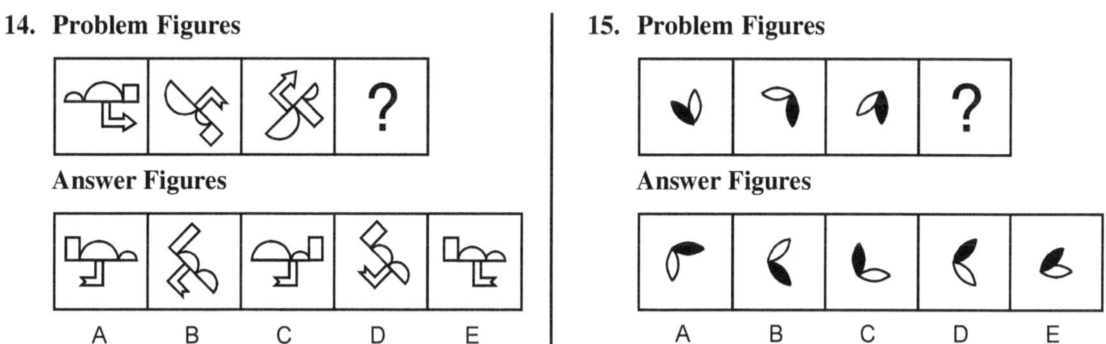

16.

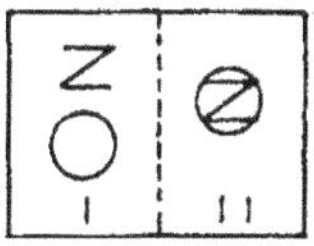

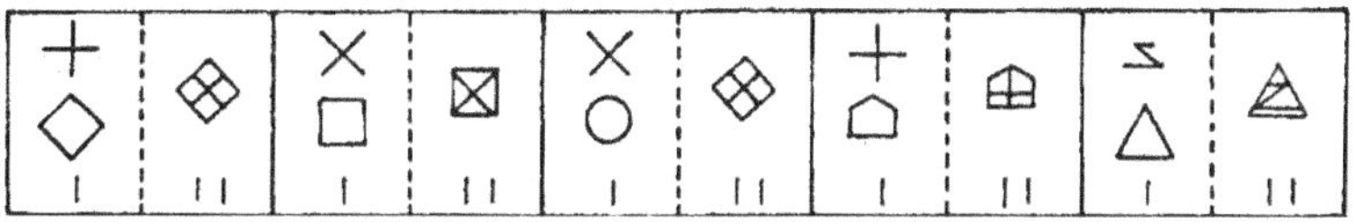

A   B   C   D   E

17.

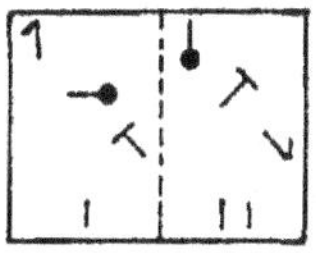

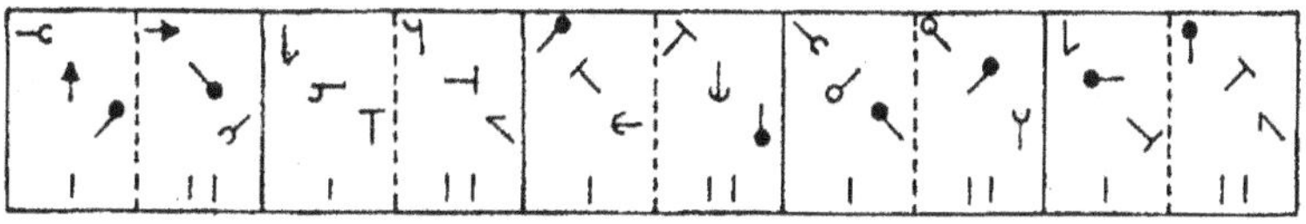

A   B   C   D   E

18.

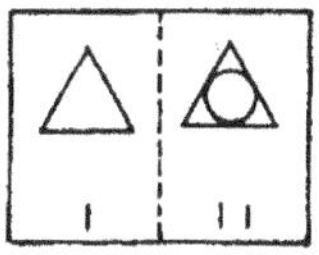

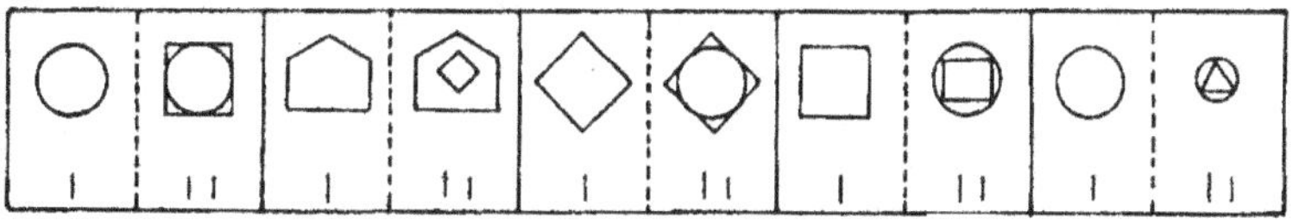

A   B   C   D   E

19.

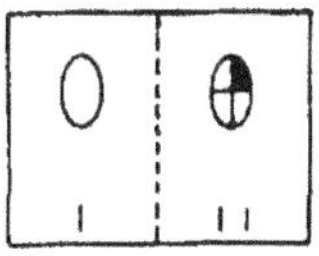

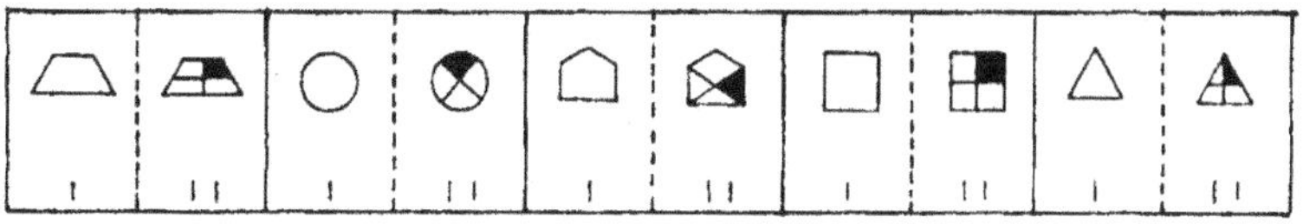

A   B   C   D   E

20.

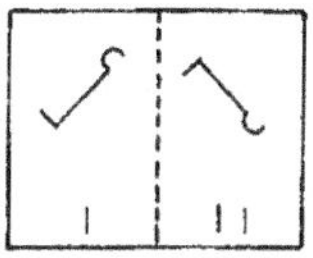

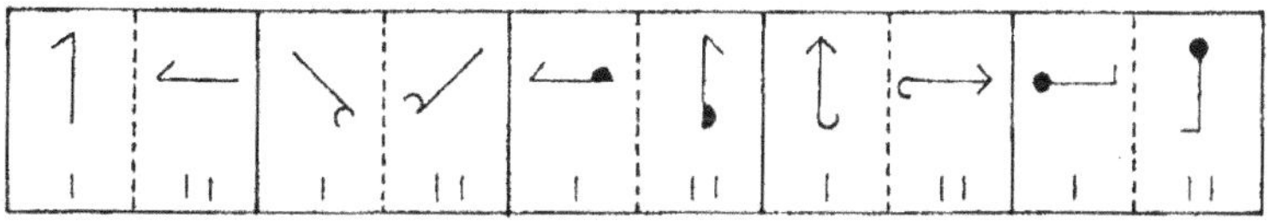

A   B   C   D   E

ANSWERS

1	2	3	4	5	6	7	8	9	10
B	C	B	A	E	D	A	E	A	B

11	12	13	14	15	16	17	18	19	20
B	B	A	E	D	B	A	E	D	E

SOME SELECTED EXPLANATORY ANSWERS

2. The element in the top left corner is turned 90° anticlockwise and moved to the centre, the element in the centre is turned 90° clockwise and moved to the bottom left corner position, the element in the bottom left corner is laterally inverted and moved to the top right corner position, and the element in the top right corner is laterally inverted and moved to the bottom right corner position.

4. The first figure is turned 135° clockwise, the inner element is moved out towards the base, the blank circle is shaded and a circle is added on its opposite side to get the second figure.

5. All arcs in the first figure except the left are below the line segment are turned to the other side to get the second figure.

7. The human sketch is moved to the right side and its hands and legs are extended and shortened respectively in a particular manner. The other two elements are turned upside down, the smaller one is enclosed within the larger one and then the two together are moved to the left and rotated 45° anticlockwise.

9. The left most element is made new and then the two corner elements are moved inbetween the two middle elements.

11. The triangle inside the circle is moved one and a half steps clockwise and turned outside. The elements on the side arc moved one step anticlockwise, the arrow and the triangle are turned 90° clockwise, and 90° anticlockwise respectively.

12. The first figure is turned 90° anticlockwise, one arc is turned to the other side to be in front of the line with a dot to get the second figure.

13. The petals in first figure are turned 135° anticlockwise to get the second figure.

14. Of the three elements the right most element is moved to the left, the design is turned 135° anticlockwise, the arrow is turned to the other side and the lines making the arrowhead are turned inwards.

15. The blank and shaded petals in first figure are turned 90° and 135° anticlockwise respectively to get the second figure.

16. The uppermost design enters into innerside side of the lower design from Ist figure to the IInd figure.

17. In element I to II upper left design comes at lower right rotating 135° C.W. Middle design goes to upper left and rotates 90° CW. While lower right design goes to middle and it also rotates 90° C.W. The same changes occur in option A.

18. In element I to II and ellipse is put in the triangle. Similarly in option E a triangle is put in the ellipse.

19. From first figure to IInd figure, design is divided into four equal parts and right side of the upper portion becomes shaded.

20. From Ist figure to IInd figure, design is reversed after moving 90° anticlockwise direction.

❉ ❉ ❉

Classification or Odd-One Out

Classification means arranging the given content in groups or classes having qualities of same kind. In classification type questions, the figures or items are sorted out in groups on the basis of their similarities in qualities in shapes, size, pattern, structure, genus, order, species, grade, style, constituents and other specifications, and thus the answer is found out.

Example

Which one of the following figures is different from the rest. Spot the figure.

1. 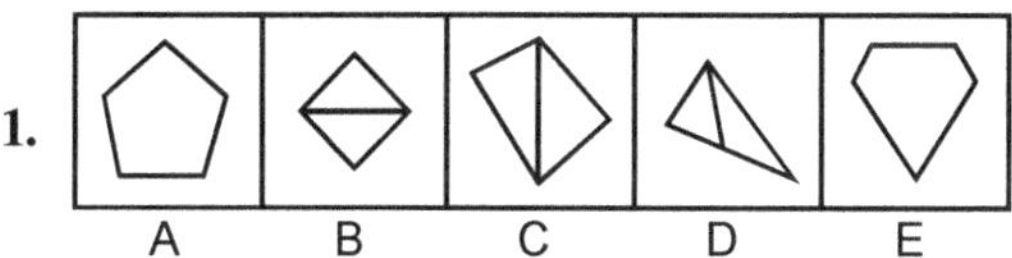

Answer D : Figures A, B, C and E are made of 5 straight lines, while D has only four straight lines. Thus A, B, C and E have a common characteristic (they have 5 straight lines each), but D does not have this characteristic. Therefore, D is different from the other four figures.

EXERCISE

Directions : *In each of the following questions one of the figures is different from the rest. Spot the figure.*

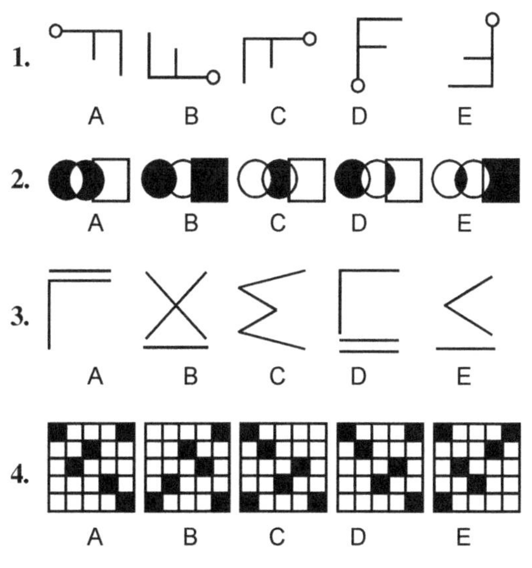

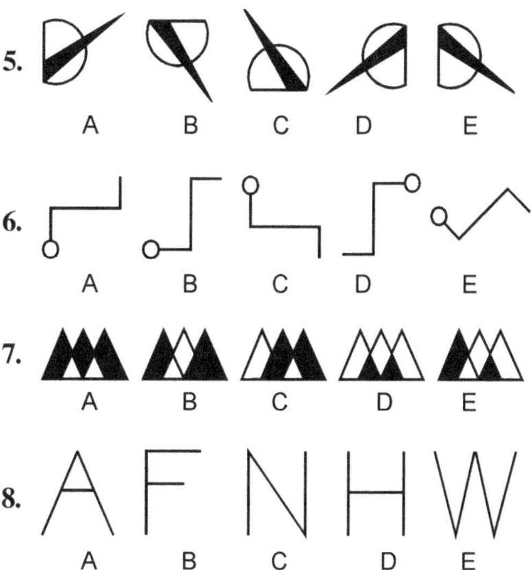

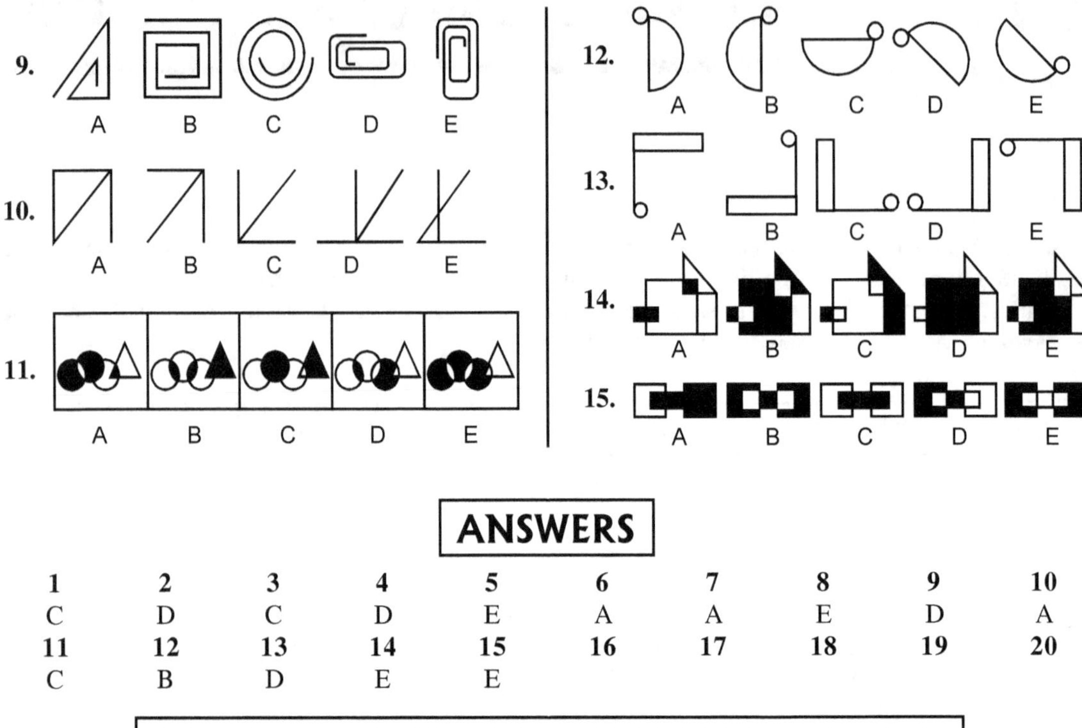

ANSWERS

1	2	3	4	5	6	7	8	9	10
C	D	C	D	E	A	A	E	D	A
11	**12**	**13**	**14**	**15**	**16**	**17**	**18**	**19**	**20**
C	B	D	E	E					

SOME SELECTED EXPLANATORY ANSWERS

1. All other figures are identical. The two line segments are to the left of the line with a circle in this option.

2. Figures A and E and figures B and C form opposite pairs. Only figure D is left single.

3. All other figures are Roman Numerals rotated 90° anticlockwise.

4. All other figures have identical squares shaded. In this option one shaded square is on the diagonally opposite corner.

5. All other figures are identical. In this option the shaded part is rising from the left of the base.

6. In all other figures the line segment with the circle is to the right of the straight line. In this option it is on the left side.

7. In all other figures only two sections are shaded.

8. All other figures are made of three straight lines.

9. In all other figures the line forming the pattern is drawn clockwise from outside to inside.

10. All other figures contain three straight lines.

11. Figures A and D and figures B and E are matched opposite pairs. Only figure C is left single.

12. All other figures can be rotated into each other.

13. In all other figures the line with the circle is to the right side at the rectangle base.

14. Only this figure has two segments shaded, all others have three.

15. This is the only figure with a white/blank middle square.

QUANTITATIVE ABILITY

PROBLEM BASED ON NUMBERS

MULTIPLE CHOICE QUESTIONS

1. Three numbers are in the ratio of 5 : 4 : 3. The difference of the largest and the smallest numbers is exceeds by 24. The middle number is:
   - A. 18
   - B. 24
   - C. 30
   - D. 48

2. Three consecutive numbers such that twice the first, 3 times the second and 4 times the third together make 182. The numbers are:
   - A. 18, 19 and 20
   - B. 19, 20 and 21
   - C. 20, 21 and 22
   - D. 21, 22 and 23

3. There is a number of two digits, the sum of whose digits is 9. If the digits of that number are reversed, the new number is $\frac{3}{8}$th of the original number, then the original number is:
   - A. 27
   - B. 45
   - C. 54
   - D. 72

4. The sum of three numbers is 68. If the ratio between first and second is 2 : 3 and that between second and third is 5 : 3, then the second number is:
   - A. 20
   - B. 30
   - C. 18
   - D. None of these

5. The sum of the digits of a number less than 100 is 6. If the digits be interchanged, the resulting number will be less by 18 than the original number, the number is:
   - A. 51
   - B. 15
   - C. 24
   - D. 42

ANSWERS

1	2	3	4	5
D	B	D	B	D

SOME SELECTED EXPLANATORY ANSWERS

1. Let the numbers be $5x$, $4x$ and $3x$.
   Then $5x - 3x = 24$
   $\Rightarrow \quad 2x = 24$ or $x = 12$
   $\therefore$ Middle number is $4 \times 12 = 48$

2. Let three consecutive numbers be $x, x + 1, x + 2$.
   $\therefore 2x + 3(x + 1) + 4(x + 2) = 182$
   $\Rightarrow \quad 2x + 3x + 3 + 4x + 8 = 182$

   $\Rightarrow \quad 9x = 182 - 11 = 171$

   $\therefore \quad x = \dfrac{171}{9} = 19$

   Required numbers are 19, 20 and 21.

3. Let the two digits be x and y and the number be $10x + y$.

Then $\qquad x + y = 9 \qquad$ ...(1)

and $\qquad 10y + x = \dfrac{3}{8}(10x + y)$

$\Rightarrow \qquad 80y + 8x = 30x + 3y$

$\Rightarrow \qquad 77y - 22x = 0$

$\Rightarrow \qquad 7y - 2x = 0$

or $\qquad 2x - 7y = 0 \qquad$ ...(2)

Multiplying equation (1) by (2), we get

$\qquad 2x + 2y = 18 \qquad$ ...(3)

Subtract (3) from (2),

$\qquad -9y = -18 \quad \therefore \quad y = 2$

From (1), $\quad x = 9 - y = 9 - 2 = 7$

Hence, the original number is 72.

4.

First		Second		Third
2	:	3	:	3
		5		3

$\Rightarrow \quad 2 \quad : \quad 3 \quad : \quad \dfrac{3}{5} \times 3$

or $\quad 10 \quad : \quad 15 \quad : \quad 9$

Let the three numbers be $10x$, $15x$ and $9x$.

Then, $10x + 15x + 9x = 68$

$\Rightarrow \qquad 34x = 68 \qquad \therefore \ x = \dfrac{68}{34} = 2$

The numbers are 20, 30, 18,

i.e., second number = 30.

5. Let the digits be x and y

and the number be $10x + y$

According to the given conditions,

$\qquad x + y = 6$

$\qquad 10y + x = 10x + y - 18$

$\Rightarrow \quad 9y - 9x = -18$ or $x - y = 2$

Adding (1) and (2),

$\qquad 2x = 8 \quad \therefore \quad x = 2$

Subtracting (2) from (1),

$\qquad 2y = 4 \quad \therefore \quad y = 2$

Hence, the required number is 42.

H.C.F. & L.C.M.

Solved Examples

Example 1: *Find the H.C.F. of 120, 240 and 300.*

Solution: I. Factor method:

$\qquad 120 = 2 \times 2 \times 2 \times 3 \times 5$

$\qquad 240 = 2 \times 2 \times 2 \times 2 \times 3 \times 5$

$\qquad 300 = 2 \times 2 \times 3 \times 5 \times 5$

Clearly, the common factors are $2 \times 2 \times 3 \times 5$.

$\therefore \qquad$ H.C.F. = 60.

Example 2: *Find the LCM of 3.6, 4.5 and 6.3.*

Solution: $\qquad 36 = 2^2 \times 3^2$

$\qquad 45 = 3^2 \times 5$

$\qquad 63 = 3^2 \times 7$

$\overline{\qquad \text{L.C.M.} = 2^2 \times 3^2 \times 5 \times 7 = 1260}$

$\therefore$ Required L.C.M. = 126.0 = 126

Alternative Method:

$$3.6 = \frac{36}{10}, \ 4.5 = \frac{45}{10},$$

$$6.3 = \frac{63}{10}$$

Required L.C.M. $= \dfrac{\text{LCM of 36, 45 and 63}}{\text{HCF of 10, 10 and 10}}$

$$= \frac{1260}{10} = 126.$$

Example 3: *Find the least perfect square number which is divisible by 2, 3, 4, 5, 6.*

Solution: The least number divisible by 2, 3, 4, 5, 6 is clearly their LCM which is 60.

Since $60 = 2 \times 2 \times 3 \times 5$.

Multiply it by 3×5 to make it a perfect square.

Hence, the required least perfect square number

$$= 60 \times 15 = 900.$$

Example 4: *Find the least number which is a multiple of 5, but when it is divided by 18, 21 and 24, the remainders are 7, 10 and 13 respectively.*

Solution: $18 - 7 = 21 - 10 = 24 - 13 = 11$, constant

L.C.M. of 18, 21, 24 = 504

$\therefore$ Required number = 504 M - 11, will be a multiple of 5 for M = 4

$$= 504 \times 4 - 11$$

$$= 2016 - 11 = 2005.$$

MULTIPLE CHOICE QUESTIONS

1. The H.C.F. of 1233, 726, 531 and 345 is:
A. 5
B. 3
C. 4
D. 2

2. The L.C.M. of 18, 28, 35, 60 and 100 is:
A. 6300
B. 6200
C. 6400
D. 6500

3. If the H.C.F. of two numbers is 5, their L.C.M. is 165 and one of the number is 55, then the other number is:
A. 5
B. 15
C. 75
D. 2475

4. The smallest number of 4 digits which when divided by 6, 8, 12 and 20 leaves remainder 5 in each case is:
A. 1285
B. 1200
C. 1085
D. 1080

5. The greatest number of 6 digits which is exactly divisible by 27, 45, 60, 72 and 96 is:
A. 998000
B. 989980
C. 997920
D. 999999

6. Four bells ring at an interval of 8, 12, 15 and 18 second respectively. All the four begin to ring together. How many times will they ring together in one hour excluding the one at the start?
A. 10 times
B. 20 times
C. 30 times
D. 40 times

7. Three different persons buy some notebooks for ₹ 92.50, ₹ 129.50 and ₹ 166.50. The maximum price of the notebook is:
A. ₹ 15.50
B. ₹ 18.50
C. ₹ 21.50
D. ₹ 23.50

8. The circumferences of the front wheel and hind wheel of a cart are $5\frac{1}{2}$ m and $14\frac{2}{3}$ m respectively. A mark is put at the point of contact of each wheel with the ground. Find the distance travelled by the cart so that the mark points on each wheel touch the ground together again:
A. 22 m
B. 44 m
C. 66 m
D. 88 m

ANSWERS

1	2	3	4	5	6	7	8
B	A	B	C	C	A	B	B

SOME SELECTED EXPLANATORY ANSWERS

3. Other number $= \dfrac{\text{H.C.F.} \times \text{L.C.M.}}{\text{First number}}$

$$= \frac{5 \times 165}{55} = 15$$

4. Smallest number of 4 digits = 1000
LCM of the given number = 120
When 1000 is divided by 120 gives remainder = 40
Required number
= 1000 + (120 – 40) + Common remainder
= 1080 + 5 (1085

8. L.C.M. of $5\frac{1}{2}$ and $14\frac{2}{3}$

i.e., $\dfrac{11}{2}$ and $\dfrac{44}{3}$

i.e., $\dfrac{\text{L.C.M. of 11 and 44}}{\text{H.C.F. of 2 and 3}}$

$= \dfrac{44}{1} = 44$

∴ Required distance = 44 m

TIME WORK, PIPE AND CISTERN

Solved Examples

Example 1: *A can complete a piece of work in 8 days, whereas A and B together can complete the same work in 6 days. How long will it take for B alone to complete the work?*

Solution: A's one day's work = $\dfrac{1}{8}$

(A + B)'s one day's work = $\dfrac{1}{6}$

B's one day's work = $\left(\dfrac{1}{6} - \dfrac{1}{8}\right) = \dfrac{1}{24}$

∴ B can complete the work in 24 days.

Example 2: *Two pipes A and B can separately, fill a cistern in 8 hours and 12 hours respectively while a third pipe C can empty it in 24 hours. In what time will the cistern be full, if all the pipes are opened together?*

Solution: In 1 hour, the pipe A fills $\dfrac{1}{8}$ th of the cistern.

In 1 hour, the pipe B fills $\dfrac{1}{12}$ th of the cistern.

In 1 hour, the pipe C can empty $\dfrac{1}{24}$ th of the cistern.

Net filling of the cistern in 1 hour

$$= \left(\dfrac{1}{8} + \dfrac{1}{12}\right) - \dfrac{1}{24}$$

$$= \dfrac{5}{24} - \dfrac{1}{24} = \dfrac{4}{24} = \dfrac{1}{6}$$

So, the cistern will be full in 6 hours.

MULTIPLE CHOICE QUESTIONS

1. If 36 binders bind 900 books in 10 days, how many binders will be required to bind 1,200 books in 12 days?
   A. 30
   B. 32
   C. 40
   D. 42

2. If A can complete a work in 30 days and B can complete the same work in 25 days, then in how many days will 'A' and 'B' together complete the work?
   A. $\dfrac{11}{150}$ days
   B. $\dfrac{150}{11}$ days
   C. 55 days
   D. $\dfrac{1}{55}$ days

3. If 100 men can do 100 jobs in 100 days, then 1 man can do one job in:
   A. 1 day
   B. 100 days
   C. 50 days
   D. 10 days

4. Ajit can complete a job in 4 days, Manoj can complete the same job in 6 days and Ravi can complete it in 12 days. In how many days will Ajit, Manoj and Ravi together complete the same job?
   A. 2 days
   B. 3 days
   C. $\dfrac{1}{2}$ day
   D. 1 day

5. A and B can finish a work in 16 days while A alone can do the same work in 24 days. Therefore B alone can finish the same work in ...... days.
   A. 24
   B. 36
   C. 48
   D. 56

6. A, B and C undertake to complete a piece of work for ₹ 1,950. A works for 8 days, B for 9 days and C for 12 days to complete the work. If their daily wages are in the ratio of 3 : 5 : 4, what does C get?
   A. ₹ 400
   B. ₹ 750
   C. ₹ 675
   D. ₹ 800

7. Two taps A and B can fill a cistern in 30 minute and 45 minute respectively. There is third exhaust tap C at the bottom of the tank. If all the taps are opened at the same time the cistern will be full in 45 minute. In what time can exhaust tap C empty the cistern when full?

A. 10 min   B. 15 min
C. 18 min   D. 20 min

8. Two taps A and B can separately fill a cistern in 24 minute and 30 minute respectively. Both the pipes are opened together. Find when the pipe B must be turned off so that the cistern may be full in 18 minute.

A. $6\frac{1}{2}$ min   B. $6\frac{3}{4}$ min

C. 7 min   D. $7\frac{1}{2}$ min

9. Efficiency of B is 80% of A. If both can complete a work in 24 days, in how many days B alone will complete the same work?
A. 54   B. 50
C. 49   D. 56

10. The efficiency of A is twice that of B. A completes a work in 9 days less than taken by B. In how many days A alone will complete this work?
A. 12 days   B. 10 days
C. 9 days   D. 13 days

11. If 3 men or 6 boys can finish a work in 20 days, then 6 men and 8 boys finish twice the work in:
A. 9 days   B. 11 days
C. 3 days   D. 12 days

12. 6 boys and 4 girls together complete a work in 5 days. The same work is done in 5 days by 10 boys. How many girls would be required if only the girls can finish this work in 5 days?
A. 20   B. 10
C. 15   D. 12

13. A man and a boy can complete digging in 40 days. The ratio of their speed of digging is 8 : 5. How many days the boys alone will take to do this work?
A. 68 days   B. 52 days
C. 104 days   D. 80 days

14. 104 men are employed to complete a work in 56 days working 8 hours per day. After 30 days $\frac{2}{5}$th work is finished. How many more men should be employed to finish the remaining work within time working 9 hours per day?
A. 52   B. 54
C. 56   D. 58

15. 5 persons prepare an admission list in 8 days working 7 hours per day. If two more persons are included to finish the work in 4 days, how much hours per day they should do the work?
A. 10 hours   B. 9 hours
C. 12 hours   D. 8 hours

16. A and B take 15 days and 10 days respectively to complete a job. Both of them together started the job, but after 2 days B have to leave the job due to any reason and the remaining work was finished by A. In how many days the job was completed?
A. 10 days   B. 8 days
C. 12 days   D. 15 days

17. A work can be finished in 100 days by some persons, but due to the absence of 10 persons, the work is finished in 110 days. How many persons were employed initially?
A. 100   B. 110
C. 55   D. 56

18. The efficiencies of two workmen A and B are in the ratio of 5 : 4. If A can do a piece of work in 12 hours, then B can do it in:
A. 18 hours   B. 16.5 hours
C. 16 hours   D. 15 hours

19. A pipe can fill a cistern in 12 hours and another pipe can empty completely filled cistern in 18 hours. If both the pipes are opened together, the cistern will be filled in:
A. 30 hours   B. 36 hours
C. 40 hours   D. 44 hours

ANSWERS

1	2	3	4	5	6	7	8	9	10
C	B	B	A	C	D	A	D	A	C

11	12	13	14	15	16	17	18	19
D	B	C	C	A	C	B	D	B

SOME SELECTED EXPLANATORY ANSWERS

1. less books, less number of binders (direct)
more days, less number of binders (indirect)

$$\left.\begin{array}{lr}\text{books} & 900:1,200 \\ \text{days} & 12:10\end{array}\right\} :: 36:x$$

Compounding the ratio,
$(900 \times 12) : (1,200 \times 10) = 36 : x$

$$\Rightarrow \quad x = \frac{1,200 \times 10 \times 36}{900 \times 12} = 40$$

Hence, 40 binders will be required.

2. A's work for one day $= \dfrac{1}{30}$

B's work for one day $= \dfrac{1}{25}$

(A + B)'s work for one day $= \dfrac{1}{30} + \dfrac{1}{25} = \dfrac{11}{150}$

$\therefore$ A and B together can complete the work in
$\dfrac{150}{11}$ days.

3. 100 men can do 100 jobs in days = 100
$\therefore$ 1 man can do 100 jobs in days
$\qquad = 100 \times 100$ days
$\therefore$ 1 man can do 1 job in days

$$= \frac{100 \times 100}{100} \text{ days} = 100 \text{ days.}$$

4. Ajit's one day's work $= \dfrac{1}{4}$

Manoj's one day's work $= \dfrac{1}{6}$

Ravi's one day's work $= \dfrac{1}{12}$

(Ajit + Manoj + Ravi)'s one day's work

$$= \frac{1}{4} + \frac{1}{6} + \frac{1}{12} = \frac{1}{2}$$

$\therefore$ Ajit, Manoj and Ravi together can complete
the work in 2 days.

7. Taps (A + B)'s one minute work

$$= \frac{1}{30} + \frac{1}{45} = \frac{5}{90} = \frac{1}{18}$$

Taps (A + B + C)'s one minute work $= \dfrac{1}{45}$

$\therefore$ Exhaust tap C's one minute work

$$= \frac{1}{45} - \frac{1}{18} = -\frac{1}{10}$$

Thus, tap C can empty $\dfrac{1}{10}$ th of tank in 1 minute.

Tap C can empty the full tank in 10 minute.

9.

	A	B	A + B
Efficiency	100	80	
	5 :	4 :	9
	E_1 :	E_2	
	D_1 :	$D_2 = 24$	

$\therefore \qquad D_1 E_1 = D_2 E_2$

$\Rightarrow \qquad 4 \times D_1 = 9 \times 24$

$\therefore \qquad D_1 = \dfrac{9 \times 24}{4} = 54$ days.

10. Let A completes this work in x days.
Then B completes this work in $(x + 9)$ days.

	A	B
Efficiency	2 :	1
Days	x :	$x + 9$

$\Rightarrow \qquad 2 : 1 :: x + 9 : x$

$\Rightarrow \qquad 2 \times x = (x + 9) : x$

$\qquad \qquad 2 \times x = (x + 9) \times 1$

$\qquad \qquad 2x = x + 9 \qquad \therefore x = 9.$

11. 3 men's work = 6 boy's work
$\therefore$ 6 men's work = 12 boy's work
6 men's + 8 boy's work = (12 + 8) boy's work
$\qquad\qquad\qquad$ *i.e.*, 20 boy's work
Now, 6 boys can do the work in 20 days.

$\therefore$ 20 boys can do the work in $\dfrac{20 \times 6}{20}$ days

i.e., 6 days
$\therefore$ 20 boys can do twice the work in 12 days.
Thus, 6 men and 8 boys finish twice the work
in 12 days.

12. $\quad (6B + 4G) \times 5 = 10B \times 5$
$\qquad\qquad 6B + 4G = 10B$
$\qquad\qquad 4B = 4G$ *i.e.*, $1B = 1G$

Thus, the work of 1 boy = The work of 1 girl
The work of 10 boys = The work of 10 girls
Hence the required number of girls = 10.

13.　　　　M : B = 8 : 5 Efficiency

∴　　　M : B = 5 : 8 No. of days

Let the number of days be $5x$ and $8x$. Then

$$\frac{1}{5x}+\frac{1}{8x} = \frac{1}{40}$$

$$\frac{8+5}{40x} = \frac{1}{40} \qquad \therefore \ x = 13$$

Hence the required number of days
$$= 8 \times 13 = 104.$$

14. Formule : $\dfrac{M_1 D_1 H_1}{W_1} = \dfrac{M_2 D_2 H_2}{W_2}$

$$\Rightarrow \qquad \frac{104 \times 30 \times 8}{\dfrac{2}{5}} = \frac{M_2 \times (56-30) \times 9}{\left(1-\dfrac{2}{5}\right)}$$

$$\Rightarrow \qquad M_2 = \frac{3}{5} \times \frac{5}{2} \times \frac{104 \times 30 \times 8}{26 \times 9} = 160$$

Required number of men = 160 – 104 = 56.

15.　　　$M_1 D_1 H_1 = M_2 D_2 H_2$

$\Rightarrow \quad 5 \times 8 \times 7 = (5+2) \times 4 \times H_2$

$$\Rightarrow \qquad H_2 = \frac{5 \times 8 \times 7}{7 \times 4} = 10 \text{ hours.}$$

16. Let A alone finish the remaining job in T days. Then

$$\frac{2}{15}+\frac{2}{10}+\frac{T}{15} = 1$$

$$\Rightarrow \qquad \frac{T}{15} = 1-\left(\frac{2}{15}+\frac{2}{10}\right) = 1-\frac{1}{3} = \frac{2}{3}$$

$$\therefore \qquad T = \frac{2}{3} \times 15 = 10.$$

Hence the required number of days
$$= 2 + 10 = 12.$$

17.　　　$M_1 D_1 = M_2 D_2$

$\Rightarrow \quad M_1 \times 100 = (M_1 - 10) \times 110$

$\Rightarrow \quad 10M_1 = 1100 \qquad \therefore \ M_1 = 110.$

18.　　　$E_1 : E_2 : : D_2 : D_1$

$$D_2 = \frac{E_1 D_1}{E_2} = \frac{5 \times 12}{4} = 15 \text{ hours.}$$

19.

$$\frac{1}{12}-\frac{1}{18} = \frac{1}{T}$$

or

$$\frac{T}{12}-\frac{T}{18} = 1$$

$$\Rightarrow \qquad \frac{3T-2T}{36} = 1$$

$$\therefore \qquad T = 36 \text{ hours.}$$

SPEED, TIME AND DISTANCE

Solved Examples

Example 1: *In how much time will a car cover a distance of 4,500 m with a speed of 45 km/hour?*

Solution:　　Time $= \dfrac{\text{Distance}}{\text{speed}}$

$$= \frac{4.5}{45} = 0.1 \text{ hour (or 6 min.)}$$

$$(\because 4,500 \text{ m} = 4.5 \text{ km})$$

Example 2: *A man travels a certain distance at the rate of 70 km/hour and returns the same point at the rate of 55 km/hour. What is his average speed of journey?*

Solution: Using formula,

$$\text{Average speed} = \frac{2xy}{x+y} = \frac{2 \times 70 \times 55}{70+55}$$

$$= 61.6 \text{ km/hour.}$$

Example 3: *A train 270 m long passes a standing man in 24 sec. What is the speed of the train?*

Solution: Required speed $= \dfrac{270}{24}$ m/sec

$$= \frac{270}{24} \times \frac{18}{5} \text{ km/hour}$$

$$= 40.5 \text{ km/hour.}$$

MULTIPLE CHOICE QUESTIONS

1. A man travels a certain distance at the rate of 10 km per hour and returns the same point at the rate of 15 km per hour. His average rate for the whole journey is:

   A. 12 km/hour
   B. $12\frac{1}{2}$ km/hour
   C. 13 km/hour
   D. None of these

2. Walking at the rate of 4 km an hour, a man covers a distance in 2 hrs. 45 min. Running at a speed of 11 km per hour, the man will cover this much distance in:

   A. $\frac{1}{2}$ hour
   B. 1 hour
   C. $1\frac{3}{4}$ hour
   D. 2 hours

3. If a person takes as much time in running 20 metre as a car takes in covering 50 m; the distance covered by the person during the time car covers 1 km is:
   A. 100 m
   B. 140 m
   C. 400 m
   D. 500 m

4. A motorist travels a distance of 10 km at a speed of 50 km/hour in the onward journey and 60 km/hour while returning. His average speed is:

   A. $54\frac{6}{11}$ km/hr
   B. 55 km/hr
   C. $55\frac{6}{11}$ km/hr
   D. 54 km/hr

5. On a tour a man travels at the rate of 35 km an hour for the first 160 km, then travels the next 160 km at the rate of 45 km an hour. What is the average speed in km per hour for the first 320 km of the tour?

   A. $39\frac{1}{4}$
   B. $39\frac{1}{2}$
   C. $39\frac{1}{16}$
   D. $39\frac{3}{8}$

6. X and Y are 15 km apart. X can walk at the speed of 14 km/hr and Y at the speed of 16 km/hr. They start walking towards each other at 7 a.m. At what time will they meet:
   A. 7.15 a.m.
   B. 7.30 a.m.
   C. 7.45 a.m.
   D. 8.00 a.m.

7. A train 600 metre long is running with a speed of 54 km/hr. In what time will it pass a tunnel 200 metre long?
   A. 48 sec
   B. 50 sec
   C. $53\frac{1}{3}$ sec
   D. $55\frac{1}{4}$ sec

8. A man travels 3/4th of the distance of his journey by bus, 1/6th by rickshaw and 4 km on foot. How many km does he travel in the journey?
   A. 40 km
   B. 46 km
   C. 48 km
   D. 50 km

9. A man walks from his house at an average speed of 5 km/hr and reaches his office 6 minute late. If he walks at an average speed of 6 km/hr he reaches 2 minute early. What is the distance of the office from his house?
   A. 4 km
   B. 4.5 km
   C. 5.0 km
   D. 5.5 km

10. If a man can row 30 km downstream and 18 km upstream, each in 3 hours, what is the speed of boat in still water?
   A. 8 km/hr
   B. 10 km/hr
   C. 12 km/hr
   D. 15 km/hr

ANSWERS

1	2	3	4	5	6	7	8	9	10
A	B	C	A	D	B	C	C	A	A

SOME SELECTED EXPLANATORY ANSWERS

1. Using formula,

$$\text{Average speed} = \left(\frac{2 \times 10 \times 15}{10 + 15}\right) \text{km/hr}$$

$$= 12 \text{ km/hr}$$

2. 2 hours 45 min. $= 2\dfrac{3}{4}$ hours $= \dfrac{11}{4}$ hours

Distance covered by man = speed × time

$$= 4 \times \frac{11}{4} = 11 \text{ km}$$

So, the time taken by man to cover 11 km distance when speed in 11 km/hr. is

$$= \frac{11}{11} = 1 \text{ hour}$$

3. Clearly, $20 : 50 = x : 1,000$, x being the distance covered the person.

So, $\qquad x = \dfrac{20}{50} \times 1,000 = 400 \text{ m}$

4. Using formula,

$$\text{Average speed} = \frac{2 \times 50 \times 60}{50 + 60}$$

$$= \frac{6,000}{110} = 54\frac{6}{11} \text{ km/hour}$$

5. Using formula,

$$\text{Average speed} = \frac{2 \times 35 \times 45}{35 + 45}$$

$$= \frac{3,150}{80} = 39\frac{3}{8} \text{ km/hour}$$

6. X and Y are moving towards each other, so their relative speed

$$= (14 + 16) \text{ km/hour}$$
$$= 30 \text{ km/hour}$$

$$\text{Time taken} = \frac{\text{Distance}}{\text{Speed}}$$

$$= \frac{15}{30} \text{ hour} = \frac{1}{2} \text{ hour}$$

Since, they start at 7 a.m., they will meet at 7.30 a.m.

7. Speed of train $= \left(54 \times \dfrac{5}{18}\right) \text{m/sec}$

$$= 15 \text{ m/sec}$$

In passing a tunnel, train will have to cover a distance of $(200 + 600)$ m *i.e.,* 800 m.

$$\therefore \text{ Time it will take to pass} = \frac{800}{15} = 53\frac{1}{3} \text{ sec.}$$

8. Let the total distance be x km. Then,

$$\frac{3}{4}x + \frac{1}{6}x + 4 = x$$

$$\Rightarrow \qquad \frac{9x + 2x + 48}{12} = x$$

$$\Rightarrow \qquad 11x + 48 = 12x \qquad \therefore \quad x = 48 \text{ km}$$

9. Let the distance of office from the house be x km.

Difference of two timings $= 6 + 2 = 8$ min.

$$= \frac{8}{60} \text{ hour} = \frac{2}{15} \text{ hour}$$

Then, $\qquad \dfrac{x}{5} - \dfrac{x}{6} = \dfrac{2}{15}$

$$\Rightarrow \qquad \frac{6x - 5x}{30} = \frac{2}{15}$$

$$\therefore \qquad x = \frac{2 \times 30}{15} = 4 \text{ km}$$

10. Let speed of boat $= x$ km/hr
and speed of stream $= y$ km/hr

Then, $\qquad \dfrac{30}{x + y} = 3$

and $\qquad \dfrac{18}{x - y} = 3$

$$\Rightarrow \qquad 3x + 3y = 30 \qquad\qquad ...(i)$$
$$\text{and} \qquad 3x - 3y = 18 \qquad\qquad ...(ii)$$

Adding (i) and (ii),

$$6x = 48 \quad \therefore \ x = 8$$

$\therefore$ Speed of boat in still water is 8 km/hr.

PERCENTAGE

Solved Examples

Example 1: *35% of a number is 315. What is the number?*

Solution: Let the number be x. Then,

$$35\% \text{ of } x = 315$$

or

$$\frac{35}{100}x = 315$$

$$\therefore \quad x = \frac{315 \times 100}{35} = 900$$

Thus, the required number is 900.

Example 2: *Mohan spent 20% of his income on food, 30% on house rent and 25% on clothes. If he saved ₹ 750, then find his income.*

Solution:

$$750 = I\left(1 - \frac{20 + 30 + 25}{100}\right)$$

$$= \frac{I[100 - (20 + 30 + 25)]}{100}$$

$$\Rightarrow \quad I = \frac{750 \times 100}{100 - 75}$$

$$= 750 \times \frac{100}{25} = ₹\ 3{,}000$$

Example 3: *Rakesh spends 20% on food, 25% of the rest on education and 10% of the remaining on house rent. If still he has ₹ 120 with him, find his income.*

Solution: Formula:

$$\text{Income} = \frac{\text{Saving} \times 100 \times 100 \times 100}{(100 - 20)(100 - 25)(100 - 10)}$$

$$= \frac{120 \times 100 \times 100 \times 100}{80 \times 75 \times 90}$$

$$= ₹\ \frac{20{,}000}{9} = ₹\ 2{,}222.22$$

MULTIPLE CHOICE QUESTIONS

1. What percent is 25 paise of ₹ 100?
   A. 250%
   B. 25%
   C. 2.5%
   D. 0.25%

2. In a co-educational school 35% of the students are boys. If there are 416 girls in the school, the number of boys in the school is:
   A. 220
   B. 224
   C. 228
   D. 230

3. In an examination a candidate has to secure 40% of the marks to pass. If a candidate secures 190 marks and fails by 10 marks, the total number of marks in the examination is:
   A. 600
   B. 500
   C. 400
   D. 360

4. If Ram's salary is 50% more than Shyam's, how much percent is Shyam's salary less than Ram's salary?

   A. 33.5%
   B. $33\frac{1}{3}\%$
   C. 50%
   D. 15%

5. Surinder appears in an examination, in which a student has to secure 36% of the marks to pass. If he secures 198 marks and fails by 18 marks, find the total marks in examination:
   A. 800
   B. 600
   C. 700
   D. 900

6. If 2 litre of water are evaporated on boiling 8 litre of sugar solution containing 6% of sugar, the % of sugar in the remaining solution is:
   A. 0.6%
   B. 0.8%
   C. 6%
   D. 8%

7. The population of a city is 15,00,000. It increases by 10% during 1st year, decreases by 20% in 2nd year and increases by 30% in the 3rd year. The population after 3 years is:
   A. 17,16,000
   B. 17,50,000
   C. 16,50,000
   D. 16,00,000

8. A man spends 80% of his income. His income is increased by 20% and his expenditure is

also increased by 15%. What is the % increase/decrease in his savings?

A. 40% increase
B. 10% decrease
C. 5% increase
D. 20% decrease

9. If the price of sugar is increased by 1%, what percentage should be the reduction in the consumption so that there is no extra expenditure:

A. 1%
B. 10%
C. $\dfrac{101}{100}\%$
D. $\dfrac{100}{101}\%$

10. The ratio of boys and girls in a school is 3 : 2. 20% boys and 25% girls get scholarship. How many students do not get scholarship?

A. 22%
B. 40%
C. 60%
D. 78%

ANSWERS

1	2	3	4	5	6	7	8	9	10
B	B	B	B	B	D	A	A	D	D

SOME SELECTED EXPLANATORY ANSWERS

1. Required % = $\dfrac{25}{100} \times 100$ = 25%

2. Let the total number of students = x

% of boys = 35,

∴ % of girls = 100 − 35 = 65%

So, 65% of x = 416

or $\dfrac{65}{100} \times x$ = 416

∴ $x = \dfrac{416 \times 100}{65}$ = 640

Hence, no. of boys = 35% of 640

$= \dfrac{35}{100} \times 640$ = 224

3. Let the total marks in the examination = x

Pass marks = 190 + 10 = 200

So, 40% of x = 200

or $\dfrac{40}{100} \times x$ = 200

∴ $x = \dfrac{200 \times 100}{40}$ = 500

4. Let Ram's salary = ₹ 100

Then,

Shyam's salary = ₹ 100 + 50% of 100

$= ₹100 + \dfrac{50}{100} \times 100 = ₹ 150$

∴ Ram's salary is ₹ 50 less from Shyam's salary.

Required percentage = $\dfrac{50}{150} \times 100 = 33\dfrac{1}{3}\%$

6. Sugar in 8 litre of solution = sugar in (8 − 2) *i.e.,* 6 litre of solution

So, 6% of 8 = x% of 6

or $\dfrac{6}{100} \times 8 = \dfrac{x}{100} \times 6$

∴ $x = \dfrac{6 \times 8}{6}$ = 8%

7. Required population

$= \dfrac{15,00,000 \times (100 + 10)(100 - 20)(100 + 30)}{100 \times 100 \times 100}$

= 17,16,000

8. Let the monthly income be ₹ 100. Then, the man spends ₹ 80 and saves ₹ 20.

His increased income = ₹ 120

His increased expenditure = ₹ 80 + 15% of ₹ 80

$= ₹ 80 + ₹\dfrac{15}{100} \times 80 = ₹ 92$

New savings = ₹ 120 − ₹ 92 = ₹ 28

% increase in savings = $\dfrac{28 - 20}{20} \times 100 = 40\%$

10. Let number of boys = $3x$ and number of girls = $2x$

Total number of students = $3x + 2x = 5x$

Students who get scholarship

$$= \frac{3x \times 20}{100} + \frac{2x \times 25}{100} = \frac{110x}{100} = \frac{11x}{10}$$

Number of students who do not get scholarship

$$= 5x - \frac{11x}{10} = \frac{39x}{10}$$

$\therefore$ Required Percentage $= \dfrac{39x}{10} \times \dfrac{1}{5x} \times 100 = 78$

Alternative Method:

Let the number of students be 100. Then

B	:	G	Total
3	:	2	5
$\downarrow \times 20$		$\downarrow \times 20$	$\downarrow \times 20$

Note : 20% of 60 + 25% of 40

$$= 12 + 10 = 22$$

$\therefore$ Required percentage $= 100 - 22 = 78$

PROFIT AND LOSS

Solved Examples

Example 1: *A person buys an article at $\dfrac{3}{4}$ of its value and sells it for 20% more than its value. What is his gain %?*

Solution: Let the value of the article $= ₹\ x$

$\therefore$ The person buys it for $₹\dfrac{3}{4}x$

and sells it for $₹\ (x + 20\%\ \text{of}\ x)$

i.e., $\left(x + \dfrac{20}{100}x\right) = ₹\dfrac{6x}{5}$

$$\text{Gain} = \frac{6}{5}x - \frac{3}{4}x = \frac{24x - 15x}{20} = \frac{9}{20}x$$

$$\text{Gain \%} = \frac{\dfrac{9}{20}x}{\dfrac{3}{4}x} \times 100 = 60\%$$

Example 2: *Manu buys a radio at 20% discount of its value and sells it for 20% more than its value. What will be his profit %?*

Solution: Let List price of radio be $₹\ x$.

C.P. of radio $= ₹\ (x - 20\%\ \text{of}\ x)$

$$= ₹\left(x - \frac{x}{5}\right) = ₹\frac{4}{5}x$$

S.P. of radio $= ₹\ (x + 20\%\ \text{of}\ x)$

$$= ₹\left(x + \frac{x}{5}\right) = \frac{6}{5}x$$

$$\text{Profit} = \frac{6}{5}x - \frac{4}{5}x = \frac{2}{5}x$$

$$\text{Profit\%} = \frac{\dfrac{2}{5}x}{\dfrac{4}{5}x} \times 100 = 50\%$$

MULTIPLE CHOICE QUESTIONS

1. Surabhi sold a washing machine for ₹ 9,499 at a gain of 15%. Find the cost price of the washing machine:

   A. ₹ 8,000
   B. ₹ 8,100
   C. ₹ 8,260
   D. ₹ 8,300

2. A fruit seller buys mangoes at the rate of 15 for ₹ 12 and sells them at the rate of ₹ 15 per dozen. Find his gain %:

   A. 25.65%
   B. 32.25%
   C. 51.35%
   D. 56.25%

3. Raj Kumar sold 2 calculators for ₹ 990 each. On one calculator he gained 10% and on the other he lost 10%; find his gain or loss in the transaction:

   A. no loss-no gain
   B. 1% gain
   C. 1% loss
   D. 5% loss

4. Mickey sells an article to Minnie at a profit of 20% and Minnie sells it to Meha at a profit of 25%. If Meha pays ₹ 450 for it, the cost price for Mickey is:

A. ₹ 300	B. ₹ 325
C. ₹ 350	D. ₹ 375

5. A shopkeeper buys 2 varieties of rice, one costing him ₹ 26 per kg and another ₹ 30.50 per kg. He mixes them in the ratio of 3 : 4 and this blended variety of rice is sold off at rate of ₹ 30 per kg. Gain % is:

A. 2%	B. 3%
C. 4%	D. 5%

6. Mudit purchases 5 shirts and 10 trousers for ₹ 5,000. He sells the shirts at 15% profit and trousers at 10% loss. Thus he gets ₹ 375 as profit. The cost of one shirt is:

A. ₹ 650	B. ₹ 675
C. ₹ 700	D. ₹ 725

7. Shobit marks his goods 25% above cost price, but allows 17.5% discount for cash payment. If he sells the article for ₹ 825, find the cost price of the article:

A. ₹ 800	B. ₹ 810
C. ₹ 820	D. ₹ 823

8. The selling price of two cows is ₹ 500 each. There is a gain of 20% on one and a loss of 10% on the other. Total gain or loss is:

A. $1\frac{5}{9}\%$	B. $3\frac{4}{5}\%$
C. 1.44%	D. $2\frac{6}{7}\%$

9. By selling an article in ₹ 480, the loss is 20%. The selling price for gaining 20% is:

A. ₹ 720	B. ₹ 600
C. ₹ 620	D. ₹ 700

10. Mohan sells a radio at 10% profit. If the purchasing price would be 10% less and selling price ₹ 132 less, then there is a loss of 10% to him. The purchasing price of the radio is:

A. ₹ 264	B. ₹ 728
C. ₹ 1,200	D. ₹ 2,100

ANSWERS

1	2	3	4	5	6	7	8	9	10
C	D	C	A	D	C	A	D	A	C

SOME SELECTED EXPLANATORY ANSWERS

1. Cost Price $= ₹\dfrac{100}{100+15}\times 9,499 = ₹ 8,260$

2. C.P. of 15 mangoes $= ₹ 12$

$\therefore$ C.P. of 1 mango $= ₹\dfrac{12}{15}$

$\therefore$ C.P. of 12 mangoes $= ₹\dfrac{12}{15}\times 12 = ₹\dfrac{48}{5}$

$$= ₹ 9.60$$

Given, S.P. of 12 mangoes $= ₹ 15$

$$\text{Gain} = ₹\left(15-\dfrac{48}{5}\right) = ₹\dfrac{27}{5} = ₹ 5.40$$

$$\text{Gain\%} = \dfrac{5.40}{9.60}\times 100 = 56.25\%$$

3. $\text{Loss\%} = \left(\dfrac{\text{Common loss and gain}}{10}\right)^2 = \left(\dfrac{10}{10}\right)^2 = 1$

4. Cost Price for Mickey $= ₹ 450\times\dfrac{100}{120}\times\dfrac{100}{125}$

$$= ₹ 300$$

Another Method:

Since it is a case of successive profit,

resultant profit $= x+y+\dfrac{xy}{100}$,

formula for $x\%$ and $y\%$ profit

$$= 20+25+\dfrac{20\times 25}{100} = 50\%$$

$\therefore$ C.P. $= ₹ 450\times\dfrac{100}{150} = ₹ 300$

5. Let the shopkeeper boys 3 kg of the 1st variety and 4 kg of the 2nd variety of rice.

C.P. of 3 kg of rice at the rate ₹ 26 per kg

$$= ₹ 26\times 3 = ₹ 78$$

C.P. of 4 kg of rice at the rate of ₹ 30.50 per kg
$$= ₹\ 30.50 \times 4 = ₹\ 122$$
∴ C.P. of 7 kg of rice = ₹ 78 + ₹ 122 = ₹ 200
S.P. of 7 kg of rice = ₹ 30 × 7 = ₹ 210
Gain = ₹ 210 – ₹ 200 = ₹ 10

∴ Gain % = $\dfrac{10}{200} \times 100 = 5\%$

6. Let the cost of one shirt be ₹ x.
Then, total S.P.

$$= 5x\left(\frac{115}{100}\right) + (5{,}000 - 5x)\left(\frac{90}{100}\right)$$

$$= 5{,}375 \text{ (given)}$$

$$\Rightarrow\quad 5\frac{3}{4}x + 4{,}500 - 4\frac{1}{2}x = 5{,}375$$

$$\Rightarrow\quad \frac{5}{4}x = 875 \quad \therefore\ x = 700$$

∴ Cost of one shirt = ₹ 700.

7. Market Price = $₹\,825 \times \dfrac{100}{100 - 17.5}$

$$= ₹\ 825 \times \frac{100}{82.5} = ₹\ 1000$$

$$\text{C.P.} = ₹\ 1000 \times \frac{100}{100 + 25} = ₹\ 800$$

8. Percentage gain or loss = $\dfrac{100(P - L) - 2PL}{200 + P - L}$

$$= \frac{100(20 - 10) - 2 \times 20 \times 10}{200 + 20 - 10}$$

$$= \frac{1{,}000 - 400}{210} = \frac{600}{210} = \frac{20}{7} \text{ positive}$$

∴ Total percentage gain = $\dfrac{20}{7}\%$ or $2\dfrac{6}{7}\%$

9. 100 – 20 = 80
When SP ₹ 80 then CP = ₹ 100

When SP ₹ 480 then CP = $\dfrac{100}{80} \times 480 = ₹\ 600$

Again 100 + 20 = ₹ 120
When CP ₹ 100 then SP ₹ 120

When CP ₹ 600 then SP = $\dfrac{120}{100} \times 600 = ₹\ 720$

∴ SP = ₹ 720

10. Let purchasing price be ₹ 100.
Then selling price = ₹ 100 + 10 = ₹ 110
New purchasing price = 100 – 10 = ₹ 90

and new selling price = $90\left(1 + \dfrac{10}{100}\right)$

$$= 90 \times \frac{11}{10} = ₹\ 99$$

Difference in the two selling prices
$$= 110 - 99 = ₹\ 11$$
When difference is ₹ 11, then P.P. = ₹ 100
When difference is ₹ 132, then P.P.

$$= \frac{100}{11} \times 132 = ₹\ 1{,}200$$

RATIO, PROPORTION AND VARIATION

MULTIPLE CHOICE QUESTIONS

1. What should be added to each of the numbers 12, 30, 40 and 86, so that they are in proportion:
A. 6
B. 4
C. – 6
D. – 4

2. The mean proportional to $6 + \sqrt{27}$ and $6 - \sqrt{27}$ is:
A. 3
B. 9
C. 10
D. $\sqrt{10}$

3. If $x : y = 9 : 11$, the value of $\dfrac{5x + 3y}{3x + 5y}$ is:
A. 45 : 55
B. 18 : 22
C. 37 : 41
D. 39 : 41

4. The ratio of males and females of a village is 5 : 3. If there are 800 males in the village, females are :

A. 240   B. 480
C. 840   D. 488

5. In a mixture of 60 litre, the ratio of ethanol to ether is 4 : 1. How much ether must be added to the mixture to make this ratio 2 : 1?

A. 10 litre   B. 12 litre
C. 18 litre   D. 24 litre

6. A mixture of 45 litre of spirit and water, contains 20% of water in it. How much water must be added to it make the water 25% in the new mixture?

A. 5 litre   B. 3 litre
C. 4 litre   D. 6 litre

ANSWERS

1	2	3	4	5	6
A	A	D	B	B	B

SOME SELECTED EXPLANATORY ANSWERS

1. Let x be added to each of the numbers. Then,

$(12 + x) : (30 + x) : : (40 + x) : (86 + x)$

$\Rightarrow (86 + x)(12 + x) = (30 + x)(40 + x)$

$\Rightarrow 1{,}032 + 86x + 12x + x^2$

$\qquad\qquad = 1{,}200 + 30x + 40x + x^2$

$\Rightarrow \qquad 28x = 168 \;\therefore\; x = 6$

2. Mean proportion $= \sqrt{(6 + \sqrt{27})(6 - \sqrt{27})}$

$\qquad\qquad = \sqrt{36 - 27} = \sqrt{9} = 3$

3. $\dfrac{5x + 3y}{3x + 5y} = \dfrac{5\left(\dfrac{x}{y}\right) + 3}{3\left(\dfrac{x}{y}\right) + 5}$, dividing both num.

and denom. by y

$= \dfrac{5\left(\dfrac{9}{11}\right) + 3}{3\left(\dfrac{9}{11}\right) + 5}, = \dfrac{\dfrac{45 + 33}{11}}{\dfrac{27 + 55}{11}} = \dfrac{78}{82} = \dfrac{39}{41}$

4. $5 : 3 = 800 : x$, where x represent females of the village.

$\therefore \qquad x = \dfrac{800 \times 3}{5} = 480$

5. Quantity of ethanol in the mixture

$\qquad\qquad = \dfrac{4}{5} \times 60 = 48$ litre

Quantity of ether in the mixture

$\qquad\qquad = \dfrac{1}{5} \times 60 = 12$ litre

Let x litre of ether be added to mixture to get the desired ratio. Then,

$\qquad \dfrac{48}{12 + x} = \dfrac{2}{1} \Rightarrow 24 + 2x = 48$

$\Rightarrow \qquad\qquad 2x = 24 \qquad\qquad \therefore\; x = 12$

$\therefore$ 12 litre of ether is to be added.

6. Quantity of water in the mixture

$\qquad\qquad = \dfrac{20}{100} \times 45$ litre $= 9$ litre

Quantity of spirit in the mixture

$\qquad\qquad = \dfrac{80}{100} \times 45$ litre $= 36$ litre

Let x litre of water be added to make the water 25% in the new mixture. Then,

$\qquad \dfrac{9 + x}{36} = \dfrac{25}{75} \quad \therefore\; x = 3$ litre

INTEREST

Solved Examples

Example 1: *What sum of money will produce ₹ 2,430 interest in 3 years at 3% simple interest?*

Solution: We have,

$$\text{S.I.} = \frac{\text{PRT}}{100}$$

Here, S.I. = ₹ 2,430, R = 3%, T = 3 years

So, $P = \dfrac{\text{SI} \times 100}{\text{R} \times \text{T}} = ₹\dfrac{2,430 \times 100}{3 \times 3} = ₹\,27,000$

Example 2: *In what time does a money becomes double at simple interest rate of 5% per annum?*

Solution: Let the money be ₹ 100.

After T years, it becomes ₹ 200, so interest = ₹ 100

$$\therefore \text{ Time, } \quad \text{T} = \frac{100 \times (\text{S.I.})}{\text{Principal} \times \text{Rate}} = \frac{100 \times (100)}{100 \times 5}$$

$$= 20 \text{ years}$$

Example 3: *A sum of ₹ 300 amounts to ₹ 420 in 4 years. What will it amount to if rate of interest is increased by 2%?*

Solution: Rate of interest before increase

$$= \frac{100 \times 120}{300 \times 4} = 10\%$$

∴ New rate of interest = 12%

S.I. with new rate of interest

$$= \frac{300 \times 12 \times 4}{100} = ₹\,144$$

Amount = ₹ 300 + ₹ 144 = ₹ 444

Example 4: *What annual instalment will discharge a debt of ₹ 1,326 due in 4 years at 7% simple interest?*

Solution: Let the annual payment be ₹ x. Then,

Amount of x for 3 years $= x + \dfrac{x \times 7 \times 3}{100}$

Amount of x for 2 years $= x + \dfrac{x \times 7 \times 2}{100}$

Amount of x for 1 year $= x + \dfrac{x \times 7 \times 1}{100}$

The three payments along with last payment of ₹ x will discharge the debt.

According to question,

$$\left(x + \frac{21x}{100}\right) + \left(x + \frac{14x}{100}\right) + \left(x + \frac{7x}{100}\right) + x = 1,326$$

or $442x = 1,32,600$

∴ $x = 300$

Hence, annual payment = ₹ 300

Example 5: *Find the compound interest on ₹ 8,000 at the rate of 5% p.a. for 2 years.*

Solution: Amount $= ₹\left[8,000 \times \left(1 + \dfrac{5}{100}\right)^2\right]$

∴ Amount $= ₹\left[8,000 \times \dfrac{21}{20} \times \dfrac{21}{20}\right]$

$$= ₹\,8,820$$

Compound interest = ₹ 8,820 – ₹ 8,000 = ₹ 820

MULTIPLE CHOICE QUESTIONS

1. In how many years will a sum of ₹ 1,500 yield an interest of ₹ 1,080 at 12 per cent per annum?

A. 5 years   B. $5\dfrac{1}{4}$ years

C. $5\dfrac{1}{2}$ years   D. 6 years

2. The principal which yields an interest of ₹ 2,500 in $2\dfrac{1}{2}$ years at 10% per annum at simple interest is:

A. ₹ 8,000   B. ₹ 9,000

C. ₹ 10,000   D. ₹ 11,000

3. A sum of ₹ 7,800 is lent out in 2 parts in such a way that the interest on one part at 10% for 5 years is equal to that on the other part at 9% for 6 years. The sum lent out at 10% is:

A. ₹ 4,050   B. ₹ 3,750

C. ₹ 4,500   D. ₹ 3,300

4. The simple interest on a sum of money is $\dfrac{1}{16}$ of the principal and the number of years is equal to the rate percent per annum. The rate percent per annum is:

A. $2\dfrac{1}{2}\%$ B. $2\dfrac{1}{3}\%$

C. $2\dfrac{1}{6}\%$ D. $6\dfrac{1}{4}\%$

5. What is the compound interest on ₹ 6,250 at 4% p.a. compounded annually for 3 years?
A. ₹ 780.40
B. ₹ 789.00
C. ₹ 788.80
D. ₹ 780.40

6. At what rate percent compound interest ₹ 800 amounts to ₹ 926.10 in $1\dfrac{1}{2}$ years interest compounded semi-annually?
A. 8% p.a.   B. 10% p.a.
C. 12% p.a.   D. 14% p.a.

7. A sum of money doubles itself at compound interest, compounded annually in 15 years. In how many years will it become 8 times, the remaining rate the same?
A. 40 years   B. 45 years
C. 50 years   D. 55 years

8. A loan ₹ 50,440 at 5% compound interest is to be paid in three equal annual instalments. What will be the amount of each annual instalment?
A. ₹ 18,522   B. ₹ 2,089
C. ₹ 2,689   D. ₹ 9,522

ANSWERS

1	2	3	4	5	6	7	8
D	C	A	A	D	B	B	A

SOME SELECTED EXPLANATORY ANSWERS

1. Here, P = ₹ 1,500; R = 12%; S.I. = ₹ 1,080

$$\text{Time, T} = \frac{₹\,1,080 \times 100}{₹\,1,500 \times 12} = 6 \text{ years}$$

3.
$$\frac{\text{I part} \times 5 \times 10}{100} = \frac{\text{II part} \times 9 \times 6}{100}$$

or
$$\frac{\text{I part}}{\text{II part}} = \frac{9 \times 6}{5 \times 10} = \frac{27}{25}$$

$\therefore$ $\text{I part} = \dfrac{7,800}{27+25} \times 27 = ₹\,4,050$

and   II part = ₹ 7,800 − ₹ 4,050 = ₹ 3,750

4. Time = R years, P = the sum in ₹

$$\frac{P}{16} = \frac{P \times R \times R}{100}$$

or
$$R^2 = \frac{100}{16}$$

or
$$R = \frac{10}{4} = 2\frac{1}{2}\% \text{ p.a.}$$

5. $\text{Amount} = ₹\,6,250 \times \left(1 + \dfrac{4}{100}\right)^3$

$$= ₹\,6,250 \times \left(\frac{26}{25}\right)^3$$

$$= ₹\,7,030.40$$

$\therefore$ Compound Interest
$$= ₹\,7,030.40 - ₹\,6,250$$
$$= ₹\,780.40$$

8. Let the annual instalment be ₹ a. Then,

$$a\left[\left(\frac{100}{100+5}\right) + \left(\frac{100}{100+5}\right)^2 + \left(\frac{100}{100+5}\right)^3\right] = 50,440$$

$$\Rightarrow a\left[\frac{100}{105}\left\{1 + \frac{100}{105} + \left(\frac{100}{105}\right)^2\right\}\right] = 50,440$$

$$\Rightarrow \qquad a = ₹\,18,522$$

DISCOUNT

MULTIPLE CHOICE QUESTIONS

1. A suitcase of ₹ 240 is sold for ₹ 202. The rate of discount is:

   A. $15\dfrac{5}{6}\%$ B. $15\dfrac{5}{8}\%$

   C. $18\dfrac{41}{50}\%$ D. $18\dfrac{5}{8}\%$

2. A merchant allows a discount of 15% on the clothes purchased. Manohar purchases clothes worth ₹ 470. The money he will give is:
   A. ₹ 70.50   B. ₹ 399.50
   C. ₹ 469   D. ₹ 270

3. A trader allows 10% trade discount and 20% cash discount. If the list price is ₹ 500, then selling price is:
   A. ₹ 360   B. ₹ 350
   C. ₹ 355   D. ₹ 340

4. A retailer gains 20% after allowing 10% discount on the cost price. If the cost price is ₹ 100, then selling price is:
   A. ₹ 120   B. ₹ 108
   C. ₹ 95   D. ₹ 115

5. The printed price of an electric fan is ₹ 500. It is sold at 10% discount. But due to change of season the shopkeeper, declares 10% additional discount. The sale price of the fan is:
   A. ₹ 455   B. ₹ 405
   C. ₹ 450   D. ₹ 400

6. The true discount of ₹ 12,100 due to two years, hence at 10% per annum compound interest is:
   A. ₹ 1,000   B. ₹ 1,100
   C. ₹ 2,100   D. ₹ 1,200

ANSWERS

1	2	3	4	5	6
A	B	A	B	B	C

SOME SELECTED EXPLANATORY ANSWERS

1. Amount of Discount

$$= \text{List price} - \text{Selling price}$$
$$= 240 - 202 = ₹\ 38$$

$$\text{Rate of Discount} = \dfrac{\text{Discount} \times 100}{\text{List Price}}$$

$$= \dfrac{38 \times 100}{240} = \dfrac{95}{6}$$

$$= 15\dfrac{5}{6}$$

i.e., $\text{Discount} = 15\dfrac{5}{6}\%$

2.   Cost price $= ₹\ 470$

   Rate of Discount $= 15\%$

$$\text{Amount of Discount} = \dfrac{470 \times 15}{100}$$

$$= \dfrac{141}{2}$$

$$= ₹\ 70.50$$

∴   Amount Due $= 470 - 70.50$

$$= ₹\ 399.50$$

3. Selling Price

$$= \text{List price}\left(1 - \dfrac{10}{100}\right)\left(1 - \dfrac{20}{100}\right)$$

$$= 500 \times \dfrac{9}{10} \times \dfrac{4}{5} = ₹\ 360$$

Alternative Method:

List price	500
Less : Trade Discount @ 10%	
$\left(\dfrac{500 \times 10}{100}\right)$	$\dfrac{50}{450}$
Less : Cash Discount @ 20%	
$\left(\dfrac{450 \times 20}{100}\right)$	$\dfrac{90}{360}$

4. Selling Price = Cost Price $\left(1+\dfrac{20}{100}\right)\left(1-\dfrac{10}{100}\right)$

$$= 100\left(1+\dfrac{1}{5}\right)\left(1-\dfrac{1}{10}\right)$$

$$= 100 \times \dfrac{6}{5} \times \dfrac{9}{10} = ₹\ 108$$

5. Sale price = Printed price $\left(1-\dfrac{d_1}{100}\right)\left(1-\dfrac{d_2}{100}\right)$

$$= 500\left(1-\dfrac{10}{100}\right)\left(1-\dfrac{10}{100}\right)$$

$$= 500 \times \dfrac{9}{10} \times \dfrac{9}{10}$$

$$= ₹\ 405$$

6. Present value $= \dfrac{12{,}100}{\left(1+\dfrac{10}{100}\right)^2}$

$$= ₹\ 10{,}000$$

$\therefore$ True Discount $= ₹\ 12{,}100 - ₹\ 10{,}000$

$$= ₹\ 2{,}100$$

AVERAGE

MULTIPLE CHOICE QUESTIONS

1. The heights of 7 buildings are 12 m, 13 m, 14 m, 15 m, 16 m, 17 m and 18 m. The average height of 7 buildings is:

A. 15 m   B. 16 m
C. 17 m   D. 18 m

2. The average height of 10 students is computed as 153 cm. But it was found later on that 151 cm was wrongly read as 141 cm. The correct average height is:

A. 155 cm   B. 154 cm
C. 152 cm   D. 151 cm

3. In a school 85 boys and 35 girls appeared in an examination. The average marks of the boys were found to be 40% whereas the average marks of the girls were 60%. The average marks percentage of the school is:

A. $50\dfrac{3}{5}$ B. 45

C. $45\dfrac{5}{6}$ D. 60

4. If the average of 5 observations x, $x + 2$, $x + 4$, $x + 6$, $x + 8$ is 11, then the average of the last three observations is:

A. 11   B. 13
C. 15   D. 17

5. The average age of 8 persons is 87 years. Of these the age of oldest is 2 years more than the one next. If these two persons are ignored, then the average age of the remaining 6 persons is 85 years. The age of the oldest person is (in years):

A. 90   B. 94
C. 96   D. 98

ANSWERS

1	2	3	4	5
A	B	C	B	B

SOME SELECTED EXPLANATORY ANSWERS

1. Average height

$$= \frac{12+13+14+15+16+17+18}{7}$$

$$= \frac{105}{7} = 15 \text{ m}$$

2. Wrong average $= \overline{x} = 153$ cm

Wrong sum of heights,

$$\Sigma x = n\overline{x} = 10 \times 153 = 1{,}530 \text{ cm}$$

Correct sum of heights

$$\Sigma'x = \Sigma x - 141 + 151$$
$$= 1{,}530 + 10 = 1{,}540 \text{ cm}$$

$\therefore$ Correct average height,

$$\overline{x}' = \frac{\Sigma'x}{n} = \frac{1{,}540}{10} = 154 \text{ cm}$$

3. Let the maximum marks be 100

Then average marks of boys = 40

and average marks of girls = 60

$\therefore$ Required average $= \dfrac{85 \times 40 + 35 \times 60}{85 + 35}$

$$= \frac{3{,}400 + 2{,}100}{120}$$

$$= \frac{5{,}500}{120} = 45\frac{5}{6}$$

4. $\overline{x} = \dfrac{x+(x+2)+(x+4)+(x+6)+(x+8)}{5} = 11$

$\Rightarrow \qquad 5x + 20 = 11 \times 5 = 55$

$\therefore \qquad x = \dfrac{55-20}{5} = \dfrac{35}{5} = 7$

This average of the last three numbers

$$= \frac{(x+4)+(x+6)+(x+8)}{3}$$

$$= \frac{(7+4)+(7+6)+(7+8)}{3}$$

$$= \frac{11+13+15}{3} = \frac{39}{3} = 13$$

5. Let $x_1, x_2, x_3, x_4, x_5, x_6, x_7, x_8$ be the ages of 8 persons where x_8 is the age of the oldest person.

Thus, total of ages of the 8 persons

$$= 8 \times 87 = 696$$

Total of ages of the 6 persons

$$= 6 \times 85 = 510$$

$\therefore \qquad x_7 + x_8 = 696 - 510 = 186 \qquad ...(i)$

But $\qquad x_8 - x_7 = 2$ (given) $\qquad\qquad ...(ii)$

Adding these two equations

$$2x_8 = 188$$

$\therefore \qquad x_8 = \dfrac{188}{2} = 94$ years

PARTNERSHIP

MULTIPLE CHOICE QUESTIONS

1. A, B and C share the profit in the ratio of 3 : 5 : 7. If the gain is ₹ 2,040, then C's share is :

A. ₹ 360

B. ₹ 600

C. ₹ 840

D. ₹ 120

2. Mishra, Sharma and Shukla started a business with ₹ 47,000. Mishra puts ₹ 5,000 more than Sharma and Sharma ₹ 3,000 more than Shukla. The share of Mishra out of the profit of ₹ 14,100 will be:

A. ₹ 3,600   B. ₹ 4,500

C. ₹ 6,000   D. ₹ 6,300

3. A, B and C are three partners in a business.

The profit share of A is $\dfrac{3}{16}$ of the profit and

B's share is $\dfrac{1}{4}$ of the profit. If C receives ₹ 243, then the amount received by B will be:

A. ₹ 90   B. ₹ 96
C. ₹ 108   D. ₹ 120

4. A starts a business with ₹ 5,000. After 4 months B joins him with a sum of ₹ 4,000. In the end of the year there is a profit of ₹ 8,970. The share of A in the profit will be:

A. ₹ 3,120   B. ₹ 4,020
C. ₹ 5,850   D. ₹ 6,360

5. A, B and C share the profit in the ratio of 2 : 3 : 7. If the average gain is ₹ 8,000, then B's share is:

A. ₹ 2,000   B. ₹ 1,000
C. ₹ 1,500   D. ₹ 3,000

ANSWERS

1	2	3	4	5
C	C	C	C	A

SOME SELECTED EXPLANATORY ANSWERS

1. C's share $= \dfrac{7}{3+5+7} \times 2,040 = ₹\ 840$

2. Let Shukla's capital $= ₹\ x$

Then Sharma's capital $= ₹\ (x + 3,000)$

and Mishra capital $= ₹\ (x + 3,000 + 5,000)$

$\Rightarrow x + (x + 3,000) + (x + 3,000 + 5,000)$
$$= 47,000$$
$$\Rightarrow \qquad 3x = 47,000 - 11,000$$
$$= 36,000$$
$$\therefore \qquad x = ₹\ 12,000$$

Thus, capitals of Mishra, Sharma and Shukla are:
$$₹\ 20,000;\ ₹\ 15,000;\ ₹\ 12,000$$

$\therefore$ Profit sharing ratio $= 20 : 15 : 12$,
$$\text{Sum} = 47$$

$\therefore \qquad$ Profit of Mishra $= \dfrac{20}{47} \times 14,100$
$$= ₹\ 6,000$$

3. Let the profit be ₹ 1. Then

$$A : B : C = \dfrac{3}{16} : \dfrac{1}{4} : \left[1 - \left(\dfrac{3}{16} + \dfrac{1}{4}\right)\right]$$

$$= \dfrac{3}{16} : \dfrac{1}{4} : \dfrac{9}{16}$$

$$= \dfrac{3}{16} : \dfrac{4}{16} : \dfrac{9}{16}, \ i.e.,\ 3 : 4 : 9$$

When C's share is ₹ 9, then B's share = ₹ 4

When C's share is ₹ 243, then B's share

$$= \dfrac{4 \times 243}{9} = ₹\ 108$$

4. $\qquad ₹\ 5,000 \times 12 = ₹\ 60,000$ for A
$$₹\ 4,000 \times (12 - 4) = ₹\ 32,000 \text{ for B}$$

Ratio of profit sharing $= 60,000 : 32,000$
$$\text{or } 60 : 32 \text{ or } 15 : 8$$

$\therefore$ A's share $= \dfrac{15}{15+8} \times 8,970$

$$= 15 \times 390 = ₹\ 5850$$

5. $\qquad$ B's share $= \dfrac{3}{2+3+7} \times 8,000$

$$= \dfrac{3 \times 8,000}{12}$$

$$= ₹\ 2,000$$

STOCK AND SHARES

MULTIPLE CHOICE QUESTIONS

1. The 6% stock at 125 which can be purchased to get an annual income of ₹ 4,320 will be:
   A. ₹ 24,000
   B. ₹ 48,000
   C. ₹ 36,000
   D. ₹ 72,000

2. The rate of interest obtained by investing in 8% stock at ₹ 160 will be:
   A. $2\frac{1}{2}\%$
   B. 5%
   C. $7\frac{1}{2}\%$
   D. 10%

3. The investment required in "5% stock at 102" to obtain an annual income of ₹ 600 will be:
   A. ₹ 6,120
   B. ₹ 12,240
   C. ₹ 9,120
   D. ₹ 12,000

4. Ramesh holds ₹ 2,100 of 3% stock. He sells them at ₹ 121 and invests the proceeds in 5% stock. Thereby, his income increases by ₹ 14. The market price of 5% stock is:
   A. ₹ 125
   B. ₹ 135
   C. ₹ 155
   D. ₹ 165

5. Mohan invests ₹ 3,467.25 in a company paying 4% per annum when its ₹ 35 shares are selling for ₹ 51.75 each. His annual income will be:
   A. ₹ 93.80
   B. ₹ 39.80
   C. ₹ 98.30
   D. ₹ 39.08

ANSWERS

1	2	3	4	5
D	B	B	D	A

SOME SELECTED EXPLANATORY ANSWERS

1. $\text{Stock} = \dfrac{\text{Income} \times 100}{\text{Rate}}$

   $= \dfrac{4,320 \times 100}{6} = ₹\ 72,000$

2. ∵ On an investment of ₹ 160, interest = ₹ 8
   ∴ On an investment of ₹ 100, interest

   $= \dfrac{8 \times 100}{160} = ₹\ 5$

3. $\text{Investment} = \dfrac{\text{Income} \times \text{Market Value}}{\text{Rate}}$

   $= \dfrac{600 \times 102}{5} = ₹\ 12,240$

4. Income from ₹ 100 stock = ₹ 3

   Income from ₹ 2,100 stock $= \dfrac{3 \times 2,100}{100} = ₹\ 63$

   The income from new stock = 63 + 14 = ₹ 77
   The cost of ₹ 100 stock = ₹ 121

   The cost of ₹ 2,100 stock $= \dfrac{121 \times 2,100}{100}$

   $= ₹\ 2,541$

   When the income is ₹ 77, then cost = ₹ 2,541
   When the income is ₹ 5, then cost

   $= \dfrac{2,541 \times 5}{77} = ₹\ 165$

5. Market value of a share of ₹ 35 = ₹ 51.75
   ∴ No. of such shares purchased by ₹ 3,467.25

   $= \dfrac{3467.25}{51.75} = 67$

   Face value of 67 shares = 35 × 67 = ₹ 2,345
   Hence, divided @ 4% of the face value

   $= 2,345 \times \dfrac{4}{100} = ₹\ 93.80$

PROBLEM ON AGE

Solved Examples

Example 1: *The ratio of ages of Kavya and Neha is 4 : 5. After 12 years, this ratio will become 5 : 6. What will be the age of Kavya after 2 years?*

Solution: Let the age of Kavya be $4x$ years and age of Neha be $5x$ years.

Age of Kavya after 12 years = $(4x + 12)$ years

Age of Neha after 12 years = $(5x + 12)$ years

Hence, $\dfrac{4x+12}{5x+12} = \dfrac{5}{6}$

$\Rightarrow$ $24x + 72 = 25x + 60$ $\therefore x = 12$

Present age of Kavya = $4 \times 12 = 48$ years

Thus, age of Kavya after 2 years

= $48 + 2 = 50$ years

Example 2: *The age of a father is four times the age of his son. If the age of father is x years, find the age of his son after 8 years.*

Solution: Age of the father = x years

$\therefore$ Age of the son = $\dfrac{1}{4}x$ years

$\therefore$ Age of the son after 8 years = $\left(\dfrac{x}{4}+8\right)$ years

MULTIPLE CHOICE QUESTIONS

1. A father's age is four times that of his son. Eight years before, the father's age was sixteen times that of the son. Father's age is:
    A. 40 years   B. 35 years
    C. 42 years   D. 36 years

2. A is older than B by 5 years. Seven years hence, thrice A's age shall be equal to four times that of B. The present age of A is:
    A. 13 years   B. 8 years
    C. 9 years   D. 7 years

3. The ages of Ram and Mohan are in the ratio of 5 : 7 and the difference between them is 12 years. The ages (in years) of Ram and Mohan are respectively:
    A. 30, 42   B. 42, 30
    C. 15, 21   D. 21, 15

4. The ages of A and B are in the ratio of 9 : 4. 7 years hence, the ratio of their ages will be 5 : 3. The age of A is:
    A. 8 years   B. 18 years
    C. 26 years   D. 52 years

5. The ratio between the present ages of X and Y is 4 : 5. The ratio between the present age of X and the age of Y before 3 years is 7 : 8. The ratio between the present age of X and his age after 7 years will be:
    A. 5 : 4   B. 8 : 7
    C. 7 : 8   D. 4 : 5

6. The ratio between Rahim's and Karim's ages two years ago was 3 : 2 and at present it is 7 : 5. The present age of Karim is:
    A. 10 years   B. 14 years
    C. 12 years   D. 16 years

7. The sum of the ages of Ram and Shyam is 40 years. 5 years hence, the ratio of their ages will be 3 : 7. The age of Ram is:
    A. 10 years   B. 30 years
    C. 15 years   D. 25 years

8. The ratio of ages of the mother and her daughter is 12 : 5. The difference of their ages is 28 years. The ratio between the present age of the mother and the age of the daughter 4 years after will be:
    A. 2 : 1   B. 1 : 2
    C. 3 : 2   D. 2 : 3

9. The ratio of present ages of Mahesh and Dinesh is 7 : 8. If 4 years ago the ratio of their ages be 5 : 6, then present age of Dinesh is:
    A. 10 years   B. 12 years
    C. 14 years   D. 16 years

10. Six years back Seema was half that of Rupa in age. Four years hence, the respective ratio of their ages would be 3 : 5. The present age of Rupa is:
    A. 46 years   B. 40 years
    C. 32 years   D. 16 years

26

ANSWERS

1	2	3	4	5	6	7	8	9	10
A	A	A	B	D	A	A	A	D	A

SOME SELECTED EXPLANATORY ANSWERS

1. Let the age of the son = x years
   Then age of the father = $4x$ years
   Before 8 years,
   Son's age = $x - 8$
   Father's age = $4x - 8$
   $$4x - 8 = 16(x - 8)$$
   $\Rightarrow \quad 4x - 8 = 16x - 128$
   $\Rightarrow \quad 12x = 120 \quad \therefore x = 10$
   Thus, father's age = $4 \times 10 = 40$ years

2. Let the age of A be x years
   $\therefore$ the age of B = $(x - 5)$ years
   Seven years hence,
   Age of A = $x + 7$
   Age of B = $(x - 5) + 7$
   $3(x + 7) = 4(x - 5 + 7)$
   $\therefore \quad 3x + 21 = 4x - 20 + 28 = 4x + 8$
   $\Rightarrow \quad 3x + 21 = 4x - 20 + 28 = 4x + 8$
   $\therefore \quad x = 13$

3. Let the ages of Ram and Mohan be $5x$ and $7x$
   Then, $7x - 5x = 12 \Rightarrow 2x = 12 \therefore x = 6$
   Age of Ram = $5 \times 6 = 30$ years
   Age of Mohan = $7 \times 6 = 42$ years

4. Let the ages of A and B be $9x$ and $4x$.
   Then $\dfrac{9x + 7}{4x + 7} = \dfrac{5}{3}$
   $\Rightarrow \quad 3(9x + 7) = 5(4x + 7)$
   $\Rightarrow \quad 27x + 21 = 20x + 35$
   $\Rightarrow \quad 7x = 35 - 21 = 14 \quad \therefore x = 2$
   Hence, age of A = $9 \times 2 = 18$ years.

5. Let the present ages of X and Y be $4x$ and $5x$
   $\therefore \quad \dfrac{4x}{5x - 3} = \dfrac{7}{8}$
   $\Rightarrow \quad 8 \times 4x = 7(5x - 3)$
   $\Rightarrow \quad 32x = 35x - 21$
   $\Rightarrow \quad 3x = 21 \quad \therefore x = 7$
   Thus, age of X = $4 \times 7 = 28$ years
   Age of X after 7 years = $28 + 7 = 35$ years

$\therefore$ Required ratio = $\dfrac{28}{35} = \dfrac{4}{5}$ or $4 : 5$

6. Let the present ages of Rahim and Karim be $7x$ and $5x$.
   Then $\dfrac{7x - 2}{5x - 2} = \dfrac{3}{2}$
   $\Rightarrow \quad 14x - 4 = 15x - 6$
   $\Rightarrow \quad x = 2$
   $\Rightarrow$ The present age of Karim is $5 \times 2 = 10$ years

7. Let the ages of Ram and Shyam 5 years hence be $3x$ and $7x$.
   The sum of their present ages
   $$= (3x - 5) + (7x - 5) = 40$$
   $\Rightarrow \quad 10x = 40 + 10 = 50 \quad \therefore x = 5$
   Hence, age of Ram = $3 \times 5 - 5 = 15 - 5$
   $$= 10 \text{ years.}$$

8. Let the ages of mother and her daughter be $12x$ and $5x$.
   Then, $12x - 5x = 28 \Rightarrow x = \dfrac{28}{7} = 4$
   $\therefore$ Present age of the mother
   $$= 12 \times 4 = 48 \text{ years}$$
   and age of daughter after 4 years
   $$= 5x + 4$$
   $$= 5 \times 4 + 4 = 24$$
   $\therefore$ Required ratio = $\dfrac{48}{24} = \dfrac{2}{1}$, *i.e.*, $2 : 1$

9. Let present ages of Mahesh and Dinesh be $7x$ and $8x$.
   4 years ago,
   Mahesh's age = $7x - 4$
   Dinesh's age = $8x - 4$
   $\therefore \quad \dfrac{7x - 4}{8x - 4} = \dfrac{5}{6}$
   $\Rightarrow \quad 6(7x - 4) = 5(8x - 4)$

$\Rightarrow \qquad 42x - 24 = 40x - 20$

$\Rightarrow \qquad\qquad 2x = 4 \qquad \therefore x = 2$

$\therefore$ Dinesh's present age $= 8 \times 2 = 16$ years.

10. Let the present ages of Seema and Rupa be x and y. Six years back,

Seema's age $= x - 6$

Rupa's age $= y - 6$

$$(x - 6) = \frac{1}{2}(y - 6)$$

or $\qquad 2x - y = 6 \qquad\qquad ...(i)$

Four years hence,

Seema's age $= x + 4$

Rupa's age $= y + 4$

$$\frac{x+4}{y+4} = \frac{3}{5}$$

$5x + 20 = 3y + 12$

$5x - 3y = -8 \qquad\qquad ...(ii)$

Multiply equation (i) by 3,

$\qquad 6x - 3y = 18 \qquad\qquad ...(iii)$

Subtract eq. (iii) from eq. (ii),

$\qquad\qquad x = 26$

Substitute this value of x in (i),

$\qquad\qquad y = 2x - 6 = 2 \times 26 - 6$

$\qquad\qquad\qquad = 52 - 6 = 46.$

ALLIGATION, MIXTURE

MULTIPLE CHOICE QUESTIONS

1. In a mixture of 60 litre, the ratio of ethanol to ether is 4 : 1. The quantity of ether to be added to the mixture to make this ratio 2 : 1 will be:

A. 10 litre   B. 12 litre

C. 18 litre   D. 24 litre

2. The price of a variety of a commodity is ₹ 5 per kg and that of another is ₹ 8 per kg. The ratio in which two varieties should be mixed so that the price is ₹ 7 per kg will be:

A. 1 : 2   B. 2 : 1

C. 3 : 1   D. 8 : 5

3. A confectioner sells the milk after mixing some water in it at the same rate at which he bought. If he gains 25% in this way, the quantity of water mixed with per litre of milk is:

A. 0.25 litre   B. 2.5 litre

C. 1.5 litre   D. 0.35 litre

4. A milk seller bought some milk at the rate of ₹ 16 per litre. He mixed water $\frac{1}{4}$th of it and sold the mixture at the cost price. Assuming the price of water as ₹ 0.00 per litre. The gain % is:

A. 16%

B. 20%

C. 25%

D. None of these

5. Ramesh has ₹ 3,600. He invests a part of it at 3% per annum and the remaining at 5% higher rate of simple interest. He gets in all ₹ 540 at the end of 3 years. The sum invested at 3% per annum is:

A. ₹ 1,440   B. ₹ 2,000

C. ₹ 2,160   D. ₹ 2,200

ANSWERS

1	2	3	4	5
B	A	A	C	C

SOME SELECTED EXPLANATORY ANSWERS

1. The quantity of ethanol $= \dfrac{4}{5} \times 60 = 48$ litre

The quantity of ether $= \dfrac{1}{5} \times 60 = 12$ litre

$\therefore \quad \dfrac{48}{12+x} = \dfrac{2}{1}$

$\Rightarrow \qquad 48 = 2(12 + x)$

$\Rightarrow \qquad 48 = 24 + 2x$

$\Rightarrow \qquad 2x = 48 - 24 = 24$

$\therefore \qquad x = 12$

2.

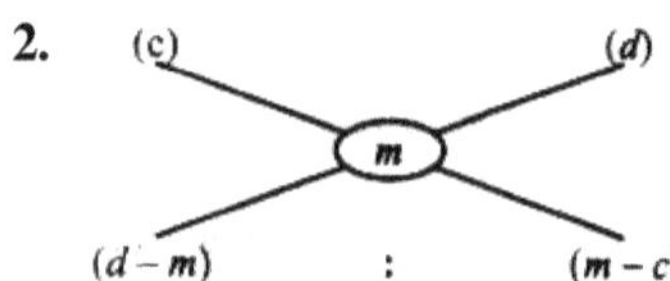

Required ratio $= \dfrac{d-m}{m-c} = \dfrac{\text{cheaper variety}}{\text{dearer variety}}$

$= \dfrac{8-7}{7-5}$

$= \dfrac{1}{2}$ i.e., $1 : 2$

3. Let the cost price of 1 litre milk $= ₹\ 100$
Profit on 1 litre $= ₹\ 25$ ...(1)
Suppose he mixes x litre of water in 1 litre milk.
Then selling price of $(1 + x)$ litre milk
$= (1 + x) \times 100$
and Profit = Selling Price − Cost Price

$= 100\ (1 + x) - 100$
$= 100x$ ...(2)

Comparing (1) and (2),
$100x = 25$

$\therefore \qquad x = ₹\ 0.25$

4. Suppose he bought 1 litre of milk,
Cost price $= ₹\ 16$/litre
Mixture = Milk + Water

$= 1 + \dfrac{1}{4} = \dfrac{5}{4}$

Cost price of the mixture $= ₹\ 16$

Selling price of the mixture $= \dfrac{5}{4} \times 16 = ₹\ 20$

$\therefore \qquad$ Gain % $= \dfrac{20-16}{16} \times 100$

$= \dfrac{4}{16} \times 100 = 25\%$

5. Average rate of interest $= \dfrac{100 \times 540}{3,600 \times 3} = 5$

By Rule of Alligation :

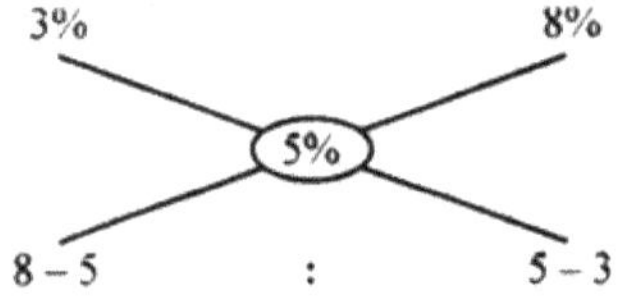

Investment at 3% per annum

$= \dfrac{3}{3+2} \times 3,600 = ₹\ 2,160$

CLOCK AND CALANDER

MULTIPLE CHOICE QUESTIONS

1. How many times the hands of a clock are at right angle in a day?
A. 24
B. 16
C. 44
D. 48

2. At what angle the hands of a clock are inclined at 15 minute past 5?

A. $58\dfrac{1}{2}°$
B. $64°$

C. $67\dfrac{1}{2}°$
D. $72\dfrac{1}{2}°$

3. What angle do the hands of a clock form at 20 past 7?
A. 70° B. 80°
C. 90° D. 100°

4. What will be the time when the hour hand makes an angle of 50° with the minute hand?
A. 1.15 hrs B. 1.20 hrs
C. 1.10 hrs D. 1.25 hrs

5. What is the time when the hands of the clock make an angle of 90° with each other?
A. 3.10 hrs B. 3.30 hrs
C. 3.20 hrs D. 3.25 hrs

6. What angle is formed when the hour hand is at 6.00 and the minute hand is at 12.00?
A. 100° B. 120°
C. 180° D. 90°

7. The angle subtended by the small hand of the clock in 20 minutes will be:
A. 10° B. 15°
C. 20° D. 25°

8. There are 5 Saturday in a month. The first day of the month will be:
A. Sunday B. Friday
C. Wednesday D. Monday

9. The first day of a year is Sunday what day of the week lies on the first day of the next year?
A. Saturday B. Friday
C. Monday D. Thursday

10. December 3, 1990 is Sunday; what day of the week will fall on Jan. 3, 1991?
A. Tuesday B. Wednesday
C. Thursday D. Friday

11. If 7th day of a month is a 3 days before Friday, then the 19th day of the same month will be:
A. Sunday B. Monday
C. Wednesday D. Friday

ANSWERS

1	2	3	4	5	6	7	8	9	10
C	C	D	A	B	C	A	B	C	B

11
A

SOME SELECTED EXPLANATORY ANSWERS

1. It is clear from the properties of the clock that both hands of a clock are at right angle twice in every hour, except at 3.00 o'clock and 9.00 o'clock. At 3.00 o'clock and 9.00 o'clock the positions are identical. So, they are at right angle 22 times in 12 hrs. Thus, in 24 hrs they are $22 \times 2 = 44$ times at right angles.

2. Whan the minute hand is at 3 and hour hand is slightly ahead of 5, only then the time is 15 past 3. The angle through which the four hand shifts in 15 minute $= 15 \times \dfrac{1}{2}° = 7\dfrac{1}{2}°$

Hence, angle at 15 minute past 5

$$= 60 + 7\dfrac{1}{2}° = 67\dfrac{1}{2}°$$

3. The hands of a clock form an angle of 100° at 20 past 7.

4. When the hour hand makes an angle of 50°, the time is 1.15 hrs.

5. The time is 3.30 hrs, when the hands make an angle of 90°.

6. An angle of 180° is formed when the hour hand is at 6.00 and the minute hand is at 12.00.

7. The small hand of the clock rotates 0.5° in one minute.

Hence, required angle $= 20 \times 0.5° = 10°$.

8. In a month of 31 days, there are 4 weeks + 3 days.

The three days may be

Thursday, Friday, Saturday

Friday, Saturday, Sunday

Saturday, Monday, Tuesday

The first day of the week may be

Thursday, *Friday* or Saturday

9. The answer depends on the year.

   If the year is an ordinary year then next day.
   If the year is a leap year then beyond 2 days.
   Thus, possible answers are *Monday* or Tuesday.

10. No. of days from Dec. 3, 1990 to Jan. 3, 1991

    = 31

No. of odd days in this period = 3

Hence, the required day is 3 days beyond Sunday, *i.e.,* Wednesday.

11. *Tuesday,* Wednesday, Thursday, Friday

    7th day of the month = Tuesday

    14th day of the month = Tuesday

15,	16,	17,
Wednesday,	Thursday,	Friday,
Saturday,	*Sunday*	
18,	19	

THE EXPONENTIAL SERIES

If x is any real number (whether rational or irrational), then

1. $e^x = 1 + \dfrac{x}{1!} + \dfrac{x^2}{2!} + \dfrac{x^3}{3!} + ...$

   The series on the right hand side of the above relation is called the exponential series.

2. $e^{-x} = 1 - \dfrac{x}{1!} + \dfrac{x^2}{2!} - \dfrac{x^3}{3!} + \dfrac{x^4}{4!} - ....$

3. $e^x + e^{-x} = 2\left[1 + \dfrac{x^2}{2!} + \dfrac{x^4}{4!} + ...\right]$

4. $e^x - e^{-x} = 2\left[\dfrac{x}{1!} + \dfrac{x^3}{3!} + \dfrac{x^5}{5!} + ...\right]$

5. $e = 1 + \dfrac{1}{1!} + \dfrac{1}{2!} + \dfrac{1}{3!} + \dfrac{1}{4!} + ...$

6. $e^{-1} = 1 - \dfrac{1}{1!} + \dfrac{1}{2!} - \dfrac{1}{3!} + \dfrac{1}{4!} - ....$

7. $e + e^{-1} = 2\left[1 + \dfrac{1}{2!} + \dfrac{1}{4!} + ...\right]$

8. $e - e^{-1} = 2\left[\dfrac{1}{1!} + \dfrac{1}{3!} + \dfrac{1}{5!} + ...\right]$

9. For $a > 0$, $a^x = e^{x \log_e a}$

   $= 1 + \dfrac{x \log_e a}{1!} + \dfrac{x^2 (\log_e a)^2}{2!} + \dfrac{x^3 (\log_e a)^3}{3!} + ...$

The Logarithmic Series

The expansion of $\log_e (1 + x)$ in ascending powers of x is given by

1. $\log(1 + x) = x - \dfrac{x^2}{2} + \dfrac{x^3}{2} - \dfrac{x^4}{4} + ...$ to ∞,

   where $-1 < x \le 1$.

   The series on the right hand side is called the logarithmic series which holds for $|x| < 1$.

2. $\log (1 - x) = -\left(x + \dfrac{x^2}{2} + \dfrac{x^3}{3} + ... \text{ to } \infty\right)$,

   where $-1 \le x < 1$.

3. $\dfrac{1}{2}\log\left(\dfrac{1+x}{1-x}\right) = x + \dfrac{x^3}{3} + \dfrac{x^5}{5} + ...$

   where $-1 < x < 1$.

4. $\log 2 = 1 - \dfrac{1}{2} + \dfrac{1}{3} - \dfrac{1}{4} + ...$ to ∞.

   This series is called *Libnitz series*.

Solved Examples

Example 1: *Find the coefficient of x^n in*

$$1 + \frac{a+bx}{1!} + \frac{(a+bx)^2}{2!} + ... + \frac{(a+bx)^n}{n!} + ...$$

Solution: $1 + \dfrac{a+bx}{1!} + \dfrac{(a+bx)^2}{2!} + ... + \dfrac{(a+bx)^n}{n!} + ...$

$= e^{a + bx}, = e^a . e^{bx},$

$= e^a\left[1 + bx + \dfrac{b^2 x^2}{2!} + \dfrac{b^3 x^3}{3!} + ... + \dfrac{b^n x^n}{n!} + ...\right]$

$\therefore$ The required coefficient of $x^n = \dfrac{e^a b^n}{n!}$.

Example 2: *For what value of x,*

$\log 2 + \log (x + 2) - \log (3x - 5) = \log 3$.

Solution: $\log 2 + \log (x + 2) - \log (3x - 5) = \log 3$

$\Rightarrow \qquad \log \dfrac{2(x+2)}{3x-5} = \log 3 \Rightarrow \dfrac{2(x+2)}{3x-5} = 3$

$\Rightarrow \qquad 2x + 4 = 9x - 15$

$\Rightarrow \qquad -7x = -19 \quad \therefore \ x = \dfrac{19}{7}$

Example 3: *Find the value of* $\log_{b^3} a^2 . \log_{c^3} b^2 . \log_{a^3} c^2$.

Solution: Given expression may be written as,

$$= \frac{\log_{10} a^2}{\log_{10} b^3} \cdot \frac{\log_{10} b^2}{\log_{10} c^3} \cdot \frac{\log_{10} c^2}{\log_{10} a^3}$$

$$\left(\text{Using} \log_a m = \frac{\log_b m}{\log_b a} \right)$$

$$= \frac{2\log_{10} a}{3\log_{10} b} \cdot \frac{2\log_{10} b}{3\log_{10} c} \cdot \frac{2\log_{10} c}{3\log_{10} a}$$

$$= \frac{2}{3} \times \frac{2}{3} \times \frac{2}{3} = \frac{8}{27}$$

Example 4: *If* $\dfrac{\log(2x-1)}{\log x} = 2$, *find* x.

Solution: $\dfrac{\log(2x-1)}{\log x} = 2$

$\Rightarrow \qquad \log (2x - 1) = 2 \log x = \log x^2$

$\Rightarrow \qquad 2x - 1 = x^2$

$\Rightarrow \qquad x^2 - 2x + 1 = 0$

$\Rightarrow \qquad (x - 1)^2 = 0 \qquad \therefore \ x = 1$

MULTIPLE CHOICE QUESTIONS

1. The value of $2^{\log_{2\sqrt{2}} 27}$ is:

   A. 27   B. $\dfrac{1}{9}$

   C. 9   D. $\dfrac{1}{27}$

2. The value of $\log_{11} \left[\dfrac{121\sqrt{14,641}}{\sqrt[3]{1,331}} \right]$ is:

   A. 3   B. 4

   C. 11   D. 12

3. The value of the expression
$\log 18^{3/2} + 3 \log (2 \times 2) - 2 \log (3 \times 2)$ is:

   A. $\log 96\sqrt{2}$ B. $\log 45\sqrt{3}$

   C. 0   D. 1

4. The value of $\sqrt{\left(\dfrac{1}{\sqrt{27}} \right)^2 - \dfrac{\log_5 13}{\log_5 81}}$ is:

   A. $3\sqrt{3}$ B. $\dfrac{1}{3\sqrt{3}}(2,197)^{1/16}$

   C. 1   D. 0

5. The value of $\log_7 \left[\log_7 \sqrt{7\sqrt{7\sqrt{7}}} \right]$ is:

   A. 7   B. $\log 7$

   C. $\log_7 \sqrt{7}$ D. $1 - 3 \log_7 2$

6. Evaluate $\log_{\sqrt{q}} p^2 \cdot \log_{\sqrt{r}} q^2 \cdot \log_{\sqrt{p}} r^2$:

   A. 1   B. $\log pqr$

   C. 64   D. $\log (p/q/r)$

7. Find x, if:
$\log_{10} x \times \log_{10} 64 = \log_{10} 8 \times \log_{10} 256$:

   A. 16   B. 32

   C. 64   D. 128

8. If $\log_{10} (x - 9) + \log_{10} x = 1$, then x equals to:

   A. 9   B. 1

   C. 0   D. 10

9. If $\log_{27} \left(\log_4 \sqrt{x^9} \right) = \dfrac{2}{3}$, then x equals to:

   A. 3   B. 8

   C. 4   D. 16

10. If $a^x = b^y = ab$, the value of $\dfrac{1}{x} + \dfrac{1}{y}$ is:

   A. a B. 1

   C. b D. ab

11. If $\log_4 \log_3 \log_2 x = 0$, the value of x is:

   A. 6   B. 8

   C. 12   D. 16

12. If $\log\left(\dfrac{x-y}{3}\right) = \dfrac{1}{2}(\log x + \log y),$ then $x^2 + y^2$ is equal to:

A. $9xy$
B. x^2y^2
C. $6xy$
D. $11xy$

13. If $\log_{16}(\log_2 a) = \log_4 b,$ then 2^{b^2} is:

A. a
B. $\dfrac{1}{a}$
C. a^2
D. $\dfrac{1}{a^2}$

14. The value of $\log_{10} 125,$ (given $\log_{10} 2 = 0.30$), is:

A. 2.05
B. 2.10
C. 2.15
D. 2.21

15. $\log_{10}\dfrac{26}{51} + \log_{10}\dfrac{119}{91} - \log_{10}\dfrac{13}{32} - \log_{10}\dfrac{64}{39}$

is equal to:

A. 0
B. 1
C. 2
D. 3

16. The expansion $e^x = 1 + \dfrac{x}{1!} + \dfrac{x^2}{2!} + \dfrac{x^3}{3!} + \dots$ to ∞ is valid for

A. $-1 < x < 1$
B. all real x
C. $-1 \le x \le 1$
D. $0 < x < 1$

17. $\dfrac{1}{2!} - \dfrac{1}{3!} + \dfrac{1}{4!} - \dfrac{1}{5!} + \dots$ equals

A. $\log 2$
B. $\log e$
C. e
D. e^{-1}

18. Co-efficient of x^4 in the expansion of $\dfrac{1 - 3x + x^2}{e^x}$ is

A. $\dfrac{25}{24}$
B. $\dfrac{24}{25}$
C. $\dfrac{4}{25}$
D. $\dfrac{5}{24}$

19. $\dfrac{1 + \dfrac{1}{2!} + \dfrac{1}{4!} + \dfrac{1}{6!} + \dots}{1 + \dfrac{1}{3!} + \dfrac{1}{5!} + \dfrac{1}{7!} + \dots}$ is equal to

A. $\dfrac{e^2 + 1}{e^2 - 1}$
B. $\dfrac{e^2 - 1}{e^2 + 1}$
C. $e^2 + 1$
D. $e^2 - 1$

20. $e^{\log_e x}$ is equal to

A. x
B. e
C. 1
D. None of these

ANSWERS

1	2	3	4	5	6	7	8	9	10
C	A	A	B	D	C	A	D	D	B

11	12	13	14	15	16	17	18	19	20
B	D	A	B	A	B	D	A	A	A

SOME SELECTED EXPLANATORY ANSWERS

2. $\sqrt{14,641} = 121,\ \sqrt[3]{1,331} = 11$

$\therefore$ Given expression $= \log_{11}\left(\dfrac{121 \times 121}{11}\right)$

$= \log_{11} 11^3 = 3\log_{11} 11 = 3$

4. Given expression $= \left(\dfrac{1}{\sqrt{27}}\right)(27)^{\frac{1}{8}\log_9 13}$

$= \dfrac{1}{3\sqrt{3}} 3^{3/8 \log_9 13} = \dfrac{1}{3\sqrt{3}} 3^{3/16 \log_3 13}$

$= \dfrac{1}{3\sqrt{3}} 3^{\log_3 13^{3/16}} = \dfrac{1}{3\sqrt{3}} \cdot 13^{3/16}$

$= \dfrac{1}{3\sqrt{3}} \cdot (2,197)^{1/16}$

5. $\log_7\left[\log_7\sqrt{7\sqrt{7\sqrt{7}}}\right]$

$$= \log_7\left[\log_7\sqrt{7\sqrt{7^{3/2}}}\right]$$

$$= \log_7\left[\log_7\sqrt{7^{1+3/4}}\right]$$

$$= \log_7\left[\log_7 7^{7/8}\right]$$

$$= \log_7\frac{7}{8} = \log_7 7 - \log_7 8$$

$$= 1 - 3\log_7 2$$

6. Given expression

$$= \frac{\log p^2}{\log\sqrt{q}}\cdot\frac{\log q^2}{\log\sqrt{r}}\cdot\frac{\log r^2}{\log\sqrt{p}}$$

$$= \frac{2\log p}{\frac{1}{2}\log q}\cdot\frac{2\log q}{\frac{1}{2}\log r}\cdot\frac{2\log r}{\frac{1}{2}\log p}$$

$$= 4\times 4\times 4 = 64$$

7. $\dfrac{\log_{10} x}{\log_{10} 8} = \dfrac{2\log_{10} 16}{2\log_{10} 8}$

$\Rightarrow \quad \log_8 x = \log_8 16 \qquad \therefore\ x = 16$

8. $\log_{10}(x-9) + \log_{10} x = 1$

$\Rightarrow \qquad \log_{10}(x-9)\,x = 1$

$\Rightarrow \qquad\qquad (x-9)\,x = 10^1 = 10$

$\Rightarrow \qquad\qquad x^2 - 9x - 10 = 0$

$\Rightarrow \qquad (x-10)(x+1) = 0 \ \therefore\ x = -1,\ 10$

Since $x = -1$ is not possible, $x = 10$

9. $\log_{27}\left(\log_4\sqrt{x^9}\right) = \dfrac{2}{3}$

$\Rightarrow \qquad \log_4\sqrt{x^9} = 27^{2/3}$

$\Rightarrow \qquad \log_4 x^{9/2} = (3^3)^{2/3} = 3^2 = 9$

$\Rightarrow \qquad\qquad x^{9/2} = 4^9$

$\Rightarrow \qquad\qquad x^{9/2} = (16)^{9/2} \ \therefore\ x = 16$

11. $\log_4 \log_3 \log_2 x = 0 \Rightarrow \log_3 \log_2 x = 4^0 = 1$

$\Rightarrow \log_2 x = 3^1 = 3 \Rightarrow x = 2^3 = 8$

12. $\log\left(\dfrac{x-y}{3}\right) = \dfrac{1}{2}(\log x + \log y)$

$\Rightarrow \quad \log\left(\dfrac{x-y}{3}\right) = \dfrac{1}{2}\log xy$

$\Rightarrow \quad 2\log\left(\dfrac{x-y}{3}\right) = \log xy$

$\Rightarrow \quad \log\left(\dfrac{x-y}{3}\right)^2 = \log xy$

$\Rightarrow \qquad \left(\dfrac{x-y}{3}\right)^2 = xy$

$(\because\ \log$ is a one-one function$)$

$\Rightarrow \quad \dfrac{x^2 + y^2 - 2xy}{9} = xy \Rightarrow x^2 + y^2 = 11xy$

14. $\log_{10} 125 = \log_{10} 5^3$

$$= 3\log_{10} 5$$

$$= 3\log_{10}\left(\frac{10}{2}\right)$$

$$= 3\log_{10} 10 - 3\log_{10} 2$$

$$= 3 - 3\times 0.30 = 3 - 0.90 = 2.10$$

15. Given expression

$$= \log_{10}\frac{13\times 2}{17\times 3} + \log_{10}\frac{17\times 7}{13\times 7} - \log_{10}\frac{13}{32} - \log_{10}\frac{32\times 2}{13\times 3}$$

$$= \log_{10}\left[\frac{13\times 2 + 17\times 7}{17\times 3 \times 13\times 7}\times\frac{32}{13}\times\frac{13\times 3}{32\times 2}\right] = \log_{10} 1$$

$$= 0$$

③ Linear and Quadratic Equation

1. An equation of the form $ax^2 + bx + c = 0$, $a \neq 0$ in which the highest power of x is 2 and a, b, c are any three numbers free from x but $a \neq 0$ is called a *quadratic equation* or second *degree equation* in x.

2. A quadratic equation is satisfied by two values of x, *i.e.*, there are two roots of the quadratic equation.

3. The formula for solving a quadratic equation $ax^2 + bx + c = 0$ is:

$$x = \frac{-b \pm \sqrt{b^2 - 4ac}}{2a}$$

where $b^2 - 4ac$ is called *discriminant*.
 (i)   If $b^2 - 4ac > 0$, the two roots are real and different.
 (ii) If $b^2 - 4ac = 0$, the two roots are real and equal.
 (iii) If $b^2 - 4ac < 0$, the two roots are imaginary.
 (iv) If $b^2 - 4ac$ is a perfect square and a, b, c are rational, the two roots are rational.
 (v)   If $b^2 - 4ac$ is not a perfect square and a, b, c, are rational, then the two roots are irrational.

4. *Linear Equations in two variables* : The equation of the form $ax + by + c = 0$, where a, b, c are real constants, is called a linear equation in two variables x and y. Two equations

$$a_1 x_1 + b_1 y_1 + c_1 = 0$$
$$\text{and} \quad a_2 x + b_2 y + c_2 = 0$$

which satisfy the same values of x and y are called linear simultaneous equations in two variables.

Important Rule:

(i)   The solution is unique, if $\dfrac{a_1}{a_2} \neq \dfrac{b_1}{b_2}$.

(ii) The solutions are infinite, if $\dfrac{a_1}{a_2} = \dfrac{b_1}{b_2} = \dfrac{c_1}{c_2}$.

(iii) No solution, if $\dfrac{a_1}{a_2} = \dfrac{b_1}{b_2} \neq \dfrac{c_1}{c_2}$.

The equation $a_1 x - b_1 y = c$ and $a_2 x^3 + b_2 y^3 = c_2$ say are non-linear simultaneous equations in x and y.

Solved Examples

Example 1: *Solve the equation:*
$$2(x - 3) = 9 + 3(x - 9)$$
Solution: $\quad 2(x - 3) = 9 + 3(x - 9)$
or $\quad 2 \times x - 2 \times 3 = 9 + 3 \times x - 3 \times 9$
or $\quad 2x - 6 = 9 + 3x - 27$
or $\quad 2x - 3x = 9 - 27 + 6$
or $\quad -x = -12$
$\therefore \quad x = 12$

Example 2: *Find two numbers whose sum is 64, and whose difference is 16.*

Solution: Let the smaller number be x.
  Then another number $= 64 - x$
Difference, $(64 - x) - x = 16$
$\Rightarrow \quad 64 - 2x = 16$
$\Rightarrow \quad -2x = 16 - 64 = -48$

$$\therefore \qquad x = \frac{-48}{-2} = 24$$

$\therefore$ Second number = 64 – 24 = 40.

Example 3: *Solve: $x^2 + (1 - p)x - p = 0$.*

Solution:
$$x^2 + (1 - p)x - p = 0$$
$$\Rightarrow \qquad x^2 + x - px - p = 0$$
$$\Rightarrow \qquad x(x + 1) - p(x + 1) = 0$$
$$\Rightarrow \qquad (x + 1)(x - p) = 0$$
$$\Rightarrow \qquad x + 1 = 0$$
$$\text{or} \qquad x - p = 0$$
$$\therefore \qquad x = -1$$
$$\text{or} \qquad x = p$$

Thus, the two roots of the quardratic equation are –1 and p.

Example 4: *If the equations $4x + 7y = 10$ and $10x + ky = 25$ represent coincident lines, then find value of k.*

Solution: Since the two lines $y = -\dfrac{4}{7}x + \dfrac{10}{7}$,

$y = -\dfrac{10}{k}x + \dfrac{25}{k}$ represent coincident lines.

$$-\frac{10}{k} = -\frac{4}{7}$$
$$\therefore \qquad k = \frac{70}{4} = \frac{35}{2}$$

Example 5: *If the quadratic equation $2x^2 + 3x + p = 0$ has equal roots, then find the value of p.*

Solution: Since the given equation has equal roots,
$$b^2 - 4ac = 0$$
$$\text{or} \qquad 3^2 - 4.2.p = 0$$
$$\text{or} \qquad 9 - 8p = 0$$
$$\therefore \qquad p = \frac{9}{8}$$

MULTIPLE CHOICE QUESTIONS

1. The value of x in the equation $\dfrac{x+2}{x-1} = \dfrac{5}{2}$ is:

   A. 3   B. 7

   C. 5   D. 9

2. 32 is divided into two parts such that if the larger is divided by the smaller, the quotient is 2 and the remainder is 5. The larger part is:

   A. 9   B. 18

   C. 23   D. 27

3. If the sum of the roots of the equation $qx^2 + 2x + 3q = 0$ is equal to their product, then the value of q is:

   A. $-\dfrac{2}{3}$ B. $\dfrac{3}{2}$

   C. 3   D. – 6

4. If $(x - 2)(x + 6) \geq 0$, then the solution set is:

   A. $\{x : x \geq 2\}$

   B. $\{x : x \leq 6\}$

   C. $\{x : x \leq -6\}$

   D. $\{x : x \geq 2 \text{ or } x \leq -6\}$

5. If α, β are the roots of the quadratic equation $4x^2 - 4x + 1 = 0$, then $\alpha^3 + \beta^3$ is equal to:

   A. $\dfrac{1}{4}$ B. $\dfrac{1}{8}$

   C. 16   D. 32

6. If the roots of the equation:
   $$\lambda^2 + 8\lambda + \mu^2 + 6\mu = 0$$
   are real, then μ lies between:

   A. –2 and 8   B. –3 and 6

   C. –8 and 2   D. –6 and 3

7. The values of x satisfying the equation $5^{2x} - 5^{x+3} + 125 = 5^x$ are:

   A. 0 and 2   B. –1 and 3

   C. 0 and –3   D. 0 and 3

8. Two students while solving a quadratic equation in x, one copied the constant term incorrectly and got the roots 3 and 2; while the other copies the constant term and coefficient of x^2 as –6 and 1 respectively. The correct roots are:

   A. 3, –2   B. –3, 2

   C. –6, –1   D. 6, –1

9. For a given value of k, the product of roots of $x^2 - 2kx + 3k^2 - 4 = 0$ is 5. The roots may be characterised as:

A. integral
B. rational but not integral
C. irrational
D. imaginary

10. If the roots of the equation $x^2 - 6x + 10 = 0$ are α and β, then $\alpha^2 + \beta^2$ is:
A. -16 B. 4
C. 60   D. 16

11. Total salary of A and B is equal. If A gets 65% allowance of his basic salary and B gets 80% of his basic salary. If the basic salary of B is ₹ 1,100, then the basic salary of A is:
A. ₹ 1,200   B. ₹ 1,980
C. ₹ 1,800   D. ₹ 1,100

12. The length of a field is twice its breadth. If the length is reduced by 5 metre and breadth is increased by 3 metre, the area remains as before. The length of the field is:

A. 15 m   B. 30 m
C. 12 cm   D. 25 m

13. A student starts for a hostel 24 km away from his house on bicycle. If he increases his speed by 2 km per hour, he reaches 2 hours early. His speed in km/hour is:
A. 8   B. 6
C. 4   D. 3

14. Ravi, after giving away 80% of his pocket money to Komal and 6% of the remaining to Kavita, has ₹ 47 left with him. The money with Ravi in the beginning was:
A. ₹ 200   B. ₹ 250
C. ₹ 500   D. ₹ 700

15. The solution of the simultaneous linear equations $2x - 3y = 3$ and $4x - y = 11$ is:
A. $x = 1, y = 1$ B. $x = 3, y = 2$
C. $x = 2, y = 3$ D. $x = 3, y = 1$

ANSWERS

1	2	3	4	5	6	7	8	9	10
A	C	A	D	A	C	D	D	D	D

11	12	13	14	15
A	B	C	B	D

SOME SELECTED EXPLANATORY ANSWERS

1.
$$\frac{x+2}{x-1} = \frac{5}{2}$$
$$2(x + 2) = 5(x - 1)$$
$$2x + 4 = 5x - 5$$
$$2x - 5x = -5 - 4$$
$$-3x = -9$$
$$x = \frac{-9}{-3} = 3$$

2. Let smaller number $= x$

∴ larger number $= 32 - x$

According to the condition given,

larger number $= 2 \times$ smaller number $+ 5$

$\Rightarrow \quad (32 - x) = 2 \times x + 5$

$\Rightarrow \quad 3x = 32 - 5 = 27$

∴ $\quad x = 9$

$\Rightarrow$ larger number $= 32 - 9 = 23$

3.
$$\alpha + \beta = \alpha\beta$$

or
$$\frac{-2}{q} = \frac{3q}{q} = 3$$

$\Rightarrow \quad q = \dfrac{-2}{3}$

4.
$$(x - 2)(x + 6) \geq 0$$
$\Rightarrow \quad (x - 2) \geq 0$ and $(x + 6) \geq 0$
$\Rightarrow \quad x \geq 2$ and $\quad x \geq -6$

Also $(x - 2)(x + 6) \geq 0$
$\Rightarrow \quad (x - 2) \leq 0$ and $(x + 6) \leq 0$
$\Rightarrow \quad x \leq 2$ and $\quad x \leq -6$

5.
$$\alpha + \beta = \frac{4}{4} = 1, \; \alpha\beta = \frac{1}{4}$$

∴ $\alpha^3 + \alpha^3 = (\alpha + \beta)^3 - 3\alpha\beta(\alpha + \beta)$

$$= 1^3 - 3 \times \frac{1}{4} \times 1 = 1 - \frac{3}{4} = \frac{1}{4}$$

6. $\lambda^2 + 8\lambda + \mu^2 + 6\mu = 0$ \qquad (quadratic in λ)

Since roots are real,

$$b^2 - 4ac \geq 0$$

or $\quad 8^2 - 4(\mu^2 + 6\mu) \geq 0$

$\Rightarrow \quad \mu^2 + 6\mu - 16 \leq 0$

$\Rightarrow \quad (\mu + 8)(\mu - 2) \leq 0$

$\Rightarrow \qquad\qquad \mu \geq -8$ and $\mu \leq 2$

or $\qquad\qquad\qquad \mu \leq -8$ and $\mu \geq 2$

It means μ lies between -8 and 2.

7. $\qquad\qquad 5^{2x} - 5^{x+3} + 125 = 5^x$

or $\quad 5^{2x} - 5^x(125 + 1) + 125 = 0$

or $\quad 5^x(5^x - 125) - 1(5^x - 125) = 0$

or $\quad (5^x - 1)(5^x - 125) = 0$

$\therefore \qquad\qquad 5^x - 1 = 0$

or $\qquad\qquad 5^x - 125 = 0$

or $\qquad\qquad\qquad 5^x = 1 = 5^0$

$\therefore \qquad\qquad\qquad x = 0$

or $\qquad\qquad\qquad 5^x = 125 = 5^3$

$\therefore \qquad\qquad\qquad x = 3$

8. Suppose the correct equation be

$$ax^2 + bx + c = 0$$

Taking c and the correct roots α and β, wrong roots as 3 and 2.

$\therefore \qquad \alpha + \beta = 3 + 2 = 5 \qquad\qquad ...(i)$

Also $a = 1$ and $c = -6$,

$$\alpha\beta = c/a = -6 \qquad\qquad ...(ii)$$

Solving, we get the correct roots are 6 and -1.

9. By hypothesis,

$$3k^2 - 4 = 5$$

or $\qquad\qquad 3k^2 = 9$

$\Rightarrow \qquad\qquad k^2 = 3$

$\qquad$ Disc. $= 4k^2 - 4(3k^2 - 4)$

$$= -8 < 0$$

Hence, roots are imaginary.

10. $\qquad\qquad x^2 - 6x + 10 = 0 \qquad\qquad ...(1)$

$\therefore \quad x - (\alpha + \beta)x + \alpha\beta = 0 \qquad\qquad ...(2)$

$\qquad\qquad\qquad \{\because \alpha, \beta$ are the roots of (1)

Comparing (1) and (2),

$$\alpha + \beta = 6 \text{ and } \alpha\beta = 10$$

$\therefore \qquad \alpha^2 + \beta^2 = (\alpha + \beta)^2 - 2\alpha\beta$

$$= 6^2 - 2 \times 10$$

$$= 36 - 20 = 16$$

11. Let the basic salary of A $= x$

$\therefore$ A's total salary

$$= x + 65\% \text{ of } x$$

$$= x + x \times \frac{65}{100} = x + \frac{65x}{100} \qquad ...(i)$$

B's total salary

$$= 1{,}100 + 80\% \text{ of } 1{,}100$$

$$= 1{,}100 + \frac{80 \times 1{,}100}{100}$$

$$= 1{,}100 + 880 = 1{,}980 \qquad ...(ii)$$

A's total salary = B's total salary (given)

$\Rightarrow \qquad x + \dfrac{65x}{100} = 1{,}980$

$\Rightarrow \quad 100x + 65x = 1{,}980 \times 100$

$\Rightarrow \qquad 165x = 1{,}980 \times 100$

$\therefore \qquad\qquad x = \dfrac{1{,}980 \times 100}{165}$

$$= ₹\ 1{,}200$$

12. Let the breadth of the field $= x$ metre

$\therefore$ length of the field $= 2x$ metre

and area of the room $= 2x \times x = 2x^2$ metre^2 ...(i)

New area $= (2x - 5)(x + 3) = 2x^2 + x - 15$ ...(ii)

Comparing (i) and (ii),

$$2x^2 = 2x^2 + x - 15$$

$\Rightarrow \qquad x - 15 = 0$

$\therefore \qquad\qquad x = 15$

Hence, $\quad$ length $= 2 \times 15 = 30$ metre

11. Let the speed of the student be x km/hour

$\therefore$ Time taken to cover 24 km

$$= \frac{24}{x} \text{ hour} \qquad\qquad ...(1)$$

When speed is $(x + 2)$ km/hour

Then time taken to cover 24 km

$$= \frac{24}{x+2} \text{ hours} \qquad\qquad ...(2)$$

According to the condition given,

$$\frac{24}{x} - \frac{24}{x+2} = 2$$

$\Rightarrow \quad 24(x + 2) - 24x = 2x(x + 2)$

$\Rightarrow \quad 24x + 48 - 24x = 2x^2 + 4x$

$\Rightarrow \quad 2x^2 + 4x - 48 = 0$

$\Rightarrow \quad x^2 + 2x - 24 = 0$

$\Rightarrow \quad (x + 6)(x - 4) = 0$

$\therefore \qquad\qquad x = -6 \text{ or } x = 4$

neglecting negative value, the speed of the student is 4 km/hour.

14. Let the pocket money be x

$\therefore \quad 80\% \text{ of } x = \dfrac{80x}{100} = \dfrac{4x}{5}$

$\quad \text{Balance} = x - \dfrac{4x}{5} = \dfrac{x}{5}$

$\text{Again } 6\% \text{ of } \dfrac{x}{5} = \dfrac{6}{100} \times \dfrac{x}{5} = \dfrac{3x}{250}$

The amount left with Ravi $= \dfrac{x}{5} - \dfrac{3x}{250} = 47$

$\Rightarrow \quad \dfrac{50x - 3x}{250} = 47 \Rightarrow \dfrac{47x}{250} = 47$

$\therefore \qquad\qquad x = ₹\ 250$

15.

$\qquad 2x - 3y = 3 \qquad\qquad ...(1)$

$\qquad 4x - y = 11 \qquad\qquad ...(2)$

Multiply equation (2) by (3), which gives

$\qquad 12x - 3y = 33 \qquad\qquad ...(3)$

Subtracting equation (1) from (3), we get

$\qquad\qquad 10x = 30$

$\therefore \qquad\qquad x = 3$

Substituting this value of x in (2), we have

$\qquad\qquad 4 \times 3 - y = 11$

$\therefore \qquad\qquad y = 12 - 11 = 1$

④ Sequences and Series

SEQUENCE

A sequence is a function whose domain is the set N of natural numbers.

Series: If $a_1, a_2, a_3, a_4, ..., a_n, ...$ is a sequence, then the expression $a_1 + a_2 + a_3 + a_4 + a_5 + ... + a_n + ...$ is a series.

A series is finite or infinite according as the number of terms in the corresponding sequence is finite or infinite.

Arithmetic Progression (A.P.)

A sequence is called an arithmetic progression if the difference of a term and the previous term is always same, *i.e.*, $a_{n+1} - a_n$ = constant ($= d$) for all $n \in$ N.

The constant difference, generally denoted by d is called the common difference.

The nth term of the A.P., $a, a + d, a + 2d, ...$ a_n is

$$a_n = a + (n - 1)d.$$

Sum to *n* Terms of an A.P.

The sum S_n of n terms of an A.P. with first term 'a' and common difference 'd' is given by

$$S_n = \frac{n}{2}[2a + (n-1)d]$$

or $\qquad S_n = \frac{n}{2}[a + l]$

where l = last term = $a + (n - 1)d$.

The nth term,

$$a_n = S_n - S_{n-1}$$

Arithmetic Mean (A.M.)

If three terms are in A.P. the middle term is called the A.M. between the other two.

Single A.M. Between two numbers *a* and *b*

If A is the arithmetic mean between a and b, then a, A, b are in A.P.

$$\therefore \qquad A = \frac{a+b}{2}$$

If $x_1, x_2 ...., x_n$ are n numbers then their A.M. is given by $\dfrac{x_1 + x_2 + ... + x_n}{n}$.

Insertion of *n* arithmetic means between any two given numbers

The numbers $A_1, A_2, ..., A_n$ are said to be n arithmetic means between any two given numbers a and b if $a, A_1, A_2, ..., A_n, b$ are in A.P. Obviously $b - t_{n+2} = a + (n + 1)\,d,$

$$\therefore \qquad d = \frac{b-a}{n+1} \text{ and so } A_1 = a + \frac{b-a}{n+1},$$

$$A_2 = a + \frac{(b-a)}{n+1}, \ A_3 = a + \frac{3(b-a)}{n+1}, ...,$$

$$A_n = \frac{n(b-a)}{n+1}.$$

Geometric Progression

A sequence of non-zero number is called a *geometric progression* (abbreviated as G.P.) if the ratio of a term and the term preceding to it is always a constant quantity.

The constant ratio is called the *common ratio* of the G.P.

The *n*th or General Term of a G.P.

The nth term of a G.P. with first term a and common ratio r is given by $a_n = ar^{n-1}$.

Sum of n terms of a G.P.

The sum of n terms of a G.P. with first term 'a' and common ratio 'r' is given by:

$$S_n = a\left(\frac{r^n - 1}{r - 1}\right) \text{ or } S_n = a\left(\frac{1 - r^n}{1 - r}\right), \ r \neq 1.$$

Sum of an Infinite G.P.

The sum of an infinite G.P. with first term a and common ratio $r(-1 < r < 1, \textit{ i.e., } |r| < 1)$ is:

$$S = \frac{a}{1 - r}$$

If $r \geq 1$, then the sum of an infinite G.P. tends to infinity.

Geometric Mean (G.M.)

If a, b, c are in G.P., then b is called *geometric mean* between a and c.

Single geometric mean between a and b

If G be the geometric mean between a and b, then a, G, b are in G.P.

$$\therefore \qquad G = \sqrt{(ab)}$$

If a_1, a_2, ..., $a_n > 0$, then their geometric mean is given by $(a_1 \cdot a_2 \cdot a_3 \ ... \ a_n)^{1/n}$.

Insertion of n geometric means between any two given positive numbers

Let a and b be two given positive real numbers and G_1, G_2, ..., G_n be the n G.Ms. to be inserted between them.

$\therefore a$, G_1, G_2, ..., G_n, b are in G.P.

Let r be the common ratio of this G.P.

$$\text{Then, } b = ar^{n+1} \Rightarrow r = \left(\frac{b}{a}\right)^{\frac{1}{n+1}}$$

$$\therefore \ G_1 = ar = a\left(\frac{b}{a}\right)^{\frac{1}{n+1}}, \ G_2 = ar^2 = a\left(\frac{b}{a}\right)^{\frac{1}{n+2}},$$

$$... \ G_n = ar^n = a\left(\frac{b}{a}\right)^{\frac{n}{n+2}}.$$

Harmonic Progression

A sequence a_1, a_2, a_3, ... a_n, ... of non-zero numbers is called a Harmonic Progression if the sequence

$$\frac{1}{a_1}, \frac{1}{a_2}, \frac{1}{a_3}, ..., \frac{1}{a_n}, ... \text{ is an A.P.}$$

Harmonic Mean

If a and b are two non-zero numbers then harmonic mean of a and b denoted by H is given by

$$H = \frac{1}{2}\left(\frac{1}{a} + \frac{1}{b}\right) \text{ or } H = \left(\frac{2ab}{a+b}\right)$$

If a, H, b are in H.P., then H is called single harmonic mean between a and b.

If a_1, a_2, a_3, ..., a_n be n non-zero numbers, then their harmonic mean H is given by

$$\frac{1}{H} = \frac{1}{2}\left(\frac{1}{a_1} + \frac{1}{a_2} + ... + \frac{1}{a_n}\right).$$

Insertion of n Harmonic Means between any two given numbers

Let a and b be any two given numbers and H_1, H_2, ... H_n be n harmonic means between them.

$\therefore a$, H_1, H_2, ..., H_n, b are in H.P.

$$\therefore \frac{1}{a}, \frac{1}{H_1}, \frac{1}{H_2}, ... \frac{1}{H_n}, \frac{1}{b} \text{ are in A.P.}$$

Let d be the common difference of this A.P.,

$$\text{then } (n + 2)^{\text{th}} \text{ term} = \frac{1}{b} = \frac{1}{a} + (n + 2 - 1)d$$

$$\Rightarrow \quad d = \frac{a - b}{ab(n+1)}$$

$$\therefore \ \frac{1}{H_1} = \frac{1}{a} + \frac{a-b}{ab(n+1)} \Rightarrow H_1 = \frac{ab(n+1)}{bn+a}.$$

$$\text{Similarly, } \frac{1}{H_2} = \frac{1}{a} + 2d, \ \frac{1}{H_3}\frac{1}{a} + 3d,....$$

$\therefore H_2$, H_3, ..., H_n can be calculated.

Properties of AM, GM and HM between two given Number, a and b

$$A = \frac{a+b}{2}, \ G = \sqrt{ab}$$

$$\text{and} \qquad H = \frac{2ab}{a+b}$$

These three means possess the following properties:

Prop. I : $A > G > H$

Prop. II : A, G, H form a GP, *i.e.*, $G^2 = AH$

Prop. III : The equation having a and b as its roots is $x^2 - 2Ax + G^2 = 0$.

Solved Examples

Example 1: *If the sum of n terms of an AP is $S_n = 3n^2 + 2n$, then find the value of d.*

Solution: Formula :
$$S_n = An^2 + Bn \Rightarrow A = 3$$
$$\Rightarrow \qquad d = 2A = 2 \times 3 = 6.$$

Example 2: *If $x > 1$, $y > 1$, $z > 1$ are in G.P., then*
$$\frac{1}{1+\log x}, \frac{1}{1+\log y}, \frac{1}{1+\log z} \text{ are in A.P., prove.}$$

Solution: Since x, y, z are in G.P.
$$y^2 = xz$$
$$\Rightarrow \qquad \log y^2 = \log (xz)$$
$$\Rightarrow \qquad 2 \log y = \log x + \log z$$
$$\Rightarrow \qquad 2(1 + \log y) = (1 + \log x) + (1 + \log z)$$
$$\Rightarrow 1 + \log x, 1 + \log y, 1 + \log z \text{ are in A.P.}$$
$$\Rightarrow \frac{1}{1+\log x}, \frac{1}{1+\log y}, \frac{1}{1+\log z} \text{ are in H.P.}$$

Example 3: *A GP consists of 2n terms. If the sum of the terms occupying the odd places is S_1 and that of the terms in the even places is S_2, then S_2 / S_1 dependent on r.*

Solution: We have :
$$S_1 = a + ar^2 + ar^4 + ... + ar^{2n-2}$$
$$S_2 = ar + ar^3 + ar^5 + ... + ar^{2n-1}$$
Clearly, $S_2/S_1 = r$, which depends on r.

MULTIPLE CHOICE QUESTIONS

1. If the sum of first n positive integers is $\frac{1}{5}$ times the sum of their squares, then n equals:
   - A. 5
   - B. 6
   - C. 7
   - D. 8

2. If $\log_3 2$, $\log_3 (2^x - 5)$ and $\log_3 (2^x - 7/2)$ are in A.P., then x is equal to:
   - A. 2
   - B. 3
   - C. 4
   - D. 2, 3

3. If a, b, c, are in A.P., b, c, d are in G.P., c, d, e are in H.P., then a, c, e will be in:
   - A. A.P.
   - B. G.P.
   - C. H.P.
   - D. None of these

4. The value of 0.423 is:
   - A. $\frac{419}{999}$
   - B. $\frac{419}{990}$
   - C. $\frac{423}{1000}$
   - D. None of these

5. The following consecutive terms $\frac{1}{1+\sqrt{x}}$, $\frac{1}{1-x}$, $\frac{1}{1-\sqrt{x}}$ of a series are in:
   - A. H.P.
   - B. G.P.
   - C. A.P.
   - D. A.P., G.P.

6. $\log_3 2$, $\log_6 2$, $\log_{12} 2$ are in:
   - A. A.P.
   - B. G.P.
   - C. H.P.
   - D. None of these

7. The fourth, seventh and tenth terms of a GP are p, q, r respectively, then:
   - A. $p^2 = q^2 + r^2$
   - B. $q^2 = pr$
   - C. $p^2 = qr$
   - D. $pqr + pq + 1 = 0$

8. In a GP of postive terms, any term is equal to the sum of the next two terms. Then the common ratio of the GP is:
   - A. $2 \cos 18°$
   - B. $\sin 18°$
   - C. $\cos 18°$
   - D. $2 \sin 18°$

9. If $\log (x + z) + \log (x - 2y + z) = 2 \log (x - z)$, then x, y, z are in:
   - A. H.P.
   - B. G.P.
   - C. A.P.
   - D. None of these

10. If $< a_n >$ is an arithmetic sequence, then
$$\Delta = \begin{vmatrix} a_m & a_n & a_p \\ m & n & p \\ 1 & 1 & 1 \end{vmatrix} \text{ equals:}$$
   - A. 1
   - B. -1
   - C. 0
   - D. None of these

11. If $a_1, a_2, a_3, \ldots$ is an A.P. such that
$a_1 + a_5 + a_{10} + a_{15} + a_{20} + a_{24} = 225,$
then $a_1 + a_2 + a_3 + \ldots + a_{23} + a_{24}$ is equal to:
A. 909   B. 75
C. 750   D. 900

12. The value of $2.\overline{357}$ is:

A. $\dfrac{2355}{1001}$ B. $\dfrac{2355}{999}$

C. $\dfrac{2355}{1111}$ D. None of these

13. The third term of a GP is 4. The product of first five terms is:

A. 4^3
B. 4^5
C. 4^4
D. None of these

14. The second, third and sixth terms of an A.P. are consecutive terms of a G.P. The common ratio of the G.P. is:
A. 1   B. -1
C. 3   D. -3

15. If x, y, z are in G.P. and $x + 3, y + 3, z + 3$ are in H.P., then:
A. $y = 2$ B. $y = 3$
C. $y = 1$ D. $y = 0$

ANSWERS

1	2	3	4	5	6	7	8	9	10
C	D	B	B	C	C	B	D	A	C

11	12	13	14	15
D	B	B	C	B

SOME SELECTED EXPLANATORY ANSWERS

1.
$$\Sigma n = \frac{1}{5}\Sigma n^2$$

$$\Rightarrow \quad \frac{n(n+1)}{2} = \frac{1}{5}\cdot\frac{n(n+1)(2n+1)}{6}$$

$$\Rightarrow \quad n = 7$$

2. The terms are in A.P., hence

$$2\log_3 (2^x - 5) = \log_3 2 + \log_3\left(2^x - \frac{7}{2}\right)$$

$$\Rightarrow \quad (2^x - 5)^2 = 2\times\left(2^x - \frac{7}{2}\right)$$

$$\Rightarrow \quad (y - 5)^2 = 2\left(y - \frac{7}{2}\right), \text{ where } y = 2^x$$

$$\Rightarrow \quad y = 4 \text{ or } 8$$
$$\Rightarrow \quad 2^x = 4 \text{ or } 8 - 2^2 \text{ or } 2^3$$
$$\therefore \quad x = 2 \text{ or } 3$$

3. We have $2b = a + c$, $c^2 = bd$ and $d = \dfrac{2ce}{c+e}$

$$\Rightarrow \quad c^2 = \left(\frac{a+c}{2}\right) d = \left(\frac{a+c}{2}\right)\left(\frac{2ce}{c+e}\right)$$

$$\Rightarrow \quad c^2 = ae$$
$\therefore$ a, c, e are in G.P.

4. $S = 0.42323232\ldots$
$$= 0.4 + 0.023 + 0.00023 + \ldots$$
$$= 0.4 + 23\times 10^{-3} + 23\times 10^{-5} + \ldots$$
$$= 0.4 + \frac{23\times 10^{-3}}{1 - 10^{-2}}$$
$$= 0.4 + \frac{23}{990} = \frac{419}{990}$$

5. Here $\dfrac{1}{1-x} - \dfrac{1}{1+\sqrt{x}} = \dfrac{\sqrt{x}}{1-x}$

Also, $\dfrac{1}{1-\sqrt{x}} - \dfrac{1}{1-x} = \dfrac{\sqrt{x}}{1-x}$

Hence, the terms are in A.P.

6. Consider $\log_2 3, \log_2 6, \log_2 12$
We have
$$\log_2 6 = \log_2 (3\times 2) = 1 + \log_2 3$$
$$\log_2 12 = \log_2 (2^2\times 3) = 2 + \log_2 3$$
Since $\log_2 3$, $1 + \log_2 3$ and $2 + \log_2 3$ are in A.P., we have

$\log_2 3$, $\log_2 6$ and $\log_2 12$ are in A.P.

$\Rightarrow \dfrac{1}{\log_2 3}, \dfrac{1}{\log_2 6}, \dfrac{1}{\log_2 12}$ are in H.P.

$\Rightarrow \log_3 2, \log_6 2, \log_{12} 2$ are in H.P.

7. Let A = first term, R = common ratio

Then $\qquad p = AR^3$, $q = AR^6$

and $\qquad r = AR^9$

$\therefore \qquad (AR^6)^2 = (AR^3)(AR^9)$

$\Rightarrow \qquad q^2 = pr$

8. $\qquad a_n = a_{n+1} + a_{n+2}$

$\Rightarrow \quad a_1 r^{n-1} = a_1 r^n + a_1 r^{n+1}$

$\Rightarrow \qquad r^{-1} = 1 + r$

$\Rightarrow \quad r^2 + r - 1 = 0$

$\Rightarrow \qquad r = \dfrac{\sqrt{5}-1}{2} \qquad (\because r > 0)$

$\qquad\qquad\quad = 2 \sin 18°$

9. $\log (x + z) + \log (x - 2y + z) = 2 \log (x - z)$

$\Rightarrow (x + z)(x - 2y + z) = (x - z)^2$

$\Rightarrow \qquad xy + yz = 2xz$

$\Rightarrow \qquad \dfrac{1}{z} + \dfrac{1}{x} = \dfrac{2}{y}$

$\Rightarrow x, y, z$ are in H.P.

10. $\qquad a_m = a + (m - 1)d \qquad\qquad ...(i)$

$\qquad a_n = a + (n - 1)d \qquad\qquad ...(ii)$

$\qquad a_p = a + (p - 1)d \qquad\qquad ...(iii)$

Multiply (i) by $(n - p)$, (ii) by $(p - m)$ and (iii) by $(m - n)$ and add,

$a_m(n - p) + a_n(p - m) + a_p(m - n) = 0$

Expanding along the first row, we have

$\qquad \Delta = a_m(n - p) + a_n(p - m) + a_p(m - n)$

$\qquad\quad = 0$

11. We have

$a_1 + a_5 + a_{10} + a_{15} + a_{20} + a_{24} = 225$

$\Rightarrow (a_1 + a_{24}) + (a_5 + a_{20}) + (a_{10} + a_{15}) = 225$

$\Rightarrow \qquad\qquad 3(a_1 + a_{24}) = 225$

$\Rightarrow \qquad\qquad a_1 + a_{24} = \dfrac{225}{3}$

$\Rightarrow a_1 + a_2 + a_3 + ... + a_{24} = \dfrac{24}{2}(a_1 + a_{24})$

$\qquad\qquad\qquad = 12 \times \dfrac{225}{3} = 900$

12. $\quad 2.\overline{357} = 2 + 0.357357357357...$

$\qquad\qquad = 2 + 0.357 + 0.000357 +$

$\qquad\qquad\qquad\qquad 0.000000357 + ...$

$\qquad\quad = 2 + \dfrac{357}{10^3} + \dfrac{357}{10^6} + \dfrac{357}{10^9} + ...$

$\qquad\quad = 2 + \dfrac{\dfrac{357}{10^3}}{1 - \dfrac{1}{10^3}} = 2 + \dfrac{357}{999} = \dfrac{2355}{999}$

13. Let a be the first term and r be the common ratio. Then

$\qquad ar^2 = 4$ (given)

$\therefore$ Product of first five terms

$\qquad = a \cdot ar \cdot ar^2 \cdot ar^3 \cdot ar^4 = (ar^2)^5 = 4^5$

14. Let a be the first term and d be the common difference of the A.P. Then $a + d$, $a + 2d$, $a + 5d$ are in G.P.,

$\Rightarrow \quad (a + 2d)^2 = (a + d)(a + 5d)$

$\Rightarrow \quad 4d^2 + 4ad = 6ad + 5d^2 \Rightarrow d = -2a$

So, the terms are $-a, -3a, -9a$ which are in G.P. with common ratio 3.

15. x, y, z are in G.P. $\Rightarrow y^2 = xz$

$x + 3, y + 3, z + 3$ are in H.P.

$\Rightarrow \qquad y + 3 = \dfrac{2(x+3)(z+3)}{(x+3)+(z+3)}$

$\Rightarrow \qquad y + 3 = \dfrac{2[xz + 3(x+z) + 9]}{[(x+z)+6]}$

$\Rightarrow \qquad y + 3 = \dfrac{2[y^2 + 3(x+z) + 9]}{[x+z+6]}$

Obviously, $y = 3$ satisfies it.

⑤ Binomial Theorem

THE FACTORIAL FUNCTION

For any natural number $n(i.e., n \in N)$, factorial of n, denoted by $n!$ or $\lfloor n$ is defined as

$$n! = n(n-1)(n-2)\ldots 3\cdot 2\cdot 1$$

$0!$ is defined as $= 1$.

Thus $n!$ is defined only for whole numbers.

Remarks: $n! = n.(n-1)! = n(n-1)\cdot(n-2)!$ etc.

The notation ^nC_r, i.e., $C(n, r)$

$$^nC_r = \frac{n!}{(n-r)!r!}, \text{ where } 0 < r < n, \text{ and } n, r \in N$$

(i) $^nC_0 = {}^nC_n = 1$ and $^nC_r = 0$ for $r > n$

(ii) $^nC_{n-r} = {}^nC_r$

(iii) $^nC_r = {}^nC_s$ iff $r = s$ or $r + s = n$

(iv) $^nC_r = \dfrac{n(n-1)(n-2)\ldots(n-r+1)}{r!}$

$$\therefore {}^nC_1 = \frac{n}{1} = n, \ {}^nC_2 = \frac{n(n-1)}{2!}, \text{ etc.}$$

Greatest value of ^nC_r

^nC_r is greatest for $r = \dfrac{n}{2}$, if n is even and is greatest

for $r = \dfrac{n-1}{2}$ or for $r = \dfrac{n+1}{2}$, if n is odd. These value of ^nC_r will be equal if n is odd.

Binomial Theorem: (Statement for positive integral index). For any positive integral n and $x, y \in C$,

$$(x + y)^n = {}^nC_0x^n + {}^nC_1x^{n-1}y + {}^nC_2x^{n-2}y^2 + \ldots + {}^nC_rx^{n-r}y^r + \ldots + {}^nC_ny^n. \quad \ldots(i)$$

Also $(1 + x)^n = {}^nC_0 + {}^nC_1x + {}^nC_2x^2 + \ldots + {}^nC_rx^r + \ldots + {}^nC_nx^n. \quad \ldots(ii)$

where $^nC_0, {}^nC_1, \ldots, {}^nC_n$ are called binomial

coefficients and $^nC_r = \dfrac{n!}{r! \times (n-r)!} \quad \ldots(iii)$

Replacing y by $-y$ in (i), we get

$$(x - y)^n = {}^nC_0x^n - {}^nC_1x^{n-1}y + {}^nC_2x^{n-2}y^2 + \ldots + (-1)^r x^{n-r}y^r + \ldots + (-1)^n {}^nC_ny^n \quad \ldots(iv)$$

The last term is positive or negative according as n is even or odd respectively.

Note: (a) Adding (i) and (iv), we get

$$(x + y)^n + (x - y)^n$$
$$= 2[x^n + {}^nC_2 x^{n-2} y^2 + \ldots] \quad \ldots(v)$$
$$= 2 \text{ (sum of terms of odd number)}$$

The last term is $^nC_n y^n$ or $^nC_{n-1} y^{n-1}$ according as n is even or odd respectively.

(b) Subtracting (iv) from (i), we get

$$(x + y)^n - (x - y)^n$$
$$= 2[{}^nC_1 x^{n-1} y + {}^nC_3x^{n-3}y^3 + \ldots] \quad \ldots(vi)$$
$$= 2 \text{ [sum of terms of even number]}.$$

The last term is $^nC_{n-1} x y^{n-1}$ or $^nC_n y^n$ according as n is even or odd respectively.

Some important points to remember

In the binomial expansion of $(x + y)^n$, where n is a positive integer

(i) The number of terms in the expansion is $(n + 1)$.

(ii) In each term of the expansion, the sum of the exponents (powers of x and y) is n (i.e., each term is of degree n).

(iii) The binomial coefficients of terms at the same positions from the beginning and from the end are equal since $^nC_r = {}^nC_{n-r}$.

45

PROPERTIES OF BINOMIAL THEOREM

(*i*) The number of terms in the expansion of $(x + y)^n$ is $n + 1$.

(*ii*) In each term, the sum of the indices of x and y is n.

(*iii*) **General term:** In the expansion (1), $(r + 1)^{th}$ term, *i.e.*, the general term denoted by T_{r+1} is given by
$$T_{r+1} = {}^nC_r x^{n-r} y^r.$$

(*iv*) **Middle term (s):**

(*a*) If n is even, the number of terms in the expansion (1) is $n + 1$, which is an odd number.

$\therefore$ there is only one middle term $\left(\dfrac{n}{2}+1\right)$ th term.

$\therefore$ The middle term $= \left(\dfrac{n}{2}+1\right)$ th term

$= {}^nC_{n/2}\, x^{n/2}\, y^{n/2}.$

Example: If $n = 8$, then the middle term is

$\left(\dfrac{8}{2}+1\right)$ th term = 5th term, *i.e.*, T_5.

And is given by $T_5 = {}^8C_4 x^{8-4} y^4 = 70x^4y^4$

(*b*) If n is odd, the number of terms in the expansion (1) will be even.

Thus there will be two middle terms in the expansion, *i.e.*, $\dfrac{1}{2}(n+1)$ th and $\dfrac{1}{2}(n+3)$ th terms.

i.e., middle terms are
$$T_{(n+1)/2} = {}^nC_{(n-1)/2}\, x^{(n+1)/2} \cdot y^{(n-1)/2}.$$
$$\text{and } T_{(n+3)/2} = {}^nC_{(n+1)/2}\, x^{(n-1)/2}\, y^{(n+1)/2}.$$

Example: If $n = 7$, then the number of terms in the expansion of $(x + y)^7$ is $7 + 1 = 8$.

$\therefore$ The middle terms are 4th and 5th terms (*i.e.*, T_4 and T_5) are given by
$$T_4 = {}^7C_3\, x^{7-3}\, y^3 = 35x^4y^3 \text{ and}$$
$$T_5 = {}^7C_4\, x^{7-4}\, y^4 = 35x^3y^4.$$

PROPERTIES OF BINOMIAL COEFFICIENTS

(*i*) $C_0 + C_1 + C_2 + ... + C_n = 2^n$

(*ii*) $C_0 + C_2 + C_4 + ... = C_1 + C_3 + C_5 + ... = 2^{n-1}$

(*iii*) $C_1 + 2C_2 + 3C_3 + ... + {}^nC_n = n.2^{n-1}$

(*iv*) $C_1 - 2C_2 + 3C_3 - ... = 0$

(*v*) $C_0 + 2C_1 + 3C_2 + ... + (n + 1) C_n$
$$= (n + 1) 2^{n-1}$$

(*vi*) $C_0C_r + C_1C_{r-1} + ... + C_{n-r}C_n$
$$= \frac{(2n)!}{(n-r)! \cdot (n+r)!}$$

(*vii*) $C_0^2 + C_1^2 + C_2^2 + ... + C_n^2 = \dfrac{(2n)!}{(n!)^2}$

(*viii*) $C_0^2 - C_1^2 + C_2^2 - C_3^2 + ...$
$$= \begin{cases} 0, & \text{if } n \text{ is odd} \\ (-1)^{n/2}\, {}^nC_{n/2}, & \text{if } n \text{ is even} \end{cases}$$

Some Important equations

(*i*) $(1 - x)^{-1} = 1 + x + x^2 + x^3 + ... + x^r + ...$

(*ii*) $(1 + x)^{-1} = 1 - x + x^2 - x^3 + ... + (-1)^r x^r + ...$

(*iii*) $(1 - x)^{-2} = 1 + 2x + 3x^2 + 4x^3 + ... + (r + 1) x^r + ...$

(*iv*) $(1 + x)^{-2} = 1 - 2x + 3x^2 - 4x^3 + ... + (-1)^r (r + 1) x^r + ...$

Solved Examples

Example 1: *Use Binomial Theorem to find* $(999)^3$.

Solution: $(999)^3 = (10^3 - 1)^3$
$$= (10^3)^3 - {}^3C_1 (10^3)^2 + {}^3C_2 (10^3) - {}^3C_3$$
$$= 10^3 [10^6 - 3(10^3 - 1)] - 1$$
$$= 10^3 (1000000 - 2997) - 1$$
$$= 1000 \times 997003 - 1 = 997002999$$

Example 2: *Find the middle term or terms in the expansion of*

(*i*) $\left(\dfrac{x}{a} - \dfrac{a}{x}\right)^{10}$ (*ii*) $\left(3x - \dfrac{x^3}{6}\right)^9$

Solution:

(*i*) In this case the number of terms in the expansion are $10 + 1 = 11$, so the middle term is T_6

$\therefore \quad T_6 = {}^{10}C_5 \left(\dfrac{x}{a}\right)^5 \left(-\dfrac{a}{x}\right)^5 = -252$

(ii) In this case the number of terms in the expansion are $9 + 1 = 10$, so the middle terms are T_5 and T_6.

Now
$$T_5 = {}^9C_4 (3x)^{9-4} \left(-\frac{x^3}{6}\right)^4$$
$$= \frac{9.8.7.6}{4.3.2} \cdot 3^5 \cdot \frac{x^{17}}{6^4} = \frac{189}{8} x^{17}$$

$$T_6 = {}^9C_5 (3x)^{9-5} \left(-\frac{x^3}{6}\right)^5 = -\frac{21}{16} x^{19}.$$

Example 3: *Find the coefficient of x^4 in the expansion of $(2 - x + 3x^2)^6$.*

Solution: Put $(2 - x + 3x^2)^6 = [2 - x(1 - 3x)]^6$
$$= 2^6 - {}^6C_1 \cdot 2^5 x(1 - 3x) + {}^6C_1 \cdot 2^4 \cdot x^2(1 - 3x)^2$$
$$- {}^6C_3 \cdot 2^3 \cdot x^3 (1 - 3x)^3 + {}^6C_4 \cdot 2^2 \cdot x^4 (1 - 3x)^4$$
$$- {}^6C_5 \cdot 2 \cdot x^5 (1 - 3x)^5 + x^6 (1 - 3x)^6$$

Coefficient of x^4 occurs in 3rd, 4th and 5th terms
$$= 15.16.9 + 20.8.9 + 15.4$$
$$= 2160 + 1440 + 60$$
$$= 3660.$$

MULTIPLE CHOICE QUESTIONS

1. The number of integral terms in the expression of

$$\left(5^{\frac{1}{2}} + 7^{\frac{1}{8}}\right)^{1024}$$ is

A. 127   B. 129
C. 131   D. 133

2. If the sum of the co-efficients in the expansion of $(a + b)^n$ is 1024, then the greatest co-efficient in the expansion is
A. 252   B. 352
C. 452   D. 552

3. If the sum of the co-efficients in the expansion of $(1 + 2x)^n$ is 6561, the greatest term in the expansion for $x = \dfrac{1}{2}$ is
A. 3rd   B. 4th
C. 5th   D. None of these

4. The positive integer just greater than $(1 + 0.0001)^{1000}$ is
A. 2   B. 3
C. 4   D. None of these

5. The number $101^{100} - 1$ is divisible by
A. 100   B. 1000
C. 10000   D. All of them

6. The remainder when 2^{2003} is divisible 17 is
A. 1   B. 2
C. 8   D. None of these

7. The digit at unit's place in the number $17^{1995} + 11^{1995} - 7^{1995}$ is
A. 0   B. 1
C. 2   D. 3

8. The sum to $(n + 1)$ terms of the series
$$\frac{C_0}{2} - \frac{C_1}{3} + \frac{C_2}{4} - \frac{C_3}{5} + \ldots \ldots \text{ is}$$

A. $\dfrac{1}{n + 1}$ B. $\dfrac{1}{n + 2}$

C. $\dfrac{1}{n (n + 1)}$ D. $\dfrac{1}{(n + 1) (n + 2)}$

9. If $|x| = 1$, then the co-efficient of x^n in the expansion of $(1 + x + x^2 + \ldots\ldots)^2$ is
A. n B. $n - 1$
C. $n + 2$ D. $n + 1$

10. If a_1, a_2, a_3, a_4 are the co-efficients of any four consecutive terms in the expansion of $(1 + x)^n$, then $\dfrac{a_1}{a_1 + a_2} + \dfrac{a_2}{a_3 + a_4}$ is equal to

A. $\dfrac{a_2}{a_2 + a_3}$ B. $\dfrac{1}{2} \cdot \dfrac{a_2}{a_2 + a_3}$

C. $\dfrac{2a_2}{a_2 + a_3}$ D. $\dfrac{2a_3}{a_2 + a_3}$

11. The remainder when 5^{99} is divided by 13 is
A. 6   B. 8
C. 9   D. 10

12. If the co-efficient of x^7 and x^8 in $\left[2 + \dfrac{x}{3}\right]^n$ are equal then n is

A. 15   B. 25

C. 45   D. 55

13. The value of $\dfrac{1}{n!} + \dfrac{1}{2!\,(n-2)!} + \dfrac{1}{4!\,(n-4)!} + \dots$

A. $\dfrac{2^{n-1}}{(n-1)!}$ B. $\dfrac{2^{n-1}}{n!}$

C. $\dfrac{2^n}{n!}$ D. None of these

14. The approximate value of $(7.995)^{\frac{1}{3}}$ correct to four decimal places is

A. 1.9995   B. 1.9996

C. 1.9990   D. 1.9991

15. The co-efficient of the term independent of x in the expansion of

$$\left(\frac{x+1}{x^{\frac{2}{3}} - x^{\frac{1}{3}} + 1} - \frac{x-1}{x - x^{\frac{1}{2}}} \right)^{10} \text{ is}$$

A. 210   B. 105

C. 70   D. 112

ANSWERS

1	2	3	4	5	6	7	8	9	10
B	A	C	B	D	C	B	C	D	C

11	12	13	14	15
B	D	B	B	A

SOME SELECTED EXPLANATORY ANSWERS

6. We have $2^{2000} = \left(2^4\right)^{500} = (17 - 1)^{500}$

$= {}^{500}C_0.17^{500} - {}^{500}C_1 17^{499} + \dots - {}^{500}C_{499}.17 + (-1)^{500}.$

$= 17m + 1$ where m is some positive integer.

$\therefore \quad 2^{2003} = 8\,(2^{2000}) = 8\,(17m+8)$

$\qquad\qquad = 17\,(8m) + 8$

$\therefore$ Required remainder is 8.

9. Given $\left(1 + x + x^2 + \dots\right)^2$

$= \left\{(1-x)^{-1}\right\}^2 = (1-x)^{-2}$

Now coefficient of x^n in $(1 - x)^{-r}$ is ${}^{n+r-1}C_{r-1}$

$\therefore$ Coefficient of x^n in $(1 - x)^{-2}$ is ${}^{n+2-1}C_{2-1}$

$\qquad\qquad = {}^{n+1}C_1 = n + 1.$

13. Given $\dfrac{1}{n!} + \dfrac{1}{2!\,(n-2)!} + \dfrac{1}{4!\,(n-4)!} + \dots$

$= \dfrac{1}{n!}\left[\dfrac{n!}{n!} + \dfrac{n!}{2!\,(n-2)!} + \dfrac{n!}{4!\,(n-4)!} + \dots\right]$

$= \dfrac{1}{n!}\left({}^nC_0 + {}^nC_2 + {}^nC_4 + \dots\right)$

$= \dfrac{2^{n-1}}{n!}.$

(6) Permutations And Combinations

COMBINATIONS

A group of r things (r can be equal to n also) chosen out of given n things is called a combination. Here the order of things is not taken into consideration.

Important Formulae of Combination

1. The number of combinations of r dissimilar things chosen out of n things is denoted by ^nC_r and is given by:

$$^nC_r = \frac{n!}{r!(n-r)!}$$

$$= \frac{n(n-1)(n-2)......(n-r+1)}{1.2.3....r}$$

2. $^nC_r = {}^nC_{n-r}$
3. $^nC_r + {}^nC_{r-1} = {}^{n+1}C_r$
4. $^nC_r + {}^nC_{r+1} = {}^{n+1}C_{r+1}$
5. $^nC_1 + {}^nC_2 + ... + {}^nC_n = 2^n - 1$

   This is the number of combinations of n things in which at least one thing is selected.

6. The number of *combinations* of $(p + q + r)$ things when p are alike of one kind q are alike of second kind, and r are alike of third kind, is

   $(p - 1)\ (q - 1)\ (r - 1) - 1$.

7. The number of *combinations* of n distinct things taken r at a time when p-particular *thing always taken is* $^{(n-p)}C_{(r-p)}$.

8. The number of *combinations* of n distinct things taken r at a time when p-particular *things* never taken is:

   $^{(n-p)}C_r$.

9. The number of *ways* to make a selection by taking some or all of $p_1 + p_2 + ... + p_r$ things, when p_1 are alike of one kind, p_2 are alike of second kind, ..., p_r are alike of rth kind, is given by:

   $[(p_1 + 1)(p_2 + 1) ... (p_r + 1) - 1]$.

10. The number of *combinations* of n distinct things taken r at a time when anything or object may be repeated any number of times is:

    $^{n+r-1}C_r$ = Coeff. of x^r in the expansion of $(1 - x)^n$.

Permutations

A group of r or all things chosen out of the given n things and arranged in a definite order is called a *permutation*.

The number of permutations of r things out of the given n thigns is denoted by ^nP_r or P(n, r).

Circular Permutations

When the objects are arranged in a circle then it is called a circular permutation.

Important Rules

(*i*) The number of circular permutations of n different things taken r at a time is $\dfrac{^nP_r}{r}$.

(*ii*) The number of ways of permuting n distinct objects along a circle is $(n - 1)!$

(*iii*) The number of ways of arranging n distinct objects along a circle when clockwise and anti-clockwise arrangements are considered alike is $\dfrac{1}{2}(n - 1)!$.

Solved Examples

Example 1: *There are three roads from A to B and four roads from B to C. In how many ways a person can go to place C from place A via place B?*

Solution:

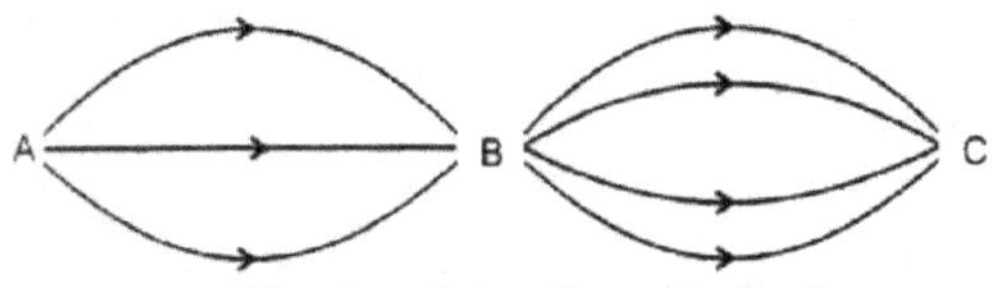

Number of ways from A to B = 3

Number of ways from A to B = 3

and number of ways from B to C = 4

∴ Required number of ways = 3 × 4 = 12

[By multiplication rule]

Example 2: *In how many ways the letters BLEEDE can be rearranged?*

Solution: Required number of different arrangements

$$= \frac{6!}{3!} = \frac{6 \times 5 \times 4 \times 3 \times 2 \times 1}{3 \times 2 \times 1}$$

$$= 6 \times 5 \times 4 = 120.$$

Example 3: *If a polygon has 27 diagonals, then how many sides does it have?*

Solution: A n-sided polygon has $^nC_2 - n = \dfrac{n(n-3)}{2}$ diagonals.

$$\therefore \qquad \frac{n(n-3)}{2} = 27$$

$$\Rightarrow \qquad n(n-3) = 54 \Rightarrow n^2 - 3n - 54 = 0$$

$$\therefore \qquad n = 9$$

Example 4: *If $^nP_r = 120$, $^nC_r = 20$, then what are the values of n and r?*

Solution: $\qquad r! = \dfrac{^nP_r}{^nC_r} = \dfrac{120}{20} = 6 = 3!$

$$\therefore \qquad r = 3$$

Now $\qquad ^nP_r = 120$

$$\Rightarrow \qquad ^nP_3 = 120 = 6 \times 5 \times 4 = {}^6P_3$$

$$\therefore \qquad n = 6$$

Example 5: *Find the number of ways in which 5 boys and 5 girls can sit in a ring.*

Solution: Given that total members to sit in a ring = 10

∴ Number of ways of sitting = (10 – 1)! = 9!

MULTIPLE CHOICE QUESTIONS

1. The number of triangles that are formed by choosing the vertices from a set of 12 points, seven of which lie on the same straight line, is:
   A. 175　　　　B. 715
   C. 75　　　　D. 185

2. Out of 18 points in a plane, no three are in the same straight line except five points which are collinear. The number of straight lines which can be formed joining them, is:
   A. 133
   B. 144
   C. 145
   D. None of these

3. A, B, C and D are four non-coplanar points. The number of planes that can be drawn passing through any three of these points, is:
   A. 3　　　　B. 4
   C. 5　　　　D. 6

4. If $^nC_r + {}^nC_{r+1} = {}^{n+1}C_x$, then x is:
   A. $r - 1$　　　　B. r
   C. n　　　　D. $r + 1$

5. The digits 4, 5, 6, 7, 8 are written in every possible order. The number of numbers greater than 56,000 is:
   A. 98　　　　B. 90
   C. 96　　　　D. 70

6. the sum of all numbers greater than 1,000 formed by using digits 1, 3, 5, 7 no digit being repeated in any number is:
   A. 72,215　　　　B. 83,911
   C. 1,06,656　　　　D. 1,14,712

7. There are 10 lamps in a hall. Each one of them can be switched on independently. The number of ways in which the hall can be illuminated, is:
   A. 10 !　　　　B. 1,023
   C. 2^{10}　　　　D. 100 !

8. There are 10 true-false questions. The number of ways in which they can be answered is:
A. $10\,!$ B. 10^2
C. 2^{10} D. $100\,!$

9. The number of all possible selections when a student can make for answering one or more questions out of eight given questions in a paper when each question have an alternative is:
A. $^8C_1 + {}^8C_2 + {}^8C_3 + \dots + {}^8C_8$
B. 2×2^8
C. 3^8
D. $3^8 - 1$

10. The number of 3-digit numbers which can be formed from the digit 1, 2, 3, 4 and 5 if repetitions of digits is allowed, is:
A. 15   B. 125
C. $5\,!$ D. $3\,!$

11. The number of ways in which a team of eleven players can be selected from 22 players always including 2 of them and excluding 4 of them is:
A. $^{16}C_5$ B. $^{16}C_{11}$
C. $^{16}C_9$ D. $^{20}C_9$

12. The number of divisors of 9,600 including 1 and 9,600 is:
A. 46   B. 58
C. 48   D. 60

13. In a college examination, a candidate is required to attempt 6 out of 10 questions which are divided into two sections each containing 5 questions. Further, the candidate is not permitted to attempt more than 4 questions from either of the section. The number of ways in which he can make up a choice of 6 questions, is:
A. 15   B. 60
C. 100   D. 200

14. A class is composed of two brothers and six other boys. In how many ways can all the boys be seated at a round table so that the two brothers are not seated besides each other?
A. 720   B. 1,440
C. 3,600   D. 4,320

15. On a railway route, there are 15 stations. The number of different tickets required in order that it may be possible to book a passenger from every station to every other (one way), is:
A. $\dfrac{15!}{2!}$ B. $15!$
C. $\dfrac{15!}{13!}$ D. $\dfrac{15!}{13!2!}$

16. An examination paper contains 8 questions of which 4 have 3 possible answers, 3 have 2 possible answers each and the remaining one question has 5 possible answers. The total number of possible answers to all the questions, is:
A. 3,240   B. 94
C. 78   D. 2,880

ANSWERS

1	2	3	4	5	6	7	8	9	10
D	B	B	D	B	C	B	C	D	B

11	12	13	14	15	16
C	C	D	C	D	D

SOME SELECTED EXPLANATORY ANSWERS

1. No. of triangles $= {}^{12}C_3 - {}^7C_3 = 185$.

2. The number of straight lines $= {}^{18}C_2 - ({}^3C_2 - 1)$
$= 144$.

3. Number of planes passing through any three of given four points.
A, B, C, D $= {}^4C_3 = {}^4C_{4-3} = {}^4C_1 = 4$

4. We have
$$^{n+1}C_x = {}^nC_r + {}^nC_{r+1} = {}^{n+1}C_{r+1}$$
or $x = r + 1$.

5. A number would be less than 56,000 only if either 4 occurs in the first place or 5, 4 occurs on the first two places.

Hence, required number of ways
$$= 5! - 4! - 3!$$
$$= 120 - 24 - 6 = 90.$$

6. As each digit occurs 3! times in unit place, ten's place, hundred's place and thousand's place. Hence, required sum
$$= 3! \ [1 + 3 + 5 + 7][1 + 10 + 100 + 1,000]$$
$$= 6[16][1,111] = 96[1,111] = 1,06,656.$$

7. For each bulb there are two choices; either switched on or off.

$\therefore$ Required number $= 2^{10} - 1 = 1,023.$

8. Since each questions can be answered in two ways.

$\therefore$ Required number
$$= 2 \times 2 \times 2 \times 2 \times 2 \times 2 \times 2 \times 2 \times 2 \times 2$$
$$= 2^{10}.$$

9. Since a student can solve every question in 3 ways–either he can attempt the first alternative or a second or he does not attempt it.

Hence, required number $= 3^8 - 1.$

10. Since each place out of unit, ten, hundred can be filled up in 5 ways.

Hence, required number of ways
$$= 5 \times 5 \times 5 = 125.$$

11. Leaving 4 from 22, we must select 9 from the reamining $22 - 4 - 2 = 16.$

Hence, number of selection $= {}^{16}C_9.$

12. As $9,600 = 2^7 \times 3 \times 5^2$

$\therefore$ Number of divisors
$$= (7 + 1) \times (1 + 1) \times (2 + 1) = 48.$$

13. Required number of ways
$$= {}^5C_4 \cdot {}^5C_2 + {}^5C_3 \cdot {}^5C_3 + {}^5C_2 \cdot {}^5C_4$$
$$= 50 + 100 + 50 = 200.$$

14. Required number of ways $= (6 - 1)! \times {}^6P_2$
$$= 5! \times 30 = 120 \times 30 = 3,600.$$

15. Here desired number of tickets $= {}^{15}C_2 = \dfrac{15!}{13!2!}$

16. Required number of possible answers
$$= 4^3 \times 3^2 \times 5$$
$$= 64 \times 9 \times 5 = 2,880.$$

(7) Matrices and Determinants

Matrices (Def.): A system of mn numbers (real or complex) arranged in a rectangular array of m rows and n columns is called a matrix of order $m \times n$ or an $m \times n$ matrix. Such an array is enclosed by [ ] or ( ). Each of the mn numbers constituting the matrix, is called an element or an entry of the matrix.

Examples:

(i) $A = \begin{bmatrix} 3 & 5 & -4 \\ 0 & 1 & 9 \end{bmatrix}$ is a matrix, having 2 rows and 3 columns. Its order is 2×3 and it has 6 elements.

(ii) $B = \begin{bmatrix} 5+3i & 4 & \sqrt{2} & -1 \\ 1 & i & -3 & 2 \\ 6 & 0 & 5 & 7 \end{bmatrix}$ is a matrix, having 3 rows and 4 columns. Its order is 3×4 and it has 12 elements.

How to represent a matrix?

An element occurring in the ith row and j^{th} column of a matrix A will be called the $(i, j)^{th}$ element of A, denoted by a_{ij}. In general, an $m \times n$ matrix A may be written as

$$A = \begin{bmatrix} a_{11} & a_{12} & a_{13} & \cdots & a_{1n} \\ a_{21} & a_{22} & a_{23} & \cdots & a_{2n} \\ \cdots & \cdots & \cdots & \cdots & \cdots \\ a_{i1} & a_{i2} & a_{i3} & a_{i4} & a_{i5} \\ \cdots & \cdots & \cdots & \cdots & \cdots \\ a_{m1} & a_{m2} & a_{m3} & \cdots & a_{mn} \end{bmatrix} = \begin{bmatrix} a_{ij} \end{bmatrix}_{m \times n}$$

TYPES OF MATRICES

Row Matrix

A matrix having only one row and any number of columns is known as a row matrix or a row vector.

Column Matrix

A matrix having only one column and any number of rows is known as a column matrix or a column vector.

Null (or zero) matrix: If all the elements of a matrix are equal to zero, then it is called a null matrix.

Square Matrix

A matrix which has the same number of rows and columns, is called a square matrix.

Any matrix of order $(n \times n)$ is called a square matrix of order n or an n rowed square matrix.

Any matrix of order $m \times n$, where $m \neq n$, is called a rectangular matrix.

Singular and non-singular square matrix

A square matrix is singular or non-singular according to the corresponding determinant of the matrix is zero or non-zero. It is non-zero if the matrix is invertible. (Invertibility of a matrix is explained later.)

Diagonal Matrix

A square matrix in which every non-diagonal elements are zero, is called a diagonal matrix.

If $A = [a_{ij}]_{n \times n}$ be a diagonal matrix, ($a_{ij} = 0$, when $i \neq j$). We can also write A as

$$A = \text{diag } [a_{11}, a_{22}, a_{33} ...., a_{nn}].$$

Scalar Matrix

A square matrix in which every non-diagonal element is zero and all diagonal elements are equal, is known as a scalar matrix.

Unit Matrix or Identity Matrix: A square matrix in which all its diagonal elements are equal to 1 and all other elements are equal to zero is called a **unit matrix or identity matrix.**

A unit matrix of order n will be denoted by I_n or simply by I.

Thus, a square matrix $[a_{ij}]_{n \times n}$ is a unit matrix, if

$$a_{ij} = \begin{cases} 0 & \text{when } i \neq j; \\ 1 & \text{when } i = j. \end{cases}$$

Equal Matrices

Two matrices A and B are said to be equal, written as A = B, if they are of the same order and their corresponding elements are equal.

PROPERTIES OF MATRIX ADDITION

(*i*) **Matrix Addition is Commutative:** If A and B be two $m \times n$ matrices, then A + B = B + A.

(*ii*) **Matrix Addition is Associative:** If A, B and C be three $m \times n$ matrices, then

(A + B) + C = A + (B + C).

(*iii*) If A is an $m \times n$ matrix and O is an $m \times n$ null matrix, then

A + O = O + A = A

Note: The null matrix O of order $m \times n$ is the *additive identity* in the set of all $m \times n$ matrices.

Negative of a Matrix

Let A = $[a_{ij}]_{m \times n}$, obtained by replacing each element of A with its corresponding additive inverse.

PROPERTIES OF SCALAR MULTIPLICATION

1. If A and B are two matrices of the same order and k is a scalar, then $k(A + B) = (kA + kB)$.
2. If A is any matrix and k_1, k_2 are any scalars, then

   (*i*) $(k_1 + k_2) A = k_1 A + k_2 A$

   (*ii*) $k_1 (k_2 A) = (k_1 k_2) A$

Transpose of a Matrix: Let A be an $m \times n$ matrix. Then the matrix of order $n \times m$ obtained by changing its rows into columns and columns into rows is called the transpose of A and is denoted by A' or A^T. Thus,

(*i*) if the order of A is $m \times n$, then, the order of A' is $n \times m$.

(*ii*) $(i, j)^{\text{th}}$ element of A = $(j, i)^{\text{th}}$ element of A'.

Properties of transpose of matrices

1. For any matrix A, (A')' = A
2. If A and B are two matrices of the same order, then (A + B)' = A' + B'.
3. If A is any matrix and k is a scalar, then $(kA)' = kA'$.

Some important results of transposed matrices

(*i*) (A + B)' = A' + B'

(*ii*) $(kA)' = kA'$, where k is constant

(*iii*) (AB)' = B'A'.

Symmetric Matrix: A square matrix A is said to be symmetric if A' = A.

Thus a square matrix A = $[a_{ij}]$ is symmetric if $a_{ij} = a_{ji}$ for all values of i and j.

Skew-symmetric Matrix: A square matrix A is said to be skew-symmetric if A' = –A.

Thus a square matrix A = $[a_{ij}]$ is skew-symmetric if $a_{ij} = -a_{ji}$ for all values of i and j.

Properties of symmetric and skew-symmetric matrices

1. (*i*) the sum of two symmetric matrices is always symmetric.

   (*ii*) the sum of two skew-symmetric matrices is always skew-symmetric.

2. Let A be a square matrix and k be a scalar.

   (*i*) If A is symmetric, then kA is symmetric;

   (*ii*) If A is skew-symmetric, then kA is skew-symmetric.

3. If A is any square matrix, then

   (*i*) (A + A') is symmetric and

   (*ii*) (A – A') is skew-symmetric.

4. Every square matrix is uniquely expressible as the sum of a symmetric matrix and a skew-symmetric matrix.

5. Every diagonal element of a skew-symmetric matrix is zero.

where the first matrix on right hand side is symmetric and the second one is skew-symmetric.

PROPERTIES OF MATRIX MULTIPLICATION

(*i*) **Associative Law for multiplication:** If A, B and C be three matrices of order $m \times n$, $n \times p$ and $p \times q$ respectively, then $(AB)C = A(BC)$.

(*ii*) **Distributive Law:** If A, B, C be three matrices of order $m \times n$, $n \times p$ and $n \times p$ respectively, then

A. (B + C) = A.B + A.C.

(*iii*) Matrix multiplication is not commutative in general, *i.e.,* A.B ≠ B.A (in general).

(*iv*) The product of two non-zero matrices can be a zero matrix.

Determinant: Corresponding to each square matrix

$$A = \begin{bmatrix} a_{11} & a_{12} & a_{13} & \dots & a_{1n} \\ a_{21} & a_{22} & a_{23} & \dots & a_{2n} \\ \dots & \dots & \dots & \dots & \dots \\ a_{n1} & a_{n2} & a_{n3} & \dots & a_{nn} \end{bmatrix},$$

there is an associated expression, which is called the *determinant* of A, denoted by det A or |A|, written as

$$\det A = |A| = \begin{vmatrix} a_{11} & a_{12} & a_{13} & \dots & a_{1n} \\ a_{21} & a_{22} & a_{23} & \dots & a_{2n} \\ \dots & \dots & \dots & \dots & \dots \\ a_{n1} & a_{n2} & a_{n3} & \dots & a_{nn} \end{vmatrix}$$

A matrix is an arrangement of numbers and so it has no fixed value, while each determinant has a fixed value.

A determinant having n rows and n columns is knonw as a determinant of order n.

Thus, the determinants of non-square matrices are not defined.

Minor of an element: The minor M_{ij} of an element a_{ij} of a square matrix A is the determinant of the matrix that remains after deleting the i-th row and j-th column in given matrix A.

Cofactor of an element: The cofactor C_{ij} of an element a_{ij} of a square matrix A is $(-1)^{i+j}$ times the determinant of the matrix that reamins after deleting the i-th row and j-th column in the given matrix A.

Example: Find the minors and co-factors of the elements of the determinant

$$\Delta = \begin{vmatrix} a_{11} & a_{12} & a_{13} \\ a_{21} & a_{22} & a_{23} \\ a_{31} & a_{32} & a_{33} \end{vmatrix}$$

Let M_{ij} denote the minor of a_{ij} in Δ.

Now, a_{11} occurs in 1st column. So, in order to find the minor of a_{11}, we delete the 1st row and 1st column of Δ. The minor M_{11} of a_{11} is given by

$$M_{11} = \begin{vmatrix} a_{22} & a_{23} \\ a_{32} & a_{33} \end{vmatrix} = (a_{22}a_{33} - a_{32}a_{23}).$$

Similarly, we have:

$$M_{12} = \begin{vmatrix} a_{21} & a_{23} \\ a_{31} & a_{33} \end{vmatrix} = (a_{21}a_{33} - a_{31}a_{23})$$

$$M_{13} = \begin{vmatrix} a_{21} & a_{22} \\ a_{31} & a_{32} \end{vmatrix} = (a_{21}a_{32} - a_{31}a_{22})$$

$$M_{21} = \begin{vmatrix} a_{12} & a_{13} \\ a_{32} & a_{33} \end{vmatrix} = (a_{12}a_{33} - a_{32}a_{13})$$

Similarly, we may obtain the minor of each one of the remaining elements.

Now, if we denote the co-factor of a_{ij} by c_{ij}, then

$C_{11} = (-1)^{1+1} \cdot M_{11} = M_{11} = (a_{22}a_{33} - a_{32}a_{23})$;
$C_{12} = (-1)^{1+2} \cdot M_{12} = -M_{12} = (a_{31}a_{23} - a_{21}a_{33})$;
$C_{13} = (-1)^{1+3} \cdot M_{13} = M_{13} = (a_{21}a_{32} - a_{31}a_{22})$
$C_{21} = (-1)^{2+1} \cdot M_{21} = -M_{21} = (a_{32}a_{13} - a_{12}a_{33})$.

Similarly, the co-factor of each one of remaining elements of Δ can be determined.

PROPERTIES OF DETERMINANTS

(*i*) The value of the determinant does not change when rows and columns are interchanged.

(*ii*) If all the elements of a rwo (column) are zero, then the value of the determinant is zero.

(*iii*) The interchange of any two rows (columns) of the determinant changes its sign.

(iv) If all the elements of a row (column) of a determinant are multiplied by a *non-zero* constant, then the value of the determinant gets multiplied by the same constant.

(v) If all the elements of a row (column) are *proportional (identical)* to the elements of some other row (column), then the value of the determinant is zero.

(vi) If each element of any row (column) is sum of two numbers, the determinant can be expressed as the sum of two determinants of the same order.

(vii) The value of a determinant remains unaltered under an operation of the form

$$R_i \rightarrow R_i + pR_j = qR_k, \; j, \, k \neq i$$

and $C_i \rightarrow C_i + pC_j + qC_k, \; j, \, k \neq i.$

SOME MORE PROPERTIES

(i) If a determinant $\Delta(x)$ becomes zero on putting $x = \alpha$, then $(x - \alpha)$ is a factor of $\Delta(x)$.

(ii) Determinant, which have all elements equal to zero except the diagonal elements, is equal to the product of the diagonal elements.

Solution of System of Linear Equations in Three variables by Cramers Rule: Solution of three linear equations in three unknown

$$a_1 x_1 + b_1 x_2 + c_1 x_3 = d_1$$
$$a_2 x_1 + b_2 x_2 + c_2 x_3 = d_2$$
$$a_3 x_1 + b_3 x_2 + c_3 x_3 = d_3$$

is given by $x_1 = \dfrac{D_1}{D}$, $x_2 = \dfrac{D_2}{D}$ and $x_3 = \dfrac{D_3}{D}$.

Where $D = \begin{vmatrix} a_1 & b_1 & c_1 \\ a_2 & b_2 & c_2 \\ a_3 & b_3 & c_3 \end{vmatrix}$, $D_1 = \begin{vmatrix} d_1 & b_1 & c_1 \\ d_2 & b_2 & c_2 \\ d_3 & b_3 & c_3 \end{vmatrix}$,

$D_2 = \begin{vmatrix} a_1 & d_1 & c_1 \\ a_2 & d_2 & c_2 \\ a_3 & d_3 & c_3 \end{vmatrix}$ and $D_3 = \begin{vmatrix} a_1 & b_1 & d_1 \\ a_2 & b_2 & d_2 \\ a_3 & b_3 & d_3 \end{vmatrix}$, provided that $D \neq 0$.

Conditions for Consistency and Inconsistency

(i) If $D \neq 0$ and out of D_1, D_2, D_3 at least one is $\neq 0$, then the system of equation is consistent and has a unique solution.

(ii) If $D = 0$ and also $D_1 = D_2 = D_3 = 0$, then the given system of equation is consistent and has infinite number of solutions.

(iii) If $D = 0$ and at least one of D_1, D_2, D_3 is non-zero, then the given system of equation is inconsistent.

MULTIPLE CHOICE QUESTIONS

1. If $M(\theta) = \begin{bmatrix} \cos \theta & \sin \theta \\ -\sin \theta & \cos \theta \end{bmatrix}$, then $M(\alpha)\, M(\beta)$ is equal to

A. $M(0)$
B. $M(\alpha\beta)$
C. $M(\alpha + \beta)$
D. $M(\alpha - \beta)$

2. If the product of matrices

$$A = \begin{bmatrix} \cos^2 \theta & \cos \theta \sin \theta \\ \cos \theta \sin \theta & \sin^2 \theta \end{bmatrix}$$

$$B = \begin{bmatrix} \cos^2 \phi & \cos \phi \sin \phi \\ \cos \phi \sin \phi & \sin^2 \phi \end{bmatrix}$$

is a null matrix, then θ and ϕ differ by

A. an odd multiple of π
B. an even multiple of π
C. an odd multiple of $\dfrac{\pi}{2}$
D. an even multiple of $\dfrac{\pi}{2}$

3. If $D = \text{diag}\,(d_1, d_2, d_3, \ldots, d_n)$, where $d_i \neq 0$ for all $i = 1, 2, \ldots, n$ then D^{-1} is equal to

A. D
B. $\text{diag}\left(d_1^{-1}, d_2^{-1}, \ldots, d_n^{-1}\right)$
C. I_n
D. None of these

4. If $X = \begin{bmatrix} 3 & -4 \\ 1 & -1 \end{bmatrix}$, the value of X^n is

A. $\begin{bmatrix} 3n & -4n \\ n & -n \end{bmatrix}$ B. $\begin{bmatrix} 2+n & 5-n \\ n & -n \end{bmatrix}$

C. $\begin{bmatrix} 3^n & (-4)^n \\ 1^n & (-1)^n \end{bmatrix}$ D. None of these

5. The matrix, $A = \begin{bmatrix} 2 & -2 & -4 \\ -1 & 3 & 4 \\ 1 & -2 & -3 \end{bmatrix}$ is

A. non-singular   B. idempotent
C. nilpotent   D. orthogonal

6. If $A = \begin{bmatrix} 1 & 0 \\ 0 & 1 \end{bmatrix}$, $B = \begin{bmatrix} 0 & 1 \\ -1 & 0 \end{bmatrix}$ and

$C = \begin{bmatrix} \cos\theta & \sin\theta \\ -\sin\theta & \cos\theta \end{bmatrix}$, then which of the following is true?

A. $C = A\cos\theta - B\sin\theta$
B. $C = A\sin\theta + B\cos\theta$
C. $C = A\sin\theta - B\cos\theta$
D. $C = A\cos\theta + B\sin\theta$

7. The inverse of the matrix

$\begin{bmatrix} 2 & -5 & 1 \\ 8 & 6 & 7 \\ \lambda & -10 & 2 \end{bmatrix}$ does not exist if λ equals to

A. 0   B. 2
C. 4   D. 5

8. The characteristic roots of the matrix

$A = \begin{bmatrix} 8 & -6 & 2 \\ -6 & 7 & -4 \\ 2 & -4 & 3 \end{bmatrix}$ are

A. 0, 3, 15   B. 0, −3, −15
C. 0, 3, −15   D. 0, −3, 15

9. The rank of

$A = \begin{bmatrix} 6 & 1 & 3 & 8 \\ 4 & 2 & 6 & -1 \\ 10 & 3 & 9 & 7 \\ 16 & 4 & 12 & 15 \end{bmatrix}$ is

A. 4   B. 3
C. 2   D. 1

10. The transformation matrix $\begin{bmatrix} 1 & 0 & 0 \\ 0 & 0 & 1 \\ 0 & 1 & 0 \end{bmatrix}$ represents

A. Rotation about x-axis by $90°$
B. Reflection about $y = z$
C. Reflexion about x-axis
D. None of these

11. The matrix $\begin{bmatrix} 1 & 5-i & 3 \\ 5+i & 2 & 3i \\ 3 & -3i & 0 \end{bmatrix}$ is

A. Symmetric   B. Skew-Symmetric
C. Hermitian   D. Skew-Hermitian

12. The eigen values of the matrix

$\begin{bmatrix} 2 & 2 & 1 \\ 1 & 3 & 1 \\ 1 & 2 & 2 \end{bmatrix}$ are

A. 1, 3, 1   B. 2, 3, 2
C. 5, 1, 1   D. 3, 5, 2

13. Given that $xyz = -1$, the value of the determinant

$\begin{vmatrix} x & x^2 & 1+x^3 \\ y & y^2 & 1+y^3 \\ z & z^2 & 1+z^3 \end{vmatrix}$ is

A. 0   B. Positive
C. Negative   D. None of these

14. If the value of the determinant $\begin{vmatrix} a & 1 & 1 \\ 1 & b & 1 \\ 1 & 1 & c \end{vmatrix}$ is positive, then

A. $abc > 1$ B. $abc > -8$
C. $abc < -8$ D. $abc > -2$

15. If $\omega = \dfrac{\left(-1+\sqrt{3}i\right)}{2}$, then the value of

$\begin{vmatrix} 1 & 1 & 1 \\ 1 & \omega & \omega^2 \\ 1 & \omega^2 & \omega \end{vmatrix}$ is

A. $3\sqrt{3}i$ B. $-3\sqrt{3}i$
C. $-\sqrt{3}i$ D. $\sqrt{3}i$

16. If $\Delta = \begin{vmatrix} \cos\alpha & -\sin\alpha & 1 \\ \sin\alpha & \cos\alpha & 1 \\ \cos(\alpha+\beta) & -\sin(\alpha+\beta) & 1 \end{vmatrix}$, then

A. $\Delta \in \left[1 - \sqrt{2}, 1 + \sqrt{2}\right]$

B. $\Delta \in [-1, 1]$

C. $\Delta \in \left[-\sqrt{2}, \sqrt{2}\right]$

D. None of these

17. If $a_1, a_2, a_3, \ldots, a_m, \ldots$ are in G.P., then the determinant

$$\Delta = \begin{vmatrix} \log a_n & \log a_{n+1} & \log a_{n+2} \\ \log a_{n+3} & \log a_{n+4} & \log a_{n+5} \\ \log a_{n+6} & \log a_{n+7} & \log a_{n+8} \end{vmatrix} \text{ is equal}$$

to

A. 0

B. 1

C. 2

D. None of these

18. $\Delta_r = \begin{vmatrix} 2r & x & n(n+1) \\ 6r^2 - 1 & y & n^2(2n+3) \\ 4r^3 - 2nr & z & n^3(n+1) \end{vmatrix}$, then

$\sum\limits_{r=1}^{n} \Delta_r$ is independent of

A. x, y, z only

B. x, y, z and n

C. x only

D. None of these

19. Let a, b, c be positive real numbers. The following system of equations in $x, y,$ and z

$$\frac{x^2}{a^2} + \frac{y^2}{b^2} - \frac{z^2}{c^2} = 1, \quad \frac{x^2}{a^2} - \frac{y^2}{b^2} + \frac{z^2}{c^2} = 1,$$

$$-\frac{x^2}{a^2} + \frac{y^2}{b^2} + \frac{z^2}{c^2} = 1 \text{ has}$$

A. no solution

B. unique solution

C. infinitely many solutions

D. finitely many solutions

20. The system of linear equations

$x + y + z = 2$

$2x + y - z = 3$

$3x + 2y + kz = 4$ has unique solutions if

A. $k \neq 0$

B. $-1 < k < 1$

C. $-2 < k < 1$

D. $k = 0$

ANSWERS

1	2	3	4	5	6	7	8	9	10
C	C	B	D	B	D	C	A	A	B
11	12	13	14	15	16	17	18	19	20
C	C	A	B	B	A	A	B	B	A

SOME SELECTED EXPLANATORY ANSWERS

4. Given $X = \begin{bmatrix} 3 & -4 \\ 1 & -1 \end{bmatrix}$

$$\Rightarrow \quad X^2 = \begin{bmatrix} 3 & -4 \\ 1 & -1 \end{bmatrix}\begin{bmatrix} 3 & -4 \\ 1 & -1 \end{bmatrix}$$

$$= \begin{bmatrix} 5 & -8 \\ 2 & -3 \end{bmatrix}$$

Putting $n = 2$ in all the given option, *i.e.*, *(a)*, *(b)* and *(c)*, it is seen that none of them talies. Thus *(d)* is the required choice.

5. Given $A = \begin{bmatrix} 2 & -2 & -4 \\ -1 & 3 & 4 \\ 1 & -2 & 3 \end{bmatrix}$

$$\Rightarrow \quad A^2 = \begin{bmatrix} 2 & -2 & -4 \\ -1 & 3 & 4 \\ 1 & -2 & 3 \end{bmatrix}\begin{bmatrix} 2 & -2 & -4 \\ -1 & 3 & 4 \\ 1 & -2 & 3 \end{bmatrix}$$

$$\Rightarrow \quad A^2 = \begin{bmatrix} 2 & -2 & -4 \\ -1 & 3 & 4 \\ 1 & -2 & -3 \end{bmatrix} = A$$

Hence, A is idempotent.

6. By closely inspecting and w.r.t. $A = \begin{bmatrix} 1 & 0 \\ 0 & 1 \end{bmatrix}$

and $B = \begin{bmatrix} 0 & 1 \\ -1 & 0 \end{bmatrix}$ we conclude that

$$A\cos\theta + B\sin\theta = \begin{bmatrix} 1 & 0 \\ 0 & 1 \end{bmatrix}\cos + \begin{bmatrix} 0 & 1 \\ -1 & 0 \end{bmatrix}\sin\theta$$

$$= \begin{bmatrix} \cos\theta & \sin\theta \\ -\sin\theta & \cos\theta \end{bmatrix} = C$$

11. All the elements of the given matrix are of the form $a_{ji} = \overline{a}_{ij}$.

12. Let $A = \begin{bmatrix} 2 & 2 & 1 \\ 1 & 3 & 1 \\ 1 & 2 & 2 \end{bmatrix}$

The characteristic equation of A is

$$|A - \lambda I| = 0$$

$$\Rightarrow \begin{vmatrix} 2-\lambda & 2 & 1 \\ 1 & 3-\lambda & 1 \\ 1 & 2 & 2-\lambda \end{vmatrix} = 0$$

$$\Rightarrow (\lambda-1)^2 (\lambda-5) = 0$$

$$\Rightarrow \lambda = 1, 1, 5.$$

19. Let $\dfrac{x^2}{a^2} = X,\ \dfrac{y^2}{b^2} = Y,\ \dfrac{z^2}{c^2} = Z.$

Then the given system of equation reduces to

$X + Y - Z = 1$

$X - Y + Z = 1$

$- X + Y + Z = 1$

The coefficient matrix is

$$A = \begin{bmatrix} 1 & 1 & -1 \\ 1 & -1 & 1 \\ -1 & 1 & 1 \end{bmatrix}$$

Here $|A| \neq 0$, so the given system of equations has unique solution.

20. The given system will have unique solution if

$$|A| \neq 0$$

$$\Rightarrow \begin{vmatrix} 1 & 1 & 1 \\ 2 & 1 & -1 \\ 3 & 2 & k \end{vmatrix} \neq 0$$

$$\Rightarrow 1\begin{vmatrix} 1 & -1 \\ 2 & k \end{vmatrix} - 1\begin{vmatrix} 2 & -1 \\ 3 & k \end{vmatrix} + 1\begin{vmatrix} 2 & 1 \\ 3 & 2 \end{vmatrix} \neq 0$$

$$\Rightarrow (k+2) - (2k+3) + (4-3) \neq 0$$

$$\Rightarrow -k \neq 0 \Rightarrow k \neq 0.$$

SETS

A well defined class or collection of objects is called a set and these objects are called elements of the set.

Finite and Infinite Sets

If the number of elements in a set is finite, then the set is called a finite set and if the number of elements in the set is infinite, then the set is called an infinite set.

Null Set

A set containing no element is called a null set.

Non-Empty Set

Any set which is not a null / void / empty set.

Singleton Set

Which contains one element only, *e.g.,* {0}, {1}, {Ram}.

Equivalent Sets

Two sets are equivalent if the number of elements in one set is equal to the number of elements in the other set, *e.g.,* {1, 2, 3} is equivalent to {*a, b, c*}.

Equal Sets (A = B)

If every element of set 'A' is in set 'B' and vice-versa.

Set of Sets/Family of Sets/Class of Sets

When the elements of a set are sets themselves.

e.g.,   A = {{ϕ}, {2}, {1}, {1, 2}},

B = {ϕ} because ϕ itself is a set called as null set.

Subset (A $\subseteq$ B)

If every element of 'A' is an element of 'B', then 'A' is a subset of 'B'.

Proper Subset (A $\subset$ B)

'A' is a proper subset of 'B', if all the elements of 'A' are elements of 'B' but not vice-versa. *e.g.,*

if   A = {1, 2, 3, 4}, and

B = {A, B, 1, 2, 3, 4, 5}, then A $\subset$ B

i.e., A is a proper subset of B if A $\subset$ B but B $\not\subset$ A.

i.e., A is a proper subset of B if A $\subset$ B but B $\neq$ A.

Improper Subset (A $\subseteq$ B)

i.e., A is an improper subset of 'B', if A = B, *i.e.,* all the elements of A are elements of B and vice-versa.

Super Set (A $\supset$ B)

{*i.e.,* A contains B}. If B is a sub-set of A, then A is called a super set of B.

Universal Set (U)

If a set contains all the sets under consideration, then it is called universal set.

Largest non-empty set of which all the sets under consideration, is universal set.

Power Set (P(A))

P(A) is the "power set of A" if P(A) contains all the possible subsets of A.

Thus power set is a "set of sets" or "class of sets", *e.g.,* if A = {2, 3, 4} then

P(A) = {{ϕ}, {2}, {3}, {4}, {2, 3}, {2, 4}, {3, 4}, {2, 3, 4}}

Disjoint set

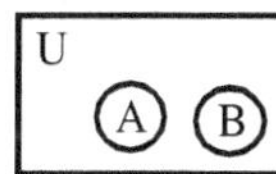

If two sets A and B do not have any common element, then A and B are disjoint sets, *i.e.*, $(A \cap B) = \phi$.

Representation of Sets

(*a*) **Rester Method or Tabular Method**

Here we list out all the elements as such within curly brackets, *e.g.*,

A = {1, 2, 3, 4, 5, ..., n)

(*b*) **Property of Set Builder Method**

By starting all the properties of the elements in the set, which will define all the elements of the set but nothing else, *e.g.*,

A = {2, 4, 6, 8} is written as

A = {$x : x$ is even natural number ≤ 8}

Cartesian Product (A × B)

Let A and B be two sets, then the set of all the ordered pairs of the form (a, b) such that $a \in A$ and $b \in B$ is A × B (read as A cross B).

Symbolically,

A × B = {$(a, b) / a \in A$ and $b \in B$}

Complement of A Set (A^C or A′)

Complement of a set is always with respect to one of its universal sets or super sets.

If X is an universal set of A, then the set of all the elements which are in X but not in A is A^c, *i.e.*, complement of A with respect to X.

Symbolically,

A′ or A^c = (X \ A), *i.e.*, (X – A)

Results on Number of Elements in Sets

If A, B and C are finite sets, and U be the finite universal set, then

(*i*) $n(A \cup B) = n(A) + n(B) - n(A \cap B)$

(*ii*) $n(A \cup B) = n(A) + n(B) \Leftrightarrow$ A, B are disjoint non-void sets.

(*iii*) $n(A - B) = n(A) - n(A \cap B)$

    i.e., $n(A - B) + n(A \cap B) = n(A)$

(*iv*) $n(A \Delta B)$ = No. of elements which belong to exactly one of A or B

$= n [(A - B) \cup (B - A)]$

$= n (A - B) + n (B - A)$

    [$\because$ (A – B) and (B – A) are disjoint]

$= n (A) - n (A \cap B) + n (B) - n (A \cap B)$

$= n (A) + n (B) - 2n (A \cap B)$

(*v*) $n (A \cup B \cup C) = n (A) + n (B) + n (C) - n (A \cap B) - n (B \cap C) - n (A \cap C) + n (A \cap B \cap C)$

(*vi*) No. of elements in exactly two of the sets A, B, C $= n (A \cap B) + n (B \cap C) + n(C \cap A) - 3n (A \cap B \cap C)$

(*vii*) No. of elements in exactly one of the sets A, B, C $= n(A) + n(B) + n(C) - 2n (A \cap B) - 2n (B \cap C) - 2n (A \cap C) + 3n (A \cap B \cap C)$

(*viii*) $n (A' \cup B') = (n (A \cap B)') = n (U) - n (A \cap B)$

(*ix*) $n (A' \cap B') = (n (A \cap B)') = n (U) - n (A \cap B)$

(*x*) $n(A' \cap B') = n (A \cup B)' = n (U) - n (A \cup B)$

RELATION

Let there be two sets A and B, then a "relation R from set A to set B" is a sub-set of A × B.

A is called 'Domain of R'

B is called 'Co-domain of R'

And the set of the corresponding second entries in the ordered pairs comprising the relation R is called the 'Range of R'.

Inverse Relation (R⁻¹)

Let R be a relation from A to B (*i.e.*, from set A to set B), then the inverse relation R^{-1} (which will be from set B to set A) is defined by

$R^{-1} = \{(b, a) : (a, b) \in R\}$

(*i*) **Reflexive relation**

If "$a\ R\ a$" holds good for all $a \in A$.

(*ii*) **Symmetric relation**

Here "$a\ R\ b$" implies "$b\ R\ a$". This means R is symmetric, if

$(a, b) \in R \Rightarrow (b, a) \in R$ for all $a, b \in A$.

(*iii*) **Transitive relation**

If "$a\ R\ b$" and "$b\ R\ c$" together imply "$a\ R\ c$". A relation R is transitive on set A if

$(a, b) \in R$ and $(b, c) \in R \Rightarrow (a, c) \in R$ for all $a, b, c \in A$.

(*iv*) **Equivalence relation**

If a relation is reflexive and symmetric as well as transitive, it is called an "equivalence relation".

FUNCTIONS

Cartesian Product of 2 sets A and B (A × B)

Cartesian Product of two sets A and B denoted by A × B is the set of all ordered pairs (a, b) such that

$a \in$ A and $b \in$ B.

Symbolically,

A × B = $\{(a, b) : a \in$ A and $b \in$ B$\}$

Function

Let X and Y be two non-empty sets. A subset f of X × Y is called a function from X into Y iff (*i.e.*, if and only if) for each $x \in$ X, there exists a unique y in Y such that $(x, y) \in f$.

Representation of Function

A function from a set X into a set Y is denoted as

$f : X \longrightarrow Y$ or as $X \xrightarrow{f} Y$.

Domain and co-domain: If f be the function defined from the set X into the set Y, then the set X is called domain of the function f denoted by (D_f) or dom (f) and the set Y is called co-domain of the function f.

Image: The unique element y in Y assigned to $x \in$ X is called the image of x under f or value of f at x. It is denoted by $f(x)$. It is also written as:

Pre-image: If y is image of x, then x is called a pre-image of y.

Inverse Image of B ∀ B ⊂ Y: (Read — Inverse image of B where B is a sub-set of Y)

If B ⊂ Y, then the set $\{x \in X : f(x) \in B\}$ is called the inverse image of B under f and is denoted as f^{-1} [B].

"Onto" and "Into" functions: Onto function is also known as surjection or surjective mapping.

If range of f is the set Y, *i.e.*, range = co-domain, then f is called *onto function*. However, if range of f is a proper subset of the set Y, then f is said to be an *into function*.

Two-one / Many-one function: If two or more elements in X have the same image in Y, then f is called a two-one or many-one function, respectively.

One-one function: Also known as "Injection Function" or "Injective Mapping".

If different elements in X have different images in Y then f is a one-one function.

Hence, if f is a one-one function, it means $f(x_1) = f(x_2) \Rightarrow x_1 = x_2$.

One-one onto function: When for each $x \in$ X, there is a unique $f(x) \in$ Y and for each $f(x) \in$ Y there is a unique $x \in$ X, then the function is an "one-one onto function".

In case of an inverse function,

dom (f^{-1}) = range (f)

where f^{-1} is the inverse of the function f.

Solved Examples

Example 1: *If A = {1, 2, 3, 4}, define relation on A which have properties of being*
(i) reflexive, transitive but not symmetric
(ii) symmetric but netither reflexive nor transitive
(iii) reflexive, symmetric and transitive.

Solution:

(*i*) Let R$_1$ = $\{(1, 1), (2, 2), (3, 3), (4, 4), (1, 3), (3, 4), (1, 4)\}$, This relation is reflexive, transitive but not symmetric.

(*ii*) Let R$_2$ = $\{(1, 3), (3, 1)\}$
Here R$_2$ is symmetric but neither reflexive nor transitive.

(*iii*) Let R$_3$ = $\{(1, 1), (2, 2), (3, 3), (4, 4), (1, 2), (2, 1)\}$.
Here R$_3$ is reflexive, symmetric and transitive.

Example 2: *If A = {1, 3, 5, 7, 11, 13, 15, 17}, B = {2, 4, 6, ..., 18} and N is the univeral set, then find A′ ∪ ((A ∪ B) ∩ B′).*

Solution: We have

$(A \cup B) \cap B' = A$ [∵ A, B are disjoint sets]

∴ $A' \cup ((A \cup B) \cap B') = A' \cup A = N$.

Example 3: *Three relations R$_1$, R$_2$ and R$_3$ are defined on set A = {a, b, c} as follows:*
(i) R$_1$ = {(a, a), (a, b), (a, c), (b, b), (b, c), (c, a), (c, b), (c, c)}
(ii) R$_2$ = {(a, b), (b, a), (a, c), (c, a)}
(iii) R$_3$ = {(a, b), (b, c), (c, a)}
Find whether each of R$_1$, R$_2$ and R$_3$ is reflexive, symmetric and transitive.

Solution:

(*i*) **Reflexive:** Clearly, $(a, a), (b, b), (c, c), \in$ R$_1$.
So, R$_1$ is reflexive on A.

Symmetric: We observe that $(a, b) \in R_1$ but $(b, a) \notin R_1$.
So, R_1 is not symmetric on A.
Transitive: We find that $(b, c) \in R_1$ and $(c, a) \in R_1$ but $(b, a) \notin R_1$. So, R is not transitive on A.

(ii) Reflexive: Since (a, a), (b, b) and (c, c) are not in R_2. So, it is not a reflexive relation on A.
Symmetric: We find that the ordered pairs obtained by interchanging the components of ordered pairs in R_2 are also in R_2. So, R_2 is a symmetric relation on A.
Transitive: Clearly $(a, b) \in R_2$ and $(b, a) \in R_2$ but $(a, a) \in R_2$.

(iii) Reflexive: Since none of (a, a), (b, b) and (c, c) is an element of R_3. So, R_3 is not reflexive on A.
Symmetric: Clearly, $(b, c) \in R_3$ but $(c, b) \notin R_3$. So, R_3 is not symmetric on A.
Transitive: Clearly, $(a, b) \in R_3$ and $(b, c) \in R_3$ but $(a, c) \notin R_3$. So, R_3 is not transitive on A.

Example 4: *If $A \times B = \{(a, 1), (a, 5), (a, 2), (b, 2), (b, 5), (b, 1)\}$, find $B \times A$.*

Solution: Clearly, $B \times A$ can be obtained from $A \times B$ by interchanging the entries (or components) or ordered pair in $A \times B$.

$\therefore B \times A = \{(1, a), (5, a), (2, a), (3, a), (5, b), (1, b)\}$

MULTIPLE CHOICE QUESTIONS

1. If $A = \{1, 3, 5, 7, 9, 11, 13, 15, 17\}$, $B = \{2, 4, ..., 18\}$ and N is the universal set, then $A' \cup ((A\ B)\ B')$ is
   - A. A
   - B. N
   - C. B
   - D. None of these

2. If $X = \{4^n - 3n - 1 | n \in N\}$ and $Y = 9\ (n - 1) | n \in N\}$, then $X \cup Y$ is equal to
   - A. X
   - B. Y
   - C. N
   - D. None of these

3. Let $A = \{x, y) \mid y = e^x, x \in R\}$
   $B = \{(x, y) \mid y = e^x, x \in R\}$, then
   - A. $A \cap B = \phi$
   - B. $A \cap B \neq \phi$
   - C. $A \cup B = R^2$
   - D. None of these

4. Suppose $A_1, A_2, ..., A_{30}$ are thirty sets each with five elements and $B_1, B_2, ..., B_n$ are n sets each with three elements such that

   $$\bigcup_{i=1}^{30} A_i = \bigcup_{i=1}^{n} B_i = S.$$ If each element of S belongs to exactly ten of the A_i's and exactly 9 of the B_i's, then the value of n is
   - A. 15
   - B. 135
   - C. 45
   - D. 90

5. If sets A and B are defined as

   $$A = \left\{(x, y) \mid y = \frac{1}{x'} 0 \neq x \in R\right\}$$

   $B = \{(x, y) \mid y = -x, x \in R\}$, then

   - A. $A \cap B = A$
   - B. $A \cap B = B$
   - C. $A \cup B = \phi$
   - D. None of these

6. A set contains n elements. The power set contains
   - A. n elements
   - B. 2^n elements
   - C. n^2 elements
   - D. None of these

7. If $A = \{1, 2, 3\}$ and $B = \{3, 8\}$, then $(A \cup B) \times (A \cap B)$ is
   - A. $\{(3, 1), (3, 2), (3, 3), (3, 8)\}$
   - B. $\{(1, 3), (2, 3), (3, 3), (8, 3)\}$
   - C. $\{(1, 2), (2, 2), (3, 3), (8, 8)\}$
   - D. $\{(8, 3), (8, 2), (8, 1), (8, 8)\}$

8. The number of subsets of a set containing n elements is
   - A. n
   - B. $2^n - 1$
   - C. n^2
   - D. 2^n

9. The symmetric difference of A and B is
   - A. $(A - B) \cap (B - A)$
   - B. $(A - B) \cup (B - A)$
   - C. $(A \cup B) - (B \cap A)$
   - D. $\{(A - B) - A\} \cup (A - B) - B\}$

10. If $A = \{1, 2, 3\}$, $B = \{4, 5, 6\}$ and $C = \{1, 2\}$, then $(A - B) \times (A \cap C)$ is
    - A. $\{(1, 3), (1, 5\}$
    - B. $\{(2, 1), (2, 2), (2, 3)\}$
    - C. $\{(1, 2), (1, 3), (1, 5)\}$
    - D. None of these

11. If R is a relation from a finite set A having m elements to a finite set B having n elements, then the number of relations from A to B is

  A. 2^{mn} B. $2^{mn} - 1$

  C. $2mn$ D. m^n

12. Let R be a relation on a set A such that R = R^{-1}, then R is

  A. reflexive   B. symmetric

  C. transitive   D. None of these

13. Let R_1 be a relation defined by $R_1 = \{(a, b) \mid a \le b, a, b \in R\}$. Then R_1 is

  A. an equivalence relation on R

  B. reflexive, transitive but not symmetric

  C. symmetric, transitive but not reflexive

  D. neither transitive nor reflexive but symmetric

14. The relation R = $\{(1, 1), (2, 2), (3, 3), (1, 2), (2, 3), (1, 3)\}$ on set A = $\{1, 2, 3\}$ is

  A. reflexive but not symmetric

  B. reflexive but not transitive

  C. symmetric and transitive

  D. neither symmetric nor transitive

15. Let P = $\{(x, y) \mid x^2 + y^2 = 1, x, y \in R\}$. Then P is

  A. reflexive   B. symmetric

  C. transitive   D. antisymmetric

16. If R be a relation $<$ from A = $\{1, 2, 3, 4\}$ to B = $\{1, 3, 5\}$, i.e., $(a, b) \in R \Leftrightarrow a < b$, then $R \, o \, R^{-1}$ is

  A. $\{(1, 3), (1, 5), (2, 3), (2, 5), (3, 5), (4, 5)\}$

  B. $\{(3, 1), (5, 1), (3, 2), (5, 2), (5, 3), (5, 4)\}$

  C. $\{(3, 3), (3, 5), (5, 3), (5, 5)\}$

  D. $\{(3, 3), (3, 4), (4, 5)\}$

17. Let A = $\{p, q, r\}$. Which of the following is not an equivalence relation on A?

  A. $R_1 = \{(p, q), (q, r), (p, r), (p, p)\}$

  B. $R_2 = \{(r, q), (r, p), (r, r), (q, q)\}$

  C. $R_3 = \{(p, p), (q, q), (r, r), (p, p)\}$

  D. None of these

18. Let R be a relation on the set N of natural numbers defined by $nRm \Leftrightarrow n$ is a factor of m (i.e., $n|m$). Then R is

  A. reflexive and symmetric

  B. transitive and symmetric

  C. equivalence

  D. reflexive, transitive but not symmetric

19. Let X = $\{1, 2, 3, 4, 5\}$ and Y = $\{1, 3, 5, 7, 9\}$. Which of the following is/are relations from X to Y?

  A. $R_1 = \{(x, y) \mid y = 2 + x, x \in X, y \in Y\}$

  B. $R_2 = \{(1, 1), (2, 1), (3, 5), (9, 4)\}$

  C. $R_3 = \{(1, 5), (2, 7), (4, 7), (7, 2)\}$

  D. $R_4 = \{(1, 3), (2, 5), (2, 4), (7, 9)\}$

20. Let R = $\{(1, 3), (2, 2), (3, 2)$ and S = $\{(2, 1), (3, 2), (2, 3)\}$ be two relations on set A = $\{1, 2, 3\}$. Then RoS =

  A. $\{(1, 3), (2, 2), (3, 2), (2, 1), (2, 3)\}$

  B. $\{(3, 2), (1, 3)\}$

  C. $\{(2, 3), (3, 2), (2, 2)\}$

  D. $\{(2, 3), (3, 2)\}$

21. Let A and B be two finite sets having m and n elements, respectively. Then the total number of mappings from A to B is

  A. mn B. 2^{mn}

  C. m^n D. n^m

22. Then total number of injective mappings from a set with m elements to a set with n elements, $m \le n$, is

  A. m^n B. n^m

  C. $\dfrac{n!}{(n-m)!}$ D. $n!$

23. If $f(x) = \cos(\log_e x)$, then $f(x)\,f(y) - \dfrac{1}{2}[f(x/y), f(x\,y)]$ is equal to

  A. 0 B. $\dfrac{1}{2}f(x)\,f(y)$

  C. $f(x + y)$ D. None of these

24. Let $f(x)$ be defined on $[-2, 2]$ and is given by

$$f(x) = \begin{cases} -1, & -2 \le x \le 0 \\ x - 1, & 0 < x \le 2 \end{cases}$$

and $g(x) = f(|x|) + |f(x)|$. Then $g(x)$ is equal to

  A. $\begin{cases} -x, & -2 \le x < 0 \\ 0, & 0 \le x < 1 \\ x - 1, & 1 \le x \le 2 \end{cases}$

  B. $\begin{cases} -x, & -2 \le x < 0 \\ 0, & 0 \le x < 1 \\ 2(x - 1), & 1 \le x \le 2 \end{cases}$

C. $\begin{cases} -x & -2 \le x < 0 \\ x-1 & 0 \le x \le 2 \end{cases}$

D. None of these

25. Let $f : R \to R$ be a function defined by $f(x)$ = cos $(5x + 2)$. Then f is

A. injective B. surjective
C. bijective D. None of these

26. If $f(x) = \dfrac{3x+2}{5x-3}$, then

A. $f^{-1}(x) = f(x)$ B. $f^{-1}(x) = -f(x)$

C. $(fof)(x) = -x$ D. $f^{-1}(x) = -\dfrac{1}{19}f(x)$

27. If $f(x) = \dfrac{x-1}{x+1}$, then $f(2x)$ is

A. $\dfrac{f(x)+1}{f(x)+3}$ B. $\dfrac{3f(x)+1}{f(x)+3}$

C. $\dfrac{f(x)+3}{f(x)+1}$ D. $\dfrac{f(x)+3}{3f(x)+1}$

28. If $f(x) = \log\left(\dfrac{1+x}{1-x}\right)$ and $g(x) = \dfrac{3x+x^3}{1+3x^2}$, then $fog\,(x)$ equals

A. $-(f)(x)$ B. $3f(x)$
C. $[f(x)]^3$ D. None of these

29. The number of bijective functions from set A to itself when A contains 106 elements is

A. 106 B. $(106)^2$
C. 106! D. 2^{106}

30. Let $f : R \to R$ be a function defined by $f(x)$ = $\dfrac{e^{|x|} - e^{-x}}{e^x + e^{-x}}$. Then

A. f is a bijection
B. f is an injection only
C. f is a surjection only
D. f is neither an injection nor a surjection

ANSWERS

1	2	3	4	5	6	7	8	9	10
B	B	B	C	C	B	B	D	B	D
11	**12**	**13**	**14**	**15**	**16**	**17**	**18**	**19**	**20**
A	B	B	A	B	C	D	D	A	C
21	**22**	**23**	**24**	**25**	**26**	**27**	**28**	**29**	**30**
D	C	A	B	D	A	B	B	C	D

DEFINITION OF LIMIT

A quantity l is said to be the limit of a function $f(x)$ at $x = a$, written as $\underset{x \to a}{\text{Lim}}\, f(x) = l$, if for a given small positive number $\in$ there exists a number δ such that $|f(x) - l| < \in$ for every $|x - a| < \delta$.

Existence of A Limit at A Point

$\underset{x \to a}{\text{Lim}}\, f(x)$ exists only if $\underset{x \to a+0}{\text{Lim}}\, f(x)$ and $\underset{x \to a-0}{\text{Lim}}\, f(x)$ both exist and are equal, *i.e.*, both right and left hand limits exist and are equal. This common value is known as the limit of the function $f(x)$ as $x \to a$.

Working Methods of Finding Limit on the Right and Left

(*i*) To find the limit on the right we put $a + h$ for x in $f(x)$ and then take the limit as $h \to 0$. Thus

$$\underset{x \to a+0}{\text{Lim}}\, f(x) = \underset{h \to 0}{\text{Lim}}\, f(a+h).$$

(*ii*) To find the limit on the left we put $a - h$ for x in $f(x)$ and then take the limit as $h \to 0$. Thus

$$\underset{x \to a-0}{\text{Lim}}\, f(x) = \underset{h \to 0}{\text{Lim}}\, f(a-h).$$

Some Important Limits

(*i*) $\underset{n \to \infty}{\text{Lim}}\left(1+\dfrac{1}{n}\right)^n = e;$

(*ii*) $\underset{n \to 0}{\text{Lim}}\,(1+n)^{1/n} = e;$

(*iii*) $\underset{x \to 0}{\text{Lim}}\left(\dfrac{\sin x}{x}\right) = 1;$

(*iv*) $\underset{x \to 0}{\text{Lim}}\left(\dfrac{\tan x}{x}\right) = 1;$

(*v*) $\underset{x \to 0}{\text{Lim}}\left[\dfrac{\log_e(1+x)}{x}\right] = 1;$

(*vi*) $\underset{x \to 0}{\text{Lim}}\left(\dfrac{e^x - 1}{x}\right) = 1;$

(*vii*) $\underset{x \to 0}{\text{Lim}}\left(\dfrac{a^x - 1}{x}\right) = \log_e a;$

(*viii*) $\underset{x \to a}{\text{Lim}}\left(\dfrac{x^n - a^n}{x - a}\right) = na^{n-1};$

where n is an integer, $n \neq 0$.

Some Important Expansions

(*i*) $\sin x = x - \dfrac{x^3}{3!} + \dfrac{x^5}{5!} - \dots \text{ to } \infty;$

(*ii*) $\cos x = 1 - \dfrac{x^2}{2!} + \dfrac{x^4}{4!} - \dots \text{ to } \infty;$

(*iii*) $\tan x = x + \dfrac{x^3}{3} + \dfrac{2}{15}x^5 + \dots \text{ to } \infty;$

(*iv*) $\tan^{-1} x = x - \dfrac{x^3}{3} + \dfrac{x^5}{5} - \dfrac{x^7}{7} + \dots \text{ to } \infty;$

(*v*) $\log_e(1+x) = x - \dfrac{1}{2}x^2 + \dfrac{1}{3}x^3 - \dfrac{1}{4}x^4 + \dots$ to ∞, where $|x| < 1;$

(*vi*) $\log_e(1-x) = -x - \dfrac{1}{2}x^2 - \dfrac{1}{3}x^3 - \dfrac{1}{4}x^4 - \dots$ to ∞, where $|x| < 1;$

(*vii*) $e^x = 1 + x + \dfrac{x^2}{2!} + \dfrac{x^3}{3!} + \dots \text{ to } \infty \sum\limits_{n=0}^{\infty}\left(\dfrac{x^n}{n!}\right)$

$(viii)$ $a^x = 1 + x(\log_e a) + \dfrac{x^2}{2!}(\log_e a)^2 + \ldots$ to ∞;

(ix) $(1 - x)^{-1} = 1 + x + x^2 + \ldots + x^r + \ldots$ to ∞.

DEFINITION OF CONTINUITY

A function $f(x)$ is continuous at a point $x = a$ if

$$\lim_{x \to a-0} f(x) = \lim_{x \to a+0} f(x) = f(a)$$

i.e., $\lim_{x \to a} f(x)$ exists and is equal to the value of the function $f(x)$ at $x = a$.

Continuity in An Interval

A function $f(x)$ is said to be continuous in the closed interval $[a, b]$ if it is continuous at every point in this interval and the continuity at the end points is defined as $f(x)$ is continuous at $x = a$ if

$$\lim_{x \to a+0} f(x) = f(a)$$

and at $x = b$, if

$$\lim_{x \to b-0} f(x) = f(b)$$

Discontinuity

A function which is not continuous at a point is said to have a discontinuity at that point.

Differentiability

If $f(x)$ be a function defined on an interval $[a, b]$ and $x_0 \in\,] a, b [$ then $f(x)$ is said to be derivable (or differentiable) at $x = x_0$ if

$$\lim_{x \to x_0} \frac{f(x) - f(x_0)}{x - x_0}$$

or $\lim_{h \to 0} \dfrac{f(x_0 + h) - f(x_0)}{h}$ exists and is denoted by $f'(x_0)$ or $Df(x_0)$.

Right-Hand Derivative

$\lim_{h \to 0} \dfrac{f(x_0 + h) - f(x_0)}{h}$, $h > 0$ is called the right hand or progressive derivative of $f(x)$ at $x = x_0$ and is denoted by

$$Rf'(x_0) \text{ or by } f'(x_0 + 0).$$

Left-Hand Derivative

$\lim_{h \to 0} \dfrac{f(x_0 - h) - f(x_0)}{-h}$, $h > 0$ is called the left hand or regressive derivative of $f(x)$ at $x = x_0$ and is denoted by

$$Lf'(x_0) \text{ or by } f'(x_0 - 0).$$

Differentiability at the end points of $[a, b]$ and in $[a, b]$:

A function $f(x)$ is said to be differentiable at $x = a$ if $Rf'(a)$ exists and is equal to $f'(a)$.

Similarly a function $f(x)$ is said to be differentiable at $x = b$ if $Lf'(b)$ exists and is equal to $f'(b)$.

Also a function $f(x)$ is said to be differentiable in $[a, b]$ if and only if it is differentiable at every point of $] a, b [$ and is differentiable at the end points of $[a, b]$.

Indeterminate Forms and L-Hospital's Rule

$$\frac{0}{0}, \frac{\infty}{\infty}, \infty - \infty, 0 \times \infty, 1^\infty, 0^\infty, \infty^0 \text{ are}$$

indeterminate forms.

If a function takes the form $\dfrac{0}{0}$ or $\dfrac{\infty}{\infty}$ at $x = a$, then L-Hospital's Rule applies.

L-Hospital's Rule

If $\phi(x)$ and $\Psi(x)$ are functions of x such that

$$\phi(a) = 0$$
$$\text{and} \quad \Psi(a) = 0$$
$$\text{or} \quad \phi(a) = \Psi(a) = \infty$$

$$\text{Then} \quad \lim_{x \to a} \frac{\phi(x)}{\Psi(x)} = \lim_{x \to a} \frac{\phi'(x)}{\Psi'(x)}$$

Solved Examples

Example 1: *If $f(a) = 2$, $f'(a) = 1$, $g(a) = -1$, $g'(a) = 2$, then evaluate*

$$\underset{x \to a}{Lt} \frac{g(x)f(a) - g(a)f(x)}{x - a}$$

Solution: $\text{Lt}_{x \to a} \dfrac{g(x)f(a) - g(a)f(x)}{x - a}$, of the form 0/0

$$= \text{Lim}_{x \to a} \dfrac{\dfrac{d}{dx}[g(x)f(a) - g(a)f(x)]}{\dfrac{d}{dx}[x - a]}$$

by De L. Hospital's rule

$$= \text{Lim}_{x \to a} \dfrac{g'(x)f(a) - g(a)f'(x)}{1}$$

$$= g'(a)\,f(a) - g(a)\,f'(a)$$

$$= (2)\,(2) - (-1)\,(1) = 5.$$

Example 2: *A function f(x) is defined by*

$$f(x) = 1 + x, \text{ if } x \le 2$$

$$= 5 - x, \text{ if } x \ge 2$$

Is the function f(x) differentiable at x = 2?

Solution: $Rf'(2) = \text{Lim}_{h \to 0} \dfrac{f(2+h) - f(2)}{h}$

$$= \text{Lim}_{h \to 0} \dfrac{\{5 - (2 + h)\} - (5 - 2)}{h}$$

$$[\because f(x) = 5 - x, \text{ if } x \ge 2 - 1]$$

And $\quad Lf'(2) = \text{Lim}_{h \to 0} \dfrac{f(2-h) - f(2)}{-h}$

$$= \text{Lim}_{h \to 0} \dfrac{\{1 + (2 - h) - (1 + 2)\}}{-h}$$

$$[\because f(x) = 1 + x, \text{ if } x \le 2]$$

$$\therefore \qquad Rf'(2) \ne Lf'(2)$$

i.e., f(x) is not differentiable at x = 2.

MULTIPLE CHOICE QUESTIONS

1. $\lim_{x \to 27} \dfrac{x^{1/3} - 3}{x - 27}$ is equal to

   A. 3   B. $\dfrac{1}{3}$

   C. 27   D. $\dfrac{1}{27}$

2. If $\lim_{x \to 0} (1 + x)^{1/x} = e$, then $\lim_{x \to \infty} \left(\dfrac{n}{1 + n}\right)^{2n}$ is

   A. e B. e^2

   C. $1/e$ D. $1/e^2$

3. If $f(x) = \dfrac{\sin^2 ax}{x^2}$, when $x \ne 0$

$$= P, \qquad \text{when } x = 0$$

is discontinuous at $x = 0$, then for what value of P, $f(x)$ will be continuous at $x = 0$?

   A. 1   B. 2

   C. a D. a^2

4. If $\quad f(x) = 2, \qquad x \le 3$

$$= ax + b \qquad 3 < x < 5$$

$$= 7, \qquad x \ge 5$$

is continuous, then

   A. $a = 2, b = 5$ B. $a = 3, b = -8$
   C. $a = -3, b = 8$ D. $a = 5, b = 7$

5. Let $f(x) = \cos x$, then

   A. $f(x)$ is continuous at $x \in R$ excepting odd multiple of $\dfrac{\pi}{2}$

   B. $f(x)$ is continuous at $x \in R$ excepting even multiple of $\dfrac{\pi}{2}$

   C. $f(x)$ is continuous at $x \in R$ excepting $x = 0$

   D. $f(x)$ is always a continuous function.

6. If $f(x) = \dfrac{1}{1 + 2^{1/x}}$, then at $x = 0$ the function is

   A. Continuous

   B. Discontinuous, because $\lim_{x \to 0^+} f(x)$ does not exist.

   C. Discontinuous, because $\lim_{x \to 0^-} f(x) \ne \lim_{x \to 0^+} f(x)$

   D. Discontinuous, because $\lim_{x \to 0} f(0) \ne f(0)$

7. $\lim_{x \to 0} \left(\dfrac{1 + 2x}{1 - 2x}\right)^{\frac{1}{x}}$ is given by

   A. e^2 B. e^3

   C. e^4 D. e^5

8. $\lim\limits_{x\to 0}\dfrac{\log(3+x)-\log 3}{\sqrt{1+x}-1} =$

  A. 1/2   B. 1/3

  C. $\dfrac{2}{3}$ D. $\dfrac{3}{2}$

9. If $\lim\limits_{x\to 0} kx \csc x = \lim\limits_{x\to 0} x \csc kx$, then $k =$

  A. 2   B. -3

  C. ± 1 D. ± 3

10. $\lim\limits_{x\to 0}\dfrac{2^x-1}{(1+x)^{1/2}-1} =$

  A. $\log 3$ B. $\log 4$

  C. $\log\sqrt{3}$ D. None of these

11. If $f(x) = \begin{cases} \dfrac{e^{[x]+x}-1}{[x]+x}, & x\neq 0 \\ 1 & x=0 \end{cases}$ then

  A. $f(x)$ is continuous at $x=0$

  B. $f(x)$ is discontinuous at $x=0$

  C. $\lim\limits_{x\to 0^+} f(x)=1$

  D. Both B and C

12. Let $f(x) = \begin{cases} \dfrac{\sqrt{1+ax}-\sqrt{1-ax}}{x} & -1\leq x<0 \\ \dfrac{2x+1}{x-2}, & 0\leq x\leq 1 \end{cases}$

If $f(x)$ is continuous in the interval $[-1, 1]$, then a equals

  A. 1   B. -2

  C. 1/2   D. $-1/2$

13. If $f(x) = x \sin 1/x,\ x\neq 0$, then the value of the function at $x=0$, so that the function is continuous at $x=0$, is

  A. 1   B. -1

  C. 0   D. indeterminate

14. Let $f(x) = \begin{cases} \dfrac{1-\sin\pi x}{1+\cos 2\pi x} & \text{if}\ \ x<1/2 \\ \dfrac{a}{\sqrt{2x-1}} & \text{if}\ \ x=1/2 \\ \sqrt{4+\sqrt{2x-1}}-2 & \text{if}\ \ x>1/2 \end{cases}$

Determine the value of a, if positive, so that the function is continuous at $x=1/2$

  A. 1/2   B. 1/3

  C. 1/4   D. 1/5

15. If $f(x) = \begin{cases} \dfrac{x^2+3x+p}{2(x^2-1)} & x\neq 1 \\ 5/4 & x=1 \end{cases}$ is

continuous at $x=1$, then

  A. $P=1$ B. $P=-2$

  C. $P=3$ D. $P=-4$

ANSWERS

1	2	3	4	5	6	7	8	9	10
D	D	D	B	D	C	C	C	C	B

11	12	13	14	15
D	D	C	C	D

SOME SELECTED EXPLANATORY ANSWERS

3. $\lim\limits_{x\to 0} f(x) = \lim\limits_{x\to 0} a^2\left(\dfrac{\sin ax}{ax}\right)^2 = a^2\times 1 = a^2$

$\therefore f(x)$ is continuous,

if $f(0)=f(0)=\lim\limits_{x\to 0} f(x) \Rightarrow p=a^2$

5. Given function is $f(x)=\cos x$

Let $a\in \mathrm{R}$

$\because \lim\limits_{x\to a^-} f(x) = \lim\limits_{h\to 0} f(a-h) = \lim\limits_{h\to 0}\cos(a-h)$

$= \lim\limits_{h\to 0} [\cos a\cdot\cos h + \sin a\cdot\sinh] = \cos a$

$$\lim_{x \to a^+} f(x) = \lim_{h \to 0}(a+h) = \lim_{h \to 0}\cos(a+h)$$

$$= \lim_{h \to 0}[\cos a \cdot \cos h - \sin a \sin h] = \cos a.$$

Also $f(a) = \cos a$

7. $\lim_{x \to 0}\left(\dfrac{1+2x}{1-2x}\right)^{\frac{1}{x}} = \dfrac{\lim_{x \to 0}(1+2x)^{\frac{1}{x}}}{\lim_{x \to 0}(1-2x)^{\frac{1}{x}}}$

$$= \dfrac{\lim_{x \to 0}\left[(1+2x)^{\frac{1}{2x}}\right]}{\lim_{x \to 0}\left[(1-2x)^{\frac{-1}{2x}}\right]^{-2}} = \dfrac{e^2}{e^{-2}} = e^4$$

9. $\lim_{x \to 0} kx \operatorname{cosec} x = \lim_{x \to 0} x \operatorname{cosec} kx$

$$\Rightarrow k \cdot \lim_{x \to 0}\dfrac{x}{\sin x} = \dfrac{1}{k}\lim_{x \to 0}\dfrac{kx}{\sin kx}$$

$$\Rightarrow k = \dfrac{1}{k} \Rightarrow k = \pm 1$$

10. $\lim_{x \to 0}\dfrac{2^x - 1}{(1+x)^{1/2} - 1}$

$$= \lim_{x \to 0}\dfrac{2^x \cdot \log 2}{\dfrac{1}{2}(1+x)^{-1/2}} \quad \left\{\because \lim_{x \to a}\dfrac{f(x)}{g(x)} = \lim_{x \to a}\dfrac{f'(x)}{g'(x)}\right\}$$

$$= 2 \log 2 = \log 4$$

13. For $f(x)$ to be continuous at $x = 0$, we must have $f(0)$ $\lim_{x \to 0} f(x)$

$$\Rightarrow f(0) = \lim_{x \to 0} x.\sin\dfrac{1}{x} = 0 \times \text{a finite quantity}$$

$$= 0$$

Hence, $f(0) = 0$

$\boxed{10}$ **Differentiation**

SOME STANDARD RESULTS

Function	Differential Coefficient

1. $y = f(x) \Rightarrow \dfrac{dy}{dx}$

$$= \lim_{\delta x \to 0} \frac{f(x + \delta x) - f(x)}{\delta x}$$

2. $y = x^n \Rightarrow \dfrac{dy}{dx} = nx^{n-1}$

3. $y = \text{constant} \Rightarrow \dfrac{dy}{dx} = 0$

4. $y = c\, f(x) \Rightarrow \dfrac{dy}{dx} = c\dfrac{d}{dx} f(x)$

5. $y = e^x \Rightarrow \dfrac{dy}{dx} = e^x$

6. $y = a^x = e^{x \log a} \Rightarrow \dfrac{dy}{dx} = a^x \log a$

7. $y = \sin x \Rightarrow \dfrac{dy}{dx} = \cos x$

8. $y = \cos x \Rightarrow \dfrac{dy}{dx} = -\sin x$

9. $y = \tan x \Rightarrow \dfrac{dy}{dx} = \sec^2 x$

10. $y = \cot x \Rightarrow \dfrac{dy}{dx} = -\operatorname{cosec}^2 x$

11. $y = \sec x \Rightarrow \dfrac{dy}{dx} = \sec x \tan x$

12. $y = \operatorname{cosec} x \Rightarrow \dfrac{dy}{dx} = -\operatorname{cosec} x . \cot x$

13. $y = f_1(x) + f_2(x) \Rightarrow \dfrac{dy}{dx} = \dfrac{d}{dx} f_1(x) + \dfrac{d}{dx} f_2(x)$

14. $y = f_1 f_2 \Rightarrow \dfrac{dy}{dx} = f_1 \cdot \dfrac{d}{dx}(f_2) + f_2 \cdot \dfrac{d}{dx}(f_1)$

15. $y = \dfrac{f_1}{f_2} \Rightarrow \dfrac{dy}{dx} = \dfrac{\dfrac{d}{dx}(f_1) \cdot f_2 - f_1 \dfrac{d}{dx} f_2}{f_2^2}$

16. $y = \sin^{-1} x \Rightarrow \dfrac{dy}{dx} = \dfrac{1}{\sqrt{(1 - x^2)}}$

17. $y = \cos^{-1} x \Rightarrow \dfrac{dy}{dx} = \dfrac{1}{\sqrt{(1 - x^2)}}$

18. $y = \tan^{-1} x \Rightarrow \dfrac{dy}{dx} = \dfrac{1}{1 + x^2}$

19. $y = \cot^{-1} x \Rightarrow \dfrac{dy}{dx} = -\dfrac{1}{1 + x^2}$

20. $y = \sec^{-1} x \Rightarrow \dfrac{dy}{dx} = \dfrac{1}{x\sqrt{(x^2 - 1)}}$

21. $y = \operatorname{cosec}^{-1} x \Rightarrow \dfrac{dy}{dx} = -\dfrac{1}{x\sqrt{(x^2 - 1)}}$

Function of a function: If y is a function of u and u is a function of x, then derivative of y wrt x is obtained as

$$\frac{dy}{dx} = \frac{dy}{du} \cdot \frac{du}{dx}$$

Parametric equations: Sometimes both x and y are expressed in terms of a third variable, usually called a parameter. In such cases we always find the value of $dy/dx = (dy/dt) . (dt/dx)$.

SECOND ORDER DERIVATIVES

Let $\qquad y = f(x) \; \therefore \; \dfrac{dy}{dx} = f'(x)$

differentiating w.r.t. 'x' $\quad \dfrac{d}{dx}\left(\dfrac{dy}{dx}\right) = \dfrac{d}{dx}(f''(x))$

$$\Rightarrow \quad \frac{d^2 y}{dx^2} = f''(x)$$

We also denote

$$y' = f'(x) = \frac{dy}{dx}$$

and $\qquad y'' = f''(x) = \dfrac{d^2 y}{dx^2}$

nth Derivatives of Some Special Functions

(i) $D^n \, a^x = (\log a)^n \, a^x$

(ii) $D^n \, e^{ax+b} = a^n \, e^{ax+b}$

(iii) If $m > n$, then

$D^n (ax+b)^m = m(m-1)(m-2)\ldots\ldots(m-n+1)$
$a^n (ax+b)^{m-n}$

$$= \frac{m!}{(m-n)} a^n (ax+b)^{m-n}$$

If $m < n$, then $\qquad D^n (ax+b)^m = 0$

And if $m = n$, then $D^n (ax+b)^m = a^n \cdot n!$

(iv) $D^n (ax+b)^{-1} = (-1)^n \, n! \, a^n \, (ax+b)^{-n-1}$

(v) $D^n \log (ax+b) = \dfrac{(-1)^n (n-1)! a^n}{(ax+b)^n}$

(vi) $D^n \sin (ax+b) = a^n \sin (ax+b+n\pi/2)$

(vii) $D^n \cos (ax+b) = a^n \cos (ax+b+n\pi/2)$

(viii) $D^n \left\{ e^{ax} \sin(bx+c) \right\}$

$$= (a^2+b^2)^{n/2} \times e^{ax} \sin\left\{ bx+c+n\tan^{-1}\left(\frac{b}{a}\right) \right\}$$

(ix) $D^n \{e^{ax} \cos (ax+c)\}$

$$= (a^2+b^2)^{n/2} \times e^{ax} \cos\left\{ bx+c+n\tan^{-1}\left(\frac{b}{a}\right) \right\}$$

LEIBNITZ'S THEOREM

If u and v are any two functions of x such that their required differential coefficients exist, then the nth differential coefficient of uv is given by

$$D^n (uv) = (D^n u) \cdot v + {}^nC_1 (D^{n-1} u) \cdot (Dv) + {}^nC_2$$
$$(D^{n-2} u) (D^2 v) + \ldots + u (D^n v).$$

Solved Examples

Example 1: *If $f(x) = \log_x (\ln x)$, then evaluate $f'(x)$ at $x = e$. Here $\ln x$ means natural logarithm of x, i.e., $\log_e x$.*

Solution: We have $f(x) = \log_x (\log_e x) = \log_x y$, where $y = \log_e x$

$$= \log_e y \cdot \log_x e = \frac{\log_e y}{\log_e x}$$

Then $\qquad f'(x) = \dfrac{\dfrac{1}{y} \cdot \dfrac{dy}{dx} \cdot \log_e x - \dfrac{1}{x} \cdot \log_e y}{(\log_e x)^2}$

$$\Rightarrow \qquad f'(e) = \frac{1 \cdot \dfrac{1}{e} \cdot 1 - \dfrac{1}{e} \cdot 0}{(1)^2} = e^{-1}$$

Example 2: *Differentiate x^x*

Solution: Let $y = x^x$

Taking logarithms on both sides, we get

$$\log y = x \cdot \log x.$$

Now differentiating both the sides w.r.t. "x", we get

$$\frac{1}{y} \frac{dy}{dx} = x \cdot \frac{1}{x} + 1 \cdot \log x = 1 + \log x,$$

$$dy/dx = y (1 + \log x) = x^x (1 + \log x)$$

$$= x^x (\log e + \log x)$$

$$= x^x \log (x\,e)$$

Example 3: *Find the derivative of $\sec^{-1}\left(\dfrac{1}{2x^2-1}\right)$*

w.r.t $\sqrt{(1-x^2)}$ at $x = \dfrac{1}{2}$.

Solution: Let $y = \sec^{-1}\left(\dfrac{1}{2x^2 - 1}\right)$ and $z = \sqrt{(1 - x^2)}$

then $y = \cos^{-1}(2x^2 - 1)$

Whence putting $x = \cos\theta$, we get

$\qquad y = \cos^{-1}(2\cos^2\theta - 1)$ and $z = \sin\theta$

$\Rightarrow \qquad y = \cos^{-1}(\cos 2\theta)$ and $z = \sin\theta$

$\Rightarrow \qquad y = 2\theta$ and $z = \sin\theta$

$\therefore \qquad \dfrac{dy}{d\theta} = 2$ and $\dfrac{dz}{d\theta} = \cos\theta$

$\Rightarrow \qquad \dfrac{dy}{dz} = \dfrac{2}{(\cos\theta)} = \dfrac{2}{x}$

$\Rightarrow \left[\dfrac{dy}{dz}\right]$ at $x = \dfrac{1}{2}$ is 4.

MULTIPLE CHOICE QUESTIONS

1. If $y = \tan^{-1}\dfrac{2x}{1 - x^2}$, then the value of $\dfrac{dy}{dx}$ is

  A. $\dfrac{1}{1 + x^2}$ B. $\dfrac{2}{1 + x^2}$

  C. $\dfrac{1 - x^2}{1 + x^2}$ D. $\dfrac{1 + x^2}{1 - x^2}$

2. If $y = x^{x^{x\cdots\infty}}$, then $x\cdot\dfrac{dy}{dx}$ is

  A. $\dfrac{x^2}{1 + y\cdot\log x}$ B. $\dfrac{y^2}{1 + y\cdot\log x}$

  C. $\dfrac{x^2}{1 - y\cdot\log x}$ D. $\dfrac{y^2}{1 - y\cdot\log x}$

3. $\dfrac{d^n}{dx^n}[\log(ax + b)]$ is equal to

  A. $\dfrac{(-1)^n\, n!\, a^n}{(ax + b)^n}$

  B. $\dfrac{(-1)^{n-1}(n - 1)!\cdot a^n}{(ax + b)^{n+1}}$

  C. $\dfrac{(-1)^{n+1}(n - 1)!\cdot a^{n-1}}{(ax + b)^{n+1}}$

  D. $\dfrac{(-1)^{n-1}(n - 1)!\cdot a^n}{(ax + b)^n}$

4. Differentiate u with respect to v where $u = e^x$. $\cos x$ and $v = e^x \sin x$.

  A. $\dfrac{\cos x - \sin x}{\cos x + \sin x}$ B. $\dfrac{\sin x + \cos x}{\sin x - \cos x}$

  C. 1   D. 0

5. If $y = x^5 \cdot e^{x^2} \cdot \sqrt{\sin x}$, $\dfrac{dy}{dx} =$

  A. $x^5 \cdot e^{x^2} \cdot \sqrt{\sin x} \cdot \left[\dfrac{5}{x} + 2x + \dfrac{1}{2}\cot x\right]$

  B. $x^5 \cdot e^{x^2} \cdot \sqrt{\sin x} \cdot \left[\dfrac{5}{x} - 2x - \dfrac{1}{2}\cot x\right]$

  C. $x^5 \cdot e^{x^2} \cdot \sqrt{\sin x} \cdot \left[\dfrac{5}{x} - 2x + \dfrac{1}{2}\cot x\right]$

  D. None of these

6. Differentiate $x^x + (\sin x)^x$ with respect to x

  A. $x^x(1 + \log x) + (\sin x)^x[x\cot x + \log(\sin x)]$

  B. $x^x(1 + \log x) - (\sin x)^x[x\cot x + \log(\sin x)]$

  C. $x^x(1 + \log x) + (\sin x)^x[x\cot x - \log(\sin x)]$

  D. $x^x(1 + \log x) - (\sin x)^x[x\cot x - \log(\sin x)]$

7. If $y = \dfrac{\cos\alpha}{\cos x} + \dfrac{\sin\alpha}{\sin x}$, then $\dfrac{d^2 y}{dx^2} =$

  A. $\cos\alpha.\sec x[1 + 2\tan^2 x] + \sin\alpha.\mathrm{cosec}\, x$ $[1 + 2\cot^2 x]$

  B. $\sin x.\sec x[1 + 2\tan^2 x] + \cos\alpha.\sec x$ $[1 + 2\cot^2 x]$

  C. $\cos\alpha.\sec x[1 - 2\tan^2 x] + \sin\alpha.\mathrm{cosec}\, x$ $[1 - 2\cot^2 x]$

  D. None of these

8. The nth derivative of the function $y = a_0 + a_1 x + a_2 x^2 + \ldots\ldots + a_n x^n$ is

  A. $n \cdot an$ B. $n \cdot an!$

  C. $n! \cdot a_n$ D. $-n!\, a^n$

9. If $y = A\cos nx + B\sin nx$, then $\dfrac{d^2y}{dx^2} =$

   A. $-y$ B. n^2y

   C. $-n^2y$ D. None of these

10. The differential coefficient of $\sin^{-1}\dfrac{1-x}{1+x}$ w.r.t. $\sqrt{x}$ is

   A. $\dfrac{3}{2\sqrt{x}}$ B. $\dfrac{\sqrt{x}}{\sqrt{1-x}}$

   C. $2\sqrt{x}$ D. None of these

11. If $y = \dfrac{x}{2}\sqrt{a^2+x^2} + \dfrac{a^2}{2}\log(x+\sqrt{x^2+a^2})$, then $\dfrac{dy}{dx} =$

   A. $\sqrt{x^2+a^2}$ B. $\dfrac{1}{\sqrt{x^2+a^2}}$

   C. $2\sqrt{x^2+a^2}$ D. $\dfrac{2}{\sqrt{x^2+a^2}}$

12. If $y = \left(x^x\right)^x$, then $\dfrac{dy}{dx} =$

   A. $\left(x^x\right)^x(1+2\log x)$ B. $\left(x^x\right)^x(1+\log x)$

   C. $x\left(x^x\right)^x(1+2\log x)$ D. $x\left(x^x\right)^x(1+\log x)$

13. If $y = \dfrac{\tan x + \cot x}{\tan x - \cot x}$, then $\dfrac{dy}{dx} =$

   A. $2\tan 2x\sec 2x$ B. $\tan 2x\sec 2x$

   C. $-\tan 2x\sec 2x$ D. $-2\tan 2x\sec 2x$

14. If $y = \sqrt{\sin x + \sqrt{\sin x + \sqrt{\sin x + \ldots\ldots\infty}}}$, then

   A. $(2y-1)\dfrac{dy}{dx} = \sin x$

   B. $(2y-1)\dfrac{dy}{dx} = -\sin x$

   C. $(2y-1)\dfrac{dy}{dx} = -\cos x$

   D. $(2y-1)\dfrac{dy}{dx} = \cos x$

15. $\dfrac{d}{dx}\left\{(\sin x)^{\log x}\right\} =$

   A. $(\sin x)^{\log x}\left[\dfrac{1}{x}\log\sin x + \cot x\right]$

   B. $(\sin x)^{\log x}\left[\dfrac{1}{x}\log\sin x + \cot x\log x\right]$

   C. $(\sin x)^{\log x}\left[\dfrac{1}{x}\log\sin x + \log x\right]$

   D. None of these

16. $\dfrac{d}{dx}\left[\log\sqrt{\sin\sqrt{e^x}}\right] =$

   A. $\dfrac{1}{4}e^{x/2}\cot(e^{x/2})$ B. $\dfrac{1}{4}e^x\cot(e^x)$

   C. $\dfrac{1}{2}e^{x/2}\cot(e^{x/2})$ D. None of these

17. If $y = x^2 e^{mx}$, where m is a constant, then $\dfrac{d^3y}{dx^3} =$

   A. $me^{mx}(m^2x^2 + 6mx + 6)$

   B. $me^{mx}(m^2x^2 + 2mx + 2)$

   C. $2m^3xe^{mx}$

   D. None of these

18. If $y = \dfrac{a^{\cos^{-1}x}}{1+a^{\cos^{-1}x}}$ and $z = a^{\cos^{-1}x}$, then $\dfrac{dy}{dx} =$

   A. $-\dfrac{1}{1+a^{\cos^{-1}x}}$ B. $\dfrac{1}{1-a^{\cos^{-1}x}}$

   C. $\dfrac{1}{(1+a^{\cos^{-1}x})^2}$ D. None of these

19. The derivative of the function $\cot^{-1}[(\cos 2x)^{1/2}]$ at $x = \dfrac{\pi}{6}$ is

   A. $(2/3)^{1/2}$ B. $(1/3)^{1/2}$

   C. $3^{1/2}$ D. $6^{1/2}$

20. If $y = (\tan x)^{(\tan x)^{\tan x}}$, then at $x = \dfrac{\pi}{4}$, $\dfrac{dy}{dx} =$

   A. 1 B. -1

   C. 2 D. None of these

ANSWERS

1	2	3	4	5	6	7	8	9	10
B	D	D	A	A	A	A	C	C	D

11	12	13	14	15	16	17	18	19	20
A	C	D	D	D	A	A	C	A	C

SOME SELECTED EXPLANATORY ANSWERS

1. $y = \tan^{-1}\dfrac{2x}{1-x^2} = 2\tan^{-1} x$

$\therefore \quad \dfrac{dy}{dx} = \dfrac{2}{1+x^2}$

3. Using TST : $8\dfrac{d^n}{dx^n}[\log(ax+b)]$

$= \dfrac{(-1)^{n-1}(n-1)!\,a^n}{(ax+b)^n}$

8. Let $y = a_0 + a_1 x + a_2 x^2 + \dots a_n x^n$.

$\dfrac{dy}{dx} = a_1 x + 2a_2 x + 3a_3 x^2 + \dots n.a_n.x^{n-1}$

$\dfrac{d2y}{dx^2} = 2a_2 + 2.3a_3 x + \dots n.(n-1)a_n.x^{n-1}$

$\dfrac{d^n y}{dx^n} = n(n-1)(n-2)\dots 3.2.1.a_n x^0 = n!a_n.$

9. $y = A\cos(nx) + B\sin(nx)$

$\therefore \dfrac{dy}{dx} = -nA\sin(nx) + nB\cos(nx)$

Again $\dfrac{d^2 y}{dx^2} = -n^2 A\cos(nx) - n^2 B\sin(nx)$

$= -n^2[A\cos(nx) + B\sin(nx)] \Rightarrow \dfrac{d^2 y}{dx^2} = -n^2 y$

10. Let $y = \sin^{-1}\dfrac{1-x}{1+x} \Rightarrow \dfrac{dy}{dx} = \dfrac{-1}{\sqrt{x}(1+x)}$ ...(i)

and $z = \sqrt{x} \Rightarrow \dfrac{dz}{dx} = \dfrac{1}{2\sqrt{x}}$ ...(ii)

By (i) and (ii) $\dfrac{dy}{dz} = \dfrac{dy/dx}{dz/dx} = \dfrac{-2}{1+x}$

12. $y = (x^x)^x \Rightarrow \log_e y = x\log_e(x)^x$

$\Rightarrow \dfrac{1}{y}\dfrac{dy}{dx} = \log(x)^x + x\dfrac{1}{(x)^x}(x^x)(1+\log_e x)$

$\therefore \dfrac{dy}{dx} = x(x^x)^x[1 + 2\log_e x]$

13. $y = \dfrac{\tan x + \cot x}{\tan x - \cot x} = \dfrac{1+\tan^2 x}{1-\tan^2 x} = -\sec 2x$

$\Rightarrow \dfrac{dy}{dx} = -2\sec 2x\tan 2x$

15. Let $y = (\sin x)^{\log x} \Rightarrow \log_e y = \log_e x\,\log_e \sin x$

$\Rightarrow \dfrac{dy}{dx} = (\sin x)^{\log_e x}\left[\dfrac{1}{x}\log_e \sin x + \cot x\log_e x\right]$

16. $\dfrac{d}{dx}\left[\log\sqrt{\sin\sqrt{e^x}}\right] = \dfrac{d}{dx}\left[\dfrac{1}{2}\log(\sin\sqrt{e^x})\right]$

$= \dfrac{1}{2}\cot\sqrt{e^x}\dfrac{1}{2\sqrt{e^x}} = \dfrac{1}{4}e^{x/2}\cot(e^{x/2})$

18. $y = \dfrac{a^{\cos^{-1}x}}{1+a^{\cos^{-1}x}}, \quad z = a^{\cos^{-1}x}$

$\Rightarrow y = \dfrac{z}{1+z} \Rightarrow \dfrac{dy}{dx} = \dfrac{(1+z)1 - z(1)}{(1+z)^2} = \dfrac{1}{(1+z)^2}$

$= \dfrac{1}{(1+a^{\cos^{-1}x})^2}$

19. $\dfrac{dy}{dx} = -\dfrac{1}{1+\cos 2x}\cdot\dfrac{1}{2\sqrt{\cos 2x}}(-2\sin 2x)$

Now substitute $x = \dfrac{\pi}{6}$, then $\dfrac{dy}{dx} = \sqrt{\dfrac{2}{3}}$

$\left[\because \cos 2x = \dfrac{1}{2} \text{ and } \sin 2x = \dfrac{\sqrt{3}}{2}\right]$

⑪ Application of Derivatives

Equation of tangent: The equation of tangent at the point $P(x_1, y_1)$ on the curve $y = f(x)$ is

$$y - y_1 = \left[\frac{dy}{dx}\right]_{(x_1, y_1)} (x - x_1)$$

If the tangent at the point $P(x, y)$ on the curve $y = f(x)$ makes an angle ψ with the positive direction of the axis of x, then

$$\tan \psi = dy/dx$$

and is called the **gradient** (or slope) of the curve at $P(x, y)$.

Tangent parallel to the axis of x: At the point where the tangent is **parallel** to the axis of x,

$$\frac{dy}{dx} = 0.$$

Tangent perpendicular to the axis of x: At the point where the tangent is perpendicular to the axis of x,

$$dx/dy = 0$$

Equation of normal: The equation of the **normal** at the point $P(x_1, y_1)$ on the curve $y = f(x)$ is

$$(y - y_1)\left[\frac{dy}{dx}\right]_{(x_1, y_1)} + (x - x_1) = 0$$

Angle of Intersection of Two Curves

Def. The angle of intersection of two curves is defined as the angle between the tangents to the two curves at their point of intersection.

If θ is the angle of intersection of the two curves at the point of intersection, then

$$\theta = \tan^{-1}\left|\frac{m_1 - m_2}{1 + m_1 m_2}\right|$$

where $m_1 = \tan \psi_1$ and $m_2 = \tan \psi_2$

where ψ_1 and ψ_2 are the angles which the tangents to the two curves at their point of intersection make with the positive direction of the axis of x.

Condition for the two curves to touch: The two curves having slope m_1 and m_2 respectively **touch** each other at their point of intersection if

$$m_1 = m_2.$$

Condition of orthogonal intersection of two curves: The two curves having slope m_1 and m_2 respectively **intersect orthogonally** (*i.e.*, at right angles) at their point of intersection if

$$m_1 m_2 = -1.$$

Lengths of Tangent, Normal, Subtangent and Subnormal

(*i*) **Length of Tangent**

$$= \left|\frac{y\sqrt{[1 + (dy/dx)^2}}{dy/dx}\right|$$

(*ii*) **Length of Normal**

$$= |y[1 + (dy/dx)^2]^{1/2}|$$

(*iii*) **Length of Sub-tangent**

$$= |y/(dy/dx)|$$

(*iv*) **Length of Sub-normal**

$$= |y(dy/dx)|.$$

Intercept of Tangent on The Axex

(*i*) Intercept of a tangent on the axis of x

$$= |x - y\,(dx/dy)|$$

(*ii*) Intercept of a tangent on the axis of y

$$= |y - x\,(dy/dx)|$$

Monotonic Function (Def.): A function $f(x)$ in an interval I is said to be **monotonic** if it follows any of the following properties:

I. Increasing if $x_1 < x_2 \Rightarrow f(x_1) < f(x_2)$

II. Non-decreasing if $x_1 < x_2 \Rightarrow f(x_1) \leq f(x_2)$

III. Decreasing if $x_1 < x_2 \Rightarrow f(x_1) > f(x_2)$

IV. Non-increasing if $x_1 < x_2 \Rightarrow f(x_1) \geq f(x_2)$.

Tests for Monotonicity : (First Derivative Test)

I. In an interval I, $f(x)$ is

II. Increasing if

$f'(x) > 0$

III. Non-decreasing if $f'(x) \geq 0$

IV. Decreasing if $f'(x) < 0$

V. Non-increasing if $f'(x) \leq 0$

Maxima and Minima: $f(x)$ has maximum at x_0 if in some interval

$$I =]x_0 - h, x_0 + h[$$

for all $x \in I, f(x) < f(x_0)$

and $f'(x)$ has minimum at x_0 if in some interval

$$I =]x_0 - h, x_0 + h[$$

for all $x \in I$ if $f(x) > f(x_0)$.

Critical Points: All such points where $f'(x) = 0$ or $f(x)$ is continuous but not differentiable are called **critical points.** So maximum or minimum can exist only at critical points.

Methods of Testing for Maxima or Minima

(*i*) **First derivative test**

Let x_0 be a critical point, then

$f'(x_0 - h) f'(x_0 + h)$

Result $> 0 < 0$ max. at x_0

$< 0 > 0$ min. at x_0

$> 0 > 0$ neither maxima

$< 0 < 0$ nor minima

where h is taken as very small positive number.

(*ii*) **Second derivative test:** If $f(x)$ has derivative, at x_0 and $f'(x_0) = 0$, then

$f''(x_0) > 0 \Rightarrow f(x)$ has minima at x_0,

$f''(x_0) < 0 \Rightarrow f(x)$ has maxima at x_0.

Derivative as a rate measure: Let $y = f(x)$ be a relation between two variables x and y. If δx be a small change in x and δy be the corresponding change in y, then $\delta y/\delta x$ represents the average rate of change in y with respect to x in the interval

$(x, x + \delta x)$ and $\lim\limits_{\delta x \to 0} \dfrac{\delta y}{\delta x} = \dfrac{dy}{dx}$, called **instantaneous rate** of change of y with respect to x.

Velocity and Acceleration: If s is the distance moved by a particle in time t, s.t.s. $= f(t)$, then the **velocity** v and the **acceleration** a of the particle at any instant t are given by

$$v = \frac{ds}{dt}$$

and $$a = \frac{dv}{dt} = \frac{d^2s}{dt^2}$$

Approximation and Error

We have $\lim\limits_{\delta x \to 0} \dfrac{\delta y}{\delta x} = \dfrac{dy}{dx}$.

$\therefore$ For smaller values of δx, we have $\dfrac{\delta y}{\delta x} = \dfrac{dy}{dx}$ (approximately)

i.e., $$\delta y = \left(\frac{dy}{dx}\right) \delta x \text{ (appr.)}$$

Thus corresponding to a small error δx in the value of x, the approximate error in the value of y is $\dfrac{dy}{dx} \delta x$, *i.e.,*

$$\delta y = \left(\frac{dy}{dx}\right) \delta x.$$

Percentage error: Let δx be an error in the variable x, then $\delta x/x$ is called the **relative error** in x and $(\delta x/x) \times 100$ is called the **percentage error** in x.

Rolle's Theorem: If function $f(x)$ is such that

(*i*) $f(x)$ is continuous in the closed interval $[a, b]$.

(*ii*) $f(x)$ is differentiable at every point in the open interval $]a, b[$.

(*iii*) $f(a) = f(b)$, then there exists at least one value of x, say c, where $a < c < b$, such that $f'(c) = 0$.

Lagrange's Mean Value Theorem

If a function $f(x)$ is such that

    (*i*) $f(x)$ is continuous in the closed interval $[a, b]$.

    (*ii*) $f(x)$ is differentiable at every point in the open interval $]a, b[$, then there exists at least one value c of x lying in the open interval $]a, b[$, such that

$$\frac{f(b)-f(a)}{b-a} = f'(c)$$

Law of Exponential Growth: The growth (increase) in some variable x is said to be according to the law of exponential,

if the rate of change in $x \propto x$

$$dx/dt = \lambda x$$
$$dx/x = \lambda \ dt = x = ce^{\lambda t}.$$

Solved Examples

Example 1: *Find the equation of the tangent to the curve* $y = x^3 + 1$ *at the point* (1, 2).

Solution: Curve is $y = x^3 + 1$

Differentiating, $\quad \dfrac{dy}{dx} = 3x^2$

$\therefore$ value of $\dfrac{dy}{dx}$ at (1, 2) $= 3(1)^2 = 3$

$\therefore$ Required equation of tangent is

$$y - 2 = \left(\frac{dy}{dx}\right)_{(1,2)} (x-1)$$

or $\qquad\qquad y - 2 = 3(x - 1)$ or $3x - y = 1$.

Example 2: *The perimeter of a rectangle is 40 cms. Find the length of sides when its area is maximum.*

Solution: Let the lengths of the sides be x and y cms.

Then perimeter of the rectangle

$$= 2(x + y) = 40 \text{ cm.} \qquad \text{(given)}$$

$\therefore \qquad\qquad y = 20 - x \text{ cms.} \qquad\qquad ...(I)$

$\therefore$ If A be the area of the rectangle, then A $= xy$

$$= x(20 - x) = 20x - x^2$$

$\therefore \qquad \dfrac{dA}{dx} = 20 - 2x, \quad \dfrac{d^2A}{dx^2} = -2 = -\text{ve}$

$\therefore \qquad (dA/dx) = 0 \Rightarrow 20 - 2x = 0$ or $x = 10$

And (d^2A/dx^2) being $-$ve, A is maximum when $x = 10$ and then from (1), $y = 10$.

$\therefore$ Rectangle with max. area and perimeter $= 40$ cms is a square whose each side is 10 cms long.

MULTIPLE CHOICE QUESTIONS

1. If m be the slope of a tangent to the curve $e^{2y} = 1 + 4x^2$, then
   - A. $m < 1$
   - B. $|m| > 1$
   - C. $|m| \le 1$
   - D. None of these

2. The values of k for which the function $f(x) = kx^3 - 9x^2 + 9x + 3$ may be increasing on R are.
   - A. $k > 3$
   - B. $k < 3$
   - C. $k \le 3$
   - D. None of these

3. The number of values of x where the function $f(x) = \cos x + \cos\left(\sqrt{2}x\right)$ attains its maximum is
   - A. 2
   - B. 1
   - C. 0
   - D. infinite

4. The local maximum value of $f(x) = \dfrac{\log x}{x}$ is
   - A. 1
   - B. e
   - C. $1/e$
   - D. None of these

5. If the radius of a circle increases from 3 cm to 3.2 cm., then the increase in the area of the circle is
   - A. $1.2\pi \text{ cm}^2$
   - B. $6\pi \text{ cm}^2$
   - C. $12\pi \text{ cm}^2$
   - D. None of these

6. The function $f(x) = x^2$ is increasing in the interval
   - A. $(-1, 1)$
   - B. $(-\infty, \infty)$
   - C. $(0, \infty)$
   - D. $(-\infty, 0)$

7. The maximum and minimum values of the function $f(x) = 3x^4 - 8x^3 + 12x^2 - 48x + 25$ in the interval $[1, 3]$ are
A. 16, –39
B. –16, 39
C. –16, –39
D. None of these

8. If $x + y = 10$, then the maximum value of xy is
A. 20
B. 30
C. 25
D. None of these

9. The slope of the tangent to the curve $x = t^2 + 3t - 8$, $y = 2t^2 - 2t - 5$ at the point $(2, -1)$ is
A. $-\dfrac{6}{7}$
B. $\dfrac{6}{7}$
C. $\dfrac{11}{7}$
D. None of these

10. The maximum value of $f(x) = \sin x + \cos x$ is
A. $\dfrac{1}{\sqrt{3}}$
B. –2
C. 1
D. $\sqrt{2}$

ANSWERS

1	2	3	4	5	6	7	8	9	10
C	A	C	C	A	C	A	C	B	D

SOME SELECTED EXPLANATORY ANSWERS

1. We have, $e^{2y} = 1 + 4x^2 \Rightarrow e^{2y} \cdot 2\dfrac{dy}{dx} = 8x$

$\Rightarrow \dfrac{dy}{dx} = \dfrac{4x}{e^{2y}} = \dfrac{4x}{1+4x^2}$

$\therefore$ Slope of tangent $= m$

$= \dfrac{4x}{1+4x^2} \Rightarrow |m| = \dfrac{4|x|}{1+4|x|^2} \le 1$

3. The maximum value of $f(x) = \cos x + \cos\left(\sqrt{2x}\right)$ is 2, which occurs at $x = 0$. Also, there is no value of x for which this value will be attained again.

5. The area of a circle is $A = \pi R^2$

$\therefore \dfrac{dA}{dt} = 2\pi R \dfrac{dR}{dt} = 1.2\pi \text{ cm}^2$

12) Integration and Area Under Curve

Anti-Derivative (or Primitive): The inverse operation of Differentiation is called Integration.

If
$$\frac{d}{dx}\{f(x)\} = \phi(x)$$

then $f(x)$ is called integral or anti-derivative or primitive of $\phi(x)$.

Integrand and Integral: The function $f(x)$ whose integral is required is called the integrand and the function $F(x)$, obtained by integration is called the integral.

STANDARD FORMULAE

1. $\displaystyle\int x^n dx = \frac{x^{n+1}}{n+1}, (n \neq -1)$

2. $\displaystyle\int \frac{1}{2} dx = \log x$

3. $\displaystyle\int e^x dx = e^x$

4. $\displaystyle\int a^x dx = \frac{a^x}{\log_e a}$

5. $\displaystyle\int \sin x\, dx = -\cos x$

6. $\displaystyle\int \cos x\, dx = \sin x$

7. $\displaystyle\int \sec^2 x\, dx = \tan x$

8. $\displaystyle\int \csc^2 x\, dx = -\cot x$

9. $\displaystyle\int \sec x \tan x\, dx = \sec x$

10. $\displaystyle\int \csc x \cot x\, dx = -\csc x$

11. $\displaystyle\int \frac{1}{\sqrt{(1-x^2)}} dx = \sin^{-1} x$

12. $\displaystyle\int \frac{-1}{\sqrt{(1-x^2)}} dx = \cos^{-1} x$

13. $\displaystyle\int \frac{1}{1+x^2} dx = \tan^{-1} x$

14. $\displaystyle\int \frac{-1}{1+x^2} dx = \cot^{-1} x$

15. $\displaystyle\int \frac{1}{x\sqrt{(x^2-1)}} dx = \sec^{-1} x$

16. $\displaystyle\int \frac{-1}{x\sqrt{(x^2-1)}} dx = \csc^{-1} x$

Standard Integral of Hyperbolic Function

(*i*) $\displaystyle\int \sinh x\, dx = \cosh x$

(*ii*) $\displaystyle\int \cosh x\, dx = \sinh x$

(*iii*) $\displaystyle\int \operatorname{sech}^2 x\, dx = \tanh x$

(*iv*) $\displaystyle\int \operatorname{cosech}^2 dx = -\coth x$

(*v*) $\displaystyle\int \operatorname{sech} x \tanh x\, dx = \operatorname{sech} x$

(*vi*) $\displaystyle\int \operatorname{cosech} x \coth x\, dx = -\operatorname{cosech} x$

Extended Forms of Fundamental Formulae

$$\int \frac{1}{a^2+x^2} dx = \frac{1}{a}\tan^{-1}\left(\frac{x}{a}\right)$$

$$\int \frac{dx}{\sqrt{(a^2 - x^2)}} = \sin^{-1}\left(\frac{x}{a}\right)$$

$$\int \frac{dx}{x\sqrt{(x^2 - a^2)}} = \frac{1}{a}\sec^{-1}\left(\frac{x}{a}\right)$$

$$\int \frac{dx}{\sqrt{(a^2 + x^2)}} = \sinh^{-1}\frac{x}{a}$$

$$\int \frac{dx}{\sqrt{a^2 + x^2}} = \log[x + \sqrt{a^2 + x^2}\,]$$

$$\int \frac{dx}{\sqrt{(x^2 - a^2)}} = \cosh^{-1}\frac{x}{a}$$

$$\int \frac{dx}{\sqrt{(x^2 - a^2)}} = \log[x + \sqrt{(x^2 - a^2)}\,]$$

$$\int \sqrt{[(a^2 - x^2)]}\,dx = \frac{1}{2}x\sqrt{(a^2 - x^2)} + \frac{1}{2}a^2 \sin^{-1}(x/a)$$

$$\int \sqrt{(a^2 + x^2)}\,dx = \frac{1}{2}x\sqrt{(a^2 + x^2)} + \frac{1}{2}a^2 \log[x + \sqrt{(a^2 + x^2)}\,]$$

$$\int \sqrt{(x^2 - a^2)}\,dx = \frac{1}{2}x\sqrt{(x^2 - a^2)} - \frac{1}{2}a^2 \log[x + \sqrt{(x^2 - a^2)}\,]$$

$$\int \frac{dx}{x^2 - a^2} = \frac{1}{2a}\log\left(\frac{x - a}{x + a}\right), x > a.$$

$$\int \frac{dx}{a^2 - x^2} = \frac{1}{2a}\log\left(\frac{a + x}{a - x}\right), \text{ when } x < a.$$

Integration by parts. The integration of the product of two functions is evaluated by the method of *integration by parts.*

The integral of the product of two functions u and v is given by

$$\int (u.v)\,dx = u.\int v\,dx - \int\left[\frac{d}{dx}(u).\int v\,dx\right]dx$$

i.e., $\int$ (first function) . (second function) dx

= (first function) . (integral of second function)

− $\int$ [(diff. coeff. of first) . (integral of second)] dx.

Solved Examples

Example 1: *Integrate the following*

(i) $\displaystyle\int \frac{(1+x)^2}{x^3}dx$ (ii) $\displaystyle\int \sqrt{1 + \cos 2x}\,dx$

Solution:

(i) $\displaystyle\int \frac{(1+x)^2}{x^3}dx = \int\left(\frac{1 + 2x + x^2}{x^3}\right)dx$

$$= \int\left(\frac{1}{x^3} + \frac{2}{x^2} + \frac{1}{x}\right)dx$$

$$= \int x^{-3}dx + 2\int x^{-2}dx + \int \frac{1}{x}dx$$

$$= \frac{x^{-2}}{(-2)} + 2.\frac{x^{-1}}{(-1)} + \log x$$

$$= -\frac{1}{2x^2} - \frac{2}{x} + \log x + c$$

(ii) $\displaystyle\int \sqrt{(1 + \cos 2x)}\,dx$

$$= \int \sqrt{(1 + 2\cos^2 x - 1)}\,dx$$

$$= \sqrt{2}.\int \cos x\,dx = \sqrt{2}.\sin x + C$$

Example 2: *Integrate the following*

(i) $\displaystyle\int \frac{dx}{(x+1)^2 - 4}$ (ii) $\displaystyle\int \frac{x^4\,dx}{(x-1)(x^2 + 1)}$

Solution:

(i) $\displaystyle\int \frac{dx}{(x+1)^2 - 4} = \int \frac{dx}{(x+3)(x-1)}$

$$= \int\left[\frac{1}{4(x-1)} - \frac{1}{4(x+3)}\right]dx$$

$$= \frac{1}{4}[\log(x-1) - \log(x+3)]$$

$$= \frac{1}{4}[\log(x-1)/(x+3)]+c$$

(ii) $\dfrac{x^4 dx}{(x-1)(x^2+1)} = x+1+\dfrac{1}{(x-1)(x^2+1)}$

$$= x+1+\frac{1}{2(x-1)}-\frac{(x+1)}{2(x^2+1)}$$

$\therefore$ The given integral

$$= \int\left[x+1+\frac{1}{2(x-1)}-\frac{1}{2(x^2+1)}-\frac{1}{2(x^2+1)}\right]dx$$

$$= \frac{1}{2}x^2+x+\frac{1}{2}\log(x-1)-\frac{1}{4}\log(x^2+1)$$

$$-\frac{1}{2}\tan^{-1}x+c.$$

MULTIPLE CHOICE QUESTIONS

1. $\displaystyle\int\frac{1}{\sqrt{x^2-a^2}}dx$ is equal to

A. $\log_e\left\{x-\sqrt{x^2-a^2}\right\}$

B. $\log_e\left\{x+\sqrt{x^2-a^2}\right\}$

C. $\log_e\left\{x^2-\sqrt{x^2-a^2}\right\}$

D. $\log_e\left\{x^2+\sqrt{x^2-a^2}\right\}$

2. $\displaystyle\int\frac{\log(\sec^{-1}x)}{x\sqrt{x^2-1}}dx$ is equal to

A. $\sec^{-1}x\cdot\log(e\cdot\sec^{-1}x)$

B. $e\cdot\sec^{-1}x.\log(\sec^{-1}x)$

C. $\sec^{-1}x\cdot\log\left(\dfrac{\sec^{-1}x}{e}\right)$

D. None of these

3. $\displaystyle\int\frac{1}{1+4\cos^2 x}dx$ is equal to

A. $\dfrac{1}{\sqrt{2}}\tan^{-1}\left(\sqrt{2}\tan x\right)$

B. $\dfrac{1}{\sqrt{5}}\tan^{-1}\left(\dfrac{\tan x}{\sqrt{5}}\right)$

C. $\dfrac{1}{\sqrt{3}}\tan^{-1}\left(\sqrt{3}\tan x\right)$

D. $\dfrac{1}{\sqrt{5}}\tan^{-1}\left(\sqrt{3}\tan x\right)$

4. $\displaystyle\int e^x(\sin x+\cos x)\,dx$ is equal to

A. $e^x . \cos x$ B. $e^x . \sin x$

C. $-e^x . \sin x$ D. $-e^x . \cos x$

5. $\displaystyle\int e^{3\log x}\left(x^4+1\right)^{-1}dx =$

A. $\dfrac{1}{3}\log(x^4+1)+c$

B. $\dfrac{1}{4}\log(x^4+1)+c$

C. $\dfrac{1}{2}\log(x^4-1)+c$

D. None of these

6. $\displaystyle\int e^{\sin x}(x\cos x-\sec x\cdot\tan x)\cdot dx =$

A. $xe^{\sin x}+e^{\sin x}\sec x+c$

B. $xe^{\sin x}-e^{\sin x}.\tan x+c$

C. $xe^{\cos x}+e^{\cos x}\tan x+c$

D. $x.e^{\sin x}-e^{\sin x}+\sec x+c$

7. $\displaystyle\int\frac{\sin x\cos x}{3\sin^2 x+5\cos^2 x}dx =$

A. $\dfrac{1}{4}\log[3\sin^2 x+5\cos^2 x]+c$

B. $-\dfrac{1}{4}\log[3\sin^2 x+5\cos^2 x]+c$

C. $\dfrac{1}{4}\log[3\sin^2 x-5\cos^2 x]+c$

D. $-\dfrac{1}{4}\log[3\sin^2 x-3\cos^2 x]+c$

8. $\int \tan^{-1}\sqrt{\dfrac{1-x}{1+x}}\, dx =$

A. $\dfrac{1}{2}\cos^{-1}x + \dfrac{1}{2}\sin(\cos^{-1}x) + c$

B. $\dfrac{1}{2}x\cos^{-1}x - \dfrac{1}{2}\sin(\cos^{-1}x) + c$

C. $\dfrac{1}{2}\cos^{-1}x - \dfrac{1}{2}\sin(\cos^{-1}x) + c$

D. $\dfrac{1}{2}x\cos^{-1}x + \dfrac{1}{2}\sin(\cos^{-1}x) + c$

9. $\int \dfrac{e^{\frac{x}{2}}}{\sqrt{e^{-x}-e^{x}}}\, dx =$

A. $\cos^{-1}(e^x) + c$ B. $\sin^{-1}(e^x) + c$

C. $\cos^{-1}(e^{-x}) + c$ D. $\sin^{-1}(e^{-x}) + c$

10. $\int \dfrac{\sec^2 x\, dx}{(\tan x+1)(2\tan x+3)} =$

A. $\log(\tan x + 1) - \log(2\tan x + 3) + c$
B. $\log(x + \tan x) - \log(x + 2\tan x) + c$
C. $\log(\tan x - 1) + \log(2\tan x - 3) + c$
D. $\log(x - \tan x) + \log(x - 2\tan x) + c$

11. $\int\limits_{0}^{\pi/2} \log\cos x\, dx$ is equal to

A. $\log 2$ B. $\pi \log 2$

C. $-\dfrac{\pi}{2}\log 2$ D. $\dfrac{\pi}{2}\log 2$

12. $\int\limits_{0}^{\pi/2} \dfrac{1}{9+16\cos^2 x}\, dx$ is equal to

A. $\dfrac{\pi}{10}$ B. $\dfrac{\pi}{20}$

C. $\dfrac{\pi}{30}$ D. $\dfrac{\pi}{40}$

13. $\int\limits_{0}^{\frac{\pi}{2}} \dfrac{\sqrt{\tan x}}{\sqrt{\tan x}+\sqrt{\cot x}}\, dx =$

A. $\dfrac{\pi}{2}$ B. $\dfrac{\pi}{3}$

C. $\dfrac{\pi}{4}$ D. $\dfrac{\pi}{12}$

14. $\int\limits_{0}^{3} \dfrac{x^2}{\sqrt{x+1}}\, dx =$

A. $\dfrac{70}{13}$ B. $\dfrac{71}{14}$

C. $\dfrac{73}{15}$ D. $\dfrac{76}{15}$

15. $\int\limits_{0}^{\frac{\pi}{2}} \dfrac{\sin x - \cos x}{1-\sin x.\cos x}\, dx =$

A. 1   B. 2
C. 3   D. 0

16. The area of the region bounded by the curve $y^2 = 16x$ and lines $x = 4$, $x = 1$ above the x-axis is

A. $\dfrac{36}{5}$ sq. units   B. $\dfrac{47}{3}$ sq. units

C. $\dfrac{56}{3}$ sq. units   D. $\dfrac{59}{7}$ sq. units

17. The area between parabola $y^2 = 4x$ and its latus-rectum, is

A. $\dfrac{2}{3}$ sq. units   B. $\dfrac{8}{3}$ sq. units

C. $\dfrac{16}{3}$ sq. units   D. $\dfrac{32}{3}$ sq. units

18. The area bounded by $y = \sin x$, the x-axis and the ordinates $x = 0$, $x = 2\pi$, is
A. 4 sq. units   B. 6 sq. units
C. 8 sq. units   D. 10 sq. units

19. The area of region bounded by the curves $y = x^2 + 2$, $y = x$, $x = 0$ and $x = 3$, is
A. 8.5 sq. units   B. 9.5 sq. units
C. 10.5 sq. units   D. 11.5 sq. units

20. The area enclosed by the two curves $y^2 = x + 1$ and $y^2 = -x + 1$, is

A. $\dfrac{2}{3}$ sq. units   B. $\dfrac{3}{5}$ sq. units

C. $\dfrac{4}{3}$ sq. units   D. $\dfrac{8}{3}$ sq. units

ANSWERS

1	2	3	4	5	6	7	8	9	10
B	C	B	B	B	D	B	B	B	A

11	12	13	14	15	16	17	18	19	20
C	C	C	D	D	C	B	A	C	D

SOME SELECTED EXPLANATORY ANSWERS

5. $\int e^{3\log x} \cdot \left(x^4+1\right)^{-1} dx$

$$= \int e^{\log x^3} \cdot \frac{dx}{x^4+1} = \int \frac{x^3}{x^4+1} dx$$

$$= \frac{1}{4}\int \frac{4x^3}{x^4+1} dx = \frac{1}{4}\log\left(x^4+1\right)+c$$

6. Let $I = \int e^{\sin x}[(x\cos x)-\sec x.\tan x]\,dx$

$$= \int x.e^{\sin x}\cdot \cos x\, dx - \int e^{\sin x}.\sec x.\tan x.dx$$

Integrating by parts, we get

$$I = \left(x.e^{\sin x} - \int e^{\sin x}.dx\right)-\left(e^{\sin x}.\sec x - \int e^{\sin x}.dx\right)$$

$$= x.e^{\sin x} - e^{\sin x} + \sec x + c$$

9. Let $I = \int \frac{e^{\frac{x}{2}}}{\sqrt{e^{-x}-e^x}}\,dx$

Multiply Numetator and Denominator by $e^{x/2}$

$$\therefore \quad I = \int \frac{e^x}{\sqrt{1-e^{2x}}}\,dx$$

Substitute $e^x = t \qquad e^x\,dx = dt$

$$\therefore \quad I = \int \frac{dt}{\sqrt{1-t^2}} = \sin^{-1} t + c$$

$$= \sin^{-1}(e^x) + c$$

10. Let $I = \int \frac{\sec^2 x}{(\tan x+1)(2\tan x+3)}\,dx$

Substitute $\tan x = t \qquad \sec^2 x\, dx = dt$

$$I = \int \frac{dt}{(t+1)(2t+3)}\,dx$$

$$= \int \left[\frac{1}{t+1}+\frac{-2}{2t+3}\right]dt$$

$$= \log(t+1)-\frac{2\log(2t+3)}{2}+c$$

$$= \log(t + 1) - \log(2t + 3) + c$$

$$= \log(\tan x + 1) - \log(2 \tan x + 3) + c$$

19. Equation of parabola is $y = x^2 + 2$

The line $y = x$ passes through origin

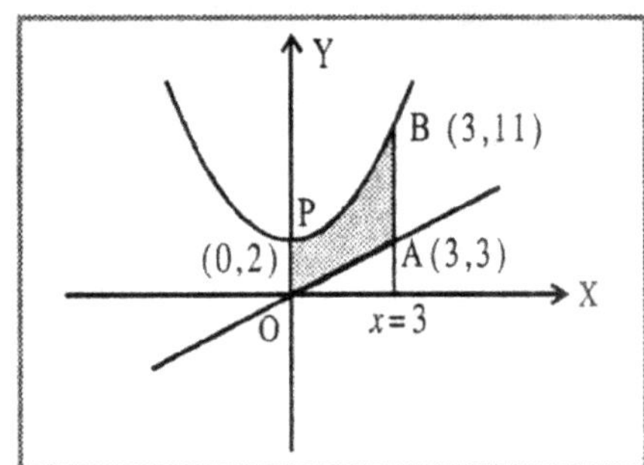

$\therefore$ Required area = Area under the parabola
　　　　　　　　　　　　　− Area under the line

$$= \int_0^3 (x^2+2)\,dx - \int_0^3 x\,dx = \left[\frac{x^3}{3}+2x\right]_0^3 - \left(\frac{x^2}{3}\right)_0^3$$

$$= (9+6)-\left(\frac{9}{2}\right) = 15-\frac{9}{2}$$

$$= \frac{21}{2} = 10.5 \text{ sq. units.}$$

(13) Straight Line and Circle

Distance Formula:

(*i*) The distance between the points (x_1, y_1) and

$$(x_2, y_2) = \sqrt{[(x_2 - x_1)^2 + (y_2 - y_1)^2]}$$

(*ii*) The distance of the point (x_1, y_1) from the

origin $= \sqrt{(x_1^2 + y_1^2)}$.

Section Formulae:

The coordinates (x, y) of a point R which divides the join of two given points $P(x_1, y_1)$ and $Q(x_2, y_2)$ in the ratio $m_1 : m_2$ are

(I) $$x = \frac{m_1 x_2 + m_2 x_1}{m_1 + m_2}$$

$$y = \frac{m_1 y_2 + m_2 y_1}{m_1 + m_2}$$

if R divides join of P and Q internally

(II) $$x = \frac{m_1 x_2 - m_2 x_1}{m_1 - m_2}$$

$$y = \frac{m_1 y_2 - m_2 y_1}{m_1 - m_2}$$

if R divides join of P and Q externally.

(III) Co-ordinates of any point dividing the join of (x_1, y_1) and (x_2, y_2) in the ratio $\lambda : 1$, are

$$\left(\frac{\lambda x_2 + x_1}{\lambda + 1}, \frac{\lambda y_2 + y_1}{\lambda + 1} \right)$$

(IV) Co-ordinates of the middle point of (x_1, y_1), and (x_2, y_2), are

$$\left(\frac{x_1 + x_2}{2}, \frac{y_1 + y_2}{2} \right)$$

Co-ordinates of Standard points connected with a triangle, the coordinates of whose vertices are

$$A(x_1, y_1),\ B(x_2, y_2)\ \text{and}\ C(x_3, y_3)$$

(I) **Centroid:** It is the point of intersection of the medians of a triangle and divides each median in the ratio 2 : 1 [*i.e.*, 2 from the vertex A(say) and 1 from the side BC]. Its coordinates are

$$\left[\frac{1}{3}(x_1 + x_2 + x_3), \frac{1}{3}(y_1 + y_2 + y_3) \right]$$

(II) **Circumcentre:** It is the point of intersection of the right bisectors of the sides of the triangle.

(III) **Incentre:** It is the point of intersection of the internal bisectors of the angles of a triangle. It is also the centre of the circle which touches the sides of the triangle internally. Its coordinates are

$$\left(\frac{ax_1 + bx_2 + cx_3}{a + b + c}, \frac{ay_1 + by_2 + cy_3}{a + b + c} \right)$$

where $a = BC$, $b = CA$, $c = AB$.

(IV) **Orthocentre:** It is the point of intersection of the altitudes of the triangle, *i.e.*, the lines through the vertices and perpendicular to the opposite sides.

(V) **Ex-centres of a triangle:** Let ABC be a triangle. There are three ex-centres. Let us denote the ex-centre opposite to vertex A, *i.e.*, touching extended sides AB and AC and the side BC from outside, by E_A. Then

$$E_A = \left(\frac{-ax_1 + bx_2 + cx_3}{-a + b + c}, \frac{-ay_1 + by_2 + cy_3}{-a + b + c} \right)$$

Other ex-centres, *i.e.*, E_B and E_C can be found like-wise.

Area of a triangle: The area of a triangle whose vertices are (x_1, y_1), (x_2, y_2) and (x_3, y_3) is

$$\frac{1}{2}[x_1(y_2 - y_3) + x_2(y_3 - y_1) + x_3(y_1 - y_2)]$$

or
$$\frac{1}{2}\begin{vmatrix} x_1 & y_1 & 1 \\ x_2 & y_2 & 1 \\ x_3 & y_3 & 1 \end{vmatrix}$$

Condition of collinearity of three points: Three points (x_1, y_1), (x_2, y_2) and (x_3, y_3) are collinear if the area of the triangle formed by these three points is zero. Hence the condition of collinearity is

$$x_1(y_2 - y_3) + x_2(y_3 - y_1) + x_3(y_1 - y_2) = 0$$

or
$$\begin{vmatrix} x_1 & y_1 & 1 \\ x_2 & y_2 & 1 \\ x_3 & y_3 & 1 \end{vmatrix} = 0$$

Area of a quadrilateral: The area of a quadrilateral whose vertices are (x_1, y_1), (x_2, y_2), (x_3, y_3) and (x_4, y_4) is

$$\frac{1}{2}[(x_1 y_2 + x_2 y_3 + x_3 y_4 + x_4 y_1)$$

$$-(x_2 y_1 + x_3 y_2 + x_4 y_3 + x_1 y_4)]$$

Note: If the area of a quadrilateral is zero, then its four vertices lie in a straight line.

LOCUS OF A POINT

The path traced out by a moving point which moves under some given geometrical conditions is called the locus of the point.

SLOPE OF A LINE

The slope of a line joining two points $A(x_1, y_1)$ and $B(x_2, y_2)$ is denoted by m and is given by $m = $

$$\frac{y_2 - y_1}{x_2 - x_1} = \tan \theta,$$ where θ is the angle which the line makes with the positive direction of x-axis.

STRAIGHT LINE

1. **Equations of straight lines in different forms:**

   (*i*) Equation of the line cutting off an intercept c on the positive side of y-axis

and making an angle θ with the positive direction (anticlock wise) of x-axis is $y = mx + c$, where $m = \tan \theta$ is called the slope of the line.

(*ii*) Equation of the line in general form is $ax + by + c = 0$

(*iii*) Any line through the origin is $y = mx$.

(*iv*) Equation of a line passing through (x_1, y_1) and having slope m is $y - y_1 = m(x - x_1)$

(*v*) Equation of a line passing through (x_1, y_1) and (x_2, y_2) is given by

$$y - y_1 = \frac{y_2 - y_1}{x_2 - x_1}(x - x_1)$$

(*vi*) Equation of the line in double intercept form is $\dfrac{x}{a} + \dfrac{y}{b} = 1$

2. Angle between the lines $y = m_1 x + c_1$ and $y = m_2 x + c_2$ is $\theta = \tan^{-1}\left(\dfrac{m_1 \sim m_2}{1 + m_1 m_2}\right)$, where $m_1 \sim m_2$ means either $m_1 - m_2$ or $m_2 - m_1$ as the case may be. If the two lines are parallel, then $m_1 = m_2$ and if perpendicular then $m_1 m_2 = -1$.

3. Equation of any straight line parallel ($\parallel$) to $ax + by + c = 0$ is $ax + by + \lambda = 0$, where λ is any constant.

4. Equation of any straight line perpendicular ($\perp$) to $ax + by + c = 0$ is $bx - ay + \lambda = 0$.

5. Length of the perpendicular from (α, β) to the line $ax + by + c = 0$ is $\left|\dfrac{a\alpha + b\beta + c}{\sqrt{(a^2 + b^2)}}\right|$.

6. General equation of a line through the intersection of two given lines $a_1 x + b_1 y + c_1 = 0$ (*i.e.*, P = 0) and $a_2 x + b_2 y + c_2 = 0$ (*i.e.*, Q = 0) is P + λ Q = 0, *i.e.*, $(a_1 x + b_1 y + c_1) + \lambda(a_2 x + b_2 y + c_2) = 0$.

7. **Distance between parallel lines:** Find the perpendicular distance of each line from the origin and retain their signs. Let them be p_1, p_2. The required distance between them is $p_1 - p_2$, *i.e.*, either $p_1 - p_2$ or $p_2 - p_1$.

8. Equations of the bisectors of the angles between two lines

Let the two lines be given by

$a_1x + b_1y + c_1 = 0$ and $a_2x + b_2y + c_2 = 0$

Then the equations of the bisectors of the angles between these two lines are

$$\left|\frac{a_1x+b_1y+c_1}{\sqrt{(a_1^2+b_1^2)}}\right| = \pm\left|\frac{a_2x+b_2y+c_2}{\sqrt{(a_2^2+b_2^2)}}\right|.$$

General Equation of Second Degree

The general equation of second degree is

$$ax^2 + 2hxy + by^2 + 2gx + 2fy + c = 0 \qquad ...(i)$$

The condition that the above equation (i) may represent a *pair of straight line* is

$$abc + 2fgh - af^2 - bg^2 - ch^2 = 0 \qquad ...(ii)$$

or

$$\begin{vmatrix} a & h & g \\ h & b & f \\ g & f & c \end{vmatrix} = 0$$

The equation to the pair of lines joining the origin to the points of intersection of the line $lx + my + n = 0$ and the curve

$$ax^2 + 2hxy + by^2 + 2gx + 2fy + c = 0$$

It is obtained by making the equation of the curve homogeneous with the help of the equation of the line.

CIRCLE

Equation of the circle in various forms:

Standard Form:

Let $p(x, y)$ be any point on the circle whose centre is origin and radius is 'r'. Join OP, then $|OP| = r$.

$$\therefore \quad \sqrt{(x-0)^2+(y-0)^2} = r$$

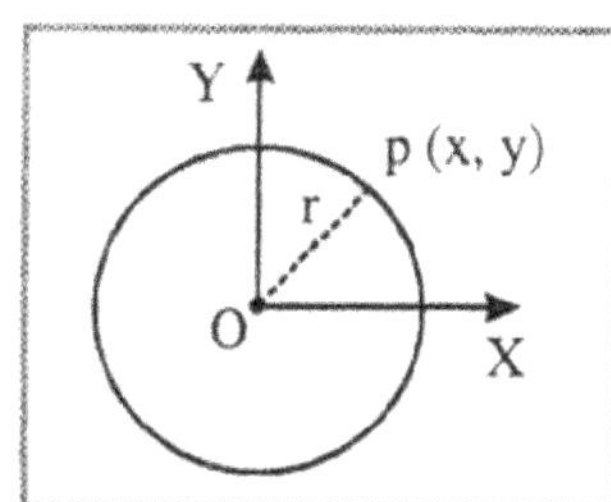

$x^2 + y^2 = r^2$ (By squaring), which is equation of a circle in standard form.

Corollory: The circle is real if $r^2 > 0$. If $r^2 < 0$, then no point in the plane satisfies the equation $x^2 + y^2 = r^2$

Central Form:

Let $p(x, y)$ by any point on the circle whose centre is $c(h, k)$ and radius is r.

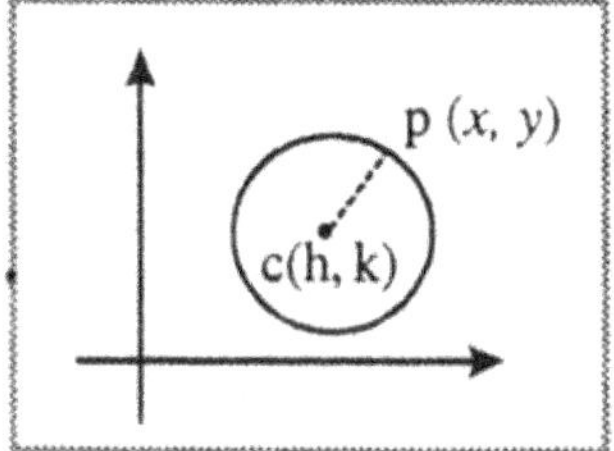

Join CP, then $|CP| = r$

$$\therefore \quad \sqrt{(x-h)^2+(y-k)^2} = r$$

Squaring, $(x - h)^2 + (y - k)^2 = r^2$, which is the required equation

$\therefore$ central form of a circle is $(x - h)^2 + (y - k)^2 = r^2$

General Form:

The equation of the circle (h, k) and radius 'r' is -
$(x - h)^2 + (y - k)^2 = r^2 \Rightarrow x^2 - 2xh + h^2 + y^2 - 2ky + k^2 = r^2$

$\Rightarrow x^2 + y^2 - 2hx - 2ky + (h^2 + k^2 - r^2) = 0$

Which can be written in the form $x^2 + y^2 + 2gx + 2fy + c = 0$ where $h = -g$, $k = -f$ and $h^2 + k^2 - r^2 = c$

$\therefore$ General form of a circle is $x^2 + y^2 + 2gx + 2fy + c = 0$

The centre and radius of the circle $x^2 + y^2 + 2gx + 2fy + c = 0$ are

$$C = (h, k) = (-g, -f)$$

and $\qquad r = \sqrt{g^2 + f^2 - c}, \ g^2 + f^2 \geq c$

Note: The equation $ax^2 + ay^2 + 2gx + 2fy + c$

$$= 0 \ a \neq 0 \Rightarrow x^2 + y^2 + \frac{2g}{a}x + \frac{2f}{a}y + \frac{c}{a} = 0$$

This represents a circle with centre at $\left(\dfrac{-g}{a}, \dfrac{-f}{a}\right)$

and radius $= \sqrt{\dfrac{g^2}{a^2} + \dfrac{f^2}{a^2} - \dfrac{c}{a}}.$

Solved Examples

Example 1: *Find the centroid of the triangle whose angular points are (2, 2), (7, 4) and (4, 7).*

Solution: If $(\overline{x}, \overline{y})$ be the required centroid, then

$$\overline{x} = \frac{1}{3}\Sigma x_1 = \frac{1}{3}(2+7+4) = \frac{13}{3}$$

and

$$\overline{y} = \frac{1}{3}\Sigma y_1 = \frac{1}{3}(2+4+7) = \frac{13}{3}$$

$\therefore$ Required centroid is (13/3, 13/3).

Example 2: *Find the equations to the straight lines passing through the point (2, 3) and inclined at an angle of 45° to the line $3x + y - 5 = 0$.*

Solution: Equation of any straight line passing through the point (2, 3) is

$$y - 3 = m\,(x - 2) \qquad \ldots(1)$$

Line DE is given by

$$3x + y - 5 = 0$$

$\Rightarrow$ Slope of line DE = –(3/1) = –3.

But the angle between the lines is ($\pm$ 45°)

$\Rightarrow \quad \tan(\pm 45°) = \dfrac{m-(-3)}{1+m(-3)};\ \Rightarrow m = -(1/2)$ or 2

Putting the values of m in (1), required equations of the stright lines are $x + 2y - 8 = 0$ and $2x - y - 1 = 0$.

Example 3: *Determine the equation of bisectors of the angles between the lines*

$$4x^2 - 16xy - 7y^2 = 0.$$

Solution: Here $a = 4;\ 2h = -16,\ b = -7$

$\therefore$ Required equation of bisectors is

$$\frac{x^2 - y^2}{a-b} = \frac{xy}{h}$$

or,

$$\frac{x^2 - y^2}{4-(-7)} = \frac{xy}{-8}$$

or, $\quad 8x^2 + 11xy - 8y^2 = 0.$

Example 4: *Find the equation of a circle with centre (–5, 4) and radius 3.*

Solution: The required circle is given by

$$[x - (-5)]^2 + [y - 4]^2 = 3^2.$$

$\therefore \quad x^2 + 10x + 25 + y^2 - 8y + 16 = 9$

$\therefore \qquad x^2 + y^2 + 10x - 8y + 32 = 0.$

Example 5: *Find the equation of the circle two of whose diameters are $x = 4$ and $y = 3$ and passing through (1, 1).*

Solution: The diameters are $x = 4$ and $y = 3$.

The centre C = (4, 3)

The circle passes through P = (1, 1).

$\Rightarrow \qquad$ radius = CP

$\therefore \qquad$ radius $= \sqrt{(4-1)^2 + (3-1)^2}$

$$= \sqrt{9+4}\ = \sqrt{13}.$$

Example 6: *Find the length of the tangent, segment to the circle $x^2 + y^2 = 4$ from the point (2, 6).*

Solution: The length of the tangent is

$$PT = \sqrt{S_1}$$

$$PT = \sqrt{(2)^2 + (6)^2 - 4}$$

$$= \sqrt{4+36-4}\ = \sqrt{36}$$

$$= 6 \text{ units.}$$

MULTIPLE CHOICE QUESTIONS

1. The point which divides the join of (1, 2) and (3, 4) externally in the ratio 1 : 1
   A. lies in the 1st quadrant
   B. lies in the IInd quadrant
   C. lies in the IIIrd quadrant
   D. cannot be found

2. Slope of any line parallel to x-axis is
   A. 1
   B. –1
   C. 0
   D. not defined

3. The vertices of a triangle are (0, 0), (3, 0) and (0, 4). Its orthocentre is at
   A. (0, 0)
   B. $\left(1, \dfrac{4}{3}\right)$
   C. $\left(\dfrac{3}{2}, 2\right)$
   D. None of these

4. The medians of a triangle meet at $(0, -3)$ and two vertices are at $(-1, 4)$ and $(5, 2)$. Then the third vertex is at
A. $(4, 15)$
B. $(-4, -15)$
C. $(-4, 15)$
D. $(4, -15)$

5. The area of a triangle is 5. Two of the vertices are $(2, 1)$ and $(3, -2)$. The thrid vertex lies on $y = x + 3$. The co-ordinates of the third vertex are given by

A. $\left(-\dfrac{7}{2}, \dfrac{13}{2}\right)$ and $\left(\dfrac{3}{2}, -\dfrac{3}{2}\right)$

B. $\left(-\dfrac{3}{2}, \dfrac{3}{2}\right)$ and $\left(\dfrac{7}{2}, \dfrac{13}{2}\right)$

C. $\left(\dfrac{3}{2}, \dfrac{9}{2}\right)$

D. $\left(\dfrac{13}{2}, \dfrac{9}{2}\right)$

6. If $u = a_1x + b_1y + c_1 = 0$

$v = a_2x + b_2y + c_2 = 0$ and $\dfrac{a_1}{a_2} = \dfrac{b_1}{b_2} = \dfrac{c_1}{c_2}$, the curve $u + kv = 0$ is
A. the same straight line
B. different straight line
C. it is not a straight line
D. None of these

7. The points $(-a, -b)$, $(0, 0)$, (a, b) and (a^2, ab) are
A. collinear
B. vertices of a parallelogram
C. vertices of a rectangle
D. None of these

8. If the lines $4x + 3y = 1$, $y = x + 5$ and $5y + bx = 3$ are concurrent, then the value of b is
A. 1
B. 3
C. 6
D. 0

9. The straight lines $x + y = 0$, $3x + y - 4 = 0$ and $x + 3y - 4 = 0$ form a triangle which is
A. isosceles
B. equilateral
C. right angled
D. None of these

10. Two points $(a, 0)$ and $(0, b)$ are joined by a straight line. Another point on this line is
A. $(3a, -2b)$
B. (a^2, ab)
C. $(-3a, 2b)$
D. (a, b)

11. If $y = 2x$ be a chord of the circle $x^2 + y^2 = 10x$, then the equation of the circle whose diameter lies on this line is
A. $x^2 + y^2 - 2x + 4y = 4$
B. $x^2 + y^2 + 2x + 4y = 3$
C. $x^2 + y^2 - 2x + 4y = 0$
D. $x^2 + y^2 - 2x - 4y = 0$

12. Radius of the circle $16x^2 + 16y^2 - 8x + 32y - 144 = 0$ is

A. $\dfrac{1}{3}\sqrt{274}$
B. $\dfrac{1}{4}\sqrt{161}$

C. $\dfrac{1}{5}\sqrt{274}$
D. $\dfrac{1}{6}\sqrt{274}$

13. Find the equation of the circle concentric with the circle $x^2 + y^2 - 6x - 2y + 4 = 0$ and passing through the point $(1, 2)$.
A. $x^2 + y^2 - 6x + 2y - 5 = 0$
B. $x^2 + y^2 - 6x + 2y + 5 = 0$
C. $x^2 + y^2 + 6x + 2y - 5 = 0$
D. $x^2 + y^2 - 6x - 2y + 5 = 0$

14. The angle between the tangent drawn from the point $(-1, 7)$ to the circle $x^2 + y^2 = 25$ is

A. $\dfrac{\pi}{2}$
B. $\dfrac{\pi}{3}$

C. $\dfrac{\pi}{4}$
D. $\dfrac{\pi}{6}$

15. If one end of the diameter of the circle $x^2 + y^2 - 4x - 2y - 5 = 0$ is $(3, 4)$, the co-ordinates of the other end are.
A. $(1, -2)$
B. $(-1, 2)$
C. $(-1, -2)$
D. $(1, 2)$

16. The circle $x^2 + y^2 - 8x + 4y + 4 = 0$ touches.
A. x-axis
B. y-axis
C. both the axis
D. neither x-axis nor y-axis

17. Find the equation of the circle passing through $(0, 0)$, $(2, 0)$ and $(0, -9)$
A. $x^2 + y^2 + 2x - 9y = 0$
B. $x^2 - y^2 + 2x - 9y = 0$
C. $x^2 + y^2 - 2x + 9y = 0$
D. $x^2 - y^2 - 2x - 9y = 0$

18. The circum circle of the triangle with vertices (0, 0), (5, 0) and (0, –6) is:
A. $x^2 + y^2 - 5x + 6y = 0$
B. $x^2 + y^2 + 5x - 6y = 0$
C. $x^2 + y^2 - 5x - 6y = 0$
D. $x^2 + y^2 + 5x + 3y = 0$

19. The tangent to the circle $x^2 + y^2 - 8x - 10y - 8 = 0$ parallel to the line $5x - 12y = 2$ is
A. $5x + 12y - 131 = 0$
B. $5x - 12y + 131 = 0$
C. $5x + 12y - 121 = 0$
D. $5x - 12y + 121 = 0$

20. Equation of the circle having normal at (3, 3) as the line $y = x$ and passing through (2, 2) is
A. $x^2 + y^2 + 5x + 5y + 12 = 0$
B. $x^2 + y^2 + 5x - 5y + 12 = 0$
C. $x^2 + y^2 - 5x - 5y + 12 = 0$
D. $x^2 + y^2 - 5x + 5y + 12 = 0$

ANSWERS

1	2	3	4	5	6	7	8	9	10
D	C	A	B	B	A	A	C	A	A

11	12	13	14	15	16	17	18	19	20
D	B	D	A	A	B	C	A	B	C

SOME SELECTED EXPLANATORY ANSWERS

12. Equation of circle is $16x^2 + 16y^2 - 8x + 32y - 144 = 0$

$$\Rightarrow x^2 + y^2 - \frac{1}{2}x + 2y - 9 = 0$$

Here, $g = -\frac{1}{4}$, $f = 1$, $c = -9$

$$\therefore \quad \text{Radius} = \sqrt{g^2 + f^2 - c}$$

$$= \sqrt{\frac{1}{16} + 1 + 9}$$

$$= \sqrt{\frac{161}{16}} = \frac{1}{4}\sqrt{161}.$$

15. We have $x^2 + y^2 - 4x - 2y - 5 = 0$. Here $g = -2, f = -1$. If one end is (x_1, y_1) the other end of the diameter is given by $(-2g - x_1; -2f - y_1)$
∴ One end (3, 4) = (x_1, y_1)
∴ other end = $(4 - 3, 2 - 4) = (1, -2)$

16. The given equation is $x^2 + y^2 - 8x + 4y + 4 = 0$
clearly $f^2 = c$, i.e., $2^2 = 4$
∴ circle touches y-axis.

17. We have equation of the circle passing through the points (0, 0), $(a, 0)$ and (0, b) is $x^2 + y^2 - ax - by = 0$.
∴ Required equation of circle is $x^2 + y^2 - 2x + 9y = 0$

19. The given equation of circle is
$$x^2 + y^2 - 8x - 10y - 8 = 0 \qquad ...(i)$$
Its centre is (4, 5) and radius is 7
Let the tangent to the circle (i) parallel to the line
$$5x - 12y = 2 \text{ is } 5x - 12y + k = 0$$
∴ Perpendicular length from the centre (4, 5) of the circle (i) to the line (ii) = radius of the circle.

$$\therefore \quad \frac{5(4) - 12(5) + k}{\sqrt{5^2 + 12^2}} = 7 \Rightarrow k = 131.$$

⑭ **Vector**

VECTOR

A directed line segment is called a vector:

Kinds of Vectors

(*i*) **Unit Vector:** The vector whose magnitude is one unit is called the unit vector.

(*ii*) **Co-planar Vectors:** A system of vectors is said to be coplanar, if their supports are parallel to the same plane.

Note that two vectors are always coplanar.

(*iii*) **Negative of a Vector:** The vector which has the same magnitude as the vector $\vec{a}$ but opposite direction is called the negative of $\vec{a}$ and is denoted by $-\vec{a}$. Thus, if $\overrightarrow{OP} = -\vec{a}$

(*iv*) **Reciprocal of a vector:** A vector having the same direction as that of a given vector $\vec{a}$ but magnitude equal to the reciprocal of the given vector is known as the reciprocal of $\vec{a}$ and is denoted by $\vec{a}^{-1}$. Thus, if $|\vec{a}| = a, |\vec{a}^{-1}| = 1/a$.

Scalar or Dot Product of Two Vectors

Definition: The scalar or dot product of two vectors $\vec{a}$ and $\vec{b}$ is defined to be the scalar $ab\cos\theta$, where $a = |\vec{a}|$, $b = |\vec{b}|$ and θ is the angle between the direction of the vectors, $\vec{a}$ and $\vec{b}$.

Algebraic Properties of Scalar or Dot Product

(I) Commutative : $\vec{a}\cdot\vec{b} = \vec{b}\cdot\vec{a}$

(II) Associative w.r.t. scalar n:

$$\vec{a}\cdot n\vec{b} = (n\vec{a})\cdot\vec{b} = n(\vec{a}\cdot\vec{b})$$

(III) Distributive Law:

$$\vec{a}\cdot(\vec{b}+\vec{c}) = \vec{a}\cdot\vec{b} + \vec{a}\cdot\vec{c}$$

Some Important Applications

(I) $\vec{a}\cdot(-\vec{b}) = (-\vec{a}\cdot\vec{b})$

(II) $(\vec{a}+\vec{b})^2 = \vec{a}^2 + \vec{b}^2 + 2\vec{a}\cdot\vec{b}$

(III) $(\vec{a}-\vec{b})^2 = \vec{a}^2 + \vec{b}^2 - 2\vec{a}\cdot\vec{b}$

(IV) $(\vec{a}+\vec{b})(\vec{a}-\vec{b}) = \vec{a}^2 - \vec{b}^2$

(V) $(\vec{a}+\vec{b}+\vec{c}...)\cdot(\vec{l}+\vec{m}+\vec{n}...)$

$$= (\vec{a}\cdot\vec{l} + \vec{a}\cdot\vec{m} + \vec{a}\cdot\vec{n} + ...) + (\vec{b}\cdot\vec{l} + \vec{b}\cdot\vec{m}$$
$$+ \vec{b}\cdot\vec{n} + ...) + (\vec{c}\cdot\vec{l} + \vec{c}\cdot\vec{m} + \vec{c}\cdot\vec{n} + ...) + ...$$

(VI) If $\vec{i}, \vec{j}, \vec{k}$ be the orthonormal trid of unit vectors, then

$$\hat{i}^2 = \hat{i}\cdot\hat{i} = 1 = \hat{i}^2 = \hat{k}$$

and $\quad \hat{i} = \hat{j} = 0 = \hat{j}\cdot\hat{k} = \hat{k}\cdot\hat{i}$

(VII) If θ be the angle between the vectors $\vec{a}$ and $\vec{b}$, then $\cos\theta = \dfrac{\vec{a}\cdot\vec{b}}{ab}$

where $a = |\vec{a}|$ and $b = |\vec{b}|$

Vector or Cross Product of Two Vectors

The vector or cross product of two vectors $\vec{a}$ and $\vec{b}$ is defined as

$$\vec{a}\times\vec{b} = (|\vec{a}||\vec{b}|\sin\theta)\hat{n}$$

or $\vec{a} \times \vec{b} = (a\, b\, \sin\theta)\,\hat{n}$

where θ is the angle between the vectors $\vec{a}$ and $\vec{b}$, and $\hat{n}$ is a unit vector perpendicular to both $\vec{a}$ and $\vec{b}$ such that $\vec{a},\ \vec{b},\ \hat{n}$ form a right handed triad of vectors.

Geometrical Interpretation of Cross Product

(*i*) If two non-parallel and non-null vectors $\vec{a}$ and $\vec{b}$ be represented along two adjacent sides of a parallelogram then $|\vec{a} \times \vec{b}|$ represents the area of that parallelogram.

(*ii*) The area of the triangle whose adjacent sides are represented by the vectors $\vec{a}$ and $\vec{b}$ is $\dfrac{1}{2}|\vec{a} \times \vec{b}|$.

(*iii*) If two diagonals of a parallelogram be represented by $\vec{a}$ and $\vec{b}$, then its area will be $\dfrac{1}{2}|\vec{a} \times \vec{b}|$.

Laws of Vector Product

(I) $(\vec{a} \times \vec{b}) = -(\vec{b} \times \vec{a})$,

where $\vec{a}$ and $\vec{b}$ are any vectors.
i.e., vector product is **not commutative.**

(II) $m(\vec{a} \times \vec{b}) = (m\vec{a}) \times \vec{b} = \vec{a} \times (m\vec{b})$,

where $\vec{a}, \vec{b}$ are vectors and m is a scalar, *i.e.,* vector product is **associative** with respect to a scalar.

(III) $\vec{a} \times (\vec{b} + \vec{c}) = (\vec{a} \times \vec{b}) + (\vec{a} \times \vec{c})$

where $\vec{a}, \vec{b}, \vec{c}$ are any three vectors.
i.e., vector product is **distributive** with respect to vector addition.

(IV) Vector products of $\hat{i}, \hat{j}, \hat{k}$

If $\hat{i}, \hat{j}, \hat{k}$ be the orthonormal triad of unit vectors, then

$\hat{i} \times \hat{j} = \hat{k} = -\hat{j} \times \hat{i}$

$\hat{j} \times \hat{k} = \hat{i} = -\hat{k} \times \hat{j}, \hat{k} \times \hat{i} = \hat{j} = -\hat{i} \times \hat{k}.$

(V) Angle between two vectors

The angle θ between two vectors $\vec{a}$ and $\vec{b}$ is given by

$$\sin\theta = \frac{|\vec{a} \times \vec{b}|}{|a|\,|b|}$$

Scalar Triple Product

Let $\vec{a},\ \vec{b},\ \vec{c}$ be three vectors. Then the scalar $(\vec{a} \times \vec{b}) \cdot \vec{c}$ is called the scalar triple product and is written as $[\vec{a}\ \vec{b}\ \vec{c}]$ or $[\vec{a},\ \vec{b},\ \vec{c}]$.

Geometrical Interpretation of Scalar Triple Product

If three coterminous edges of a parallelopiped are represented by vectors $\vec{a},\ \vec{b}$ and $\vec{c}$ respectively both in magnitude and direction, then the volume of the parallelopiped is $[\vec{a}\ \vec{b}\ \vec{c}]$, *i.e.,* the scalar triple product of the vectors $\vec{a},\ \vec{b}$ and $\vec{c}$.

Properties of Scalar Triple Product

(I) $(\vec{a} \times \vec{b}) \cdot \vec{c} = (\vec{b} \times \vec{c}) \cdot \vec{a} = (\vec{c} \times \vec{a}) \cdot \vec{b}$

(II) $(\vec{a} \times \vec{b}) \cdot \vec{c} = \vec{a} \cdot (\vec{b} \times \vec{c})$

(III) $(\vec{a} \times \vec{b}) \cdot \vec{c} = -(\vec{b} \times \vec{a}) \cdot \vec{c} = -\vec{c} \cdot (\vec{b} \times \vec{a})$

(IV) **A.** Scalar triple product is zero when two of the three vectors are equal.

B. Scalar triple product is zero when two of the three vectors are parallel.

(V) Condition for three vectors to be coplanar:
If three non-parallel and non-zero vectors $\vec{a}, \vec{b}, \vec{c}$ are **coplanar**, then their scalar triple product is zero, *i.e.,* $[abc] = 0$.

Expression of Scalar Triple Product in Determinant Form

If $\vec{a} = a_1\hat{i} + a_2\hat{j} + a_3\hat{k}, \vec{b} = b_1\hat{i} + b_2\hat{j} + b_3\hat{k}$

$\vec{c} = c_1\hat{i} + c_2\hat{j} + c_3\hat{k},$ then

$$[\vec{a}\ \vec{b}\ \vec{c}] = \begin{vmatrix} a_1 & a_2 & a_3 \\ b_1 & b_2 & b_3 \\ c_1 & c_2 & c_3 \end{vmatrix}$$

Scalar Product of Four Vectors

Definition

For four vectors $\vec{a}, \vec{b}, \vec{c}, \vec{d}$, the expression $(\vec{a}\times\vec{b})\cdot(\vec{c}\times\vec{d})$ is termed as the scalar product of four vectors and is given by

$$(\vec{a}\times\vec{b})\cdot(\vec{c}\times\vec{d}) = \begin{vmatrix} \vec{a}\vec{c} & \vec{a}\vec{d} \\ \vec{b}\vec{c} & \vec{b}\vec{d} \end{vmatrix}$$

$$= (\vec{a}\cdot\vec{c})(\vec{b}\cdot\vec{d}) - (\vec{a}\cdot\vec{d})(\vec{b}\cdot\vec{c}).$$

Vector Product of Four Vectors

Definition

The expression $(\vec{a}\times\vec{b})\times(\vec{c}\times\vec{d})$ is called the vector product of four vectors $\vec{a}, \vec{b}, \vec{c}, \vec{d}$.

Note:

1. $(\vec{a}\times\vec{b})\times(\vec{c}\times\vec{d}) = [\vec{a}\ \vec{b}\ \vec{d}]\ \vec{c} - [\vec{a}\ \vec{b}\ \vec{c}]\ \vec{d}$

   [Considering $\vec{a}\times\vec{b}$ as one single vector.]

2. $(\vec{a}\times\vec{b})\times(\vec{c}\times\vec{d}) = [\vec{a}\ \vec{c}\ \vec{d}]\ \vec{b} - [\vec{b}\ \vec{c}\ \vec{d}]\ \vec{a}$

   [Considering $\vec{c}\times\vec{d}$ as one single vector]

3. $\because\ [\vec{a}\ \vec{b}\ \vec{d}]\ \vec{c} - [\vec{a}\ \vec{b}\ \vec{c}]\ \vec{d}$

   $= [\vec{a}\ \vec{c}\ \vec{d}]\ \vec{b} - [\vec{b}\ \vec{c}\ \vec{d}]\ \vec{a}$

   $\therefore\ [\vec{a}\ \vec{b}\ \vec{c}]\ \vec{d}$

   $= [\vec{b}\ \vec{c}\ \vec{d}]\ \vec{a} - [\vec{c}\ \vec{a}\ \vec{d}]\ \vec{b} + [\vec{a}\ \vec{b}\ \vec{d}]\ \vec{c}$

   $= [\vec{b}\ \vec{c}\ \vec{d}]\ \vec{a} + [\vec{c}\ \vec{a}\ \vec{d}]\ \vec{b} + [\vec{a}\ \vec{d}\ \vec{b}]\ \vec{c}$

   $\therefore\ \vec{d} = \dfrac{[\vec{b}\ \vec{c}\ \vec{d}]}{[\vec{a}\ \vec{b}\ \vec{c}]}\vec{a} + \dfrac{[\vec{c}\ \vec{a}\ \vec{d}]}{[\vec{a}\ \vec{b}\ \vec{c}]}\vec{b} + \dfrac{[\vec{a}\ \vec{b}\ \vec{d}]}{[\vec{a}\ \vec{b}\ \vec{c}]}\vec{c}$

   Let us write $\vec{r}$ in place of $\vec{d}$ every where.

   $\vec{r} = \dfrac{[\vec{b}\ \vec{c}\ \vec{r}]}{[\vec{a}\ \vec{b}\ \vec{c}]}\vec{a} + \dfrac{[\vec{c}\ \vec{a}\ \vec{r}]}{[\vec{a}\ \vec{b}\ \vec{c}]}\vec{b} + \dfrac{[\vec{a}\ \vec{b}\ \vec{r}]}{[\vec{a}\ \vec{b}\ \vec{c}]}\vec{c}$

Thus any vector $\vec{r}$ can be written as a linear combination of any three non-coplanar vectors $\vec{a}, \vec{b}, \vec{c}$.

Solved Examples

Example 1: *Find k, if the vectors* $\overline{a} = \hat{i} - 2\hat{j} + \hat{k}$, $\overline{b} = k\hat{i} - 5\hat{j} + 3\hat{k}$, $\overline{c} = 5\hat{i} - 9\hat{j} + 4\hat{k}$ *are coplanar.*

Solution: We know that if the vectors $\overline{a}, \overline{b}, \overline{c}$ are coplanar then $[\overline{a}\ \overline{b}\ \overline{c}] = 0$.

$$\therefore\quad \begin{vmatrix} 1 & -2 & 1 \\ k & -5 & 3 \\ 5 & -9 & 4 \end{vmatrix} = 0$$

$\Rightarrow\ 1(-20 + 27) + 2(4k - 15) + 1(-9k + 25) = 0$

$\Rightarrow\ 7 + 8k - 30 - 9k + 25 = 0 \Rightarrow -k + 2 = 0$

$\Rightarrow\ -k = -2 \Rightarrow k = 2$

Example 2: *If two adjacent sides of a $\triangle ABC$ are given by* $2\overline{i} - 3\overline{j} + \overline{k}$ *and* $\overline{i} + 2j - 4\overline{k}$, *find its third side.*

Solution: For a triangle ABC, we have

$$\overline{AB} + \overline{BC} + \overline{CA} = \overline{O}$$

$\therefore\quad \overline{BC} = -(\overline{AB} + \overline{CA})$

$\qquad = -(2\overline{i} - 3\overline{j} + \overline{k} + \overline{i} + 2\overline{j} - 4\overline{k})$

$\qquad = -(3\overline{i} - \overline{j} - 3\overline{k})$

$\qquad = -3\overline{i} + \overline{j} + 3\overline{k}.$

Example 3: *If* $\overline{a} = 3\hat{i} + 2\hat{j} - \hat{k};\ \ \overline{b} = 4\hat{i} - 5\hat{j} - 3\hat{k},$ $\overline{c} = \hat{i} + \hat{j} + \hat{k}$ *find* $[\overline{a}\ \overline{b}\ \overline{c}]$.

Solution: $[\overline{a}\ \overline{b}\ \overline{c}] = \begin{vmatrix} 3 & 2 & -1 \\ 4 & -5 & 3 \\ 1 & 1 & 1 \end{vmatrix}$

$= 3(-5 - 3) - 2(4 - 3) - 1(4 + 5)$

$= 3(-8) - 2(1) - 1(9)$

$= -24 - 2 - 9 = -35$

MULTIPLE CHOICE QUESTIONS

1. $\bar{a}, \bar{b}, \bar{c}, \bar{d}$ are the position vectors of the points A, B, C and D respectively such that $2\bar{a} - \bar{d}$ $= 4\bar{c} - 3\bar{b}$, then the lines AB and CD are
   A. parallel
   B. perpendicular
   C. intersect each other
   D. None of these

2. Find the ratio in which the segment joining the points (3, 5, 6) and (4, 6, –3) is divided by yz-plane
   A. internally in the ratio 2 : 1
   B. externally in the ratio 3 : 2
   C. internally in the ratio 4 : 5
   D. externally in the ratio 3 : 4

3. Find $[\bar{a}, \bar{b}, \bar{c}]$ if $\bar{a} = \hat{i} + 2\hat{j} - 3\hat{k}$, $\bar{b} = 2\hat{i} - \hat{j} + \hat{k}$ and $\bar{c} = \hat{i} + \hat{j} - \hat{k}$
   A. 11
   B. –12
   C. –15
   D. 17

4. The position vector of a point which divides the join of the points $2\bar{a} - 3\bar{b}$ and $3\bar{a} - 2\bar{b}$ externally in the ratio 2 : 3 is:
   A. $-3\bar{b}$
   B. $4\bar{b}$
   C. $-5\bar{b}$
   D. $6\bar{b}$

5. Find the area of the tirangle whose vertices have the position vectors $\bar{a} = 2\hat{i} + 2\hat{j} + \hat{k}$, $\bar{b} = 3\hat{i} + 2\hat{k}$ and $\bar{c} = \hat{i} + 2\hat{j} + 2\hat{k}$
   A. $\sqrt{2}$ sq. units
   B. $\sqrt{3}$ sq. units
   C. $\sqrt{5}$ sq. units
   D. $\sqrt{7}$ sq. units

6. If $A \equiv (3, -2, 2)$ and $B \equiv (5, 1, -3)$ are any two points, find $\overline{AB}$ in terms of $\hat{i}, \hat{j}, \hat{k}$.
   A. $2\hat{i} + 3\hat{j} - 5\hat{k}$
   B. $2\hat{i} - 3\hat{j} + 4\hat{k}$
   C. $\hat{i} + 2\hat{j} - 3\hat{k}$
   D. $2\hat{i} + \hat{j} - 5\hat{k}$

7. The volume of the parallelopiped whose edges are $-6\hat{i} + \lambda\hat{k}$, $2\hat{i} - \hat{k}$ and $2\hat{i} + \hat{j} - 10\hat{k}$ is 130 cub. units, find the value of λ.
   A. –31
   B. –61
   C. –51
   D. –67

8. The position vector of the mid-point M of seg. BA where p.v.'s of A and B are given by $3\bar{i} + 2\bar{j} + 8\bar{k}$ and $\hat{i} - 8\hat{j} - 2\hat{k}$ is:
   A. $2\hat{i} - 3\hat{j} + 3\hat{k}$
   B. $2\hat{i} + 3\hat{j} - \hat{k}$
   C. $\hat{i} - 3\hat{j} + 2\hat{k}$
   D. None of these

9. $\bar{a} = \hat{i} + 2\hat{j} - 3\hat{k}$ and $\bar{b} = 2\hat{i} + 3\hat{j} + 5\hat{k}$ are the diagonals of a parallelogram. Find the area of the parallelogram.
   A. $\dfrac{\sqrt{359}}{2}$ sq. units
   B. $\dfrac{\sqrt{423}}{2}$ sq. units
   C. $\dfrac{\sqrt{455}}{2}$ sq. units
   D. $\dfrac{\sqrt{483}}{2}$ sq. units

10. If $A \equiv (2, 3, -3)$ and $B \equiv (5, -1, 2)$, find the vector having magnitude 5 units along $\overline{AB}$
    A. $\dfrac{1}{\sqrt{2}}(3\hat{i} - 4\hat{j} + 5\hat{k})$
    B. $\dfrac{1}{\sqrt{2}}(2\hat{i} + 3\hat{j} - 5\hat{k})$
    C. $\dfrac{1}{\sqrt{3}}(\hat{i} + 2\hat{j} + \hat{k})$
    D. $\dfrac{1}{\sqrt{3}}(\hat{i} - 2\hat{j} - \hat{k})$

11. If $\bar{a} = 5\hat{i} - 3\hat{j} + 4\hat{k}$, $\bar{b} = \hat{i} - 2\hat{j} + \hat{k}$, $\bar{c} = 3\hat{i} + 5\hat{j}$ then find $\bar{a} \cdot (\bar{b} \times \bar{c})$
    A. 8
    B. 10
    C. 14
    D. 20

12. If $A(1, 2, 3)$, $B(2, 3, 4)$, $C(p, q, 6)$ are three collinear points, find p and q.
    A. 3, 4
    B. 4, 5
    C. 5, 6
    D. 6, 7

13. If $\bar{a}, \bar{b}, \bar{c}$ are position vectors of A, B and C where $A \equiv (1, 3, 0)$, $B \equiv (2, 5, 0)$, $C \equiv (4, 2, 0)$ and $\bar{c} = x\bar{a} + y\bar{b}$, find x and y.
    A. $x = -15, y = 9$
    B. $x = -16, y = 10$
    C. $x = 17, y = -11$
    D. $x = 18, y = -12$

14. Find λ, if the vectors $\bar{a} = \hat{i} - 2\hat{j} + \hat{k}$, $\bar{b} = \lambda\hat{i} - 5\hat{j} + 3\hat{k}$, $\bar{c} = 5\hat{i} - 9\hat{j} + 4\hat{k}$ are coplanar.
    A. $\lambda = 1$
    B. $\lambda = 2$
    C. $\lambda = -2$
    D. $\lambda = 3$

15. The position vectors of the centroid of the $\triangle ABC$ when the position vectors of the vertices are (1, 3, 0) (2, 1, 1), (0, –1, 0) is:

A. (1, –1, 2)   B. (2, 1, –1)
C. (1, 1, 1)   D. None of these

16. Find the value of x such that the four points A(3, 2, 1), B(4, x, 5), C(4, 2, –2) and D(6, 5, –1) are coplanar

A. $x = 3$ B. $x = 5$
C. $x = 7$ D. $x = -1$

17. Find the volume of the parallelopiped if $\overline{a} = 4\hat{i}$, $\overline{b} = 5\hat{j}$ and $\overline{c} = 6\hat{k}$ are coterminous edges of the parallelopiped.

A. 98 cub. units   B. 100 cub. units
C. 110 cub. units   D. 120 cub. units

18. Find the unit vector along $\overline{PQ}$ if P(–2, 2, 3) and Q(–1, 4, 5)

A. $\dfrac{1}{2}(\hat{i} - \hat{j} + 2\hat{k})$ B. $\dfrac{1}{2}(2\hat{i} + \hat{j} - \hat{k})$

C. $\dfrac{1}{3}(2\hat{i} + 2\hat{j} + \hat{k})$ D. $\dfrac{1}{3}(\hat{i} + 2\hat{j} + 2\hat{k})$

19. For what value of k, the vectors $2\hat{i} + 2\hat{j} - 3\hat{k}$, $3\hat{i} + k\hat{j} + 2\hat{k}$ and $\hat{i} + 2\hat{j} + 3\hat{k}$ are coplanar.

A. 20/3   B. 30/7
C. 40/9   D. 50/13

20. Find the volume of the tetrahedron whose vertices are A(2, 6, 3), B(4, –3, 2), C(5, 4, 1) and D(7, 3 4).

A. $\dfrac{25}{3}$ cub. units   B. $\dfrac{46}{3}$ cub. units

C. $\dfrac{50}{3}$ cub. units   D. $\dfrac{53}{3}$ cub. units

ANSWERS

1	2	3	4	5	6	7	8	9	10
C	D	C	C	B	A	B	A	D	A

11	12	13	14	15	16	17	18	19	20
B	B	B	B	C	B	D	D	C	C

SOME SELECTED EXPLANATORY ANSWERS

11. We have, $\overline{a} = 5\hat{i} - 3\hat{j} + 4\hat{k}$, $\overline{b} = \hat{i} - 2\hat{j} + \hat{k}$, $\overline{c} = 3\hat{i} + 5\hat{j}$

$$\therefore \ \overline{a} \cdot (\overline{b} \times \overline{c}) = [\overline{a}\ \overline{b}\ \overline{c}] = \begin{vmatrix} 5 & -3 & 4 \\ 1 & -2 & 1 \\ 3 & 5 & 0 \end{vmatrix}$$

$$= 5(0 - 5) + 3(0 - 3) + 4(5 + 6)$$
$$= -25 - 9 + 44 = 10$$

14. Since the vectors $\overline{a}\ \overline{b}\ \overline{c}$ are coplanar, we have $[\overline{a}\ \overline{b}\ \overline{c}] = 0$.

$$\therefore \ \begin{vmatrix} 1 & -2 & 1 \\ \lambda & -5 & 3 \\ 5 & -9 & 4 \end{vmatrix} = 0$$

$\Rightarrow 1(-20 + 27) + 2(4\lambda - 15) + 1(-9p + 25) = 0$
$\Rightarrow 7 + 8\lambda - 30 - 9\lambda + 25 = 0$
$\Rightarrow -\lambda = -2 \Rightarrow \lambda = 2$

15. Let A(1, 3, 0), B(2, 1, 1) and C(0, –1, 0) be the given points. Let G($(\overline{x}, \overline{y}, \overline{z})$ be the centroid. Then

$$\overline{x} = \frac{1+2+0}{3}, \quad \overline{y} = \frac{3+1-1}{3}, \quad \overline{z} = \frac{0+1+0}{3}$$

$\Rightarrow \overline{x} = 1, \overline{y} = 1, \overline{z} = 1/3$.

17. Volume of a parallelopiped whose three coterminous edges are $\overline{a}\ \overline{b}\ \overline{c} = [\overline{a}\ \overline{b}\ \overline{c}]$

$= \overline{a} \times \overline{b} \cdot \overline{c} = 4\hat{i} \times 5\hat{j} \cdot 6\hat{k} = 120\hat{i} \times \hat{j} \cdot \hat{k}$

$= 120\ \hat{k} \cdot \hat{k} = 120$ cub. units $[\because \hat{i} \times \hat{j} = \hat{k}]$

⑮ Trigonometry

Solved Examples

Example 1: *If* $\tan\theta = \dfrac{4}{3}$, *what is the value of*

$$\sqrt{\dfrac{1-\sin\theta}{1+\sin\theta}}\ ?$$

Solution: If $\tan\theta = \dfrac{4}{3}$, then $\sin\theta = \dfrac{4}{5}$

$$\sqrt{\dfrac{1-\sin\theta}{1+\sin\theta}} = \sqrt{\dfrac{1-\dfrac{4}{5}}{1+\dfrac{4}{5}}} = \sqrt{\dfrac{1}{9}} = \dfrac{1}{3}.$$

Example 2: *If* $\cos y° = \sin(y° + 20°)$, *find the least positive value of y.*

Solution: $\cos y° = \sin(90° - y°)$

$\therefore\quad \sin(90° - y°) = \sin(y° + 20°)$

or $\qquad 90° - y° = y° + 20°$

$\Rightarrow \qquad\qquad 2y° = 70°$ or $y = 35°$.

Example 3: *If* $A = 29°$, *find the value of* $\sin^4 A + \cos^4 A + 2\sin^2 A\cos^2 A$.

Solution: Since $\sin^4 A + \cos^4 A + 2\sin^2 A\cos^2 A$

$$= (\sin^2 A + \cos^2 A)^2 = 1 \text{ for all values of } A$$

Hence the value of the given expression is 1.

Example 4: *A vertical tower stands on a horizontal plane, and from a point on the ground at a distance of 30 metres from the foot of the tower, the angle of elevation is 60°. The height of the tower is...* ($\sqrt3 = 1.73$).

Solution: From the adjoining figure, the height of the tower MP is given by

$$\dfrac{h}{30} = \tan 60°$$

$$= \sqrt3 = 1.73$$

$\therefore \qquad h = 30 \times (1.73)$

$$= 51.9 \text{ m}$$

MULTIPLE CHOICE QUESTIONS

1. On the same side of the tower two objects are located. Observed from the top of the tower, their angles of depressions are 45° and 60°. If the height of the tower is 300 m, the distance between the two objects is:

   A. $100(2-\sqrt3)\,\text{m}$ B. $300(2-\sqrt3)\,\text{m}$

   C. $100(3-\sqrt3)\,\text{m}$ D. $300(3-\sqrt3)\,\text{m}$

2. If $\cos\theta = \dfrac{3}{5}$, the value of $\sqrt{\dfrac{\sec\theta - \operatorname{cosec}\theta}{\sec\theta + \operatorname{cosec}\theta}}$ is

   A. $\sqrt7$ B. $\dfrac{1}{\sqrt7}$

   C. $\dfrac{2}{\sqrt7}$ D. $\dfrac{3}{\sqrt7}$

3. What is the value of $\dfrac{\cot\alpha\,\tan\beta\,(\tan\alpha + \cot\beta)}{\cot\alpha + \tan\beta}$?

   A. 1   B. $\sin\alpha\sin\beta$

   C. $\cos\alpha\cos\beta$ D. $\cot\alpha\tan\beta$

4. The angle of elevation of the top of a pillar is 30°, and on approaching 20 m nearer it is 60°. Find the height of the pillar.

(Given $\sqrt{3}$ = 1.732)

  A. 10.73 m   B. 173.2 m

  C. 1.732 m   D. 17.32 m

5. The value of $\dfrac{\cot(90° - A)}{\operatorname{cosec}^2 A} \cdot \dfrac{\sec A \cot^3 A}{\sin^2(90° - A)}$

  A. sec A   B. tan A

  C. $\sec^2 A$ D. $\tan^2 A$

6. The angles of depression of the top and the bottom of a 7 m tall building from the top of a tower are 45° and 60° respectively. The height of the tower is:

  A. $\dfrac{7}{2}(\sqrt{3}-1)\,\text{m}$

  B. $\dfrac{7}{2}(\sqrt{3}+1)\,\text{m}$

  C. $7(\sqrt{3}+1)\,\text{m}$

  D. $7(\sqrt{3}+2)\,\text{m}$

7. What is the value of $\cos^2 22\frac{1}{2}° + \cos^2 67\frac{1}{2}°$

$+ \cos^2 112\frac{1}{2}° + \cos^2 157\frac{1}{2}°$

  A. 4   B. 2

  C. $2\dfrac{1}{2}$ D. 3

8. If $\sin \alpha = \dfrac{12}{13}\left(0 < \alpha < \dfrac{\pi}{2}\right)$ and $\cos \beta = -\dfrac{3}{5}\left(\pi < \beta < \dfrac{3}{2}\pi\right)$, then the value of $\sin(\alpha + \beta)$ is

  A. $-\dfrac{56}{65}$ B. $\dfrac{16}{65}$

  C. $\dfrac{56}{65}$ D. $-\dfrac{16}{65}$

9. If $x = 8a \cos^3 \theta$, $y = 8b \sin^3 \theta$, what is the vlaue of $\left(\dfrac{x}{a}\right)^{\frac{2}{3}} + \left(\dfrac{y}{b}\right)^{\frac{2}{3}}$

  A. 1   B. 2

  C. 4   D. 8

10. ABC is a triangle, and BD is perpendicular to AC produced: Find BD if A = 30°, C = 120° and AC = 20

  A. $5\sqrt{3}$ B. $10\sqrt{3}$

  C. $6\sqrt{2}$ D. $8\sqrt{3}$

11. If $\cos(\alpha + \beta) = \dfrac{4}{5}$ and $\sin(\alpha - \beta) = \dfrac{5}{13}$ where α, β lie between 0° and 45°, then the value of $\tan 2\alpha$ is

  A. $\dfrac{56}{33}$ B. $\dfrac{46}{33}$

  C. $\dfrac{14}{33}$ D. $\dfrac{16}{33}$

12. A ladder is placed against the wall such that it just reaches the top of the wall. The foot of the ladder is 1.5 m away from the wall and the ladder is inclined at an angle of 60° with the ground. The height of the wall is ($\sqrt{3}$ = 1.73)

  A. 2.695   B. 2.785

  C. 2.595   D. 2.545

13. Find the numerical value of $3 \tan^2 30° + \dfrac{1}{4}$ sec 60° + $5 \cot^2 45° - \dfrac{2}{3} \sin^2 \theta = 3 \cos \theta$?

  A. $3\dfrac{1}{2}$ B. $4\dfrac{1}{2}$

  C. 5   D. 6

14. The angle of elevation of the top of a tower from a point on the ground is 30°. After walking 30 m towards the tower, the angle of elevation becomes 60°. The height of the tower is:

  A. $15\sqrt{3}$ m   B. $20\sqrt{3}$ m

  C. $30\sqrt{3}$ m   D. $10\sqrt{3}$ m

15. If $x \tan (180° + A) \tan (90° + A) \sin (-A) = \sin (180° - A) \cot (90° - A) \cos (360° - A)$, find the value of x.

A. $\sin A$
B. $\cos A$
C. $\tan A$
D. $\cot A$

16. The angle of elevation of the top and the foot of a flagstaff fixed on a wall are 60° and 45° to a man standing on the other end of a road 30 m wide, the height of the flagstaff is:

A. $30(\sqrt{3} - 1)$

B. $10(\sqrt{3} + 1)$

C. $30(\sqrt{3} + 1)$

D. $30\sqrt{3}$

17. Find the value of $\cot (90° - A) \cot A \cos (90° - A) \tan (90° - A)$

A. $\sec A$ B. $\sin A$
C. $\cos A$ D. $\tan A$

18. $4 \tan^{-1} \dfrac{1}{5} - \tan^{-1} \dfrac{1}{239}$ is equal to

A. π B. $\dfrac{\pi}{2}$

C. $\dfrac{\pi}{3}$ D. $\dfrac{\pi}{4}$

19. $\tan^{-1} \left(\dfrac{x}{y} \right) - \tan^{-1} \left(\dfrac{x-y}{x+y} \right)$ is

A. $\dfrac{\pi}{2}$ B. $\dfrac{\pi}{3}$

C. $\dfrac{\pi}{4}$

D. None of these

20. The solution of

$$\sin^{-1} \left(\frac{2a}{1+a^2} \right) - \cos^{-1} \left(\frac{1-b^2}{1+b^2} \right) = \tan^{-1} \left(\frac{2x}{1-x^2} \right) \text{ is}$$

A. $\dfrac{a-b}{1-ab}$ B. $\dfrac{1+ab}{a-b}$

C. $\dfrac{ab-1}{a+b}$ D. $\dfrac{a-b}{1+ab}$

21. The value of

$$\tan \left[\cos^{-1} \left(\frac{4}{5} \right) + \tan^{-1} \left(\frac{2}{3} \right) \right] \text{ is}$$

A. $\dfrac{6}{17}$

B. $\dfrac{7}{16}$

C. $\dfrac{17}{6}$

D. None of these

22. If $\sin^{-1} x + \sin^{-1} y + \sin^{-1} z = \dfrac{3\pi}{2}$, the value of

$$x^{100} + y^{100} + z^{100} - \frac{9}{x^{101} + y^{101} + z^{101}} \text{ is}$$

A. 0   B. 1
C. 2   D. 3

ANSWERS

1	2	3	4	5	6	7	8	9	10
C	B	A	D	A	B	B	A	C	B

11	12	13	14	15	16	17	18	19	20
A	C	D	A	A	A	C	D	C	D

21	22
C	A

SOME SELECTED EXPLANATORY ANSWERS

7. $\cos^2 112\frac{1}{2}^\circ = \cos^2\left(90^\circ + 22\frac{1}{2}\right) = \sin^2 22\frac{1}{2}^\circ$

$\cos^2 157\frac{1}{2}^\circ = \cos^2\left(90^\circ + 67\frac{1}{2}^\circ\right) = \sin^2 67\frac{1}{2}^\circ$

9. $2\cos = \left(\dfrac{x}{a}\right)^{\frac{1}{3}}$ and $2\sin\theta = \left(\dfrac{y}{b}\right)^2$

squaring and adding

$4(\cos^2\theta + \sin^2\theta) = \left(\dfrac{x}{a}\right)^{\frac{2}{3}} + \left(\dfrac{y}{b}\right)^{\frac{2}{3}} = 4$

10. $\angle ABC = 30^\circ \Rightarrow AC = BC = 20$

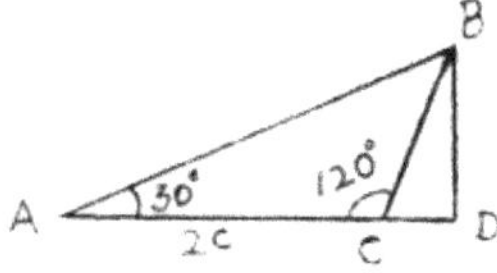

$\therefore\quad BD = BC\sin 60^\circ = 20 \times \dfrac{\sqrt{3}}{2}$

$\qquad = 10\sqrt{3}$

15. $x(\tan A)(-\cot A)(-\sin A) = \sin A \tan A(\cos A)$

$\Rightarrow x\sin A = \sin^2 A$ or $x = \sin A$

20. $\sin^{-1}\left(\dfrac{2a}{1+a^2}\right) - \cos^{-1}\left(\dfrac{1-b^2}{1+b^2}\right)$

$= \tan^{-1}\left(\dfrac{2x}{1-x^2}\right)$

$\Rightarrow 2\tan^{-1} a - 2\tan^{-1} b = 2\tan^{-1} x$

$\Rightarrow \tan^{-1} x = \tan^{-1}\left(\dfrac{a-b}{1+ab}\right)$

$\Rightarrow x = \dfrac{a-b}{1+ab}.$

1. **Event.** An *event* is an occurrence. Presence of a tail when a coin is tossed is an event.

2. **Mutually Exclusive Events.** If two or more events have no point in common, *i.e.*, they cannot occur simultaneously, the event are said to be mutually exclusive events. A head and tail are two mutually exclusive events of a coin. There are six mutually exclusive event in case of a dice, because only one event at a time can occur.

3. **Exhaustive events.** All possible outcome of an experiment are called exhaustive events.

4. **Definition of probability.** If there are n exhaustive, mutually exclusive and equally likely outcomes of an experiment and m of them are fovourable to an event A, then the probability of A is defined as

the ratio $\dfrac{m}{n}$

$$\Rightarrow \quad P(A) = \frac{\text{favourable events}}{\text{total number of events}}$$

5. Odds in favour and odds against an event. If 'a' of the outcomes are favourable to an event A and 'b' of the outcomes are *against* it as a result of an experiment, then we say that odds are 'a' to 'b' in favour of A, or odds are 'b' to 'a' against A.

6. $P(A)$ and $P(\bar{A})$ are the probabilities of occurrence and non-occurrence of an event A, then

$$P(A) + P(\bar{A}) = 1 \text{ i.e.,}$$

$$P(\bar{A}) = 1 - P(A)$$

7. If A and B are two mutually exclusive events, then $P(A \cap B) = 0$. This means that A and B cannot occur simultaneously, *i.e.*, $A \cap B = \phi$.

8. $P(A \cup B) = P(A) + P(B)$ for A and B to be mutually exclusive events.

9. $P(A \cup B) = P(A) + P(B) - P(A \cap B)$ if A and B are not mutually exclusive events.

Two Important Theorems:

(*i*) **Addition Theorem:** Probability of A or B
$P(A \cup B) \Rightarrow P(A \text{ or } B) = P(A) + P(B) - P(A \cap B)$ when A and B are not mutually exclusive
$P(A \cup B) = P(A) + P(B)$ where A and B are mutually exclusive.

(*ii*) **Multiplicative Theorem:** Two events A and B are mutually independent if and only if
$P(A \cap B) \Rightarrow P(A \text{ and } B) = P(A) \times P(B)$.
Provided $P(A) \neq 0$, $P(B) \neq 0$.

Solved Examples

Example 1: *If two coins are tossed once, what is the probability that at least one head occur?*

Solution: There are four outcomes

$$H, H; \ H, T; \ T, H, T, T$$

$\therefore$ P [at least one head] = ¾

Example 2: *Compare the chance of throwing 4 with one dice and 8 with two dice.*

Solution: There are 6 possible ways in which the dice can fall and of these one is favourable to an event.

$\therefore$ P(throwing 4 with one die) $= \dfrac{1}{6}$

Again when two dice are thrown there are 36 exhausive cases and a sum 8 can happen in 5 cases namely

(3, 5); (5, 3); (4, 4); (2, 6) and (6, 2).

$\therefore$ P (getting a sum eight) $= \dfrac{5}{36}$

$\therefore$ Ratio is $\dfrac{1}{6} : \dfrac{5}{36} \Rightarrow 6 : 5.$

Example 3: *A bag contains 6 white, 7 red and 8 black balls. Three balls are drawn at random. What is the chance that a white, red and a black ball is drawn?*

Solution: $\dfrac{6_{c_1} \times 7_{c_1} \times 8_{c_1}}{21_{c_3}} = \dfrac{6 \times 7 \times 8 \times 3 \times 2 \times 1}{21 \times 20 \times 19}$

$$= \dfrac{29}{95}.$$

MULTIPLE CHOICE QUESTIONS

1. Assuming that for a husband-wife couple the chance of their child being a boy or a girl are the same, the probability of their two children being a boy and a girl is:

   A. $\dfrac{1}{2}$ B. 1

   C. $\dfrac{1}{4}$ D. $\dfrac{1}{8}$

2. A cricket team has 15 members, of whom only 5 can bowl. If the names of the 15 members are put into a hat and 11 are drawn at random, then the chance of obtaining an eleven containing at least 3 bowlers is:

   A. $\dfrac{7}{13}$ B. $\dfrac{11}{15}$

   C. $\dfrac{12}{13}$ D. $\dfrac{12}{15}$

3. 8 coins are tossed simultaneously. The probability of getting at least 6 heads is:
   A. 57/64   B. 229/256
   C. 7/64   D. 37/256

4. From a pack of cards, two are drawn, the first being replaced before the second is drawn. The probability that the first is a diamond and the second is a king will be:
   A. 13/4   B. 5/52
   C. 1/52   D. 52

5. A number is chosen at random among the first 120 natural numbers. What is the probability of the number chosen being a multiple of 5 or 15?
   A. 1/5   B. 1/8
   C. 1/6   D. 1/15

6. Three dice are rolled. What is the probability of getting different faces?

   A. $\dfrac{1}{3}$ B. $\dfrac{1}{4}$

   C. $\dfrac{5}{9}$ D. $\dfrac{4}{9}$

7. What is the probability that three persons selected at random will be born on different days of the week?

   A. $\dfrac{48}{49}$ B. $\dfrac{2}{3}$

   C. $\dfrac{30}{49}$ D. $\dfrac{36}{49}$

8. The probability of having a king and a queen when the two cards are drawn at random from a pack of 52 cards, is:

   A. $\dfrac{16}{663}$ B. $\dfrac{8}{663}$

   C. $\dfrac{4}{663}$ D. $\dfrac{2}{663}$

9. A card is drawn from an ordinary pack and a gambler bets that it is either a spade or an ace. The odds against his winning are:
   A. 9 : 4   B. 9 : 5
   C. 9 : 6   D. 9 : 8

10. The probability that is leap year, selected at random, will contain 53 Sundays, is:

A. $\dfrac{1}{3}$ B. $\dfrac{2}{7}$

C. $\dfrac{3}{7}$ D. $\dfrac{4}{3}$

11. Which one of the following is not a fundamental approach of probability?
A. Classical   B. Empirical
C. Subjective   D. None of these

12. A bag, contains 5 white, 5 black, 7 yellow and 8 red balls the probability of getting a red ball when a ball is drawn at random is:

A. $\dfrac{1}{3}$ B. $\dfrac{1}{6}$

C. $\dfrac{1}{4}$ D. $\dfrac{7}{24}$

13. The probability of drawing a king of red colour from a pack of 52 cards is:

A. $\dfrac{1}{13}$ B. $\dfrac{1}{26}$

C. $\dfrac{1}{52}$ D. None of these

14. The probability that a non-leap year should have fifty-three Sundays is:

A. $\dfrac{1}{7}$ B. $\dfrac{2}{7}$

C. $\dfrac{3}{7}$ D. None of these

15. Probability of not getting a total of 7 in a single throw with two dice is:

A. $\dfrac{1}{9}$ B. $\dfrac{8}{9}$

C. $\dfrac{7}{18}$ D. $\dfrac{1}{8}$

16. A doctor is to visit a patient once in the month of November. The probability that he visits on date which is a multiple of 5 or 6 is:

A. $\dfrac{11}{30}$ B. $\dfrac{11}{31}$

C. $\dfrac{10}{30}$ D. $\dfrac{10}{31}$

17. A coin is tossed thrice. The probability of getting exactly one head or one tail is:

A. $\dfrac{3}{8}$ B. $\dfrac{5}{8}$

C. $\dfrac{4}{8}$ D. $\dfrac{6}{8}$ or $\dfrac{3}{4}$

18. P(A) = 0.4, then odds in favour of the event A are:
A. 2 : 3   B. 2 : 5
C. 3 : 2   D. 5 : 4

19. If $P(A \cap B) = 0$, then events A and B are:
A. mutually exclusive
B. equally likely
C. dependent
D. independent

20. The probability of getting a total 8 or at least 9 or less than 8 with two dice is:

A. $\dfrac{5}{36}$ B. $\dfrac{10}{36}$

C. $\dfrac{21}{36}$ D. 1

ANSWERS

1	2	3	4	5	6	7	8	9	10
C	D	D	C	A	C	C	B	A	B

11	12	13	14	15	16	17	18	19	20
D	A	B	C	B	C	D	A	A	D

EXPLANATORY ANSWERS

1. Clearly, $P(B) = \dfrac{1}{2} = P(G)$

Hence, required probability
$$= P(BG) = P(B)P(G)$$
$$= \frac{1}{2} \times \frac{1}{2} = \frac{1}{4}$$

3. Required probability
$$= {}^8C_6\left(\frac{1}{2}\right)^6 \cdot \left(\frac{1}{2}\right)^2 + {}^8C_7\left(\frac{1}{2}\right)^7 \cdot \left(\frac{1}{2}\right) + {}^8C_8\left(\frac{1}{2}\right)^8$$
$$= \frac{1}{256}(28+8+1) = \frac{37}{256}$$

4. Required probability $= \dfrac{{}^{13}C_1 \cdot {}^4C_1}{{}^{52}C_1 \cdot {}^{52}C_1}$
$$= \frac{13}{52} \cdot \frac{4}{52} = \frac{1}{52}$$

6. The exhaustive number of cases $= 6^3 = 216$.
The number of cases when all the three faces are distinct $= {}^6P_3 = 120$

$\therefore$ Required probability $= \dfrac{120}{216} = \dfrac{5}{9}$

7. Let A, B and C be three persons selected at random. If A can be born on any one of the day of the 7 days of the week.
However, B and C should have been born on different days.
Therefore, the required probability
$$= \frac{7}{7} \times \frac{6}{7} \times \frac{5}{7} = \frac{30}{49}.$$

10. A leap year contains 366 days and therefore 52 weeks and 2 days.
Clearly there are 52 Sundays in 52 weeks.
So, for remaining two days

Probability of Sunday $= \dfrac{2}{7}$

$\therefore$ Required probability $= \dfrac{2}{7}$

1. A land measure unit is an *are*. One *are* measures an area equal to 100 m². One *Hectare* means 100 ares and is therefore equal to 10000 m². Whenever the area of a plane or that of a solid is given in Hectares and Ares? This must be converted into m².

2. *Planes* are two dimenstionals and occupy surface area.

3. *Perimeter.* The lengths of all the sides of a polygon is called a perimeter of the polygon. The perimeter of a circle is called the circumference.

4. *Rectangle.* If the length and breadth of the rectangle be '*l*' and '*b*' and '*d*' be the length of the diagonal, then P (perimeter) = 2 (*l* + b).

   A (surface area or area) = $l \times b$

   D (diogonal) = $\sqrt{l^2 + b^2}$

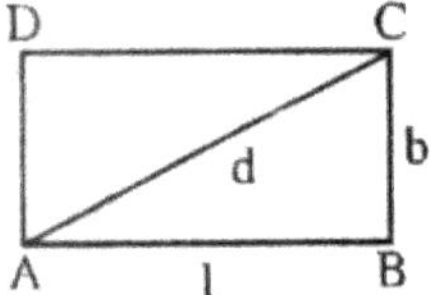

5. *Square.* If x be the side of a square, then

   $$P = 4x \text{ or } x = \frac{1}{4}P$$

   $$A = x^2 \text{ or } x = \sqrt{A}$$

   $$D \text{ (diogonal)} = \sqrt{2}x$$

   or $\qquad D^2 = 2A$

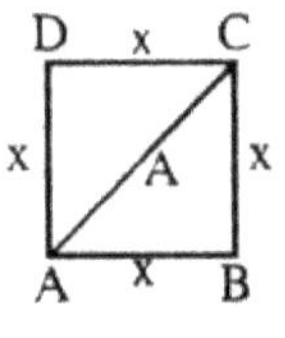

6. *Rhombus.* If x be the side the rhombus, all its side are equal and diagonal bisect at right angle.

   $$P = 4x \text{ or } x = \frac{1}{4}P$$

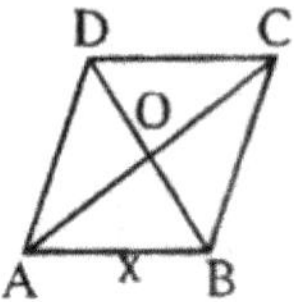

   $$A = \frac{1}{2} \times \text{Product of the diagonals}$$

   $$= \frac{1}{2} \times AC \times BD$$

7. *Triangle.* This is a polygon with minimum number of sides *i.e.,* three

   (*i*) Area of any triangle = $\frac{1}{2} \times$ base $\times$ height

   (*ii*) Area of a triangle when its sides are given as *a, b, c.*

   $$= \sqrt{s(s-a)(s-b)(s-c)}$$

   where $= s = \frac{1}{2}(a + b + c)$.

   (*iii*) Area of an equilateral triangle

   $$= \frac{\sqrt{3}}{4} \times (\text{side})^2.$$

   (*iv*) Area of an isoceles triangle whose base is '*b*' and equal sides are '*a*' each

   $$= \frac{1}{4} \times b \times \sqrt{4a^2 - b^2}$$

   Note: If a regular hexagon (6 equal side polygon) is inscribed in a circle of radius x. The area of the hexagon is equal to six time the area of the equilateral triangle of side x.

8. Area of four walls of a room = 2 $\times$ height $\times$ (length + breadth) = 2 h ($l + b$)

9. *Circle.* It is a polygon with maximum number of sides. Given the perimeter, the circle is the plane with maximum area.

10. What is π? This is ratio of the circumference of the circle with its diameter remain constant. Its approximate value is $\dfrac{22}{7}$ or 3.1416.

Thus $\pi = \dfrac{\text{Circumference}}{\text{diameter}}$

11. Circumference of a circle = $2\pi r$

$$\text{Area} = \pi r^2 \text{ or } r = \sqrt{\dfrac{\text{Area}}{\pi}}$$

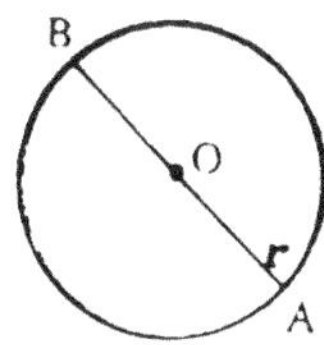

12. The radius R of a circle whose area is equal to the sum of the areas of series of a circles with radii r_1, r_2, r_3 etc. is equal to

$$R = \sqrt{r_1^2 + r_2^2 + r_3^2 + ...}$$

For example, the radius of a circle whose area is equal to the sum of the areas of two circles of radii 6 cms. and 8 cms. is = $\sqrt{6^2 + 8^2}$ cm. = 10 cm.

13. *Volume of Solids.* A solid occupies space and the space it occupies is known as its volume. A sphere, a cube are the examples of solids. It is measured in cubic units.

14. CUBOID. OA, OB, OC are called three coterminous edges of the cuboid and may be considered as length, breadth and height *i.e.*, 'l', 'b', 'h'.

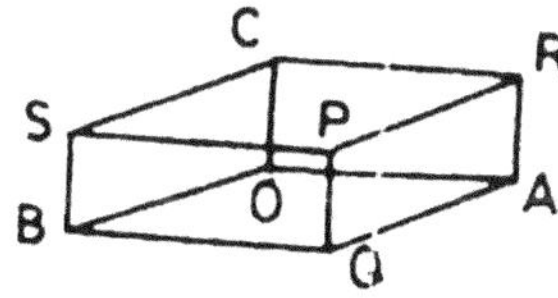

(*i*) Surface area = $2 \times (lb + bh + lh)$

(*ii*) Volume = $l \times b \times h$

(*iii*) Diagonal = $\sqrt{l^2 + b^2 + h^2}$

Note: If we want to find the quantity of paint required for painting the wooden or iron box or iron sheet required for making a box, formula (*i*) is used. In order to find, how much space a box can occupy or how much a box can contain, formula (*ii*) can be used. Formula (*iii*) be used to find the length of the longest pole which can be placed in a big hall.

15. CUBE. A cube has all its edges equal say 'e' be its length. All its faces are square faces. It has 12 edges.

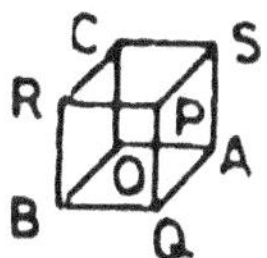

 (*i*) Perimeter = $12 \times$ edge

 (*ii*) Area = $6 \times (\text{edge})^2$

 (*iii*) Volume = $(\text{edge})^3$ or edge = $(\text{volume})^{1/3}$

 (*iv*) Diagonal = $\sqrt{3} \times$ edge.

 (*v*) Edge 'E' of a cube whose volume, is equal to the sum of volume : of cubes of edges e_1, e_2, e_3, ... is given by
$$E = (e_1^3 + e_2^3 + e_3^3 + ...)^{1/3}$$

16. *SPHERE.* A rubber ball is an example of a sphere. If the radius of the sphere is r, then

 (*i*) Surface area = $4\pi r^2$

 (*ii*) Volume = $\dfrac{4}{3}\pi r^3$

 (*iii*) Area of the solid hemisphere = $3\pi r^2$.

 (*iv*) Radius 'R' of the sphere whose volume is equal to the sum of the volumes of spheres with radii r_1, r_2, r_3, ... is given by
$$R = (r_1^3 + r_2^3 + r_3^3 + ...)^{1/3}$$

17. *CYLINDER.* When a rectangle is revolved about one of its side, a solid so formed is a cylinder.

 (*i*) Curved surface of the cylinder
   = base circumference $\times$ height
   = $2\pi r \times h$

 (*ii*) Total surface of a closed cylinder
   = $2\pi r (r + h)$

 (*iii*) Volume = based area $\times$ height
   = $\pi r^2 \times h$

(*iv*) Height of the cylinder

$$= \frac{\text{Volume of cylinder}}{\text{base area of cylinder}}$$

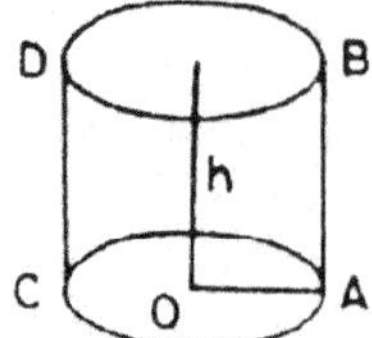

18. *CONE.* When a right angle triangle is revolved about one of its side a solid so formed is a cone. If r be the base radius, h the height and l, the slant height, then $l = \sqrt{r^2 + h^2}$

(*i*) Curved surface area $= \pi r l$

(*ii*) Total surface area $= \pi r(l + r)$

(*iii*) Volume $= \dfrac{1}{3}\pi r^2 h$

Note: Volume of the cone $= \dfrac{1}{3}$ volume of the cylinder

$$\therefore \frac{\text{Volume of cone}}{\text{Volume of cylinder}} = \frac{1}{3}$$

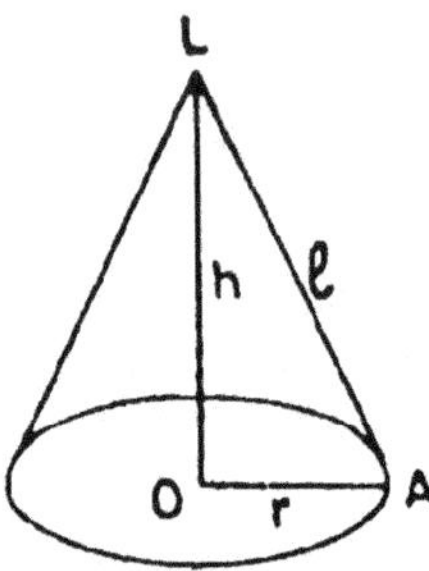

For example, if a conical vessel can hold 20 litres of milk, then a cylindrical vessel can hold 3 × 20, *i.e.*, 60 litres of milk.

19. If it is to find the canvas required for making the conical tent with given dimensions, formula (*i*) is used. How much iron sheet is required to construct a conical vessel, formula (*ii*) is used. To find the capacity of the cone, formula (*iii*) is used.

20. *Very Important Note*

If the ratio of the two similar planes or solids are as $x : y$, then their areas are as $x^2 : y^2$ and volumes are $x^3 : y^3$. This is explained by the following examples.

(*i*) If the sides of a rectangle are doubled, what percent of its area is increased?

Now it is very clear that the area of the corresponding rectangle becomes four times the original and thus the increase is 3 times or 300%.

(*ii*) If the cost of levelling the field in the form of a square is ₹ 25, what is the cost of levelling another square field whose side is three time the side of the first.

Since the area of the other field is 9 times the original, so the cost is ₹ (25 × 9), *i.e.*, ₹ 225.

(*iii*) The perimeter of a regular hexagon is 48 cm., what is the area of the hexagon.

The perimeter being 48 cm, so the side of the hexagon is (48 ÷ 6), *i.e.*, 8 cm. Hence the area of the hexagon is

$$6 \times \frac{\sqrt{3}}{4} \times (8)^2 \text{ cm}^2 \text{ or } 96\sqrt{3} \text{ cm}^2.$$

(*iv*) The perimeter of a cube is 36 cm. What is its volume?

$$\text{Now side of the cube} = \frac{1}{12} \times 36 \text{ cm.} = 3 \text{ cm.}$$

$$\therefore \text{ Volume} = 3^3 \text{ cm}^3 \text{ or } 27 \text{ cm}^3.$$

(*v*) The weight of an iron ball of radius 2 cm is 25 grams. What is the weight of another similar sphere whose radius is 6 cm.

Since the radius of the other sphere is 3 times the first the volume is 27 times the first. Now weights are proportional to their volume, so the weight of the other sphere is 27 × 25 grams or 675 grams.

(*vi*) If the ratio of areas of two cylindrical vessels are as 25 : 49, what will be the ratio of their volumes?

Since area ratio is 25 : 49

$\therefore$ dimensions ratio $= 5 : 7$

or   Volume ratio $= 125 : 343$

Solved Examples

Example 1: *The length of the room is $5\frac{1}{2}$ metres and width $3\frac{3}{4}$ metres, find the cost of paving the floor by slabs at the rate of ₹ 800 per m².*

Solution: Area of the floor of the room $= 5\frac{1}{2} \times 3\frac{3}{4}$ m²

$$= \frac{165}{8} \text{ m}^2$$

Cost for paving the floor $= ₹ \dfrac{165}{8} \times 800$

$$= ₹ \ 16500.$$

Example 2: *The area of a square field is 6050 m²; find the length of the diagonal.*

Solution: Area $= (\text{Diagonal})^2$

$\therefore$ Diagonal $= \sqrt{2 \times \text{Area}}$ meters

$$= \sqrt{2 \times 6050} \text{ m}$$
$$= \sqrt{12100} \text{ m}$$
$$= 110 \text{ m}$$

Example 3: *How many bricks 20 cm. by 10 cm. will be needed to pave the floor of a room 25 m. long and 16 m. wide?*

Solution: Area of the room $= 25$ m. $\times 16$ m.

$$= 400 \text{ m}^2$$

Area of the brick $= 20$ cm. $\times 10$ cm.

$$= \frac{1}{5} \text{ m} \times \frac{1}{10} \text{ m} = \frac{1}{50} \text{ m}^2$$

$\therefore$ Number of bricks required $= \left(400 \div \dfrac{1}{50}\right) = 20{,}000.$

Example 4: *The material of a cone is converted into the shape of the cylinder of equal radius. If the height of the cylinder is 5 cm, what is the height of the cone?*

Solution: Volume of the cone

$$= \text{Volume of the cylinder}$$

$\therefore$ $\dfrac{1}{3}\pi r^2 h = \pi r^2 \times 5$

$\therefore$ $h = 15$ cm.

Example 5: *Three solid spheres of gold whose radii are 1 cm, 6 cm and 8 cm respectively are melted into a single solid sphere. Find the radius of the sphere.*

Solution: According to the formula, radius of the new sphere is

$$= (1^3 + 6^3 + 8^3)^{1/3}$$
$$= (729)^{1/3} = 9.$$

Example 6: *A solid spherical ball is prepared by melting a cone and cylinder having the same height and same base radius equal to r. Find the radius of the sphere.*

Solution: Volume of the sphere of radius R

$$= \text{Vol. of cone} + \text{Vol. of cylinder}$$

$\therefore$ $\dfrac{4}{3}\pi R^3 = \dfrac{1}{3}\pi r^2 h + \pi r^2 h$ $(\because r = h)$

$\therefore$ $R = r.$

Hence the radius of the sphere is the same as the base radius of the other two solids.

Example 7: *Cone, a hemisphere and a cylinder stand on equal bases and have the same height. What is the ratio of their respective volumes?*

Solution: Let the radius of the cone, hemisphere and cylinder be *r*.

$\therefore$ height of the hemisphere is also *r*.

$\therefore$ $V_1 : V_2 : V_3 = \dfrac{1}{3}\pi r^2 \cdot r : \dfrac{2}{3}\pi r^3 : \pi r^2 r$

$$= \frac{1}{3} : \frac{2}{3} : 1$$

or $1 : 2 : 3.$

Example 8: *How many spherical bullets can be made out of a metre cube, if there is no loss in the process, given that the diameter of the sphere is 2 cm.?*

Solution: No. of spherical bullets

$$= \frac{\text{Volume of the cube}}{\text{Volume of the sphere}}$$

$$= \frac{(100 \text{ cm})^3}{\dfrac{4}{3} \times \dfrac{22}{7} \times r^3} = \frac{10^6 \times 7 \times 3}{88}$$

$$= 238636.36.$$

108

MULTIPLE CHOICE QUESTIONS

1. The perimeter of a rectangular field is 480 m and the ratio between the length and breadth is 5 : 3. Find the area in hectare.
   A. 135 B. 1.35
   C. 13.5 D. 13500

2. The area of a rectangular field is 3600 m². The ratio of its length and breadth is 16 : 9. Find its perimeter.
   A. 250 m B. 1250 m
   C. 500 m D. 750 m

3. Find the length of the wire required to go 15 times round a square field containing 69696 m².
   A. 15840 m B. 16840 m
   C. 15820 m D. 15640 m

4. The area of the floor of a room is 20 m², that of a longer wall 15 m² and of the shorter wall 12 m². Find the volume of the room.
   A. 45 m³ B. 10 m³
   C. 60 m³ D. 40 m³

5. Find the cost of fencing a circular field at the rate of 50 P. per metre if its area is 13860 m².
   $$\left(\pi = \frac{22}{7}\right)$$
   A. ₹ 660 B. ₹ 540
   C. ₹ 700 D. ₹ 800

6. The radii of the two circular field is in the ratio 3 : 5. The area of the first field is what per cent less than the area of the second?
   A. 50% B. 60%
   C. 40% D. 64%

7. If all the sides of a triangle be increased by 200 per cent. What is the corresponding increase in its area?
   A. 300% B. 400%
   C. 600% D. 800%

8. The edges of three iron cubes are 6 cm, 8 cm, 10 cm respectively. A new cube was made by melting them. Find the edge of the new cube.
   A. 8 cm B. 12 cm
   C. 14 cm D. 10 cm

9. The length of the room is 6 m, width 4 m and 3 m high. How many boxes will it hold if each box occupies 1.5 cubic metres of space?
   A. 64 B. 48
   C. 54 D. 60

10. If the length of a rectangle is increased by 50% and its breadth is decreased by 25%, what is the change percent in its area?
    A. 12.5% increase B. 10% increase
    C. 25% increase D. 20% decrease

11. A reservoir is 45 metres long and 12 metres broad. How many kilo litres of water must be poured into it to raise the water level by 2 metres. [1 cube metric can contain 1 kilolitre]
    A. 540 B. 1280
    C. 1080 D. 1380

12. A cubic metre of a certain metal is hammered to form a fine sheet so as to cover one hectare of land. What is the thickness of the sheet?
    A. 1 cm B. 0.1 cm
    C. 0.01 cm D. 0.001 cm

13. A conical flask of radius r and height h is full of water. It is emptied into another cylindrical flask of radius $x\,r$. If this flask becomes full, what is its height?
    A. $3x^2h$ B. $\dfrac{h}{3x^2}$
    C. $\dfrac{3h}{x^2}$ D. $\dfrac{3x^2}{h}$

14. It is required to construct a conical circus tent of radius 21 m and 35 m slant high. The width of the canvas cloth is 3 metre, what will be the length of the cloth which shall do the need full.
    A. 700 m B. 1250 m
    C. 776.5 m D. 770 m

15. Two sphere have volumes in the ratio 64 : 729. If 160 ml paint is required fot painting the surface area of the smaller sphere, how much paint is required to paint the larger one?
    A. 729 ml B. 750 ml
    C. 216 ml D. 810 ml

16. Find the volume of the right circular conical tent whose vertical height is 8 m and area of whose base is 156 m².

   A. 225 m³   B. 396 m³
   C. 416 m³   D. 516 m³

17. A solid cone is melted and converted into a cylindrical shape of equal radius. Find the height of the cone if the height of cylinder is 5 cm.

   A. 15 cm   B. 1 cm
   C. 45 cm   D. 25 cm

18. From a right circular cylinder with height 10 cm and radius of base 6 cm, a right circular cone of the same height and base is removed. Find the volume of the remaining solid.

   A. 744 cm³   B. 814 cm³
   C. 654 cm³   D. 754 cm³

19. A hollow sphere of internal and external radii 2 cm. and 4 cm. is melted into a solid of base radius 4 cm. Find the height of the cone.

   A. 12 cm   B. 7 cm
   C. 14 cm   D. 21 cm

20. The radius of a circle is 20 cm. The radii (in centimeters) of three concentric circles drawn in such a manner that the whole area is divided into four equal parts, are

   A. $20\sqrt{2},\ 20\sqrt{3},\ 20$

   B. $\dfrac{10\sqrt{3}}{3},\ \dfrac{10\sqrt{2}}{3},\ \dfrac{10}{3}$

   C. $10\sqrt{3},\ 10\sqrt{2},\ 10$

   D. 17, 14, 10

21. A surveyor in his field book has drawn the plot as shown in the given figure. The area of the plot is

   A. $\dfrac{1}{2}(az + by + ct + dx)$

   B. $\dfrac{1}{2}(bt + cx + ay + az)$

   C. $\dfrac{1}{2}(cx + bt + by + az)$

   D. $\dfrac{1}{2}(d + t)(c + x) + \dfrac{1}{2}(a + b)(y + z)$

22. The area of a quadrilateral of sides a, b, c, d inscribed in a circle is $\left(s = \dfrac{a+b+c+d}{2}\right)$

   A. $\sqrt{s(s-a)(s-b)(s-c)(s-d)}$

   B. $\sqrt{(s-a)(s-b)(s-c)(s-d)}$

   C. $s(s-a)\sqrt{(s-b)(s-c)(s-d)}$

   D. $s\sqrt{(s-a)(s-b)(s-c)(s-d)}$

23. ABCD is a square, ΔOAB is equilateral OL $\perp$ CD. The area of the quadrilateral OALB is

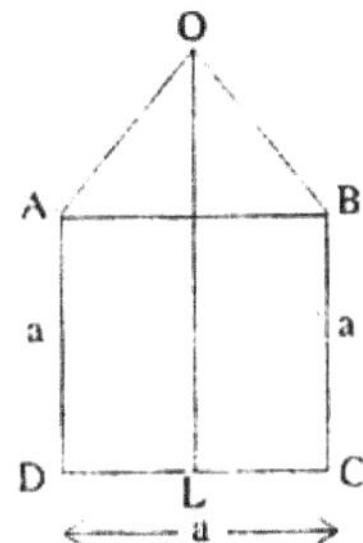

   A. $\dfrac{a^2}{8}(2+\sqrt{3})$ B. $2a^2$

   C. $a^2 + \dfrac{\sqrt{3}}{2}a^2$ D. $\dfrac{a^2}{2} + \dfrac{\sqrt{3}}{4}a^2$

24. ABC is a triangle with perimeter p and $\angle A = \dfrac{\pi}{3}$. A circle of radius r with centre O is drawn to touch BC at P, AB produced at Q and AC produced at R. The area of the portion bounded by AQ, AR and the arc QPR is

   A. $\dfrac{1}{3}(rp - \pi r^2)$ B. $\dfrac{1}{3}r(p - \pi r)$

   C. $\dfrac{1}{3}rp - \dfrac{1}{2}\pi r^2$ D. $\dfrac{1}{2}rp - \dfrac{1}{3}\pi r^2$

25. A sphere is placed in an inverted conical vessel of base radius 3 cm and slant height 5 cm and it is observed that the base of the cone touches the sphere. The ratio of the volume of the sphere of that of the cone is

   A. 2 : 7   B. 3 : 8
   C. 4 : 9   D. 5 : 11

26. A tent is formed in this shape of a prism of n sides surmounted by a pyramid. If the length of each side is 'a' and the height of the prism is h and the height of the pyramid is H, then the capacity of the tent will be

A. $(h + 3H) \dfrac{na^2}{12} \cot \dfrac{\pi}{n}$

B. $(3h + H) \dfrac{na^2}{12} \cot \dfrac{\pi}{n}$

C. $(3h + H) \dfrac{na^2}{24} \cot \dfrac{\pi}{n}$

D. $(h + 3H) \dfrac{na^2}{24} \cot \dfrac{\pi}{n}$

27. A solid is hemispherical at the bottom and conical above it. If the radius and height of the conical part are equal, the ratio of the surface area of the 2 parts is

A. $\sqrt{2} : 1$ B. $\sqrt{3} : 1$

C. $1 : 1$ D. $1 : \sqrt{3}$

28. If four isosceles right angled triangles of side 5 m are removed from the corners of a rectangular plot 20 m × 10 m, then the area of the remaining portion (in m²) is

A. 156.0   B. 156.5
C. 150.0   D. 150.6

29. The measurements in a field book are recorded as under

	To B	
	500	
To C 100	300	To D....
	100	
	From A	

The reading to D is missing in the field book. But the area of this field is mentioned as 40,000 m². Then the missing value (in m) should be

A. 60   B. 50
C. 40   D. 30

30. The diameter of two cones are equal and their slant heights are in the ratio 5 : 4. If the curved surface of the smaller cone 200 cm², then the curved surface of the bigger cone (in cm²) is

A. 200   B. 250
C. 400   D. 500

31. If the radius of the base and the height of a right circular cone are increased by 20%, then the percentage increase in volume is approximately

A. 60   B. 68
C. 73   D. 78

32. From four corners of a rectangular iron sheet of 24 m × 30 cm, four squares of side 6 cm are cut. The remaining 2 portions of the sheet is formed into an open box. The internal volume (in cm³) of the box is

A. 4300   B. 2592
C. 2542   D. 1296

33. If the volumes of a cone and a hemisphere having the same base are equal, then the height of the cone will be x times the radius of the base of the hemisphere, where x is

A. 1   B. 2
C. 3   D. π

34. An iron pipe is 3.5 m long, its external and internal diameters are 8 cm and 6 cm respectively. The volume (in cc) of the pipe is (given $\pi = 22/7$)

A. 7700   B. 1100
C. 770   D. 77

35. Within a rectangular garden 10 m wide and 20 m long, we wish to pave a walk around the borders of uniform width so as to leave an area of 96 square meters for flowers. How wide (in meter) should the walk be?

A. 1   B. 2
C. 2.1   D. 2.5

ANSWERS

1	2	3	4	5	6	7	8	9	10
B	A	A	C	A	D	D	B	B	A
11	**12**	**13**	**14**	**15**	**16**	**17**	**18**	**19**	**20**
C	C	B	D	D	C	A	D	C	C

21	22	23	24	25	26	27	28	29	30
B	A	D	D	B	A	A	C	A	B

31	32	33	34	35
C	B	C	B	B

SOME SELECTED EXPLANATORY ANSWERS

20. Since the area of each part is $\frac{1}{4}$ of the whole, the areas of the four circles (including the given one) must be

$\pi \cdot 400$ cm², $\pi \cdot 300$ cm², $\pi \cdot 200$ cm² and $\pi \cdot 100$ cm² which is valid only if the radii of the concentric circles be

$10\sqrt{3}$, $10\sqrt{2}$ and 10.

21. Area of the plot = sum of the areas of triangles.

23. Area of quadrilateral

$$OALB = \Delta OAB + \Delta ALB$$

$$= \frac{\sqrt{3}}{4}a^2 + \frac{1}{2}a^2$$

(Area of ΔALB = area of half the square ABCD)

24. Required area = Area of quadrilateral AQOR

$$- \text{ area of the sector QOR}$$

Now BL = BQ and CL = CR

$\therefore \quad p = AB + BC + AC$

$$= (AB + BL) + (LC + AC)$$

$$= AQ + AR$$

Required area

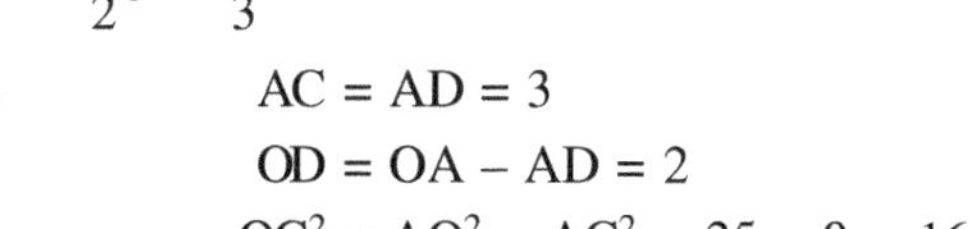

$$= \left(\frac{1}{2}AQ \times r + \frac{1}{2}AR \times r\right)$$

$$- \frac{120}{360} \times \pi r^2$$

$$= \frac{1}{2}(AQ + AR) \times r - \frac{1}{3}\pi r^2$$

$$= \frac{1}{2}pr - \frac{1}{3}\pi r^2$$

25.

$$AC = AD = 3$$

$$OD = OA - AD = 2$$

$$OC^2 = AO^2 - AC^2 = 25 - 9 = 16$$

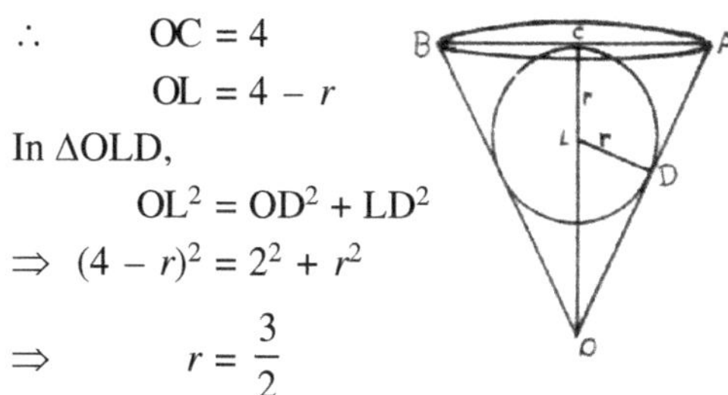

$\therefore \quad OC = 4$

$$OL = 4 - r$$

In ΔOLD,

$$OL^2 = OD^2 + LD^2$$

$$\Rightarrow (4 - r)^2 = 2^2 + r^2$$

$$\Rightarrow \quad r = \frac{3}{2}$$

Volume of the sphere $= \frac{4}{3}\pi\left(\frac{3}{2}\right)^3 = \frac{9}{2}\pi$

Volume of the cone $= \frac{1}{3}\pi \cdot 3^2 \cdot 4 = 12\pi$

Required ratio $= \frac{9}{2}\pi : 12\pi$

$$= 3 : 8$$

26. Capacity of the prism of n

sides of lenth 'a' = Base area × height

$$= n\,H\,\frac{a^2}{4}\,\cot\frac{\pi}{h}\,(i)$$

Capacity of the pyramid of n sides of length 'a'

$$= \frac{1}{3} \times \text{Base area} \times \text{height}$$

Total capacity = $(i) + (ii)$

$$= \frac{1}{3} \times n\,\frac{a^2}{4}\,\cot\frac{\pi}{4}\,h\,(ii)$$

27. $h = r$ slant height of the cone $= \sqrt{2}\,r$

$\therefore \qquad 2\pi r^2 : \pi r. \sqrt{2}\,r$

$\Rightarrow \qquad \sqrt{2} : 1$

29. $\qquad 40000 = \frac{1}{2} \times 500 \times (100 + x)$

$\Rightarrow \qquad x = 60.$

30. Radii of two cones $= r$ and r

$$\text{Slant height} = 5x \text{ and } 4x$$

$$\pi r.4x = 200 \Rightarrow \pi rx = 50$$

$$\therefore \qquad 5\pi\, rx = 5 \times 50 = 250$$

31. Let r and h be the radius and height of the cone, then $\dfrac{6}{5}r$ and $\dfrac{6}{5}h$ be the radius and height of the new cone.

$$\text{Increase in volume} = \frac{1}{3}\pi r^2 h\left(\frac{6^3}{5^3} - 1\right)$$

$$= \frac{1}{3}\pi r^2 h\left(\frac{91}{125}\right)$$

$$\text{Percentage increase} = \frac{91}{125} \times 100\%$$

$$= 73\% \quad \text{approximately.}$$

32. $\sqrt{3}x = \sqrt{300} \Rightarrow x = 10$

$\qquad$ Surface area $= 6x^2 = 600$

33. $\pi r l = 2\pi r \times 3 \Rightarrow l = 6$

35. $(20 - 2x)(10 - 2x) = 96$ only if $x = 2$.

18 Statistics

Statistics : Statistics is the science which deals mainly with collection, presentation and interpretation of numerical data.

Measures of Central Tendency : Certain methods which reduce the given data to a single representative figure is called the measure of central tendency.

The commonly used measures of central tendency are *the mean, the median* and *the mode*.

Means:

1. *The arithmetic mean* of a set of n numbers is

$$\overline{X} = \frac{x_1 + x_2 + ... + x_n}{n} = \frac{\sum x}{n}$$

If the numbers occur f_1, f_2, ..., f_n times, respectively, then

$$\overline{X} = \frac{f_1 x_1 + f_2 x_2 + ... + f_n x_n}{f_1 + f_2 + ... + f_n} = \frac{\sum fx}{\sum f}$$

If the numbers are associated with a *weighting factor* $w_i \geq 0$, then

$$\overline{X} = \frac{w_1 x_1 + w_2 x_2 + ... + w_n x_n}{w_1 + w_2 + ... + w_n} = \frac{\sum wx}{\sum w}$$

2. *The geometric mean* of a set of n numbers is

$$\overline{G} = \sqrt[n]{x_1 x_2 .... x_n}$$

If the numbers occur f_1, f_2, ... f_n times, respectively

then $\overline{G} = \sqrt[n]{x_1^{f_1} x_2^{f_2} .... x_n^{f_n}}$

where $n = f_1 + f_2 + ... + f_n$.

3. *The harmonic mean* of a set of n numbers is

$$\overline{H} = \frac{1}{\left(\dfrac{1}{n}\right)\left(\dfrac{1}{x_1} + \dfrac{1}{x_2} + ... + \dfrac{1}{x_n}\right)} = \frac{n}{\sum\left(\dfrac{1}{x}\right)}$$

If the numbers occur f_1, f_2, ..., f_n times, respectively, then

$$\overline{H} = \frac{1}{\left(\dfrac{1}{n}\right)\left(\dfrac{f_1}{x_1} + \dfrac{f_2}{x_2} + ... + \dfrac{f_n}{x_n}\right)} = \frac{n}{\sum\left(\dfrac{f}{x}\right)}$$

where $n = f_1 + f_2 + ... + f_n$.

4. *The quadratic mean* of a set of n numbers is

$$\overline{Q} = \sqrt{\frac{x_1^2 + x_2^2 + ... + x_n^2}{n}} = \sqrt{\frac{\sum x^2}{n}}$$

5. *Relation*

$$\overline{H} \leq \overline{G} \leq \overline{X}$$

Median : If the data of a series are arranged in ascending or descending order of magnitude, the value of the middle term is called the *median*.

If n is the number of terms, the median is the $\left(\dfrac{n+1}{2}\right)$th term in case n is *odd*.

If n is even then the average of the two middle terms is given by the median.

In case of grouped data, the median is given by the formula

$$\text{Median} = L + \frac{(U-L)}{f} \times \left(\frac{n}{2} - C\right) = L + \frac{\dfrac{n}{2} - C}{f} \times i$$

Where L and U are respectively the lower and upper limit of the median class.

f is the frequency of the median class.

C is cumulative frequency of the class preceding the median class.

i is the class interval and n is the total frequency.

Mode: For ungrouped data (discrete distribution)

Mode = The value of the item which occurs most frequently.

For grouped data (continuous distribution)

$$\text{Mode} = L + \frac{f_m - f_1}{(f_m - f_1) + (f_m - f_2)} \times (U - L)$$

$$= L + \frac{f_m - f_1}{2f_m - f_1 - f_2} \times h$$

Where U and L are upper and lower limit

h is width of the modal class

f is the frequency of the modal class.

f_1 is the frequency of the class preceding the modal class.

f_2 is the frequency of the class following the modal class.

Relation between Mean, Median and Mode :

$$\text{Median} = \text{Mode} + \frac{2}{3}(\text{Mean} - \text{Mode})$$

approximately.

or   Mode = 3 Median – 2 Mean.

approximately.

Average or Mean Deviation : It is defined as the arithmetic average of the absolute values of the deviations, *i.e.,* all deviations taken positive, from the mean, mode or median.

(i) The deviation from the arithmetic mean $\overline{X}$ of each number x_j in a set of numbers $x_1, x_2, ..., x_n$ is $D_j = x_j - \overline{X}$, $j = 1, 2, ..., n.$

(ii) The mean deviation of the same set is

$$\overline{D} = \frac{\left|x_1 + x_2 + ... + x_n - n\overline{X}\right|}{n} = \frac{\sum \left|x_j - \overline{X}\right|}{n}$$

Where $\left|x_j - X\right|$ is the absolute value of Dj.

If the numbers occur $f_1, f_2, ..., f_n$ times, then $n = f_1 + f_2 + ... + f_n$ and

$$\overline{D} = \frac{f_1\left|x_1 - \overline{X}\right| + f_2\left|x_2 - \overline{X}\right| + ... + f_n\left|x_n - \overline{X}\right|}{n}$$

$$= \frac{\sum f\left|n - \overline{X}\right|}{n}$$

Standard Deviation : The standard deviation in a set of number $x_1, x_2, ..., x_n$ is

$$\sigma = \sqrt{\frac{(x_1 - \overline{X})^2 + (x_2 - \overline{X})^2 + ... + (x_n - \overline{X})^2}{n}}$$

$$= \sqrt{\frac{\sum (x_j - \overline{X})^2}{n}}$$

If the numbers occurs $f_1, f_2, ..., f_n$ times, then $n = f_1 + f_2 + ... + f_n$ and

$$\sigma = \sqrt{\frac{f_1(x_1 - \overline{X})^2 + f_2(x_2 - \overline{X})^2 + ... + f_n(x_n - \overline{X})^2}{n}}$$

$$= \sqrt{\frac{\sum f_n(x - \overline{X})^2}{n}}$$

Variance: The square of standard deviation is called the variance (σ^2).

$$\therefore \ \sigma^2 = \frac{\sum (x - \overline{X})^2}{n} \quad \text{or} \quad \sigma^2 = \sum f(x - \overline{X})^2$$

7. The covariance of two sets X $(x_1, x_2, ..., x_n)$, the arithmetic means of which are $\overline{X}$ and $\overline{Y}$, respectively, is

$$\sigma_{xy} = \frac{\sum (x - \overline{X})(y - \overline{Y})}{n}$$

MULTIPLE CHOICE QUESTIONS

1. If the means of a set of observations $x_1, x_2, ...,$ x_n is $\overline{X}$, then the mean of the observations $x_i + 2i; i = 1, 2, 3, ..., n$ is

A. $\overline{X}+2$
B. $\overline{X}+2n$

C. $\overline{X}+(n+1)$
D. $\overline{X}+n$

2. The weighted AM of first n natural numbers whose weights are equal to the corresponding numbers is equal to

A. $2n + 1$
B. $\frac{1}{2}(2n+1)$

C. $\frac{1}{3}(2n+1)$
D. $\frac{2n+1}{6}$

3. 10 is the mean of a set of 7 observations and 5 is the mean of a set of 3 observations. The mean of the combined set is given by

A. 15
B. 10
C. 8.5
D. 7.5

4. Out of 50 students in a class, 10 were of the age of 10 years, 14 were of the age of 11 years and the remaining of 12 years. Then AM of students is

A. 11.5
B. 11.24
C. 11.32
D. None of these

5. The GM of the series $1, 2, 4, 8, 16, ..., 2^n$ is,

A. $2^{\frac{n+1}{2}}$
B. 2^{n+1}

C. $2^{n/2}$
D. 2^n

6. If G_1, G_2 are the geometric means of the series of observations and G is the GM of the ratios of the corresponding observations then G is equal to

A. $\dfrac{G_1}{G_2}$
B. $\log G_1 - \log G_2$

C. $\dfrac{\log G_1}{\log G_2}$
D. $\log (G_1.G_2)$

7. If a variable takes values $0, 1, 2, ..., n$ with frequencies $1, {}^nC_1, {}^nC_2, ..., {}^nC_n$, then the AM is

A. n
B. $\dfrac{2^n}{n}$

C. $n + 1$
D. $\dfrac{n}{2}$

8. The mean of the series $x_1, x_2, ..., x_n$ is $\overline{X}$. If x_2 is replaced by λ, then the new mean is

A. $\overline{X}-x_2+\lambda$
B. $\dfrac{\overline{X}-x_2-\lambda}{n}$

C. $\dfrac{(n-1)\overline{X}+\lambda}{n}$
D. $\dfrac{n\overline{X}-x_2+\lambda}{n}$

9. In a college of 100 teachers, the mean age is 30 years and in another college of 50 teachers, the mean age is 60. The mean age of the teachers of two colleges taken together is

A. 40
B. 42
C. 45
D. None of these

10. In any discrete series (when all values are not same) the relationship between M.D. about mean and S.D is

A. M.D. = S.D.
B. M.D. $\geq$ S.D.
C. M.D. $<$ S.D.
D. M.D. $\leq$ S.D.

11. Quartile deviation of the following data 32, 45, 28, 72, 63, 59, 60 is

A. 14.5
B. 15
C. 15.5
D. 16

12. The mean deviation from the mean of the AP $a, a + d, a + 2d, ..., a + 2nd$ is

A. $n (n + 1) d$
B. $\dfrac{n(n+1)d}{2n+1}$

C. $\dfrac{n(n+1)d}{2n}$
D. $\dfrac{n(n-1)}{2n+1}d$

13. The standard deviation of Q. 12 is

A. $\dfrac{n(n+1)}{3}d^2$
B. $\sqrt{\dfrac{n(n+1)}{3}}d$

C. $\dfrac{n(n-1)}{3}d^2$
D. $\sqrt{\dfrac{n(n-1)}{3}}d$

14. The standard deviation of 4, 5, 6, 7, ..., 13 is x, then the standard deviation of 14, 15, 16, ..., 23 is

A. 2   B. $10x$

C. $x + 10$ D. $x + \sqrt{10}$

15. The mean of five observations is 15 and their variance is 9.2. If three observations are 16, 17 and 19, the other two are

A. 10, 11   B. 11, 12

C. 12, 13   D. None of these

ANSWERS

1	2	3	4	5	6	7	8	9	10
C	C	C	C	A	A	D	D	A	D

11	12	13	14	15
C	B	B	A	B

SOME SELECTED EXPLANATORY ANSWERS

3. Given $n_1 = 7$, $\overline{X}_1 = 10$, $n_2 = 3$, $\overline{X}_2 = 5$

$\therefore$ Combined mean $= \dfrac{n_1\overline{X}_1 + n_2\overline{X}_2}{n_1 + n_2}$

$= \dfrac{7 \times 10 + 3 \times 5}{7 + 3} = \dfrac{85}{10} = 8.5.$

4. Required AM

$= \dfrac{10 \times 10 + 14 \times 11 + \{50 - (10 + 14)\} \times 12}{10 + 14 + \{50 - (10 + 14)\}}$

$= \dfrac{10 \times 10 + 14 \times 11 + 26 \times 12}{10 + 14 + 26}$

$= \dfrac{566}{50} = 11.32.$

5. GM of the series 1, 2, 4, 8, ..., 2^n

$= \left\{1.2.4.8....2^n\right\}^{1/n}$

$= \left\{2^1.2^2.2^3.....2^n\right\}^{1/n}$

$= \left\{2^{\frac{n(n+1)}{2}}\right\}^{1/n} = 2^{\frac{n+1}{2}}.$

13. We have

$$\sigma^2 = \dfrac{1}{2n+1}\sum_{r=0}^{2n}\left\{(a+rd) - (a+nd)\right\}^2$$

$= \dfrac{2d^2}{2n+1}(1^2 + 2^2 + ... + n^2)$

$= \dfrac{n(n+1)}{3}d^2$

$\therefore \quad \sigma = \sqrt{\dfrac{n(n+1)}{3}}.d.$